Environmental Ethics

ETHICS AND ACTION

A series edited by Tom Regan

Environmental Ethics

*Duties to and Values in
the Natural World*

Holmes Rolston, III

Temple University Press
PHILADELPHIA

The book's epigraph is from Victor Hugo's *En Voyage, Alpes et Pyrénées* (Paris: J. Hetzel, 1890), entry for 11 August 1843, pp. 180–81.

Temple University Press, Philadelphia 19122
Copyright © 1988 by Temple University. All rights reserved
Published 1988
Printed in the United States of America

Library of Congress Cataloging-in-Publication Data

Rolston, Holmes, 1932–
  Environmental ethics.

  (Ethics and action)
  Bibliography: p. 373
  Includes index.
  1. Human ecology—Moral and ethical aspects.
I. Title. II. Series.
GF80.R64 1988   179'.1   87-6499
ISBN 0-87722-501-X (alk. paper)

In the relations of humans with the animals, with the flowers, with the objects of creation, there is a whole great ethic scarcely seen as yet, but which will eventually break through into the light and be the corollary and the complement to human ethics. . . . Doubtless it was first of all necessary to civilize man in relation to his fellow men. With this one must begin and the various lawmakers of the human spirit have been right to neglect every other care for this one. That task is already much advanced and makes progress daily. But it is also necessary to civilize humans in relation to nature. There, everything remains to be done.

—Victor Hugo

Contents

Figures

Preface

THAT HUMANS must live in *response to nature,* in encounter with their natural environment, has provoked reflection since philosophy began. Explicitly or implicitly, every person, every culture has a concept of nature. That humans have a *responsibility for nature* is among the more recent philosophical discoveries, although not without precedent in the past. Humans have always had local impact on their environment, killing animals for food or plowing fields. But only when science brought enriched understanding and technological power did humans gain the possibility of dramatically altering the events of natural history.

Like no humans before us, we know Earth with its past evolutionary story; we know its present fauna, flora, ecosystems; and we hold Earth's future in our hands. The accumulation of that power is evident in the ecological crises of the latter half of the twentieth century—in the threat of catastrophic extinctions, for example. What was for so long a given has of late become an obligation. Great power, unconstrained by ethics, is subject to great abuse.

We do not yet have an adequate ethics for this Earth and its communities of life. Toward that end, we here travel through a series of chapters of widening ethical scope, exploring values carried by the natural world. We begin with an introductory account of humans valuing the natural world (Chapter 1), then develop nature-regarding duties at the levels of sentient animals, organisms, species, ecosystems (Chapters 2 through 5). From that vantage point we resurvey values in nature theoretically (Chapter 6). Environmental ethics and value theory have then to be applied to our social choices, to policy in government (Chapter 7), and to industry and business (Chapter 8). We conclude with a world view locating persons in a satisfactory residence on this historic and storied Earth (Chapter 9).

We are searching for an ethics that appropriately "follows nature." We want to optimize human fitness on Earth, and to do this morally. We seek a naturalized ethics. That is not the only human concern; a comprehensive ethics needs an account of the goods of culture, of right and wrong within personal relations, a humanized ethics. But humans inhabit natural communities as surely as they do cultural communities, and a major unfinished agenda in ethics is our responsibility for nature. What human behavior is appropriate here? Whether and in what sense such an ethics can be derived from nature, gaining an *ought* from an *is*, will have to be discovered along the way.

Two observations are worth making at the start. Environmental ethics will mix descriptions of what is the case (derived from science, from metaphysics, from judgments of intrinsic values present or absent there) with prescriptions of what ought to be (right and wrong in human conduct). It is never clearer than now that an ethics attaches to a world view, but we are also trying to see further than humans have seen before, struggling for coherence, surveying a complex historical place. The quest is ethically demanding at the same time that it is metaphysically searching.

Environmental ethics is practically urgent. Theoretical questions will make a practical difference; encounters in practice will force us back to theoretical reflection. In what follows we must map unexplored theoretical ground in philosophy, make unexpected crisscrossings from science to ethics, and reevaluate on the scene wildlife and wildland encounters in public and private life. It is sometimes thought that environmental ethics is not very important, peripheral to the urgent issues of human relations—poverty, war, crime, man's inhumanity to man—and further, that it is only a matter of application rather than theory.

But not so. Few ethical explorations run so deep or so quickly from theory to practice; few make such an evident difference on the world scene. Environmental ethics is both radical and revolutionary.

We modern humans, increasingly competent about making our way through the natural world, have been decreasingly confident about its values, its meanings. The correlation is not accidental. It is hard to discover meaning in a world where value appears only at the human touch, hard to locate meaning when we are engulfed in sheer instrumentality, whether of artifacts or natural resources. One needs a significant place to dwell.

Power without ethics is profane and destructive in any community. While many have come to see that this is so in interhuman ethics—hence the outcries for human rights, for justice and charity, for peace—few as yet have seen how the escalating human use of the world, unchecked by any ethic, prevents us from appreciating values on the Earth where we reside. The outcry for a life ethic, a land ethic has only begun.

> The great fault of all ethics hitherto has been that they believed themselves to have to deal only with the relations of man to man. In reality, however, the question is what is his attitude to the world and all life that comes within his reach. A man is ethical only when life, as such, is sacred to him, that of plants and animals as that of his fellow men, and when he devotes himself helpfully to all life that is in need of help. . . . The ethic of the relation of man to man is not something apart by itself: it is only a particular relation which results from the universal one.[1]

With that universal vision, Albert Schweitzer joins Victor Hugo in the hope for this whole great ethic, scarcely realized as yet.

For the trip you are about to take, I offer myself as a wilderness guide. Nowadays it is easier to get lost conceptually in the natural world than physically. A century ago the challenge was to know where you were geographically in a blank spot on the map, but today we are bewildered philosophically in what has long been mapped as a moral blank space. Despite our scientific and cultural taming of wild nature we still wander, confused as to how to value it. Values run off our maps. Travelers need pathfinding through strange places. But at the end of the journey we will find ourselves back home again and really know for the first time where we reside.

Environmental Ethics

1   *Humans Valuing the Natural Environment*

 THAT THERE OUGHT to be some ethic concerning the environment can be doubted only by those who believe in no ethics at all. For humans are evidently helped or hurt by the condition of their environment. Environmental quality is necessary, though not sufficient, for quality in human life. Humans dramatically rebuild their environment, in contrast to squirrels, which take the environment as they find it. But human life, filled with its artifacts, is still lived in a natural ecology where resources—soil, air, water, photosynthesis, climate—are matters of life and death. All that we have and are was grown in or gathered out of nature. Culture and nature have entwined destinies, similar to (and related to) the way minds are inseparable from bodies. So ethics needs to be applied to the environment.

Nevertheless, we are not here seeking simply to apply human ethics to environmental affairs. Environmental ethics is neither ultimately an ethics of resource use; nor one of benefits, costs, and their just distribution; nor one of risks, pollution levels, rights and torts, needs of future generations, and the rest—although all these figure large within it. Taken alone, such issues enter an ethic where the environment is *secondary* to human interests. The environment is instrumental and auxiliary, though fundamental and necessary. Environmental ethics in the *primary*, naturalistic sense is reached only when humans ask questions not merely of prudential use but of appropriate respect and duty.[1]

That there ought be an environmental ethic in this deeper sense will be doubted by many, those entrenched in the anthropocentric, personalistic ethics now prevailing in the Western world. For them, humans can have no duties to rocks, rivers, or ecosystems, and almost none to birds or bears; humans have serious duties only to each other, with nature often instrumental in such duties. The environment is the wrong kind of primary target for an ethic. It is a means, not an end in itself. Nothing there counts morally. Nature has no intrinsic value.

Just this last claim—that nature has no intrinsic value—is what we will steadily be challenging. *Value* will therefore be a principal term in the arguments that follow. If this were an inquiry into human ethics, terms such as *rights, justice, beneficence and maleficence, social contracts, promises, benefits and costs, utility, altruism, and egoism* would be regularly used. These also play a part in environmental ethics, but the fundamental term that will most help to orient us is *value.* It will be out of *value* that we will derive *duty.*

One striking thing about humans in relation to the natural environment is the richness of their "uses" of it. We will begin with an account of humans valuing their environment. Every living thing exploits its environment for biological needs. Like squirrels, humans are hurt by poisons in groundwater, helped by a renewable food supply. But humans have a power to understand, appreciate, and enjoy nature far beyond their biological uses of it. Humans are helped by scenic vistas or scientific experiments conducted in the wilderness, but squirrels never use their environment in these ways. Humans dramatically study and rebuild their environments. Further, unlike animals, humans can take an interest in sectors remote from their immediate, pragmatic needs; they can espouse a view of the whole (see Chapters 2 and 9). This means that nature carries for humans a vast array of values little shared by other species.

To begin with an account of how humans value nature may seem to lead only to a secondary environmental ethics. But appearances are deceiving. Such a beginning will prove a strategic entry point into a primary environmental ethics, owing to the rich ways in which humans value nature. Even those who believe that we only need an ethic concerning the environment can start here and see what concerns develop, what gestalts change. Valuing nature may prove a route into doing what only humans can do, transcending what is immediately given and using it as a window into the universe. This trailhead is a good place to take off for points unknown.

Over the route that follows we will not always be able to travel using well-charted ethical arguments, for these do not exist in the wilderness. Ethicists have reflected upon human-to-human relationships for thousands of years, and although interhuman ethics remains frequently unsettled, there are well-worn tracks of debate. Environmental ethics is novel, at least in the classical and modern West; it lies on a frontier. This terrain is sufficiently unexplored to make discovery possible. We may also find ourselves deeper in the woods than we anticipated.

Values Carried by Nature

Asking about values *carried* by nature will let us make an inventory of how nature is valuable to humans, with the subtle advantage that the term *carry* lets us switch-hit on the question of objectivity and subjectivity. In the spectrum of values crossed here, some (the nutritional value in a potato) seem objectively there, while others (the eagle as a national symbol) are merely assigned. Either way, desired human experiences are tied in to the existence of something out there. As we uncover these valued "functions" of nature, we can begin to press the question whether and how far value intrinsic in nature enables humans to come to own these values. Notice too that things never have value generically, but rather have specific sorts of value. Some adjective needs to be filled into a blank before the noun:———value. Analogously, objects are not just colored *simpliciter* but are crimson or sky blue.

Life-Support Value

The ecological movement has made it clear that culture remains tethered to the biosystem and that the options within built environments, however expanded, provide no release from nature. Humans depend on airflow, water cycles, sunshine, photosynthesis, nitrogen fixation, decomposition bacteria, fungi, the ozone layer, food chains, insect pollination, soils, earthworms, climates, oceans, and genetic materials. An ecology always lies in the background of culture, natural givens that support everything else. Some sort of inclusive environmental fitness is required of even the most advanced culture. Whatever their options, however their environments are rebuilt, humans remain residents in an ecosystem. Earlier ethics never paid much attention to ecosystems because humans had little knowledge of what was going on and even less power to affect these processes (though there was environmental degradation in ancient Mesopotamia). But lately, owing to human population increases, advancing technology, and escalating desires, we are drastically modifying our life-support system. Persons are helped and hurt by these alterations, and this raises ethical questions.

Ecological values contribute positively to human experiences. But they also seem to be there apart from humans being here.

Nature is an evolutionary ecosystem, with humans a late add-on; the central goods of the biosystemic Earth were in place before humans arrived. Nature is an objective value carrier; humans cash in on, and spend, what is naturally given. In many respects, though by no means all, the earthen setup is "a happy place." Those who find value to be entirely subjective will smile and say that in that kind of remark humans are only getting back their reflected emotions, as when others say that Earth is "a lonely place." But those who prefer a more objective gestalt will wonder why we find ourselves alive and well (= happy) in a life-support system that can, by means of natural selection and ecological support, evolve and sustain such a flourishing of life.

"Happy" is too subjective a word, but what if we say that Earth is a "fortunate" place or a "fertile" place, a place with significant fortunes where life has been nourished? That seems to begin to value objectively what is going on independently of humans. What if we say that Earth is a "satisfactory" place and mean by that not only that humans have prospered here but also that myriads of species have found "satisfactory" environments, life-supporting niches into which they are well fitted? Is not that objective satisfaction of life true, with or without our human experiences of satisfaction, when we reflect over the prosperous Earth? (See Chapter 5, "Assessing Satisfactory Ecosystems").

Do not humans value Earth because it is valuable, and not the other way round? Is the value in this life-support system really just a matter of latecoming human interests, or is Earth not historically a remarkable, valuable place prior to the human arrival and even now valuable antecedently to the human uses of it? The human part in the drama is perhaps the most valuable event of all. But it seems parochial, as well as uninformed ecologically, to say that our part alone in the drama establishes all its worth. Ecology is not something subjective, not something that goes on in the human mind. Perhaps the value produced and carried in an ecosystem, together with the conscious valuing of it that comes later on, is not a merely subjective affair either, although the latter does require human subjects.

In an ecological perspective, that Earth is *valuable* would mean that Earth is *able* to produce *value* and has long been doing so as an evolutionary ecosystem. A late though remarkable product of the process is humans, who are also valuable—of value in an advanced way. When humans come, they find Earth often *valuable*, able to satisfy preferences, *able* to produce *valued experiences*. The subjective value events are a subset—perhaps a capstone subset but still a superposed subset—of the larger, objective production and support (= satisfaction) of value.

Economic Value

Though humans require natural givens, they do not take the environment ready to hand. They do not usually adapt themselves to wild nature; rather they labor over nature, rebuilding it to their cultural needs, owing to the remarkably flexible powers of the human hand and brain. Any living thing makes its environment into a resource. A squirrel hides a cache of acorns; a bird builds a nest. But these activities still involve ecologies, hardly yet economies, unless we choose to call all questions of efficient food and energy use economic. Achieving economic value, in the usual sense, involves the deliberate redoing of natural things, making them over from spontaneous nature, coupled with a commerce in such remade things. Animals do not exchange in markets; by contrast, markets are basic to every culture.

The price of petroleum proves that nature has economic value, but the sense in which it does can be contested, for human labor so dramatically adds to nature's raw value that an economist may here see valuing as a kind of adding-on of labor to what is initially valueless: "crude" oil has no value, but a petroleum engineer may "refine" it. The sense of the prefix *re-* in *resource* is that nature can be refitted, turned to use by human labor, and only the latter gives it value. Valuing is a kind of laboring. If this were entirely so, we should not say, strictly speaking, that nature *has* economic value, any more than we say that an empty glass has water in it. It only *carries* the value of labor. Marxists have often argued that natural resources should be unpriced, for resources as such have no economic value.[2] But a research scientist, mindful of the remarkable natural properties on which technology depends, may immediately add that human art has no independent powers of its own, and such a scientist may give a different valuation of this natural base.

There is a foundational sense in which human craft can never produce any unnatural chemical substances or energies. All humans can do is shift natural things around, taking their properties as givens. There is nothing unnatural about the properties of a computer or a rocket; as much as a warbling vireo or a wild strawberry, both are assemblages of completely natural things operating under natural laws. This sets aside essential differences between artifacts and spontaneous nature (which we examine later), but it does so to regain the insight that nature has economic value because it has an instrumental capacity—and this says something about the material on which the craftsmanship is expended. Nature has a rich utilitarian *pliability*, due both to the plurality of natural sorts and to their splendid, multifaceted powers. This is nature's economic value in a basic and etymological sense of something we can arrange so as to make a home out of it. Nature is a fertile field for human labor, but that agricultural metaphor (which applies as well to industry) praises not only the laborers but their surrounding environment. Nature is something recalcitrant yet often agreeable and useful, frequently enough to permit us to build our entire culture on it.

Despite the prefix, *resource* preserves the word *source* and recalls these generative qualities so profuse in their applications. It is sometimes thought that the more civilized humans become, the further we get *from* nature, released from dependency on the spontaneous natural course. This is true, but science and technology also take us further *into* nature. A pocket calculator is, in this perspective, not so much an exploitation of nature as it is a sophisticated appreciation of the intriguing, mathematical structure of matter-energy, properties enjoying an even more sophisticated natural use in the brain of the fabricator of the calculator.

Such economic value is a function of the state of science, but it is also a function of available natural properties, which often quite unpredictably mix with human ingenuity to assume value. *Penicillium* was a useless mold until 1928, when Alexander Fleming found (and much amplified) the natural antibacterial agency. The bread wheat, on which civilization is based, arose from the hybridization (probably accidental) of a mediocre natural wheat with a weed, goat grass. Who is to say where the miracle foods and medicines of the future will come from? Given the striking advances of technology, an endangered ecosystem is likely to contain some members of potential use. When humans conserve nature, we hope in the genius of the mind, but we also reveal our expectations regarding the as yet undiscovered wealth of natural properties that we may someday capture and convert into economic value.

In some respects, human ingenuity makes nature an infinite resource, because humans can always figure new ways to remake nature, find substitute resources, exploit new properties. By an increasingly competent use of natural resources, the human economy can grow forever. Over the centuries, especially in the last few, more and more of nature has been brought into the human orbit. But in some respects the West has been on an unprecedented growth trip, with Americans exploiting and filling up the New World, Europeans sucking prosperity from colonies, everyone mining nonrenewable resources. The recent economic boom may be atypical, only apparent or local. More persons are starving than ever before. The idea that nature is an inexhaustible resource may be a fantasy. Moral issues regarding the conservation and distribution of resources are becoming urgent, a principal concern in environmental ethics.

Recreational Value

It may seem frivolous to move from labor to play, from life support to recreation, but the question is a quite serious one: why do humans enjoy nature even when we no longer need it for economic or life-supportive reasons, when the sense of "enjoy" alters from beneficial use to pleasurable appreciation? For some, nature is instrumental to an active human performance; they want only terrain rough enough to test a jeep, or a granite cliff sound enough for pitons. Even so, it serves as a field for skill. For others, the natural qualities are crucial in contemplating an autonomous performance. They watch the fleecy cumulus building over the Great White Throne in Zion, listen for the bull elk to bugle, laud the aerial skills of the hummingbird at the bergamot, or laugh at the comic ostrich with its head in the sand. For the one group, nature is a place to *show what they can do;* for the other, values are reached as they are *let in on nature's show*—a difference surprisingly close to that between applied and pure science, to which we soon turn.

Recreational values can be found in sports and popular pastimes and can thus be humanistic, but they are not always so. People like to recreate in the great outdoors because they are surrounded by something greater than anything they find indoors. They touch base with something missing on baseball diamonds at the city park. The pleasures found to be satisfactory, recreating, re-creating there can be in sober sensitivity to objective natural characters. When persons enjoy watching wildlife and landscapes, though this may take considerable skill, the focus is on nature as a wonderland full of eventful drama and a bizarre repertory, a rich evolutionary ecosystem where truth is stranger than fiction. Persons come to own all these recreational values, but sometimes what they seem to be valuing is *creation* more than *recreation*.

These two sorts of recreational value—the gymnasium and the theater—can often be combined, as when a botanist enjoys the exertion of a hike up a peak and also pauses en route at the Parry's primrose by the waterfall. But the two often need to be compromised and are sometimes irreconcilable. It will strike a sportsman as ridiculous to say that snail darters and Furbish louseworts, threatened with extinction by the Tellico and Dickey and Lincoln dams, have more recreational value than will the reservoirs behind those dams, stocked with game fish. It will seem obscene to the naturalist to exterminate a rare life form in exchange for one more place to water-ski. The natural history values seem lately to be counting more. Every state wildlife magazine devotes more space to the nongame species than it did a decade ago, and every national park and wilderness area is much visited. And what if these values count still more in the next generation?

In choosing whether to log a wilderness, should policy favor the preferences of the young, whom surveys reveal to be more pro-nature, over those of older persons, who are more prodevelopment and less naturalistic? Should we favor the pronature preferences of the better educated over those of the less educated?[3] In social justice, politicians try to favor the disadvantaged and frequently think that seniority carries some weight, either in wisdom or in rights. But in environmental ethics, this view can weight the prejudices against wildlife and preservation, expressed by the less well-educated or older sectors of society, against another social ideal: a harmonious, caring relationship with wildlife and a desire for ample wilderness. This ideal, emerging in the better-educated and the younger generation, initially a minority view, may be more functional socially and in the long term result in a better balance between economic and recreational values.

Humans sometimes want the wild environment as an alternative to the built environment. Leisure, in contrast to work for pay; work (climbing, setting up camp) that isn't for pay; an environment with zest, in contrast to a boring or familiar job; the spartan contrasts with the citied comforts—all these meet otherwise unmet needs. Here humans value the wilderness or the park noneconomically for its unbuilt characteristics. Is this only some sort of escape value? Or is there some more positive characteristic in wildness that re-creates us?

Scientific Value

Science in its origins was a leisurely pursuit for intellectuals, and a good test still for unalloyed scientists is to ask whether they would continue their researches if they were independently wealthy and if these had no economic or life-supporting consequences. The alliance of pure science with naturalistic recreation is seldom noticed, but this only reveals how far recent science has sold its soul to the economists. Is being a naturalist a matter of recreation or of science? Does one do it for play or pay? Some ornithologists and mineralogists hardly ask; rather, whether avocationally or vocationally, they unite in valuing nature as an object worthwhile to be known in its own right, always caring for its fascinating characteristics.

Like music and the fine arts, natural science is an intrinsically worthwhile activity, but scientists find this difficult to say and, sometimes with much ingenuity, sell their study short by retreating to some utilitarian subterfuge. But natural science per se cannot be worthwhile unless its primary object, nature, is interesting enough to justify being known. To praise cognitive science is also to praise its object, for no study of a worthless thing can be intrinsically valuable. Filtering out all applied values, one reaches a residual scientific value in nature, an interest in both the natural stuff and this study of it which has enlisted the greatest human genius.

Natural science is our latest and perhaps most sophisticated cultural achievement, but we should not forget that its focus is primitive nature. Valuing science does not devalue nature; rather, we learn something about the absorbing complexity of the natural environment when we find that it can serve as the object of such noble studies. There is an intellectual adventure in discerning how the tunicates and the vertebrates are both so structured as to be included among the chordates, which are related to the echinoderms more closely than to the cephalopods; it is an accomplishment possible only because nature is a rich developmental system. Some say that we first understand things and afterward evaluate them, but if there is anyone for whom pure science has value, then nature contains at least the raw precursors of value.

The Jurassic fossil *Archaeopteryx*, linking the reptiles with the birds, has great scientific value but no economic or life-support value. The steaming pools of Yellowstone preserve an optimal thermal habitat for primitive anaerobic bacteria which, recent studies suggest, survive little changed from the time when life evolved under an oxygen-free atmosphere.[4] Odd, useless, and often rare things typically have high scientific values—like the finches on the Galápagos—for the clues they furnish to life's development and survival. Who is to say where tomorrow's scientific values may lie? A scientist might have been pardoned a generation back for thinking the Yellowstone microhabitats unimportant.

Science tells the natural tale: how things are, how they came to be. That story cannot be worthless, not only because human roots lie in it but because we find it a delightful intellectual pursuit. But scientists can be beguiled into severing values from nature at the same time that they find their principal entertainment in unraveling an account of the physical and biological saga. The older sciences (and many abstract ones still) fastened on morphology, structure, homeostatic processes. That itself was engaging, but now no natural science, whether astrophysics or ecology, escapes the evolutionary paradigm, and humankind is only beginning to understand what *natural history*—a sometimes despised term—is all about. That history has an epic quality, a certain wandering notwithstanding, and it is surely a story worth telling—and valuing. This leads to the historical value in nature, which we presently specify.

Aesthetic Value

We value the Landscape Arch of the Canyonlands for the same reason that we value the "Winged Victory" of Samothrace: both have grace. Every admirer of the Tetons or of a columbine admits the aesthetic value carried by nature. A. F. Coimbra-Filho advocates saving three species of tiny, rare marmosets of the Atlantic rainforest because "the disappearance of any species represents a great esthetic loss for the entire world."[5] Yet justifying such value verbally is as difficult as is justifying the experience of pure science. The intrinsically valuable intellectual stimulation that the scientist defends is, in fact, a parallel to the aesthetic encounter that the aesthetician defends, for both demand a distance from everyday personal needs and yet a participatory experience that is nontransferable to the uninitiated. Sensitivities in both pure science and natural art help us see much further than is required by our pragmatic necessities. In both, one gets purity of vision.

In the discovery of such aesthetic value, it is crucial to separate this from both utility and life support, and only those who recognize this difference can value the desert or the tundra. The mist that floats about an alpine cliff, spitting out lacy snowflakes, tiny exquisite crystals, will increase the climber's aesthetic experience there even though the gathering storm may be dangerous. The glossy chestnut, half covered by the spined husk, is pretty as well as edible, and we lament its vanishing; but the head of a much too common weed, *Tragopogon*, is just as shapely. The distance that scientists cultivate, as well as the habit of looking closely, fits them to see the beauty that cold-blooded scientists are supposed to overlook. But beauty keeps turning up, and in unsuspected places, as in the stellate pubescence on the underside of a *Shepherdia* leaf or in a kaleidoscopic slide of diatoms. No one who knows the thrill of pure science can really be a philistine.

A prosaic scientist will complain that the admirer of nature overlooks as much as he or she sees: chestnuts aborted by the fungal blight, fractured snowflakes, imperfections everywhere. Contingencies sometimes add beauty, for a skein of geese is not less moving if one is out of line, nor is the cottonwood silhouetted against the wintry sky any less dramatic for the asymmetries within its symmetrical sweep. Still, every natural thing is marred by accidents and eventually destroyed by them. Does not the aesthetician repair nature before appreciating it? Sometimes—but in so doing, if we consider the case of organic beauty, the artist sees that biological ideal toward which a living thing is striving and which is rarely reached in nature. So, the artist paints a perfect lady-slipper orchid. Perhaps we could say, in the language of the geneticists, that the artist portrays that phenotype producible by the normal genotype in a congenial environment. Or, borrowing from the computer scientists, the artist executes the program built into a thing, which, owing to environmental constraints, has not been executed in nature. Such an ideal is, in a way, still nature's project. In a distinction going back to Aristotle, it is true to the poetry of a thing though not true to its history, yet the poetry directs its history.[6] The form, though not wholly executed, is as natural as is the matter. Some will simply insist that all this is not true to the plain facts of nature; others will realize that it is not so much fiction as a way of getting at what one might call a natural essence only partly expressed in any individual existence.

It is sometimes said that science tells the story as it actually is, art as it ideally ought to be. But that is not entirely so. Art can enjoy the conflict and resolution in the concrete particular expression of a natural thing; science typically seeks a universal law to which no particular ever quite conforms. The physicist who rounds out his slightly erratic lab data into a symmetrical sine wave and the botanist who describes a generic type in her herbarium specimens, ignoring anomalies, both think they are truer to nature by overlooking some data. Again, art may abstract from nature in order to help us see it better. Impressionistic painters, such as Cézanne or Monet, have often said that by exaggeration they reeducate our perceptions to help us capture qualities *in nature:* the flair in an elm, chromatic qualities in a sandstone mesa, the intricacy of a fern leaf. They may even abstract out lines, edges, solidity, or luminous qualities. But the scientist need not say that this is unrealistic, for theoretical science also abstracts in order to appreciate the generic qualities illustrated in particular things. Both science and art use nature to enrich human experience.

Genetic-Diversity Value

Humans eat remarkably few plants in any volume (about 30 out of 300,000 species), and still remarkably fewer come from North America (one or two, pecans and cranberries). With the loss of fifteen cultivars, half the world would starve. Ten species provide 80 percent of the world's calories. Given increasing pressures within agriculture (monocultures, pesticides, herbicides, hybridized strains, groundwater pollution), given increased mutation rates from radioactivity, the nuclear threat, and imported exotic blights, it seems important to preserve the genetic reservoir naturally selected in wild organisms just in case, for instance, Americans need to crossbreed against such microorganisms as produced the corn blight of 1970, or to turn to food stocks adapted to the North American habitats.

It is prudent to preserve the foreign native habitats of the major food, fiber, and medicinal plants (if they now remain), and where such foreign preservation is impossible or unlikely, it becomes all the more important to protect domestic genetic diversity. Even today's poisons in wild plants, naturally evolved defenses, are likely sources of tomorrow's pesticides, herbicides, and medicines. Such resources, at present unknown, cannot be well protected *ex situ* (in zoos, seed depositories) but only *in situ,* by preserving natural ecosystems. Nor can laboratory genetic recombinations substitute for wildlands; natural diversity is required for the startpoint materials.

We might incline to say that genetic diversity involves only a particular kind of economic value, and from a limited perspective this is true. But a full value analysis is more complex. Genetic material has been naturally selected, with the result that it serves the good of the organism, whether or not humans ever use it. In serendipity, a bit of genetic information becomes useful to humans, satisfying their biological needs or other interests. As a result it comes to be traded in the economy. The genetic material and its products certainly end up carrying economic value. But this is possible because humans tap in to capture and redirect some form of value already there. Human labor, cleverness, preferences, and value assignments mix with primitive values already present in the morphology or biochemistry. Information coded in the genes, discovered by the organism before humans arrive, is exploited by human ingenuity—somewhat as the person who eats a potato overtakes nutritional value already functional in the plant. There is a kind of genetic richness located in organisms in ecosystems, and genetic-diversity value is a puzzling hybrid between human economic values and values inlaid biologically in life itself.

Historical Value

Wildlands provide historical value in two ways, cultural and natural. Americans (North, South, Canadian) have a recent heritage of self-development against a diverse and challenging environment, seen in pioneer, frontier, and cowboy motifs. New World cultures remain close to the memory of a primitive landscape. United States history goes back four hundred years; Greek history, four thousand years. The Americans' ancestral virtues were forged with the European invasion of a (so-called) empty continent, which it was their "manifest destiny" to develop. Even the Europeans have historical memories associated with nature: the British with the moors; the Germans with the Black Forest; the Russians with the steppes; the Greeks with the sea. Every culture remains resident in some environment.

Forests, prairies, and ranges ought to be preserved as souvenir places for each generation of Americans learning (however secondarily or critically) their forefathers' moods, regained there quite as much as in the Minuteman Historical Park. Such places provide a lingering echo of what Americans once were, of a way we once passed. It would be a pity not to have accessible to youth in every state some area big enough to force a camp in crossing it, to get lost in, to face the discomforts and hazards of, if for no other reason than to rouse the spine-tingling that braced our forebears. There is nothing like the howl of a wolf to resurrect the ghost of Jim Bridger. A wilderness trip mixes the romance and the reality of the past in present experience. Further, a vice in "white" history is to forget all the "red" years. Understanding the Indian experientially (so far as this is possible at all) requires wilderness to lift historical experience out of the books and recapture it on a vivid landscape.

On the stage of natural history, the human phenomenon is even more ephemeral than is American history on the stage of human history. At this range, wildlands provide the profoundest historical museum of all, a relic of the way the world was during 99.99 percent of past time. Humans are relics of that world, and that world, as a tangible relic in our midst, contributes to our sense of duration, antiquity, continuity, and identity. An immense stream of life has flowed over this continent Americans inhabit, over this Earth. The river of life is a billion years long, and humans have traveled a million years on it, recording their passage for several thousand years. If the length of the river of life were proportioned to stretch around the globe, the human journey would be halfway across a county, and humans would have kept a journal for only a few hundred feet. The individual's reach would be a couple of steps! On this scale, even the Greeks are recent, despite their ancient history, and people in every nation need nature as a museum of what the world was like for almost forever, before we so recently came.

Natural history value couples with scientific value, as when the Yellowstone thermophiles or *Archaeopteryx* reveal something about the origins of life. Without science we cannot know this history. But doing science is something else from doing history. Science is full of laws, theories, regularities, taxa, classifications, causal explanations. A historian wants more—a historical narrative that tells a story about what happened once upon a time, and, above all, the meanings in these events, if such there are. That is why science cannot teach us all we need to know about nature. Indeed interpretive natural history is the most demanding inquiry a naturalist can undertake. Here humans evaluate the story in which they stand, and write the current chapter in the ongoing Earth narrative. This will lead to the ultimate tasks in our environmental ethic (see Chapter 9).

Using nature as a museum of natural history, a teaching place, doubtless makes nature of instrumental value, but here the living museum and the historical reality are, although in small part, one and the same. When we treasure the living museum instrumentally, we may also come to recognize intrinsic value in the natural processes that still survive in remnant wild and rural areas.

In one sense, remnants of the past may have no present value, but in another sense, for humans as historical beings, remnants of the past have great value for the clues they furnish to the story in which we find ourselves emplaced. Without fossils and natural history, the meaning of which have been appreciated only in the last hundred years, humans would be seriously blind to who and where they are. A fossil, unlike a tiger, has no intrinsic value, but it is an instrumental relic in the discovery of what was and is of intrinsic value, discovery of the truth about the value-producing evolutionary ecosystem, the historical environment in which humans were generated. A fossil is a sign that points beyond itself, and in this sense its value is not assigned but historical.

Cultural-Symbolization Value

The bald eagle symbolizes American self-images and aspirations (freedom, strength, beauty), as does the bighorn ram, a "state animal" for Coloradoans. Flowering dogwood and the cardinal characterize Virginia. The pasqueflower is the state flower of South Dakota, the alligator a symbol for Florida, the moose for Maine, the maple leaf for Canada, the trillium for Ontario, the arbutus for Nova Scotia. The lion is a British symbol; the Russians have chosen the bear. Natural areas enter local cultural moods—Grandfather Mountain in western North Carolina, Natural Bridge and the Shendandoah River in central Virginia. Horsetooth Mountain, overlooking the city, provides the logo for Fort Collins, Colorado. Every homescape has its old and familiar haunts—swimming holes, water gaps, passes—which enter our sense of belongingness and identity. Culture commingles with landscape and wildlife in places named after geomorphic, faunal, or floral features: Tinkling Springs, Fox Hollow, Aspen, Crested Butte.

However much the native wildness is domesticated, humans want some wildness preserved, for it comes to express the values of the culture superimposed on it. What would be the impact on American hopes if the bald eagle became extinct? On New Hampshire of the loss of Franconia Notch and the Great Stone Face? What are the psychological connections between the Mississippi River and the state of Mississippi? Between the Scots and Loch Lomond? Would not the death of the last bighorn lower the perceived quality of life in Colorado? Would Boulder, Colorado, not be a poorer place with the Flatirons scarred by development?

No culture develops in independence of the environment on which it is superimposed, no matter how relatively free humans are in their cultural options, no matter that the Chickahominies and the English did very different things in Virginia. In culture there is but one Virginia, and each Virginian has a proper name. The human differences include conscious self-affirmations and heritages for which nature provides little precedent. But nature first is never twice the same, and the idiographic features in nature blend with those in culture to particularize and enrich the combined story. Always in the understory there are distinctive landscape features—the Shenandoah Valley or the Chesapeake Bay—with which the Virginians interact. The Finger Lakes are part of the ethos of central New York state. Shorelines are essential to the quality of life on Prince Edward Island. The cultural-symbolization capacity of nature is no accident but has been a repeated feature in the myriad cultures on Earth.

Character-Building Value

Wildlands are used by organizations that educate character—Boy and Girl Scouts, Outward Bound, and church camps. Similar growth occurs in individuals independently of formal organizations. The challenge of self-competence, in teamwork or alone, is valued, together with reflection over skills acquired and one's place in the world. Wildlands provide a place to sweat, to push oneself more than usual, perhaps to let the adrenalin flow. They provide a place to take calculated risks, to learn the luck of the weather, to lose and find one's way, to reminisce over success and failure. They teach one to care about his or her physical condition.

Wildlands provide a place to gain humility and a sense of proportion. Doing so partly recapitulates our historical experience; it anticipates the religious experience that we soon examine. What was earlier a recreational testing of what we can do is heightened into an achievement of self-identity. In a survey of 300 geniuses, Edith Cobb found evocative experiences in natural locales characteristic of their youth, a formative factor in their creativity.[7] Not only are youth affected so; several noted writers have reported how self-actualization was fostered in a wilderness setting.[8] Nature is a place to "know thyself."

Such values associate as readily with rural as with wild nature. Once, when purchasing seed and fertilizer, I wrote a check and offered identification with a guaranteed check card. The sales clerk waved the latter aside, saying, "People don't write bad checks for fertilizer and seed corn." On another occasion, hiking with my father, we had just left the car at a stranger's place in the mountains, adjacent to a forest trail. At the edge of the homestead, realizing that I had forgotten to lock the car, I turned to go back. "Never mind," my father said, "did you see that man's tomatoes?" There seems to be something about loving the soil, the labor and patience of raising crops, that couples well with honesty—at least psychologically and statistically if not logically or inevitably. The virtues of humility, simplicity, frugality, serenity, and independence can also be learned in town, but they are nowhere better taught than in the encounter with rural nature. John Denver located this kind of value in his hit tune, "Thank God, I'm a country boy!"

Related to this is a therapeutic value in nature. An entirely normal use of wild and rural areas, reported by a majority, is for semitherapeutic recreation in a low-frustration environment. A minority use, less well explored, is as a setting to treat psychologically disturbed persons. For the mentally ill, the ambiguity and complexity in culture can be disorienting. It is hard to differentiate among friends, enemies, and the indifferent, hard to get resolve focused on what to do next or to predict the consequences of delay. But in the wilds or on the farm, supper has to be cooked; one needs firewood, and it is getting dark. There are probabilities in facing nature—maybe it won't rain when you forget your poncho—but there are no ambiguities. Exertion is demanded; visceral accomplishment is evident, again in a low-frustration environment. The self is starkly present, and the protocol is simpler. One really is on his own; or, one's friends are few, and she utterly depends on them. All this can mobilize the disturbed for recovery, perhaps using in basic form the same forces that create the character-building effect for us all.[9]

So far as humans over the evolutionary course have been selected to need challenge, adventure, exertion, and risk, society must provide avenues for such archetypal emotions or expect deviant behavior—gangs and rebels without a cause. There are alternative routes for such expression: sports, for instance, or—alas—the military. Humans are remarkably unspecialized. But perhaps wild and rural areas match some deep-seated psychosomatic needs. The lack of this may be part of the trouble in our crowded, warring world. We do not know but can suspect that encounter with nature is often related to our mental health.

Diversity-Unity Values

We may next harness a pair of complementary values. The sciences describe much natural *diversity* and also much *unity*, terms which are descriptive and yet contain dimensions of value.

Diversity is itself a diverse idea, sometimes requiring more exact specification, but we need here only the core focus on plurality, richness, variety, all unfolding from fundamental themes. Disparate sets of results are coordinated as spin-offs from simple processes; the world is simple in principles and rich in phenomena. The physical sciences have revealed the astronomical extent of matter coupled with its reduction into a few kinds of elements and particles, which dissolve into interradiating wave fields. The taxonomist has enlarged the array of natural kinds, while the biochemist has found only the materials of physics organized everywhere in parallel chemistries, such as glycolysis and the citric acid cycle or DNA and RNA at the core of life. Evolution has traced every life form back to monophyletic or a few polyphyletic origins, while ecology has interwoven these myriad forms to connect them at present as fully as they have been related by paleontology. This macroscopic web is matched by the unity revealed by the electron microscope or the X-ray spectrometer. The natural pageant is a kind of symphony of motifs, each motif interesting, often orchestrated together, sometimes chaotic, and all spun from a few simple notes.

The story of science is the discovery of a bigger universe with more things in it, and the finding of laws and structures to explain their common composition and kinship. Humans value both the diversity and the unity. A few centuries ago we supposed this universe to have far less spatiotemporal and biological diversity, and its unity was unknown or denied. Everywhere there was dualism and opposition—in heaven and earth, mind and matter, life and nonlife, humanity and nature, gods and demons. No scientist would willingly return to that universe, for it was oppressively small, less diverse, and yet also superstitious and lacking in the natural unity that we now know it to possess.

Nature is sometimes locally poor, as in a lodgepole forest with its sparse *Vaccinium* undercover, but in the ensemble the natural sorts are lush and many-splendored. This richness greatly entertains naturalists, widened as their acquaintance with it is by lenses, voyages, and books, and it will be perceptibly sacrificed if we trade snail darters or Furbish louseworts for a few more generating machines. Diversity will be substantially threatened if the present rate of extinction, accelerated by human intervention to perhaps 1,000 times over natural rates, continues unabated. The same naturalists will enjoy realizing how these natural kinds have an ecosystemic connectedness, but with this realization of facts, what *is* the case, there immediately comes a concern how often these connections are upset by ill-considered human interventions, leading to concern for what *ought* to be.

If this is too metaphysical, then perhaps one need only notice how both diversity and unity feed the human mind. Mind cannot be formed under the homogeneity of a blank wall nor before the heterogeneity of a bewildering jungle. "Great objects make great minds."[10] A complex mind evolves in order to deal with a diverse world, yet one through which unifying relationships run. That was true in Pleistocene times in the Olduvai Gorge, and it is true now, for our minds are still developing. Emerging out of nature, we have become geniuses by confronting nature's plurality-in-unity, both historically and scientifically.

But do we then say that these features are of no value until thickened by the addition of human interest? Or do we wonder that just this system, evolving so, did thicken human interest to form the mind prehistorically and that it continues to do so now? The mind is a mirror of these properties in nature, and there is even a sense in which the mind, founded on the cerebral complexity and integrating capacity, is a product of nature's tendency both to diversify and to unify (see Chapter 5, on individualizing ecosystems). When this mind reflects, in turn, on the natural world, it can assign value at once to diverse particulars and to the universal and global regularities that underlie and permeate these particulars.

Stability and Spontaneity Values

A pair of complementary natural values rests on a mixture of ordered stability with what, rather evasively, we must call the appearance of spontaneity, counterparts that are not only descriptive but also valuational. That natural processes are regular—that gravity holds, rains come, oaks breed in kind, and succession is reset and repeated—yields laws and trends rooted in the causal principle; it means that nature is dependable, as well as being unified and intelligible. Every order is not a value, but some order supports value, and why is this natural dependability not a quite basic value? A requisite of any universe is that it be ordered, but we need not despise a necessary good, nor does such minimum essential order account for the ecological and biochemical constancy that supports life and mind, upon which all knowledge and security depend.

The polar value, really a sort of freedom, is hardly known to science by any such name; indeed, it is with some risk of offense and oversimplification that we here touch the long-debated issues surrounding determinism. Still, nature sometimes provides an "appearance" of contingency. Neither landscapes nor aspen leaves nor ecological successions are ever twice the same. In the laboratory, science abstracts out the regularly recurring components in nature to attain predictive control, while in the field nature always remains in part unique and particular, nonrepetitive. What happens there is always something of an adventure: the way the cottontail evades the coyote, or just when the last leaf is tossed from this maple and where the gusting wind lands it. We hardly know how to give a complete account of this. Rigorous determinists insist that nothing in nature (or in culture) can be either of chance or of choice, believing that to say otherwise is to destroy the fundamental axiom of all science. But others require a less rigidly closed system, finding that science still prospers when positing statistical laws, which need not specify every particular.

If there are real natural possibilities in excess of what actually comes to pass, the possible event that does happen can be selected by chance or by choice or by some intermediate, partial autonomy for which we hardly yet have an adequate model. Genetic experimentation seems to rest partly on microscopic contingencies, as in crossing-over or mutation affected by random radioactivity, and these effects are sometimes amplified into phenotypic expressions. The macroscopic level to a large degree suppresses any microscopic contingencies, and yields in consequence those stabilities that humans also value, but the scene of natural history is just as repeatedly a place of emergent surprises. Stability is always a dynamic stability that leads to innovative change. The statistical trends develop into ongoing stories.

We are not sure whether *Australopithecus* had to develop in Africa or whether giraffes had to mutate so as to develop long necks, although both events may have been probable. Did the first ancestral birds storm-blown to the Galápagos Islands absolutely have to be finches? For the conservatives, it is safest to say theoretically that here we only reveal our ignorance of nature's detailed determinism, that nature's surprises are only apparent, though perhaps we cannot now or ever escape this appearance. For the liberals, it is bolder and more satisfying, as well as true to practical experience, to say that nature sometimes allows the real appearance of spontaneous novelty. What the Darwinian revolution did to the Newtonian view was to find nature sometimes a jungle and not a clock, and many have disliked the change. Contingencies do put a bit of chaos into the cosmos. But you can have a sort of adventure in Darwin's jungle that you cannot have in Newton's clock. Openness brings risk and often misfortune, but it sometimes adds excitement. Here nature's intelligibility, aesthetic beauty, dependability, and unity are checked by the presence of spontaneity, and this can be valued too.

Eventually, as a product of chance mixed with natural stabilities and evolutionary trends that we dimly understand, living things gain a partial integrity to go on their own. Causality is not altogether here denied, but it is put to a pliable organic rather than mechanistic use as a self-caused, functional organism seeks helps and avoids hurts in a mixedly stable and contingent environment. Psychical, deliberate freedom seems largely to be reserved for persons, but this capacity evolved out of choicelike precedents in the protopsychologies of animal behavior. A nearsighted person will value only the climaxing, epiphenomenal human freedom, but a farsighted person may cherish these lesser precedents, if only as a glowing of what is fully ignited in humans. That a lionness is "born free" is part of the romance of nature, not of science, but this does not make her freedom any less real. Indeed, as even scientists better observe such animals and trace human kinships with them, it becomes increasingly difficult to say why we should value human freedom so much, and animal freedom so little.

Nor are these features of constancy and contingency in nature beyond our capacity to affect them. One of our fears is that technology with its manipulations and pollutants, including radioactive ones, will destabilize long-enduring ecosystems; another is that unabated human growth will transgress virtually the whole domain of spontaneous wildness; another is lest we should make the Earth a bit less autonomous by losing snail darters.

Each wild area is nature in idiographic form. Each natural place is one of a kind, so we give it a proper name—the Rawah Mountains, the Dismal Swamp. We climb Mount Ida or canoe on the Congaree River. Even when exploring some nameless canyon or camping at a spring, one experiences a concrete locus never duplicated in idiosyncratic detail. We do not want order at the expense of spontaneous novelty, too much system and too little story. We want constancy with contingency. The regularity is valuable, but so is the element of wildness. Just this wildness, which might seem to threaten to make nature chaotic, in fact adds novelty. By making each location different, wildness makes a favorable difference. It makes each ecosystem historic, the more excellent because no two are alike.

Dialectical Value

We humans are not really bounded by our skin; rather, life proceeds within an environmental theater across a surface of dialectic. The leg muscles are the largest in the body, and we need room to roam down by the river or along the seashore. The hands have evolved for grasping natural things, but so has the brain, and sentient experience underruns mental life. The crafting of an arrow point, a rifle, or a rocket is an environmental exchange. Society and artifacts are also requisite for mind, as is abstract thought, but nature is the most fundamental foil and foundation for mind, and this diffuses the human/natural and the value/fact line. Culture is carved out *against* nature but carved out *of* nature, and this fact is not simple to handle valuationally. Superficially, so far as nature is antagonistic and discomfiting, it has disvalue. Even here a subjectivist must take care lest nature gain objective value first on the negative side of the field, only later to require it positively. We cannot count the hurts in nature as objectively bad unless we are willing to count its helps as objectively good.

With deeper insight, we do not always count environmental conductance as good and environmental resistance as bad, but the currents of life flow in their interplay. An environment that was entirely hostile would slay us; life could never have appeared within it. An environment that was entirely irenic would stagnate us; human life could never have appeared there either. All our culture, in which our classical humanity consists, and all our science, in which our modern humanity consists, has originated in the face of oppositional nature. Nature insists that we work, and this laboring—even suffering—is its fundamental economic pressure. The pioneer, pilgrim, explorer, and settler loved the frontier for the challenge and discipline that put fiber into the American soul. One reason we lament the passing of wilderness is that we do not want entirely to tame this aboriginal element in which our genius was forged. We want some wildness remaining for its historical value and for its character-building value.

But this is of a piece with the larger natural process of conflict and resolution. Half the beauty of life comes out of it, as do the yellow flowers of the nearly extinct louseworts or the exquisite nautilus shell secreted against its environment. The cougar's fang sharpens the deer's sight, the deer's fleet-footedness shapes a more supple lioness. We admire the element of fight even in the maimed and blasted, even in the inanimate, gnarled timberline fir. The coming of Darwin is often thought to have ruined nature's harmonious architectures, but the struggles he posits, if sometimes overwhelming, are not always valueless. None of life's heroic quality is possible without this dialectical stress. Take away the friction, and would the structures stand? Would they move?

When we recognize how we humans are placed within such stresses, do we then say that we wrest values from an otherwise valueless nature? Has this necessary dialectical context of life and mind no value? That humans should struggle against storm and winter is not here denied, nor that we may need to oppose wolves and thistles, rattlesnakes and malaria mosquitoes. But we add that humans can respect the alien in nature not only in its autonomous otherness but even in its stimulus, provocation, and opposition. The hardest lesson in ethics is to learn to love one's enemies.

Life Value

Reverence for life is commended by every great religion, and even moralists who shy from religion accord life ethical value. John Muir would not let Gifford Pinchot kill a tarantula at the Grand Canyon, remarking that "it had as much right there as we did."[11] A thoroughgoing humanist may say that only personal life has value, making every other life form tributary to human interests, but a sensitive naturalist will suspect that this is a callous rationalization, anthropocentric selfishness calling itself objective hard science. The first lesson learned in evolution was perhaps one of conflict, but a subsequent one is of kinship, for the life we value in persons is advanced from but allied with the life in monkeys, perch, and louseworts. Mixed with other values, this Noah principle of preserving a breeding population is powerfully present in the Endangered Species Act. But if life generically is of value, then every specific individual in some degree instances this value, and this is why, without due cause, it is a sin to kill a mockingbird.

Value in the multiple levels of life (sentient animals, plants, species, ecosystems) will be extensively considered in chapters to follow. But here at the start we can notice some features that humans value in living things. We have already observed how life is an artist; indeed, it is always a tribute to a work of art to say that it has organic unity. A further component that recent science is unfolding is what we may call life's intelligibility. Inorganic things have a passive intelligibility, as when minerals crystallize into thirty-two mathematically deducible classes or the elements form an atomic table, so that rational legibility, like aesthetic value, is broader than life. Beyond this, living things are active information systems, as is proved by genetic and biochemical "linguistics." The purines and pyrimidines of the DNA and RNA helixes serve as an "alphabet" organized by codons, word units, into chains rather like sentences and paragraphs. The double helix can be unzipped and "read"; one stereospecific molecule can "recognize" another, and by this "coded messages" are "communicated." Life continues by a steady "problem solving," and evolution accumulates a sophisticated "memory" as organisms are better programmed by natural selection to "deal with" their environment. The bio-*logical* chemistries have such a cybernetic power that, though it is preconscious, the information content routinely in every human cell is more than that in any human book.

A book can be read, but so too can a chambered nautilus. The microscopic ribs, typically thirty in a chamber, seem to be secreted daily in relation to the lunar-tidal cycle, forming a logarithmic spiral known as the Fibonacci series. With its complex physiology and ecology, *Nautilus pompilius* is an intelligible organic system quite as impressive as the atomic submarine named for it, and the beauty of its pearly orange and white spiral vault is greater. The *Nautilus* evolution may hide clues to the story of our planet and to ecological stability.[12] Under X-ray photography exquisite subsurface symmetries appear. We congratulate Leonardo Fibonacci for discovering that series, but why not value the *Nautilus* for so exquisitely graphing it? Intelligible things do not have to be produced intentionally, any more than aesthetic ones do.

Those who cannot find these organic, aesthetic, or intelligible justifications for valuing life cannot deny to it an interest value. Mind is the most interesting and, presumably, the rarest thing in the universe, but life is the second rarest phenomenon, which alone ought to prove it of interest. And all life is natural. We can bring ourselves to say that the culture which unfolds from mind is artificial, but we can never say that life is anything but natural, which makes it an unequivocal natural value. If a space probe were to find on Mars life of the complexity of the Yellowstone thermophiles, to say nothing of those louseworts or snail darters, it would be the most epochal discovery in the history of science, and we would value there what is daily despised on Earth. Lower life may be sacrificed for higher forms, of course; still, a principal task in ethics, explored in subsequent chapters, is for humans to find a suitable place for the integrity of other life forms.

Religious Value

Nature generates poetry, philosophy, and religion not less than science, and at its deepest educational capacity we are awed and humbled by staring into the stormy surf or the midnight sky, or by peering down at the reversing protoplasmic stream in a creeping myxomycete plasmodium. Mountaintop experiences, sunsets, canyon strata, or a meadow of dog's-tooth violets can generate experiences of "a motion and a spirit that impels . . . and rolls through all things."[13] Wild nature thus becomes something like a sacred text. For wilderness purists intensely, and for most persons occasionally, wildlands provide a cathedral setting. There are memories of wilderness in the origins of monotheism (Mount Sinai, Jesus in the desert). Analogies with the natural world fill the Book of Job and Jesus' parables. The wilderness elicits cosmic questions, differently from town. Those thoughts struck in contemplation of nature are thoughts about who and where we are, about the life and death that nature hands us, and our appropriate conduct in this environment.

We might say, overworking the term, that nature is a religious "resource," as well as a scientific, recreational, aesthetic, or economic one. But, using a better word here, we want a wilderness "sanctuary" (and could we begin to think of wildlife sanctuaries in this way?) as a place to escape from the secular city, as a sacrosanct, holy place where we can get near to ultimacy. There is something Greater in the outdoors. Humans are programmed to ask why, and the natural dialectic is the cradle of our spirituality. The wilderness works on a traveler's soul as much as it does on his muscles.

Surveys indicate that, on statistical average, those who do not attend religious services value nature more highly than those who do.[14] Often this is because church leaves them cold; they may be pantheists, or nonecclesiastical monotheists. They may have a diffuse, naturalistic religion, not a supernaturalistic creedal one. They may not like indoor liturgies, but prefer outdoor awe, solitude, vastness.

If nature is used as a hospital or school for character, that is clearly an instrumental use, but what shall we say when nature is used as church? Is this too an instrumental use—to generate human religious experiences, nothing more? Perhaps. But some of these experiences will involve a recognition of God's creation, or the Ultimate Reality, or a Nature sacred in itself. In fact, one profanes such experience and nature alike to see nature as merely instrumental and otherwise devoid of value.

We might sum up a major task in environmental ethics in the injunction *Keep life wonderful!* Each of the fourteen preceding values is tributary to this greater commandment. Nature is a wonderful life support, resource, cultural base; further, it is a wonderland when approached scientifically, aesthetically, dialectically, historically, philosophically, religiously. But is the admonition to keep life wonderful a humanistic or a naturalistic one? From one perspective it might seem that there is no wonder present apart from the human coming, since we do not believe that *Rhododendron* shrubs or mouse lemurs have the capacity for wonder. That would make nature an instrument of human wonder, valued for its capacity to elicit these experiences. Humans desire an environment sophisticated enough to match their wonderful brains. From another perspective, we ask whether such wonder (taking place in wonderful brains) can be generated except in the presence of something worthy enough to induce it, which suggests that nature is intrinsically a wonderland. Such a natural wonderland would generate duties when moral agents encounter it.

Humans cannot escape confrontation with nature; still, modern life can be lived at such remove from this naturalness that our wisdom is artificially led astray. Natural symbols—bread, water, wine, paths, fatherhood, motherhood, mountains, rivers, light, and darkness—are not incidentally among our richest sacramental elements. Wild nature is as necessary as the university for our valuational education. The struggling life essence emerging from and overlaid on physical existence, the arrival of intelligence and whether it has any evolutionary point, the intellectual adventure in beholding the natural scene, the complementarity of spirit and matter—these remain puzzles never completely worked out, for we are always entering deeper waters than we can fathom. We can count that a disvalue: nature outgoes and disappoints us. Or we can count it a value that nature breeds a creative discontent, keeps a distance from us, supplies a further question with each answer, and is so rich and demanding as to be at length inaccessible in the whole, knowable only in part. We are kept pilgrims and pioneers on a frontier, and to travel hopefully is better than to arrive. Meanwhile, this much at least we do value: that nature is endlessly stimulating to the mind and bores only the ignorant or the insensitive.

Value Ownership

If humans are to talk about natural values, we must be actively "in on" them; that is must share those values in personal experiences adequate to judge them. Indeed, even scientists now realize that they always bear some relationship beyond that of passive observer to whatever they seek to know. But the ownership features loom larger here. Humans are rather more "turned on" in doing evaluative judgments than in doing straightforward empirical ones, but that can mean that we are rather more "tuned in" to what is so. That does add a dimension of biography to every report about nature, but it would be valuational solipsism to conclude that in those values that natural things seem to carry we are getting back absolutely nothing but our projections.

That values are actualized in real things, often natural things, seems to warrant the view that valuing is sometimes in part a form of knowing where we register properties—aesthetic *properties* of the Grand Canyon, for instance, in the appreciating mind—notwithstanding what we may add in the appreciating process. Otherwise, we commit the fallacy of misplaced location and ascribe to the viewer what is really in the scene, or at least what comes relationally. But if we fail to recognize, on the other hand, that the canyon itself has no aesthetic *capacities*, we tumble into the pathetic fallacy, projecting onto natural things sentiments that exist only in the human mind.

Values and Human Excitement

We might first think that the phrase "experienced value" is a tautology and the phrase "unexperienced value" a contradiction in terms, somewhat like the phrases "experienced thought" and "unexperienced thought." But the existence of unexperienced value (undiscovered vitamins, genes anciently beneficial to dinosaurs, cougar predation keeping the deer herd healthy) is not a contradiction in terms unless one builds into the meaning of value that it must be experienced. We must not beg the question of objectivity in value. We want rather to examine it—a question woven through our subsequent discussion. We are trying to notice at this point that humans must come to own any values about which they deliberate. The existence of these values must come to human attention. Humans participate in them, and we realize that we are enjoying them. But it would be fatal to further analysis to conclude that since humans experientially own these values under analysis, values are found only in felt existence, nowhere else.

Value is not received as the conclusion of an argument, or by the indifferent observation of a causal series. A value or disvalue is recognized as whatever has got some bite to it. In the case of bare knowing, assuming the correspondence theory of truth at least at some ranges, the knower has an internal *representation* of what is there, perhaps calmly so. Valuing requires more, an internal *excitation.* That brings emoting, and we may be tempted to say that the marriage of a subject to its object gives birth to value. Value enters and exits with awareness. Doing science and taking holidays, for instance, are human experiences. Strip away the human presence and there is neither science nor recreation in the wilderness. So it might seem that any associated value lies entirely in the human experience, no matter how greatly features in the wilderness contribute to it. On the other hand, life support and genetic information operate in the wild regardless of whether humans are present or aware of these things. Perhaps the human valuing of nature generates new values, a kind that are experiential by logical necessity, but these seem superposed on spontaneous natural values, some kinds of which are not experiential.

If natural things have values, we cannot conceivably learn this without experiences by which we are let in on them. With every such sharing there comes a caring, and this may seem to proscribe objective neutrality. In fact, it only prescribes circumspect inquiry. All natural science is built on the experience of nature, but this does not entail that its descriptions, its "facts," are just those experiences. All valuing of nature is built on experience too, but that does not entail that its descriptions, its "values," are just those experiences. Valuing could be a further, nonneutral way of knowing about the world. We humans cannot know the value of anything in the natural world without some feeling about it, but it does not follow that the value is just how we feel about it. The value comes mediated, communicated by our experience, but it does not follow that the value just is the experience. We might suppose that value is not empirical, since we have no organs and can make no instruments for registering it. But that need not mean it is not there. Valuing could just as well be an advanced kind of experiencing where a more sophisticated, living organism/instrument is required to register natural properties. Value must be lived through, *experienced,* but so as to discern the character of the surroundings one is living through.

Values and Human Resources

Let us approach the same thought by probing the term "resource." With soil, timber, or game, the meaning of "resource" is clear enough. Humans tap into spontaneous nature, dam water, smelt ores, domesticate, manage, and harvest, redirecting natural courses to become our resources. Sometimes, humans stay so close to the natural functioning that we say we are capturing (and usually amplifying) values preexisting in nature, as when we grow and eat potatoes. More often, we rebuild the environment enough to claim that value is largely the product of our labor. We wanted potatoes, but the fields grew worthless brush. We wanted logs dovetailed around us as a home, but the world gave only standing trees. Resourceful use generates value, our intentional exploiting of natural things.

Sometimes, we rearrange natural properties creatively to meet our needs. Molybdenum serves as an alloy of steel, a use it does not have in spontaneous nature. Vincristine and vinblastine, extracted from a Madagascar periwinkle, are used to treat Hodgkin's disease and leukemia, a purpose bearing no resemblance to the function of these alkaloids in nature, where they are poisons protecting the periwinkle from browsers. Such resource use can persuade us that values are almost always invented and assigned by human desires. All values carried by nature must therefore be in one form or another a matter of resource use. All must involve human ownership, whether by capture, labor, creativity, or other experience. A park ranger may interpret the Tetons as a scientific, recreational, or aesthetic resource, but by the time that ranger calls it a philosophical or religious resource, the term is eating up everything, as if humans have no other operating modes vis-à-vis nature. Resources now seem to be coming in two kinds: the ordinary ones that are rearranged into artifacts, and the extraordinary, wild sort that we make as little impact on as possible. Contrary to typical resource use, the botanist and the mountaineer visit the Teton wilderness on its own terms and do not reform it to theirs. Humans ordinarily value resources they can make over, but here they value what they will not disturb lest they devalue it, although they do wish to visit it.

Well, some will reply, nature offers some resources that take no redoing or consuming, only looking and enjoying. Most are commodities to be drawn upon, but others are amenities left as is. There are various kinds of instrumental value. The commonest kind modifies natural resources, but an infrequent sort needs only to take natural things as they are. We capture wilderness instrumentally for human experience even though we never lay a hand on it and tread lightly afoot. So why is it not a resource? Remember, there is no science, experienced beauty, or taking holidays in the wilderness. There are only precursors of value, which can be ignited by human interest, somewhat as wood is combustible but without flame until fire appears. The human interest, making something a resource, lights up the value. "Damage to penguins, or sugar pines, or geological marvels is, without more, simply irrelevant. One must go further ... and say: Penguins are important because people enjoy seeing them walk about rocks."[15]

"Everything is a resource, really"—if it has any value at all. The argument cites ways in which humans redirect nature to their benefit, and then turns to apparent nonresources. Nevada authorities labor to save the Devil's Hole pupfish, which requires reduced water drawdown for ranching. Southwest developers agree not to build the Marble Canyon Dam, and members of the Wilderness Society contribute money to save wildernesses—some nearby, which they expect to visit, and some Alaskan, which they do not. But some humans are fascinated by the penguins and pupfish, run rafts down the Grand Canyon, visit the Indian Peaks, enjoy knowing the Alaskan wilds are there, and hope their children may visit them. SUPPORT WATCHABLE WILDLIFE! That slogan from the Oregon Department of Fish and Wildlife is a commendable step away from the fish you catch and game you shoot, both to consume. But *watchable* wildlife is a resource for looking. In every case humans enter some self-fulfilling relationships. What we want is high-quality wilderness experience that improves human life.

Use of the word "resource" gradually changes until nothing can be comprehended outside such a relationship, no matter if the paramount emotion becomes appreciating these realms for what they are in themselves. One ponders the pupfish, the Supai and Redwall strata in Marble Gorge, or spends a lonesome weekend amidst glacier-cut scenery in the Indian Peaks, wondering if a grandchild might ever share such feelings on Alaskan slopes, steadily stretched out of local concerns to the age-long flows of life over time. But these are aesthetic, epistemological, and metaphysical resource relationships. Logically, the claim has become trivial, redefining as resource whatever one "takes in," whether food, scenery, or information about natural history. Ethically, valuing has become so anthropocentric that humans cannot consider values in any naturalistic sense. Perhaps the resource orientation is only a half-truth and afterward logically misguided. Perhaps it is ethically misguided, because man is the only measure of things. Everything is defined in relation to us.

What if a daughter should say to her mother, "You know you are a resource, really," or a communicant approaching the altar were to think how the priest, in transforming bread and wine, was making better resources out of them? Before parents and the sacred, one is not so much looking to *resources* as to *sources*, seeking relationships in an elemental stream of being with transcending integrities. Our place in the natural world necessitates resource relationships, but there comes a point when humans want to know how we belong in this world, not how it belongs to us. We want to get ourselves defined in relation to nature, not just to define nature in relation to us.

The deepest task of an environmental ethics is this larger appreciation of nature, with appropriate conduct, although a subset of environmental ethics considers resource allocation, value trade-offs in human uses of the environment, pollution issues, rights of future generations, and so on. The deeper ethic is about our sources, beyond our resources, and it is also an ethic of neighboring and alien forms of life.

Values and Human Desires

Analogously to resource use, this valuing always involves human interests. Both necessarily have human owners. But just as one can twist the notion of resource into a nonnegotiable paradigm—apart from which nothing we encounter can be comprehended—by treating every human interaction with nature as a resource question, so also one can twist the notion of valuing into nonnegotiable subjectivity by treating human interest in every case as constituting the value present, merely because of the inevitable human excitement.

Sometimes we need to consider, beyond the human ownership, what the valuing is *of*, and whether humans are becoming participants in values that transcend human life. True, there are neither holidays nor scientific experiments in a wilderness. A canyon does not experience its own aesthetic properties. But it is false that when humans arrive, what they value is their experiences and nothing more. They value what these experiences are *of*. A lover has a valuable experience, but what he values is not the experience alone, reducing its object to a precursor; he values also the existence of his beloved. We concede that this is true of those who love persons; why is it not true of those who love penguins? Man may be (in some advanced senses) the only *measurer* of things, but it does not follow that man is the only *measure* of things.

Everything I value involves a value owned by me; everything I desire, a desire owned by me. But it does not follow that all my desires are selfish because they are my desires. Nor are my values merely subjective because they are experienced by me. Every time I act, I am doing something I want to do, satisfying one of my desires. But "unselfish desires" is not a contradiction in terms, nor is "selfish desires" a tautology. If I give a donation to the fund for whales, saying "I want to make a gift," the treasurer will not remonstrate, "How selfish of you! You are satisfying your own desires!" Similarly if I add, "I value those whales," the treasurer will not censure me: "There you go, looking after your human values. You are not only selfish, you are a human chauvinist! You are making a resource of whales to protect the experiences you value." Many human (owned) desires are not selfish, and many human (owned) values are not humanistic. The question of objectivity remains after subjective ownership has been admitted as inevitable. We need to go further in this other, more ethical direction, not reducing penguin value to people experience but extending value from subjective people experiences to objective penguin lives. If value is always and only a matter of satisfying our human preferences, the morality that issues from value preservation is, *ipso facto*, constrained to a class self-interest.

Following Nature

"Nature knows best" is the third law of ecology, according to Barry Commoner, and the gravity of his claim is underlined by its ranking with the first two: that everything is interconnected, and that nothing is ever destroyed, only recycled.[16] But this law is curiously normative, implying that humans, in their *valuing* of nature, ought to *follow* nature. Doing so is often a matter of prudence, but perhaps value in nature also generates human duties toward it. Perhaps in some ways nature even educates our character. Ralph Waldo Emerson once wrote, "Right is a conformity to the laws of nature so far as they are known to the human mind."[17]

But there are dissenting voices. John Stuart Mill exclaimed, "Conformity to nature has no connection whatever with right and wrong."[18] William James called us to "the moral equivalent of war" in our human resistance to amoral nature:

> Visible nature is all plasticity and indifference,—a moral multiverse . . . and not a moral universe. To such a harlot we owe no allegiance; with her as a whole we can establish no moral communion; and we are free in our dealing with her several parts to obey or to destroy, and to follow no law but that of prudence in coming to terms with such of her particular features as will help us to our private ends.[19]

Much of the puzzle lies in the way we use both the words *nature* and *follow*. We next undertake an analysis of what it might mean to follow nature, asking whether humans ought to do so.[20]

Following Nature in an Absolute Sense

Everything conducted in accordance with the laws of nature "follows nature" in a broad, elemental sense, and it is sometimes asked whether human conduct ought to follow these laws. The human species has come into evolutionary nature lately, yet dramatically and with such upset that we are driven to ask whether persons are some sort of anomaly, literally apart from the laws that have hitherto regulated and otherwise still regulate natural events. No doubt our bodies have very largely the same biochemistries as the higher animals. But in our deliberative and rational powers, in our moral and spiritual sensitivities, we do not seem to run with the same mechanisms with which the coyotes and the chimpanzees so naturally run. These faculties seem to "free" us from natural determinisms; we transcend nature and escape her clutches.

In their cultural life, humans are not entirely subject to the laws of evolutionary nature. But humans are, in a still more basic sense, subject to the operation of these natural laws that we sometimes seem to exceed. If nature is defined as the aggregate of all physical, chemical, and biological processes, there is no reason why it should not *include* human agency. The human animal, as much as the others, seems to be subject to all the natural laws so far formulated. Although we live at a higher level of natural organization than any other animals, and even though we act as intelligent agents in ways in which no other animals can, there does not seem to be any law of nature that we violate in either our biochemistry or our psychology. It is difficult, however, to get clear on the logical connections, to say nothing of the psychosomatic connections, of agency with causation.

In any case, when humans operate as agents on the world, we certainly do so by using rather than exempting ourselves from laws of nature. No one has ever broken the laws of gravity, or those of electricity, nutrition, ecology, or psychology. All human conduct is natural inasmuch as the laws of nature operate in us and on us willy-nilly. We cannot help but follow nature, and the advice to do so in this basic law-of-nature sense is idle and trivial, even while some high-level questions about the role of human deliberation in nature remain open.

Following Nature in an Artifactual Sense

Still, within this necessary obedience to the laws of nature, humans do have options. Submit we must, but we may nevertheless sometimes choose our route of submission. Something remains "up to us." Humans alter the course of spontaneous nature. That forces us to a second extreme—asking whether, in what we may call an *artifactual* sense, humans can follow nature. The feeling that deliberation exempts humans from the way nature spontaneously runs suggests the possibility that all agentive conduct is unnatural. Here nature is defined as the aggregate of all physical, chemical, and biological processes *excluding* those of human agency.

What we commonly mean by a natural course of events lies not so much in a scientific claim about human submission to natural law as it does in a contrast of the natural with the artificial, the artifactual. Nature runs automatically and, within her more active creatures, instinctively, or perhaps in rudimentarily cognitive ways. But persons do things by self-conscious design, which is different, and we for the most part have no trouble distinguishing the two kinds of events. A cabin in the woods is not natural, but the rocks, trees, and stream that form its setting are. A warbler's nest and a beaver's skull are natural, while a sign marking the way to the lake and an abandoned hiking boot are not. These things differ in their architecture. The one kind is merely caused, the other there for reasons.

By this account no human has ever acted deliberately except to interfere in the spontaneous course of nature. All human *actions* are in this sense unnatural because they are artifactual, and the advice to follow nature is impossible. We could not do so if we tried, for in deliberately trying to do so we act unnaturally.

Each extreme—the absolute and the artifactual—so strongly appeals to parts of our usages of the words *nature* and *follow* that some inquirers are stalled here and can go no further. Are there not some other, intermediate senses in which humans can follow nature?

Following Nature in a Relative Sense

Although always acting deliberately, humans may conduct themselves more or less continuously with nature as it is proceeding upon their entrance. All human agency proceeds in rough analogy with the sailing of a ship: if it had no skipper, it would be driven with the wind, but the skipper may set the sails to move crosswind or even tack against the wind, using the wind all the while. There are no unnatural energies. Human deliberative agency manages only to shift the direction of these natural forces, and it is that intervention which we call unnatural. But human interventions are variously disruptive, and we can recognize a relative range across which some are more, some less natural. Humans are the animals with options who, when they act, choose just how natural or artificial their actions will be.

Any parents who "plan" their children act unnaturally in the artifactual sense. Yet marriage, mating, and the rearing of children do proceed with the laws of nature. In between, some moralists and some medical persons dislike methods that greatly tamper with natural cycles. In contrast to the natural love of man and woman, homosexual conduct is unnatural, "queer," which is one of the strongest reasons why many condemn it. All childbirth is natural, all medically attended childbirth is unnatural, and yet we speak of natural childbirth as opposed to a more medically manipulative childbirth.

All landscaping is artificial; on the other hand, no landscaping violates the laws of nature. Some landscaping, which blends with natural contours and uses native flora or introduced plants compatible with it, is considered more natural; however, landscaping that bulldozes out half a hill and sets a building with exotic shrubbery against a scarred landscape is unnatural. Such culture lies awkwardly on the land. All farming is unnatural, against spontaneous nature, but some farming practices fit with the character of the soil and climate, while others do not. Bluegrass does well in Kentucky and in the Midwest, but the Deep South farmer is foolish to plant it. Some lakes are natural while others are man-made, but among the latter a pond with a relatively fixed shoreline that retains the natural flora seems more natural than a drawdown reservoir with barren edges.

It is sometimes thought that with increasing alteration and repair of nature, the degree of unnaturalness is roughly the same as the degree of progress—a successful shift from nature to culture. But the ecological perspective has forced us to wonder whether modern life has become increasingly out of kilter with its environment, lost to natural values. Big-city life in a high-rise apartment—to say nothing of the slums—or a day's work in a windowless, air-conditioned factory represents synthetic life filled with plastic everything from teeth to trees. Such life is foreign to our native, earthen element. We have lost touch with natural reality; life is, alas, artificial.

This relative sense of following nature has to do with the degree of alteration of our environment, with our appreciative incorporation of the natural environment into our life styles, and with our nearness to nature. Are there senses in which in culture humans can still be said to follow nature? Does culture simply oppose nature, or can cultural values remain complementary with natural values? With this question in mind, we examine four specific relative senses of following nature.

Following Nature in a Homeostatic Sense

The ecological crisis has introduced a homeostatic sense of following nature: "You ought not to upset the stability of the ecosystem." Human welfare depends upon following nature in a sense so basic that we wonder how far it is moral. In primitive times the human race had relatively inconsequential environmental impact, but technological humanity has at its option powers capable of massive environmental alteration. Humans use these clumsily, partly in ignorance, partly because of unplanned growth in society, but significantly too because of our defiant refusal to accept our environment, to fit into it. Environmental rebels, we overexploit nature and become misfits. Our modern conduct is thus unnatural.

Natural systems have considerable resilience and recuperative capacity; still, they may be pushed into deterioration and collapse. What will supersonic jets or aerosol cans do to the ozone layer? Where does all the DDT go, or the strontium 90? Humans sling natural chemicals around in unnatural volumes, allowing lead from gasoline, arsenic from pesticides, mercury from batteries, nitrogen from fertilizers, acids from coal-fired generators to find a way into places where they poison the life processes. Most industrial chemistry is exotic, not biodegradable, unnatural in the sense that nature cannot break it down and recycle it—or does so very slowly. Every rock made underground can be eroded at the surface; every compound organically synthesized has some enzyme that will digest it. But our artificial products choke up the system.

Should humans therefore behave naturally? Humans are the only animals with deliberate options, which the advance of science increases, and this capacity to command nature is a sort of escape from obeying spontaneous nature. We bring nature under our deliberate control. But technology does not release us from natural dependencies; it only shifts their location and character. The only sense in which we can ever break natural laws is to neglect to consider their implications for human welfare. The key point is that among our options some will help retain stability in the ecosystem and others will not. To follow nature means to choose a route of submission to nature that utilizes natural laws for our well-being.

It may be objected that the advice to *follow* nature has been subtly converted into the injunction to *study* nature—conduct with which no rational person will quarrel. But *studying* nature has nothing to do with *following* nature. To the contrary, its purpose is to free us from conforming to nature's spontaneous course, examining how much alteration we can get by with. This objection has force, but its scope is too narrow. We study nature to manipulate only parts of it, always within the natural givens to which we submit and with which we work. We study cancer to eradicate it, diabetes to repair a breakdown of natural insulin production. But we study the laws of health in order to follow them. We study the causes of floods to prevent them, but we study the laws of ecosystemic health in order to follow such laws. Those who study nature find items they may alter, but they also discover that the larger courses of nature are always to be obeyed, in the sense of intelligently fitting ourselves into their pattern of operation. We do study nature, in the end, to follow nature.

Much of this is moral in the humanistic sense. The jet set who insist on flying in SSTs, should these planes prove to deplete the protective ozone layer, would be acting immorally against their fellow humans. But we can isolate the moral ends here (respect for the welfare of others) and see the natural means (conformity to the limitations of our ecosystem) as nonmoral.[21] So far, there is nothing moral about following nature of itself. Our relations with nature are always technical or instrumental; the moral element emerges only when our traffic with nature hurts or helps persons. Still, we have reached a homeostatic sense in which humans both can and ought to follow nature, on the basis, however, of human interests.

Following Nature in an Imitative Ethical Sense

It is difficult to propose that humans ought to follow nature in an imitative ethical sense because our usual estimate—and here we vacillate—is that nature is either amoral or immoral. Morality appears in humans alone and is not, and never has been, present on the natural scene. The "conduct" of nature, if it can be called that, is simply amoral. No being can be moral unless free deliberatively, and nothing in nature has sufficient mental competence to be moral. Nature simply unfolds in geological forces and genetic programming, like the driven wind and developing seed. Biological and evolutionary processes are no more moral than gravity or electricity. Whether something does or must happen has nothing to do with whether it ought to happen. So we divide matters into the realm of the *is* and the realm of the *ought.* No study of nature can tell us what ought to happen, and following nature where doing so is optional is something that is never itself a moral issue. Nature is blind to this dimension of reality. It is a moral nullity.

We immediately grant that there are no moral agents in nature, whether orangutans, butterflies, wind, or rain; nor is nature as a whole a moral agent when personified as "Mother Nature." No natural forces or species do things in self-conscious deliberation, choosing the most moral routes. If anyone proposes that humans "follow nature" in something like the ethical sense in which Christians "follow Jesus," or Buddhists follow Buddha, such an ethicist has gone quite astray, and the blind does indeed lead the blind. There is no way to derive any of the familiar moral maxims from nature: *"One ought to keep promises." "Tell the truth." "Do to others as you would have them do to you." "Do not cause needless suffering."* There is no natural decalogue to endorse the Ten Commandments; nature tells us nothing about how we should be moral in this way. In this sense, Mill is undoubtedly right when he protests that conformity to nature has no connection with right and wrong.

But this does not end the matter, for there may be goods (values) in nature with which we ought to conform, even if these goods have not been produced by deliberative moral processes. Sentient animals, plants, and ecosystems may be of value that counts morally even though they are not themselves moral agents. They may be value objects, though they are not moral tutors. We do not follow nature in our interhuman ethics (we will warn humans who might drown in an impending canyon flood), but we may follow nature in our criteria for interspecific ethics (we might let unwary caribou drown in a raging river, leaving them to the forces of natural selection). The following chapters will attempt to disentangle these questions; we will progressively ask about duties as these result from responding to values in sentient animals, organisms, species, ecosystems.

But we need now to notice that because merely natural things have no moral agency, and because interhuman relations are clearly moral, it has been easy to suppose that there is nothing moral in our relations with nature. To grant, however, that morality emerges in human beings out of nonmoral nature does not settle the question whether we, who are moral, should follow nature: that is, sometimes orient our conduct in accord with value there.

When the issue of good in nature is raised, the counterclaim will usually arise that the course of nature is bad—one which, were we to follow it, would be immoral. Nature proceeds with a recklessness that is indifferent to life; this results in senseless cruelty and is repugnant to our moral sensitivities. Life is wrested from her creatures by continual struggle, usually soon lost; those few who survive to maturity only face eventual collapse in disease and death. With what indifference nature casts forth her creatures to slaughter! Everything is condemned to live by attacking or competing with other life. There is no altruistic consideration of others, no justice.

At this point we set aside a sense of following nature that we cannot recommend. Virtually no one will take this struggling and cruel indifference as a model for interhuman conduct. Offered an imitative ethical sense of following nature, we observe, first, that nature is not a moral agent and therefore really cannot be followed; and secondly, that there are elements in nature which, if we were to transfer them to interhuman conduct in culture, would be immoral and therefore ought not to be imitated. But does it follow that nature is therefore bad, a savage realm without natural goods? Is this ferocity, this recklessness, all that is to be said, or even the principal thing to be said? Can the issue be set in some different light?

Following Nature in an Axiological Sense

Three environments—the urban, the rural, and the wild—provide three human pursuits: culture, agriculture, and nature. All three environments are needed for human well-being, and all three vocations ought to be followed. Culture requires nature in life support, but culture's leading values are invented, not natural. Agriculture (and much technology) captures and mixes human desires with natural processes, following nature homeostatically. Further, gardens supply food, and rose gardens supply beauty, and many persons prefer the suburban environment: that is, the home graced with nature, landscaped, with cottontails in the fencerows and cardinals in the apple trees. We want parks and green space, a creekside path to the school, a woodlot behind the house, a mountain on the skyline, the home surrounded by the greater outdoors. All this undermines Mill's claim that "all praise of Civilization, or Art, or Contrivance, is so much dispraise of Nature."[22] Civilization can include nature selectively because humans value nature's presence in their suburban and rural environments. The good life is lived in a place of symbiosis between humankind and nature.

Our requirements for wild nature are more difficult to specify than those for tamed nature but are nonetheless real. They include the recreational, aesthetic, scientific, historical, character-building, diversity, dialectical, and religious values cataloged earlier. But in the pursuit of these values can humans be said to be following nature? It is tempting at first to say that humans are not *following* but *using* nature, yet on reflection one sees that elements in this *using* are better described as *following*. Wild nature is a place of encounter where we go not to act on it but to contemplate it, drawing ourselves into its order of being rather than drawing it into our order of being. We need wild nature in much the same way that we need other things in life that we appreciate for their intrinsic worth, except that wild nature provides our sole contact with worth independent of human activity. Wild nature has a kind of integrity, and we are the poorer if we do not recognize and enjoy it.

We may be said to follow that which is the object of our orienting interest, as when we follow sports, medicine, law, or the latest news developments. Many scientists, perhaps all the "pure" ones, "follow nature" in that they find its study to be of consuming interest—intrinsically worthwhile—and those who are also naturalists go on in varying senses to say that they appreciate nature, find satisfaction in it, and even love it. We follow what we "participate in," especially what provides goals we take to be of value. This sense of "follow" is less than "ethical imitation," but it is significantly moral. For we look to nature as a realm of natural value beyond mere natural facts, which, maintained in its integrity, humans may and ought to encounter. The notion of "following" nature, in addition, is deeper than following art, music, or sports, in that we are led through sensitive study to import nonhuman kinds of value. When I delight in the wild hawk in the windswept sky, that is not a value that I invent but one that I discover—and follow.

We take ourselves to nature and listen for its forms of expression, drawn by a realm of values not of our construction. We ought not to destroy this integrity but rather preserve and contemplate it. G. E. Moore lamented the "naturalistic fallacy," by which we mistakenly move from a natural *is* to an ethical *ought*, but even he finds that appreciation of the existence of natural beauty is a good.[23] As soon as we move from a natural *is* to a natural *is good*, our relations with nature become moral. We follow what we love, and the love of an intrinsic good is always a moral relationship. Value generates duty. In this axiological sense we ought to follow nature, to make its value one among our goals; in so doing, our conduct is guided by nature.

How far is this value so distributed that each individual is obligated to follow nature axiologically? Every person ought to be concerned with the preservation of natural goodness, if only because other humans undeniably do find values there. Nevertheless, we can allow individuals to weight their preferences, and there may be differing vocations, some seeking the social goods more than the natural ones. But a purely urban person, one who lives and dies on concrete without ever setting foot on Earth, is a one-dimensional person. Only those who add the rural and the wild are three-dimensional persons. No one has learned the full scope of what it means to be moral until he or she has learned to respect the integrity of wild things.

Following Nature in a Tutorial Sense

Although nature is not a moral agent, and neither its creatures nor ecosytems are moral tutors in interhuman ethics, we can often "draw a moral" from reflecting over nature: that is, gain a lesson in living. Nature has a "leading capacity"; it educates, leads us out (Latin: *educere*, to lead out, *educare*, to bring up) to know who and where we are, and what our vocation is. Encounter with nature integrates us, protects us from pride, gives a sense of proportion and place, teaches us what to expect and what to be content with. Living well is the catching of certain natural rhythms.

Folk wisdom is routinely cast in this natural idiom. The sage in the Book of Proverbs admonishes the sluggard to consider the ways of the ant and be wise. The farmer urges: "Work, for the night comes, when man's work is done"; "Make hay while the sun shines." The Psalmist notices how much we are like grass, which flourishes but is soon gone, and those who understand the "seasonal" character of life are the better able to rejoice in the turning of the seasons and to do everything well in its time. Jesus asks us, in our search for the goods of life, to consider the natural beauty of the lilies of the field, which the affected glory of Solomon could not surpass; he points out birds, who, although hardly lazy, are not anxious or worried about tomorrow. "What you sow, you reap." "Into each life some rain must fall." "All sunshine makes a desert." "By their fruits shall you know them." "The early bird gets the worm." "Time and tide wait for no man." "The loveliest rose has yet its thorns." "The north wind made the Vikings." "The tree stands that bends with the wind." "Every mile is two in winter." "If winter comes, can spring be far behind?" It is no accident that our major religious seasons are naturally scheduled: Christmas comes at the winter solstice, Easter with the bursting forth of spring, and Thanksgiving with the harvest.

A larger moral virtue, excellence of character, comes in large part, although by no means in the whole, from this natural attunement, and here the human lifestyle can follow nature: that is, be properly sensitive to its flow through us and its bearing on our habits of life. Otherwise, life lacks propriety; we do not know our place under the sun. Nature gives no ethical guidance in our interhuman affairs, but human conduct must also take an appropriate form toward our environment, toward what the world offers us. That is the deepest sense of an environmental ethic. It is what Emerson was trying to say with his claim that moral conduct includes conformity to the laws of nature.

Some will complain, perhaps fiercely, that nature serves only as an occasion for the construction of human virtues; that the natural wisdom gained shows only the virtues that develop in humans when we confront nature; and thus that there is no following of nature but rather a taking advantage of nature when it serves, a resisting of nature when it opposes, an opportunist surmounting of nature in which humans succeed resourcefully. But this anthropocentric account is too one-sided. Evolution and ecology have taught us that every kind of life is what it is environmentally, in its surroundings, not autonomously. Humans too are environmental reciprocals, indebted to our environment for what we have become in ways that are as complementary as they are oppositional. Dialectically, the character is achieved within us, but the context is relational. Nature is not sufficient to produce these virtues, but it is necessary for them. Humans are realizing in the strong and good life something of the strength and goodness that nature has disciplined into its creatures and is bequeathing to us.

Nature is a vast scene of birth and death, springtime and harvest, permanence and change; of budding, flowering, fruiting, and withering away; of processive unfolding; of pain and pleasure, success and failure; of ugliness giving way to beauty and beauty to ugliness. From the contemplation of it we get a feeling for life's transient beauty sustained over chaos. There is a music to it all, not the least when in a minor key. Even the religious urges within us, though they may promise a hereafter, are likely to advise that we must for now rest content with the world we have been given. Though we are required to spend our lives in struggle, yet we are able to cherish the good Earth and to accept the kind of universe in which we find ourselves. It is no coincidence that an ecological perspective often approaches a religious dimension in trying to help us see the beauty, integrity, and stability of nature within and behind its seeming indifference, ferocity, and evil.

Certainly there is struggle in nature. But there is also, and even more, adaptedness. There is resistance to life, but there is a conductance of life. The account we want—and will be seeking in subsequent chapters—contains both elements, and not merely as a nonsensical mixture of goods and evils. What one needs is a nature where the evils are tributary to the goods, where natural resistance is embraced within and made intelligible by natural conductance. Not death but life, including human life fitted to this planetary environment, is the principal mystery that has come out of nature. For several billion years the ongoing development and persistence of that life, culminating in human life, have been the principal features of eco-nature behind which the element of struggle must be contained as a subtheme. Our conduct ought to fit this natural life story.

Learning these lessons about life, bringing our conduct around to fit this world, is a following of nature. We can sometimes "seek nature's guidance" in a tutorial sense almost as one might seek guidance from the Bible, or Socrates, or Shakespeare, even though nature does not "write" or "speak." None of us lives to the fullest who does not study the natural order, and, more than that, none is wise who does not ultimately make peace with it.

2   *Higher Animals: Duties to Sentient Life*

 "THE QUESTION IS NOT, Can they *reason?* nor, Can they *talk?* but, Can they *suffer?*"[1] So Jeremy Bentham pinpointed half of a long-standing ethic toward animals. The other half is summarized by Aristotle: "Plants exist to give food to animals, and animals to give food to men—domestic animals for their use and food, wild ones, in most cases, if not in all, furnish food and other conveniences, such as clothing and various tools. Since nature makes nothing purposeless or in vain, all animals must have been made by nature for the sake of men."[2] Thus the traditional ethic was rather simple: Use animals for your needs, but do not cause needless suffering. This ethic is prohibitive on the one side, although enjoining care of domestic animals to prevent suffering. It is permissive on the other side; subject to prohibited cruelty, animals goods may be sacrificed for human interests. Decent hunters track wounded deer; humane trappers check their lines daily. Ranchers who let their horses starve are prosecuted in court. Kosher slaughter minimizes pain. An ox in the ditch is to be rescued, even on the sabbath. "A righteous man has regard for the life of his beast."[3]

Unlike many issues confronted in environmental ethics, there is a classical tradition about handling animals. Mutagens in the atmosphere, acid rain, toxic substances in groundwater, non-biodegradable wastes, extinctions of species, upsets of marine ecosystems, destruction of the ozone layer—such issues were never faced by our grandparents. But they lived in closer association with wild and domestic animals than do we, so one might expect issues concerning animals to have been carefully sifted, and settled. Nevertheless there has recently been a vigorous reassessment of human duties to sentient life, often involving novel dimensions.

This reawakening is allied with larger environmental issues, but is partly an independent movement.[4] Members of the Humane Society may or may not be members of the Sierra Club. The new ethic is due to increased scientific knowledge about an-

45

imal cognition, perception, experience, and behavior and to increased awareness of human kinship with animals. It is due to alarm over increased and increasingly callous uses of animals in medicine, industry, and research. It is due to revised religious beliefs. Animals have no immortal souls, but then persons may not either, or beings with souls may not be the only kind that count morally. We have come increasingly to believe that sensual pleasures expressed are a good thing, and even soulless animals enjoy such pleasures. All this results in a maturing of conscience, as ethicists see that morality should be nonarbitrary, nondiscriminatory, unrelated to irrelevant accidents of birth or to prejudice or power, and based only on morally significant differences.

For example, Merck Sharp & Dohme applied for a permit to import chimpanzees as the only known animal in which a vaccine for hepatitis B could be tested. About 1,500 persons a year in the United States die from this disease, a 1 percent fatality rate. But chimps are a threatened species and highly intelligent social animals. The capture of a juvenile chimp requires shooting the mother, and caged chimps are deprived of their natural life. An analyst in *Science* concluded, "The world has a growing population of 4 billion people and a dwindling population of some 50,000 chimpanzees. Since the vaccine seems unusually innocuous, and since the disease is only rarely fatal, it would perhaps be more just if the larger population could find some way of solving its problem that was not to the detriment of the smaller."[5] The permit was denied, largely for ethical reasons. Concern for the advanced sentient life of chimpanzees and the killing involved in their capture, especially where it posed the threat that such a form of life would be made extinct, overrode human interests. A community of Trappist monks even volunteered to test another form of the vaccine. It was later discovered that the vaccine might be tested on Beechey's ground squirrels, which are susceptible to a related virus. This was judged acceptable, as the squirrels are a lower form of life and are not endangered.

We will often be using the word "nonhuman" to refer to sentient animals. In a way, it is rather unkind to describe them in terms of what they are not; they need to be appreciated for what they are. Still the human/nonhuman boundary is a biologically identifiable one beyond which ethical concern is often thought to be exhausted, so the term is useful despite its limitations.

We will first explore some routes toward discovering human duties to nonhumans that seem promising, to find that we have to probe further.

Natural Rights, Goods, Interests

Animal Rights and Suffering

Interhuman ethics invokes the concept of rights so often that the question suggests itself as one of "animal rights," a term that can serve to protect certain animal goods that constrain duty. Charles S. Elton, an ecologist, reports a belief that he himself shares: "There are some millions of people in the world who think that animals have a right to exist and be left alone."[6] Arne Naess, a philosopher, says of animals that "in principle each of them have the same right to live and blossom as we and our children have."[7] In Rocky Mountain National Park, at lakes containing mineral salts frequented by bighorn sheep, a Park Service sign cautions visitors not to approach too closely because harassment of the sheep can result in their death; it concludes, "Respect their right to life." After years of trying to communicate with dolphins, John Lilly became convinced that his dolphins had a right to be free: "I no longer wanted to run a concentration camp for my friends."[8] Similarly persuaded, a graduate student in Hawaii freed two laboratory dolphins and was convicted of grand theft.[9]

Some right of dolphins to be free can seem as plausible as the right of scientists to own them—not an absolute right, but one whose overriding would require justification. The right of bighorns to live seems stronger than any right of park visitors to harass them. At the same time, "rights" might protect those values associated with (higher?) sentience but leave untouched values in nature associated with ecosystem stability, endangered plant species, or wilderness preservation.[10]

Rights belong mostly in Western culture; the idea is not well developed in ancient, preliterate, or Oriental societies though all cultures distinguish right and wrong. There is nothing about rights in the Bible or in Plato and Socrates. Still, it might be an important Western ethical discovery, or invention. In the West, rights attach most evidently to citizens in states. A citizen has a *legal* right to vote, assigned in laws. But we also think that *natural* rights exist, regardless of law. Innocent persons have a natural right not to be killed, no matter whether they have court access. Good laws should recognize natural rights. Few legal rights have been assigned to animals (though there are laws about animal welfare), so animal rights would seem to be natural rights. No "bill of rights" exists to give legal status to them; perhaps one should. An effort to introduce a Cetacean Bill of Rights failed in the Hawaiian legislature.

Animals rights may be simpler than human rights, but the concept also grows tenuous. What happens is similar to the degeneration of other concepts that work reasonably well at the human level and fade over a descending phylogenetic spectrum: what it means to be "conscious" or "aware," to "deliberate," to undergo "experience," to have "interests" and "needs," even to "suffer" and be "afflicted." We speak with some plausibility of the "mammal rights" of chimpanzees and dolphins but with difficulty of those of birds or of bats (the latter are mammals too) and perhaps not at all of any of oysters and insects. Is this a logical difficulty, cultural conditioning, a habit of language? Or does it reflect attenuating value in organisms? A connection of rights with human-allied kinds of experience?

When we say that persons have *natural* rights, we mean that there are certain values in personality (characteristics in the *nature* of personhood) that warrant protection with rights and that laws in culture ought to reflect these. But does the concept of a natural right apply to nonhuman nature? Perhaps we should not arbitrarily restrict rights to persons. But if we take persons off the scene entirely, in the wilderness the mountain lion is not violating the rights of the deer he slays. Animal rights are not natural in the sense that they exist in spontaneous nature. Rights go with legitimate claims and entitlements, but there are no titles and no laws that can be transgressed in the wilderness. Nature is amoral, though perhaps valuable.

Meanwhile, by constructing the concept of rights, Western ethicists discover a way to protect values naturally present in persons: that is, present whether or not legal systems recognize these personal values. So rights seem to be present when (Western?) persons come on the scene and to be absent when persons are gone. Do they come on the scene when persons encounter nonhuman animals? Perhaps rights are generated by the encounter of moral agents with sentient life—the more sentient, the more the sense of rights emerges. So rights are or should be clearly present in (or assigned to) persons, and significantly present (assigned) when persons encounter higher sentient animals. Rights would then fade as one went downward on the phylogenetic scale to the point where sentience disappears.

Rights would attach not just to persons but to sentience. But such rights would only be seminatural, not natural in the sense that they exist in wild nature; they would be cultural products, generated when moral agents (at least Western ones) encounter sentient animals. Animal rights, if there are such, are *unnatural* in the sense of not binding humans when they are only *observing* spontaneous nature. Any such rights emerge only with actual *intervening* in ecosystems. Such an interruption-generated right would be *artifactual*, stronger than a legal right, binding independently of law, but not natural. Humans must sometimes affect sentient life adversely; we may sometimes affect it beneficially; and when we do either, we might incline to say that living things gain a right, otherwise unknown in nature, not to be afflicted with needless suffering.

Let us try this in some boundary cases. Ducks feed on spent shot that falls into their ponds, needing grit for their gizzards, and afterward die slowly from lead poisoning. Two or three million ducks and geese die this way each year. This little affects the total duck population, since ducks reproduce amply. Steel shot is a little more expensive, wears the bore a little faster, and is unfamiliar to hunters, who must adjust for the weight difference. Some say, but most deny, that there is added crippling with steel shot, more wounded ducks that escape. Weapons manufacturers have resisted steel shot; federal agencies in some areas have required its use.[11]

A sensitive ethicist here will readily say that there ought to be no needless suffering, but it may seem odd to try to say that ducks have a "right" to steel shot! Some may say that the ducks have a right not to be shot at all. Assuming for the moment that humans have a place as predators in their ecosystems, and noticing that ducks are regularly eaten in nature, we seem to be left with the result that ducks may be sacrificed for humans but ought not to be subjected to needless suffering. Still, it seems strained to try to protect this value with the concept of a right.

After torrential rains preceding the fall migration, 10,000 caribou drowned in northern Quebec, attempting to cross the Koksoak and Caniapiscau rivers in October 1984. They were part of a herd of 400,000, the largest in the world, and many more were approaching the same treacherous stretch of rapids and waterfalls, though the survival of the herd was not in danger. Should wildlife authorities have attempted to divert the unwary caribou? Some Eskimo leaders blamed a government-owned utility, saying that too much flood water was let through a dam. Caribou have drowned this way for thousands of years, though earlier drownings have never been known to exceed 500 animals.[12] Should the flow have been regulated to maximize survival of the caribou?

Some will say that if such a drowning is a natural event, noninterference is the best policy; if the drowning is a result of human interference, an obligation arises to protect the caribou. But especially in the first case and perhaps in the second, it seems odd to say that the caribou have a right to be warned.

A few days later, ninety-four pilot whales beached themselves for unknown causes on Cape Cod. When the whales, though air-breathing, were stranded at low tide, their internal organs were crushed enough to disable them, but they did not die immediately. Humane society officials gave many of them injections to kill them swiftly, preventing their lingering death and drowning with the return of high tide. In December 1986 this happened again—about the same number of whales and at the same location. Workers pushed some back to sea and euthanized others. "It would be inhuman to let them suffer any more," said Greg Early, a biologist at Boston's New England Aquarium.[13] Sea World, a Florida marine attraction, recovers dolphins that beach themselves when they become ill and nurses them back to health. They display them for a time for tourists to enjoy and then return them to the sea. Such treatment of whales and dolphins seems permissible: the whales are doomed and no ecosystem is disrupted by euthanizing them; nor is there likely to be much adverse affect from rescuing a few dolphins.

In Alaska, Hubbard Glacier suddenly started to move in April 1986 and within weeks sealed off Russell Fjord from the sea, dooming porpoises and harbor seals, as the salt water was replaced by fresh water. Animal rights enthusiasts proposed to rescue the porpoises and seals, while scientists said that nothing should be done. This rare natural event would provide an opportunity for ecosystems research. (Later, the waters broke through.)

It does seem odd to say that the whales had a right to mercy killing, or that the dolphins had a right to be nursed back to health and then released, or that the seals and porpoises had a right to be rescued. Ducks, dolphins, whales—we seem to be treating animals differently from persons. We would at once say that persons had a right not to be shot at all; a right to be warned of an impending flood; a right to be rescued, medically treated, and released; perhaps even, if doomed to die, a right to a painless death. Rights readily attach to values we wish to protect in persons but transfer uncertainly to wild animals. A cultural discovery, really a convention, that works well to protect values associated with persons in culture, is not translating well to duties in an ecosystem.

"Rights" is a noun, and it can look like the name for something that an animal or a human has in addition to hair, teeth, skills. But there is no reference to anything biologically present; a right is more like a person's having "money" or "status"; that is, these things are subjectively, sociologically real in the conventions of culture, used to protect values that are inseparably entwined with personality. We might try to stretch such conventional rights and project them out of culture onto wild nature: a woman has a right not to suffer and so does a wombat. But this does not work convincingly if we move far from analogical contexts. The concept breaks down because nature is not culture.

Rights will perhaps then be said to go no further than centers of consciousness. This may be an arbitrary limit, but it is as good as any. Rights go with felt interests. Rights run the pleasure-pain spectrum; they rotate around a pleasure-pain axis. Rights go with a sense of intrusion on experience, with hurt or aspiration, and this experience is present in the higher sentient forms but vanishes lower down.

By contrast, "right" is an adjective, used to describe forms of behavior engaged in by moral agents. All that "rights" (the noun) really does is state some, but not all, of the claims about what is "right" behavior for moral agents. Humans do possess rights (that is, they can press claims on other humans about right behavior), and this use of "rights" may be contagious enough to work rhetorically with higher animals, whose claims can be pressed by sympathetic humans. But environmental ethics uses "rights" chiefly as a term of convenience; the real convictions here are about what is "right." The issues soon revert to what they always were, issues of right behavior by moral agents; an environmental ethicist, outside of culture, is better advised to dispense with the noun, *rights*, since this concept is not something that attaches to animals in the wild, and to use only the adjective, *right*, which applies when moral agents encounter nature and find something there judged to be good (appropriate, valuable) before human moral agents appear. It is sometimes convenient rhetorically but in principle unnecessary to use the concept of rights at all.

Animal Interests and Welfare

To say that x has rights seems like a statement of fact, a description of something present. But it is really a valuation embedding a prescription, claiming to have located value in the possessor of rights. Whether this location is an assignment or a discovery is not always clear. There are no rights present in the wild before human assignment. But values (interests, desires, needs satisfied; welfare at stake) may be there apart from the human presence. Rights are derivative from legal or moral norms that humans hold, mapped onto values located in fauna and flora. The sign that enjoins Rocky Mountain National Park visitors not to harass bighorns, "Respect their (right to) life," can now be analyzed. What an ethical visitor directly respects is their life, an objective fact in the wild, discovered there and positively evaluated. The words in parentheses can be subtracted without loss of logic or fact. What those words add is symbolic and psychological, exporting to the sheep a familiar cultural innovation for protecting human life. This can be pedagogically effective but is not theoretically important.

It is really more "natural" to say that animals have *goods* (or, more technically, utilities). Goods do exist in wild nature, while rights do not. In the case of sentient animals, their goods are best examined with the concept of *interests*, the fulfillment of which integrates into their welfare. Interests are both biological and psychological. A coyote has a *biological interest* in poisons in the stream from which she drinks, but may take no *psychological interest* in this. She both has and takes an interest in ground squirrels as prey. Water and seeds are in a ground squirrel's biological interest, good for his well-being, although he may take a psychological interest in what is not in his biological interest, when he seeks the junk foods handed out by tourists. What affects the coyote's biological interest adversely will eventually affect her psychological interest, when poisons cause a lingering death.

Can we then say that a psychological interest, with a biological interest tributary to it, when encountered by a moral agent, generates a good we are obliged to consider? Perhaps this will permit room for grading interests, which are more easily placed in a hierarchy than are rights. All animals should have equal consideration of their interests, coupled to their goods, but animal capacities differ. Some have greater, some lesser interests and goods. Putting this positively, Peter Miller says that the moral ideal is "promoting to the maximum extent possible the welfare of every being that has a welfare to promote."[14] This is the principle of universal benevolence, supported by the Golden Rule. Without using "rights" vocabulary, it says almost the same thing as does Naess with his "right to live and blossom."

To put the idea negatively, at least we ought to minimize

the suffering of every being that can suffer, since each has an interest in not suffering. Discarded papers from Polaroid camera film, laced with chemical salts, are tasty but poisonous to elk. Nature photographers who consider these interests ought to be careful with their toxic trash. We should rescue the caribou, dolphins, seals; euthanize the whales; and (for those who must hunt) mandate steel shot.

But do we really feel obligated to promote to the maximum extent possible the welfare of every being that has a welfare to promote? A sandhill crane in Texas, which lost its lower legs either in a trap or to an alligator, was fitted with artificial limbs and suction-cup feet. A golden eagle was given a cornea transplant. A Laysan albatross with sheared wing and tail feathers, found in San Francisco streets, received feather implants and was flown by airplane 5,000 miles back to the Midway Islands and released. In Las Vegas a mallard hen, shot through the chest with a target arrow by a boy, was flown by helicopter to a veterinarian, who removed the arrow and administered antibiotics. The duck pulled through and made national headlines. Researchers in Florida spent $200,000 putting artificial flippers on a sea turtle that had been attacked by a shark; they hoped to rehabilitate it and turn it loose. Some will praise such medical assistance to wild animals as charitable acts, examples of universal benevolence, but many others will think that this is a misguided treating of wild animals as though they were fellow humans.

The bighorn sheep of Yellowstone caught conjunctivitis the winter of 1981–82. On craggy slopes, partial blindness can be fatal: more than 300 bighorns, 60 percent of the herd, fell to their deaths or to predators, or were injured, slowly weakened, and starved. But park officials refused to treat the disease. The Park Service, although it can urge visitors to respect the bighorns' right to life, did not conclude that bighorns had a right to medical treatment saving their lives. Their decision was that the disease was natural and should be left to run its course.[15] If we abandon the idea that the bighorns, unlike humans with pinkeye, had a right to treatment, did humans still have a duty to promote the bighorn welfare? Had the *Chlamydia* microbe that caused the pinkeye, being an insentient animal, no welfare (or less welfare) to consider?

Colorado wildlife veterinarians, on the other hand, have made extensive efforts to rid the Colorado bighorns of lungworm (genus: *Protostrongylus*), promoting the welfare of the sheep, perhaps thinking that such treatment respects their right to life. Were they were moral than the Wyoming veterinarians? One reply here is that the lungworm parasite was contracted (some say) from imported domestic sheep and that such human interruption yields a duty to promote welfare not present in the Yellowstone case. Others say rather that the parasite is native but that the bighorns' natural resistance to it is weakened because human settlements in the foothills deprive sheep of their winter forage and force them to winter at higher elevations; there, undernourished, they contract the lungworm first and later die of pneumonia, caused by bacteria, generally genus *Pasteurella.* Is there here an obligation to promote sheep welfare against that of *Protostrongylus* and *Pasteurella?* (Some will say that there are no moral issues here at all; only different management objectives.)

The obligation to universal benevolence is too strong. It fails to incorporate any moral tolerance of the processes of wild nature— of letting a strayed albatross die, or a beached whale or dolphin, or a turtle attacked by sharks. There is no human duty to promote by intervention the richest psychological life of wild animals, or their richest biological life. What could this mean in adjusting the number of rabbits that the coyotes devour? Should we divide the harem of a dominant bull for the more equitable satisfaction of young bulls, promoting the maximum welfare of each male? We have a more restricted obligation.

Still, some obligation to benevolence sometimes seems to constrain what humans ought to do. A Wyoming rancher built a wire-mesh fence, twenty-eight miles long and five feet high, to protect his cattle-grazing land from antelope. He also hoped to scatter or destroy the herd because there was a likelihood that wildlife authorities would declare the area critical habitat for antelope, which would make stripmining his property for coal difficult or impossible. The area contains a checkerboard pattern of public and private lands, so that the fence, though entirely on private land, blocked access of the herd to both public and private lands. An early, severe winter (1983–84) followed; snows prevented the antelope from foraging elsewhere, and the fence blocked their migration to the Red Rim area, which blows free of snow. About 1,500 antelope were threatened with starvation.

At the urging of the Wyoming governor, together with the Game and Fish Department and the Wyoming Wildlife Federation, and accompanied by national news coverage of the impending starvation, the rancher agreed to have sections of the fence laid down, to be put back up the following spring. Ranchers claim that an overpopulation of antelope is destroying range, though wildlife biologists reply that cattle and antelope do not eat the same plants, their diets overlapping only about 8 percent. The fence was put up and taken down several winters, and finally the court ordered it removed or rebuilt to allow antelope to pass under it.

We might say, with mixed convictions, that the rancher had a right to protect his cattle, perhaps to protect his mineral rights, but that he had no right to destroy antelope this way, especially since it caused suffering by blocking the normal migration routes to winter range. But all that is talk of what rights a human did or did not have. Turning to the animals, we may be unclear whether to say that antelope have a right to their winter range. Certainly they do not possess any such right in the wild. We might better say that the welfare of the rightless antelope makes a claim on humans strong enough to limit even some human property rights. (Depending on the public interest in the herd, we might say that the rancher was entitled to some compensation for the loss of these rights.)

The 1983–84 winter continued a cruel one and of a herd of 8,400 in southern Wyoming about 85 percent died, or 7,200 antelope. Normal mortality is 15 to 25 percent. Many antelope migrated south into the western slope of Colorado, where thousands of deer and elk were also starving. Wildlife lovers and hunters, joined by many businesses, donated $250,000 to feed them. They pressed the Colorado Division of Wildlife into undertaking more feeding than officials really wished to do, spending $1.6 million to help 70,000 animals, the most extensive feeding program ever in the state.

Did the wildlife lovers recognize some welfare claim of the animals to be fed that the game managers failed to recognize? Biologists argued that feeding, by allowing the weaker animals to survive, only reduces the vigor of the species; they claimed to be equally concerned for the long-term welfare of the animals. Were they in fact callous about the starving deer? If not fed, the animals will damage haystacks and orchards, and ranchers and farmers will claim a right to compensation. It seems that the welfare claim works against the rancher's rights when the antelope are attempting to reach their winter range in an ecosystem, but that the welfare claim evaporates when the antelope, migrating freely throughout that ecosystem, run out of food in a rough winter.

One argument was that the winter was quite exceptional and

that humans had increasingly occupied the normal winter range of the animals; they no longer had anywhere to go; and they had a "right" either to their winter range or to supplementary feeding in lieu of it. Or at least that humans had a duty to protect animal lives that they had put in jeopardy. If human intervention, and not just the forces of natural selection, are causing the deaths, that does seem to make a difference in the welfare claim.

A Satisfactory Fit for Species

The picture gets more complicated. Negatively, there are no rights in the uncivil wild; positively, there are many animal interests and goods there. Realistically, suffering is an integral feature of sentient life in ecosystems. Nature is harsh; herbivores starve; carnivores kill. When humans encounter wild nature, animals have neither a right nor a welfare claim to be spared the pains imposed by natural selection. That is why we worry about diverting the unwary caribou from a naturally caused flood, why we feel no strong obligation to mercy-kill beached whales or rescue sick dolphins or feed hungry antelope. Backyard bird feeders to the contrary, robins have no right to be fed. Wild animals have to look out for themselves. There is no human duty to eradicate the sufferings of creation.

Worse, we are wrongheaded to meddle. When wildlife managers feed deer, they increase the herd for the hunt but upset natural forces. Wild creatures may have, asymmetrically, some negative claim not (without cause) to be harmed but no positive claim to be helped. Even among humans, with their rights, we have a strong duty not actively to harm other persons but a somewhat weaker duty to feed the poor: I can be taken to court for harming a stranger but not for refusing to feed him. Still, we may think that the starving human has a right to be fed and that government policy (as well as human charity) ought to consider this. Meanwhile, humans leave wild animals to the ravages of nature; environmental ethics has no duty to deny ecology but rather to affirm it.

Environmental ethics accepts predation as good in wild nature. But if all suffering introduces rights or welfare claims when moral agents come on the scene, a really consistent animal ethics will dislike predation and seek to eliminate it. Steve F. Sapontzis concludes: "Where we can prevent predation without occasioning as much or more suffering than we would prevent, we are obligated to do so"; animals ought to be spared needless suffering.[16] He might add that a human mother would not accept the principle that predation is the way ecosystems work if her child were being eaten by a grizzly bear, so why should she accept it when a fawn is being eaten by a cougar? The child has a right to be rescued; does not the fawn have the same right? Or at least ought we not consider its interests? What about the interests of the bear? If its act were seen simply as a value capture within the wilds, we should not say that the grizzly, acting in its interests, was violating the rights of even the child, much less the fawn. The human victim has a right only in relation to other humans, with whom it coexists in culture. The grizzly is not violating human rights when it eats a child, but other humans are if they fail to rescue the victim.

The fawn lives only in an ecosystem, in nature; the child lives also in culture. Environmental ethics is not social ethics, nor does it give us any duty to revise nature. Our attitude toward predation is not just that it is practically difficult to remove, or that removing it is an impossible ideal. We would not want to take predation out of the system if we could (though we take humans out of the predation system), because pain and pleasure are not the only criteria of value, not even the principal ones. Pain and pleasure are subsumed under a bigger picture. The maximum happiness of particular sentient animals is not what ecosystems are all about, though ecosystems select well-adapted member species, which they support with a generally satisfactory life. These play roles and flourish in their own niches, with increasingly distinctive organic individuality as one goes up the system (see Chapter 5). In the trophic pyramid the omnivores and carnivores regularly and necessarily capture values by imposing pain on others.

Meanwhile, predation does not all that obviously increase suffering. Slow death by starvation or disease is not more pleasant than nearly instantaneous death by tooth and claw. Predation prevents overpopulation from the surplus of young and culls the aged and the diseased. We may judge, in fact, that bighorns, coyotes, caribou, ducks, squirrels, bluebirds in their wild places, selected over evolutionary time as adapted fits in their niches, already have something approaching the richest psychological and biological lives available to them within the constraints of their ecosystems. Suffering, though present, has been trimmed to a level that is functional, bearable, even productive. (Again, see Chapter 5.) We can still hold that psychological lives, subjective experiences, felt interests satisfied, where these occur in nature, are intrinsic values and that they ought not to be sacrificed lightly, sometimes not at all. When humans enter an ecosystem of interwoven intrinsic values, duties can arise. But these duties of universal human benevolence must be kept in the context of beliefs about the satisfactory "benevolence" (= goodness) of ecosystems, comprehending inescapable suffering. This urges a nonmeddlesome Golden Rule and checks benevolence by the realities of ecosystemic nature.

The questions, then, are not merely, Can they suffer? or Have they rights? or Have they a welfare that claims our benevolence? These questions, while relevant, get backed up against a bigger question: Has the animal a satisfactory place in its ecosystem? Sentience is to be set in an ecosystemic context. Where that place has been blocked—as for the antelope by the fence, or the caribou by the floodwaters (if human intervention aggravated the flood), or the bighorns by their exotic parasite—we admit a claim to duty on behalf of the animals. Sometimes we may even rhetorically or symbolically speak of their rights. Where that place remains natural, no duty arises.

This satisfactory fit is to be judged collectively at the species level; it will be distributed to individuals on average. No species can flourish without flourishing individuals who are tokens of the type, who exemplify the natural kind. But in the struggle for life, for adaptive fit, many individuals will be losers; their welfare must be sacrificed to predators or competitors. That is not satisfactory to these individuals; their preferences are not satisfied. But we humans who observe this system find such a system, where many natural kinds are interwoven into a web of life, satisfactory—not just in the sense that we tolerate it but that we see how it yields a flourishing of species, manifest in individuals.

It may seem unsatisfactory that innocent life has to suffer, and we may first wish for an ethical principle that protects innocent life. This principle is persuasive in culture, and we do all we can to eliminate human suffering. But ought suffering to continue when humans do or can intervene in nature? That it ought not to continue is a tender sentiment but so remote from the way the world *is* that we must ask whether this is the way the world *ought* to be in a tougher, realistic environmental ethic. A morally satisfactory fit must be a biologically satisfactory fit. What *ought to be* is derived from what *is*. In that sense, humans do follow nature axiologically and set our moral standards accordingly. Nature is not a moral agent; we do not imitate nature for interhuman conduct. But nature is a place of satisfactory fitness, and we take that as a criterion for some moral judgments. We endorse a painful good.

Animals Captured in Culture

Once we realize that we have no duty to reform wild nature, what more? When humans tame nature, then should innocent life never suffer? Should we deny ecology, or continue to affirm it, or at least tolerate it? There seems no commanding reason to reform nature when we superimpose agricultural and industrial interactions. Whatever we say about interhuman duties within culture, humans have no duties, in interspecific environmental ethics, to interrupt the course of wild nature. Nor, when exploiting nature for human interests, have we a strong obligation to reduce the suffering below levels found independently of the human presence. Humans are not bound to inflict no innocent suffering. That is contrary to nature. In the clash and interweaving of goods in an ecosystem, pain goes with the defending and capturing of goods that characterize all sentient life. Nothing lives autonomously, not even autotrophs (plants). Everything crowds and competes with neighboring life. One good must spoil another. Heterotrophs (animals) sacrifice other lives for their own. Sentient lives both suffer and cause pain. No predator can live without causing pain.

When humans enter such an environment, they may continue to inflict innocent suffering, particularly in the regimens of securing food, shelter, and basic physical comforts. Human predation on nature, more or less within the natural patterns, cannot be condemned simply because humans are moral agents, not if nonhuman predation has been accepted as a good in the system. (Human predation in culture would be another thing.) The wild animal has no right or welfare claim to have from humans a kinder treatment than in nonhuman nature. What should happen morally in an encounter with nature (distinguished from what happens within culture) is a function of what has happened naturally. Neither in nature nor in culture-nature interactions does need imply duty. So the deer need food, the albatross and turtle need help, but have no claim on us to provide it.

Meanwhile, culture ought not to amplify the cruelty in nature, certainly not without showing that greater goods come of doing so. The way to judge whether an intervention introduces needful suffering is to ask whether the suffering is analogous to functional, baseline suffering in the ecosystemic routines. So far, this is an ethic of *nonaddition* but not of *subtraction*. *Needful* means *quasi-ecological*, and *ecological* tends to imply not rights but right. At this point, right in culture means no more than right in nature, that is, in continuity with the satisfactory fit that such an animal had in the ecosystem from which it was taken. Again, what *is* in nature is taken as a criterion for what *ought to be* when culture overtakes nature. Nature did not make plants and animals for the use of man, not in the way that Aristotle thought, but humans do live in an ecosystem where one species must capture the values of others to live. Making a resource of something else is pervasive in the system, even when it inflicts suffering; when humans do this too, they simply follow nature. There is nothing immoral about participating in the logic and biology of one's ecosystem. (Nothing here implies what "ought to be" within culture.)

In this sense those who sympathize with the pains of animals and wish to eliminate these pains are not biologically sensitive but insensitive. Pain is a pervasive fact of life, not to be wished away by a kindly ethic either in natural systems or in cultural overlays on these systems. Suffering is a necessary evil, a sad good, a dialectical value. That humans continue this pattern with their interruptions of the natural order shows no disrespect for animal life; to the contrary, it respects natural processes. We follow nature and set norms accordingly.

It might first be thought that pain is an evil wherever it occurs, in nature or in culture, and so it does not matter whether the injury is to a woman or a wombat. If the evil is that it hurts, the one has as much right to treatment as the other. But pain operates functionally in wombats in their niche; pain in a woman in a medically skilled culture is pointless. Pain in nature is situated, instrumental pain; it is not pointless in the system, even after it becomes no longer in the interests of the pained individual. The profit in the pain has vanished in culturally situated persons, but it remains in the wild. Animals have no right to be removed from their niche; neither have we a duty to remove them or a duty to reform nature when we superimpose agriculture and industry on it.

We can add that where pain in agricultural or industrial animals has also become pointless, because they too have been removed from the environment of natural selection, humans have a duty to remove that pain, as far as they can. With that we do not disagree, but this extended ethic is a duty of benevolence, not one of justice.

Where humans elect to capture animals for food, domestication, research, or other utility, our duties to them, if any arise, are generated by these animals' encounters with culture; they are not simply a matter of the animals' *capacity* to suffer pains but of their *context*. That context is as natural as it is cultural; it is a hybrid of the two. The animals do not, in their sentient life, participate in human culture; on the other hand, they are not in the wild but domesticated. Judgments about duties are not merely to sentience but to sentience in niche in ecosystem, now overtaken by culture. In the capturing of values in nature, pain is often present even in innocent life, and when culture captures values in nature, there is only a weak duty to subtract from the pain. Such pain is no longer in the context of natural selection, but it remains in the context of the transfer of ecological goods, inherited from the wilds.

The strong ethical rule is this: Do not cause inordinate suffering, beyond those orders of nature from which the animals were taken. One ought to fit culture into the natural givens, where pain is inseparable from the transfer of values between sentient lives. Culturally imposed suffering must be comparable to ecologically functional suffering—a *homologous principle*. It has a "similar logic" (Greek: *homologos*). Combining this with the principle of nonaddition, humans introduce no inordinate unnatural suffering, though they may substitute variant forms in their interests. If we wish to symbolize this with a cultural discovery, we can use rights language and say that animals gain that much right in their encounter with humans. The relevant question is not simply Bentham's "Can they suffer?" but "Is the human-inflicted suffering excessive to natural suffering?" Ethics does not require us to deny our ecology but rather to affirm it, even as we domesticate and rebuild our environment. Ecology, not charity or justice, provides the benchmark or, at least, the floor.

Going further can be commended but not required. A weak ethical rule is, reduce suffering as far as it is pointless. This ethic has an ecosystem base, though above that base it has a hedonist concern for pointless pain.

A further problem with the good-neighbor policy is that with it we are able to judge duties only to kindred life. Humans often find something attractive about primates and higher mammals. They are like ourselves; we do not wish our kin to suffer. But that is covertly anthropocentric after all; we are being "humane" by enlarging the class of those with humanlike desires. This extends to nearby nature the civility of culture. It is a homologous ethic from the other direction, that of culture. We give animals rights only so far as we can see ourselves in them. But nature is not an arena of good neighbors; the goodness there spontaneously arises in the clash of the struggle to survive and maintain adaptive fit. When humans interact with nature, the ethics that has proved appropriate within culture only partly deploys there. It may not deploy at all into our relations with alien sentient life.

Higher animals suffer the more because they can form plans and carry them out; their sentience joins with their intentions and frustrations. But we are unsure whether this is so in insects. Sentience conveniently marks the border of the capacity to suffer, but this is not quite accurate, perhaps quite inaccurate, and we do not know what sentience involves in alien forms, whether they suffer in their sentience or not. Some human sentience is without much capacity to be pained by it; there is little pain associated with seeing or smelling. On the other side, do insects enjoy their sentience? Sentience in lower life may be weakly connected with pleasure. Earthworms are to some degree sentient, they have nerves, ganglia, brains, even endorphins (natural opiates). But their form of sentience may be so alien to ours that "Do to others as you would have them do to you" is untranslatable there. One hardly knows what universal benevolence to earthworms, respecting their rights, would mean. But we can make good sense of their adaptive fit, of a satisfactory place for their natural kind in an ecosystem. And we can make some estimates of whether our cultural uses of them (as bait for fish) take place in analogy with their roles in ecosystems.

Human Dominion over Animals

Human Superiority versus Biocentrism

That humans are superior to animals is an ancient axiom. The Book of Genesis begins with a divinely ordained human dominion over the creatures. Jesus said that persons are of more value than many sparrows. Immanuel Kant claimed:

> The fact that man can have the idea "I" raises him infinitely above all the other beings living on earth. By this he is a *person* . . . that is, a being altogether different in rank and dignity from *things*, such as irrational animals, which we can dispose of as we please.

So far as animals are concerned, we have no direct duties. Animals are not self-conscious and are there merely as a means to an end. That end is man. . . . Our duties towards animals are merely indirect duties towards humanity.[17]

This position is not found only among old-fashioned theologians and metaphysicians; it has recent scientific support. Michael Polanyi, a philosopher of science, insists:

It is the height of intellectual perversion to renounce, in the name of scientific objectivity, our position as the highest form of life on earth, and our own advent by a process of evolution as the most important problem of evolution.[18]

G. G. Simpson, a paleontologist, concludes a survey of evolution by insisting on "the anthropocentric point of view," despite the fact that he finds no directional progress in the evolutionary process:

Man is an entirely new kind of animal in ways altogether fundamental for understanding of his nature. It is important to realize that man is an animal, but it is even more important to realize that the essence of his unique nature lies precisely in those characteristics that are not shared with any other animal. His place in nature and its supreme significance to man are not defined by his animality but by his humanity. . . . Man *is* the highest animal.[19]

W. H. Murdy, a biologist, warns: "An anthropocentric belief in the value, meaningfulness, and creative potential of the human phenomenon . . . may be requisite to the future survival of the human species and its cultural values."[20] Charles Darwin, defending human descent from anthropoid primates, could still write eloquently of human superiority.

Man in the rudest state in which he now exists is the most dominant animal that has ever appeared on this earth. He has spread more widely than any other highly organised form: and all others have yielded before him. He manifestly owes this immense superiority to his intellectual faculties, to his social habits, which lead him to aid and defend his fellows, and to his corporeal structure. The supreme importance of these characters has been proved by the final arbitrament of the battle for life. Through his powers of intellect, articulate language has been evolved; and on this his wonderful advancement has mainly depended. . . . He has invented and is able to use various weapons, tools, traps, etc., with which he defends himself, kills or catches prey, and otherwise obtains food. . . . He has discovered the art of making fire, by which hard and stringy roots can be rendered digestible, and poisonous roots or herbs innocuous. This discovery of fire, probably the greatest ever made by man, excepting language, dates from before the dawn of history. These several inventions, by which man in the rudest state has become so pre-eminent, are the direct results of the development of his powers of observation, memory, curiosity, imagination, and reason.

Man may be excused for feeling some pride at having risen, though not through his own exertions, to the very summit of the organic scale.[21]

Even if older versions of anthropocentrism are outdated, is there not a modern version that is reasonable? It is not necessary to deny intrinsic values in nature, or animal goods, or duties to sentient life; nor is it necessary to affirm purposive design in nature or the divinely mandated dominion; we only maintain that humans are superior to the animals. Still, any superiority will certainly color ethical judgments, for it is likely to have, or be thought to have, moral relevance for discriminatory treatment. Thus the issue is both metaphysical and of practical concern, the more urgent now that humans have almost unlimited powers over animal lives. Biocentric environmental ethics argues, to the contrary, that there is no human superiority, or much less than commonly believed, and that what there is is morally irrelevant. Paul Taylor, a philosopher pleading "the ethics of respect for nature," contends that the view by which we "regard humans to be superior in inherent worth to all other species" is "completely groundless," "at bottom nothing more than the expression of an irrational bias in our own favor," a "deep-seated prejudice." In contrast, "the biocentric outlook recommends itself as an acceptable system of concepts and beliefs to anyone who is clear-minded, unbiased, and factually enlightened, and who has a developed capacity of reality awareness with regard to the lives of individual organisms."[22]

Richard and Val Routley, although not happy with biospheric egalitarianism and preferring to speak of biospecies impartiality, nevertheless complain of "human chauvinism." "Class chauvinism . . . is *substantially* differential, discriminatory and inferior treatment . . . for items outside the class, for which there is not *sufficient* justification. Human chauvinism is class chauvinism where the class is humans." The Routleys maintain that an environmental ethic requires "the removal of humans from a dominant position in the natural order."[23] Here we can recall Arne Naess's claim that animals "in principle . . . have the same right to live and blossom as we and our children have."

Albert Schweitzer concludes: "Ethics thus consists in this, that I experience the necessity of practising the same reverence for life toward all will-to-live, as toward my own. Therein I have already the needed fundamental principle of morality. It is *good* to maintain and cherish life; it is *evil* to destroy and check life."[24] The authors quoted above often qualify their egalitarian principles to make place for human interests advanced over those of the animals, but it is not clear how they can do this consistently. John Muir puts the question we must now try to answer: "Why should man value himself as more than a small part of the one great unit of creation?"[25]

It is permissible and even morally required to treat unequals with discrimination. One should treat *equals equally* and *unequals equitably*. But two things differing evaluatively must differ descriptively in ways relevant to support the differing evaluation. Are *Homo sapiens* and *Canis lupus* unequals? And if so, what constitutes equitable treatment of each class?

Suppose we make a trial list of human uniqueness and superiority claims.

1. Humans see better.
2. Humans run faster.
3. Humans walk upright.
4. Humans copulate face to face.
5. Humans care for their young longer.
6. Humans cook their food.
7. Humans are conscious.
8. Humans are self-conscious.
9. Humans use tools.
10. Humans use language.
11. Humans reason.
12. Humans use language to reason.
13. Humans can be criticized.
14. Humans are creative.
15. Humans have free will.
16. Humans are moral agents.
17. Humans are aware of their deaths.
18. Humans laugh at themselves.
19. "Man is the only animal that blushes. Or needs to" (Mark Twain).
20. Humans deliberately defend their interests.
21. Humans form societies.
22. Humans form cultures.
23. Humans do science.
24. Humans can be religious.
25. Humans can be awe-inspired.
26. Humans espouse world views.

Some of these claims are false, some are distinctively true of humans. Some are *quantitatively* true—more true in humans; some are *qualitatively* true—present in humans and absent in animals. But if one says, for instance, that rationality is a morally relevant criterion of superiority, placing humans above animals, then does one by the same rule say that college professors have more value than freshmen? Or does one say that although professors have more rationality, fine-tuning the criterion is irrelevant; all humans have crossed a threshold of rationality that no non-humans have crossed. Excellent humans may in fact possess more value than mediocre humans, but all possess sufficient value to warrant equal treatment by law and common morality. Which of these claims are unique and significant enough to be morally relevant as a basis for discriminatory (discriminating) treatment: using animals rather than humans for food or research; shooting a rabid fox but treating a rabid person; medicating pinkeye in humans but not in bighorn sheep?

In the previous section, the ethical analysis of animal rights, goods, welfare left them in nature, while humans were removed to culture. We must now resurvey that boundary division to map what it means for human superiority in a world where culture is overlaid on ecosystems characterized by satisfactory fitness. After that, we can return to domestic and industrial uses of animals, concluding with an analysis of hunting, where culture once more returns to nature.

Equality, Discriminatory and Discriminating Treatment

"Equality" is a positive word in ethics, "discriminatory" a pejorative one. On the other hand, simplistic reduction is a failing in the philosophy of science and metaphysics; to be "discriminating" is desirable in logic and value theory. Something about treating humans as equals with wolves, monkeys, and caribou seems to "reduce" humans to merely animal levels of value, a "no more" version in ethics of the "nothing but" fallacy often met in science. Humans are "nothing but" naked apes. Humans have "no more" value than apes. Something about treating wolves, monkeys, and caribou as the equals of humans seems to elevate the animals unnaturally. There is something insufficiently discriminating in such judgments. It is species-blind in a bad sense, blind to the real differences between species, valuational differences that do count morally. A discriminating ethicist will insist on preserving the differing richness of valuational complexity, wherever found.

Admittedly, each animal is well equipped for its niche, with finely honed superiorities there. Eagles see better telescopically, and gazelles run faster than humans. In this context, "the 'degeneracy' of a parasite is as perfect as the gait of a gazelle," claims Stephen Jay Gould.[26] Humans have a developed capacity to reason; wolves reason simply, though when hunting in packs they do "figure out" how to cut an aging musk ox from the herd. Wolves have a keen capacity to smell, atrophied or never existing in humans. Neither superiority is better than the other. Goods are to be judged for the animal in its niche, and the distinctively human goods (morality, language-rationality, self-awareness, espousing world views), like the array of animal goods (agility, perception, endurance, fertility), are good only relatively in a niche, not absolutely or hierarchically better. Everything is a satisfactory fit in its place.

The human superiorities are splendidly adapted for culture, the human niche. But humans—so the egalitarian ethic argues—should not value themselves more highly for being cultured and disvalue wild animals because they are not. The latter are supposed to be not civilized but wild, and their kind is not to be judged faulty or individuals faulted for their beastly lack of civility. Animals are not morally deficient, much less immoral; they are amoral. It is pointless to blame a blue jay for "selfishly" stealing seeds at the feeder while praising a child who shares her cookies. Animals have all the capacities they need for the niches they fill; to disvalue them because they are not moral or civil is out of place.

Further, judgments of merit are inappropriate. Merit is having more, demerit having less of a value one can gain or fail to gain. An Eagle Scout has more merit than a Tenderfoot. A monkey does not have more merit than a minnow. The alpha monkey in a troop dominance order may have more merit than a delta monkey, but we base no moral judgments on this. A moral person may have more merit than an immoral one, but a person, who is moral, does not have more merit than a monkey, who is not. Such arguments improve the sensitivity of analysis in environmental ethics.

Nevertheless, the human superiority is not groundless prejudice. To say that humans should be judged by their standards of good and kangaroo rats by theirs, and that each is equally good of its kind, overlooks the kind of good realized in each. It is true that each natural kind has (more or less) equal (or at least amply satisfactory) fitness in its niche. Each kind has capacities and habitats by and within which its contextual goods are expressed. But equal fitness or goodness in differing niches does not imply equal value or goodness in the differing lives-in-context. Good they are where they are, and good we are where we are; but cross-place comparisons are possible—at least by humans, who seem to be the only animals capable of making such comparisons. This is true even if humans have quite limited entrance into what it is like to be a spider, a monkey, a tree.

Each natural kind has place, integrity, even perfections, but none of the others reaches the eminence of personality. Without faulting the animals for their lack of civility, an animal capable of culture (represented by Einstein) realizes a greater range of values in its life than does an animal incapable of culture (a kangaroo rat). Emphatically, this does not deny that kangaroo rats have intrinsic worth or that humans have duties toward them; rather, it discriminates differentials in value richness that are ethically relevant. To take an extreme, the difference between two humans (Einstein and Jesus Christ, both members of the same species) can be greater and more interesting than the difference between plant species; two moss species may be separated mostly by the length of the midrib in their leaves. And a researcher who chooses the least sentient animal that will do for the purposes of the research (using ground squirrels rather than chimpanzees) is recognizing that value richness in primates exceeds that in rodents. A parasite may have survival capacities as perfected as those of a gazelle, given the niche of each, but neither parasite nor gazelle runs the spectrum of values that humans run.

It is not so much that the "lower" organisms lack anything—they have quite satisfactorily the capacities they need to fit their niches, else they would be extinct—but rather that lower organisms do not express the richness in potential in the ecosystem as fully as do higher ones (see Chapter 5). They seek their own goods successfully, but these are limited goods, primitive ones seen in the perspective of what else eventuates in evolutionary development. It is a tragedy for a human to be a vegetable, but it is not a tragedy for a vegetable to be a vegetable; the difference lies in the value richness that has failed in the deformed human, while nothing has failed in the vegetable. To the contrary, a great deal has been realized, although the ecosystem in attaining vegetable existence has not yet fully expressed its potential in value richness. Also, vegetable existence with its photosynthesis makes human existence with its mobility possible.

It is difficult to specify any precise, single, distinctive, morally relevant human characteristic. There is perhaps no such characteristic. Some distinctive traits may be only incidental or accidental (copulating face to face), others more nearly essential (espousing world views). Even among the latter traits various abilities contribute to a valuational gestalt, like puzzle pieces forming a whole picture. Biologists no longer look for distinguishing essences in defining a species but use what is called a polytypic or polythetic definition, a gestalt of features some combination of which is sufficient for species membership but no one of which is necessary.

Contemporary philosophers, like biologists, are less inclined than their forebears were to look for single principles in anything—especially in complex things—and more inclined to welcome multidimensioned differences, to want holism and not reductions. The human richness, just because it is an integrated and complex pattern, cannot be reduced to any one feature. We can welcome transitional zones between the animal and the human skills. But since there is no one place where we can, in principle, draw a single hard line, we do not conclude that there are no significant differences between here and there, no transition zone through which we cross.

The human uses of reason and language shade through quantitative degrees of difference from animal cognition and pass over into qualitative differences in kind. Chimpanzees communicate, occasionally use symbols; humans employ mathematical systems to figure their incomes or speculate about black holes and the big bang. Higher animals are indisputably conscious, sometimes self-conscious. Chimps (and almost no others) recognize themselves in mirrors. If a red tag is placed on a chimp's ear while he is asleep, he will, upon waking and accidentally passing a mirror, reach to his ear to remove it.[27] But the human self-awareness becomes intense and deeply reflective, abetted by philosophical doctrines and religious experiences that are absent from the animal world.

In some cases the animal skills get stretched over toward culture, and domesticated animals reveal the wealth of potential animal experience when their wildness hybridizes with culture. An ailing infant gorilla was borrowed from a San Francisco zoo, raised in close association with Stanford University researchers, and taught a sign language. Koko used several hundred signs to construct such sentences as, "Koko, listen bird," "Up please," "Hurry go," "Give me drink," "Sorry me," "Me can't," "Fine animal, gorilla." When there was an earthquake, Koko signed, "Darn floor, bad bite!" She once requested a cat and was first given a toy cat, which she treated so carefully that later she was given a live kitten, whereupon she signed, "Koko love soft there." When the kitten was run over by a car, Koko grieved.

When the zoo asked for the return of this valuable animal, the researchers replied that because she had learned language it was now morally wrong to treat her as a zoo animal. She was not returned, and the zoo was reimbursed by donations. Does the learning of language, embellishing whatever communication system wild gorillas have, make a moral difference? Nim Chimsky, an educated chimpanzee, was returned to the community of zoo chimpanzees from which he had originally come and immediately established complete domination over his companions![28]

Some of the claims for Koko and Nim may be deflated by a more critical assessment of their behavior, but such cases show that we cannot draw as comfortable a line between humans and higher animals as we earlier thought. They simultaneously show that there are significant differences within the animal levels of experience as well. No squirrel could have been taught Koko's sign language, or grieved when it lost a pet cat. But just as gorillas greatly exceed the capacities of squirrels, so humans, for all our discoveries about gorillas, still greatly exceed the capacities of gorillas.

There is night and there is day, and to point out that there is twilight does not deny either. It is not arbitrary to regard one thing as living (a planarian) and another as nonliving (a quartz crystal) just because some things are intermediate (a crystallized virus). Wolves are sentient and trees nonsentient, although ants live in a twilight zone. There are gradients of passage, but emergences are real. There are no sharp lines, no neatly specifiable, philosophical essences in evolutionary theory; what we find is a valued gestalt of features present in our species and absent in other species. It does not dissolve this display of personality to find that its component dimensions fade already in some humans, and fade further into the animal world out of which we once evolved. In a unified science and value theory one does not wish it any other way. One welcomes the continuity with animal sensate life while resisting reductions and rejoicing in the distinctively novel compositions of the human coming. Quantitative differences add into qualitative differences; they shift in their interplay to recompose an emerging gestalt that exceeds previous evolutionary achievement.

Humans as Moral, Cognitive, Critical Overseers

Humans are in the world *ethically*, as no other animal is. Humans are in the world *cognitively* at linguistic, deliberative, self-conscious levels equaled by no other animal. Humans are in the world *critically*, as nothing else is. Only humans can consider, reflect upon, be right or wrong about the way they are in the world. Ducklings can make mistakes in their imprinting, but this is a mistake of instinct, not of reason. Ducklings do not cause ecological crises as a result of mistaken world views. Bats are in the world as nothing else, with superior auditory senses. But humans can reflect how bats are in the world; bats cannot reflect how humans are in the world. The bat way of being does not have the scope that the human way has.

Animals are wholly absorbed into those niches in which they have such satisfactory fitness, but humans can stand apart from the world and consider themselves in relation to it. Humans are, in this sense, eccentric to the world—in it but standouts. Humans are only part of the world in biological and ecological senses, but they are the only part of the world that can orient itself with respect to a theory of it. So humans can begin to comprehend what comprehends them; in this lies their paradox and responsibility. They have a distinct metaphysical status just because they alone can do metaphysics. The metaphysics they do may lead them to an experience of unity with nature, to responsible care for other species, but such unity paradoxically puts them beyond nature, where nothing else is capable of such experience and caring. When they assert the value of Earth and its creatures, they exceed the creatures' scope of value.

Many sectors of the environment are *open* to humans if they wish to enter there (as also is rebuilding the environment), while an animal is *closed* to surroundings outside its niche. The animal takes an interest in its own sector of the environment—prey, predators, mates, offspring—but it cannot take an interest in sectors remote from its niche or espouse a view of the whole. Some animal experiences are no doubt closed to humans (we cannot taste spruce budworms as Cape May warblers taste them), but humans can nevertheless select to know about the budworm-warbler cycle, while neither the warblers nor the budworms can select to know about humans. It is not merely in resource use, or in self-actualization, or in maximizing utility, or in projecting value onto nature, or in the complexity of their central nervous systems that humans are superior. They are superior in loving the other, perhaps even as themselves. The animal takes a gastrocentric view (centering on food), a self-centered view (protecting its own life), a species-centered view (propagating its kind), but humans can take something more than an anthropocentric view. In their complexity, they can know and value the complexity of their world.

Thus the human capacity for a transcending overview of the whole makes us superior and imposes strange duties, those of transcending human interests and linking them up with those of the whole natural Earth. Humans have little biological role in ecosystems, in the sense that were they subtracted from oak-hickory forests or African savannas or Asian steppes, those ecosystems would not be negatively affected; they would rather be improved. Humans are not important as predators or prey; they play no role in the food chains or in regulating life cycles. They are a late add-on to the system; and their cultural activities (except perhaps for primitive tribes) only degrade the system, if considered biologically and ecologically. But one human role is to admire and respect the ecosystems they culminate, as environmental ethics urges, and not merely to admire and respect themselves, as traditional ethics does. The human role is ethical, metaphysical, scientific, religious, and in this sense humans are unique and superior, but their superiority is linked in a feedback loop with the whole. (Chapter 9 returns to this theme.)

Experiences other than the capacity to reason abstractly, to be self-conscious, or to espouse world views are also valuable: pleasures in exercise, eating, the warmth of the sun, or sexual activity. Humans should value these in themselves and also in animals. There they generate constraints on permissible human interventions. But humans reach vast ranges of valuational experience unshared with the animals. If I am hiking with my dog and come to an overlook, we may both pause and enjoy the rest, but I can look at the scenery. He can look, but not at the view. Perhaps he smells what escapes my detection. But the human considers the canine perception, although not undergoing it, enjoys the exercise, rest, and also the aesthetic experience, all in the midst of a world view that sets a context of explanation for events in the scene. The animal has only its own horizon; the human can have multiple horizons, even a global horizon. The human has only a limited understanding of what is going on, but it is less limited than that of the dog, and this establishes a superior value richness. Theodosius Dobzhansky, a geneticist, concludes, "No animal asks questions about the meaning or purpose of life, because animal life cannot be doubted, it can only be embraced and enjoyed. Man is unique . . . who asks such questions."[29]

Humans should not "look down on" the "lower" orders of life, but humans alone can "look out over" or "look out for" all other orders of life. It is no evil for beasts to be beasts; rather it is their glory. But it is an evil for humans to be like beasts—without culture, without moral agency, gastrocentric, self-centered, propagating only their kind. Humans ought to see where and who humans are and comprehensively what others are. They have increasingly seen more of what there is to see in the unfolding of art, literature, philosophy, natural history, science. In this looking out, humans are the ablest form of life, the form in which valuational capacities are most (but not exclusively) developed. This is superiority based on accident of birth. Humans drew human genes; monkeys got monkey genes. But it is also superiority based on evolutionary achievement, for which humans have to be grateful. It is no mark of intelligence or morality to refuse a value endowment. Wasted talent is a sin.

"Biocentric" is not the right word, but then "anthropocentric" is not either. The system does not center indiscriminately on life, with one life being equal to another; and the system does not center functionally on humans, who in the ecological sense have little role in the system. Microbes are more important than humans instrumentally. All value does not "center" on humans, though some of it does. Everything of value that happens is not "for" humans; nonhumans defend their own values, and humans need to recognize these values outside themselves. Nevertheless, humans are of the utmost value in the sense that they are the ecosystem's most sophisticated product. They have the highest per capita intrinsic value of any life form supported by the system. The system is *bio-systemic* and *anthropo-apical*.

Just as it is unwise to protest that there ought be no innocent suffering, it is foolish to protest that there ought to be valuational equality in nature when there plainly is not. The question is not one of *equality* but of *quality*. Let us not be fooled by comparisons with culture. The difference in value richness between human races (if and where this exists) is an artifact of culture. That between species is essential in nature. A newborn Hottentot (Khoisan), removed from her native culture, might be reared to take an Oxford degree. But this was not so with Koko. A clear-headed ethicist will be nondiscriminatory in interhuman ethics, but only a sentimental egalitarian seeks to be nondiscriminating in environmental ethics. An ethic needs a grasp of reality. The way the world *is* has a bearing on the way it *ought to be.*

Peter Singer says that we must *consider* animals equally but may *treat* them differently, distinguishing among the animals and between animals and humans in view of different interests.[30] But this is wordplay that means, Consider and treat animals appropriately. We equally consider them all (all are given consideration), but what we consider is really their inequality of interests. In every case we give due consideration, but there cannot be equal consideration of unequal interests. Equal consideration of unequal interests amounts to differential treatment based on specific kind.

Nor should interests be factored out of the gestalt in which they are emplaced: for example, setting a chicken's interest in not suffering as equal to a human's interest in not suffering. The latter is Singer's real intent. Where any interest (in not suffering, for instance) is present, that interest gets both equal consideration and equal treatment. It is equally wrong to harm man or beast, based on equal capacities to suffer.

But what these interests are is analyzed not by isolating them from the larger patterns into which they figure but rather by synthesizing them into the total picture. While animals have emotions, as do humans (both fear death); humans have conceptually based emotions, even conceptually based pain (the shame, the indignity of being a slave or receiving an insult). They have ego-based, beyond merely self-based, emotions. Adequate language uses a proportionate consideration of value richness, not an isolation of analogous interests.

One should give equal consideration to equal interests, so far as they are present—so the argument first seems to run. An elk and a human both have interests in eating, but an elk has no interest in learning to read; a human does. So we do not treat them equally in all respects but only so far as like interests are present. We feed both; we educate only the human. But we cannot consider isolated interests like this. Interests figure in a gestalt. A human who can eat and take an education has more interest in eating than does an elk, since all the "upstairs" values depend on the "downstairs" value. The eating supports other interests, and the other interests enrich the significance and value of the eating. Every individual organism among the natural kinds has (if you wish to phrase it so) a right to respectful appreciation of the sorts of values (intrinsic, instrumental, ecosystemic) that it embodies and exemplifies. But since these are diverse and pluralistic values, shifting with each individual and kind along an instrumental/ecosystemic/individual spectrum, this appreciation never cashes out into equal rights or equal consideration of welfare.

Marginal Cases and Some Rationalizations

Three problems need brief attention; all come from failings in human superiority. First, on a spectrum of individuals—remembering that humans are sometimes infants, sometimes insane, senile, or ignorant, and that some animals are quite bright—we will find it possible to blur the cutoff points. Retarded humans may not espouse world views; chimpanzees may be more self-aware than infants. But the problem of fuzzy set edges is a pseudoproblem in an analysis at the species level, where capacities in value richness are statistical marks of the species. In this sense it is not, technically, the species to which humans belong biologically that makes moral demands on us; it is the personal, psychological capacities that exclusively (on this planet) and characteristically emerge in *Homo sapiens*, short of mental retardation or other malfunction. It is existential personality rather than biological humanity that we find superior to other species, but it is of course biological humanity that sponsors this existential personality, so to honor the one is to honor the other.

That some humans are nascent or deficient in these capacities requires that we class them as human by admitting potential or tragic loss. They are developing humans or, alas, broken humans who but vegetate. Marginal humans may get into our species for historical reasons, owing to their descent, despite their lost properties. The criteria for normal humanity remain unchanged. This might call for some extra kindness, going further in consideration than can really be justified by strict attention to their failed or aborted humanity, a kindness that pities their brokenness. We do not respect them for what they are but respect the full humans they were or might have been; we repair the tragedy by charity, rather than do strict justice to their tragic condition.

Meanwhile, we recognize them as underdeveloped humans because we know what the criteria for developed humans are, and it is those criteria on which we will base our interspecific theories. Humans are always persons, actually or potentially, except where some failure in the biology that places us in *Homo sapiens* results in the failure of the personality otherwise invariably present. The criteria for normal humanity remain unchanged by the marginal cases.

Driven to extremes, we might prefer a fine animal over a repugnant person (in a lifeboat: a panda bear over Hitler). But these anomalies—humans who are less than persons, persons who are notoriously demeritorious—have to be argued against a paradigm figured by class descriptions based on the type-species. Class rules can be useful (no drivers under sixteen years of age, no involuntary experimenting on humans) despite exceptions (some teenagers under sixteen more mature than others over, some chimps more self-aware than some senile persons).

Second, in ethics one learns to be wary of rationalizations. Self-interest can unconsciously defend a right, good, or benefit and cast up a show of alleged reasons that salve the conscience and convince or overwhelm oppressed opponents. "Justice" has a way of slipping into "just-us." One can see how a defense of human superiority might be rationalizing, but it is difficult to say the same of a biocentric ethic, which seems so altruistic and egalitarian. Is the more generous position not probably right? If humans are superior, it is because they move through the world ethically, cognitively, critically, culturally. If in fact they move through the world only in rationalized illusion, their alleged superiority is bogus. It is self-interest defended by bad taxonomy.

But one does not settle a dispute by noticing that rationality can fail and slip into rationalizing. It is an ad hominem reply to say that a position is suspiciously self-serving. One must assess the reasons given. One has to test the logical connections of premises with conclusions, facts against the picture into which they are fitted. Only humans can assess reasons in self-conscious deliberation, test an argument, ask about just (discriminating) versus unjust (discriminatory) treatment. Only humans can consider animal interests and rights, be glad to find that animals enjoy some values beyond the human reach, or ask about the possibility of rationalizing. But precisely such capacities are the major factors in establishing the gestalt claimed to be superior. The argument confirms itself even as it is questioned. Such a logic does not become suspect by noticing that the nonsuperiority claim is unlikely to be rationalizing.

Third, an argument for reconciling human interests with biological processes runs something like this (we could call this anthropocentric biocentrism!):

1. Unless the members of each species act to perpetuate their lives and species, natural selection will cease.
2. Natural selection is a good thing and should continue.
3 . All other species are engaged in a tooth-and-claw struggle to survive.
4. Humans cannot fairly be asked to play the game under a disadvantage, using another, more charitable set of rules. To require humans to be moral is unfair, putting them under a special burden. The rules should apply evenhandedly.
5. Humans should seek their own survival and prospering first, eliminating other animals and species as may be necessary to doing so. One should always replace an alligator with a human, where possible, not only because a human has more value than an alligator but because an alligator will replace a human with an alligator, where possible.
6. This argument is species-blind and is an argument in self-defense. All species should defend themselves, and may the fittest survive.[31]

In replying to such argument it is critical to notice that human conduct is not to be modeled on animal conduct, because of our relevant superiority, because of human power, morality, self-conscious deliberative capacities, espousing world views, and so on. Different rules do apply to those with superior talents. An *ought* follows from differences in what *is* the case.

A concluding move is important. Neither logic, nor justice, nor charity, nor biology, nor ecology, nor psychology, nor humanism, nor naturalism, nor religion, nor anything else permits stopping short at the human/nonhuman line, with all moral considerability on the one side and none on the other, although any and all these permit the discriminating treatment of humans as much as they require the discriminating treatment of nonhuman animals. From superiority we do not move merely to privilege but also to responsibility. To say that humans embody the highest levels of value is to value the goods of culture and also to value humans as a microcosm of the macrocosm. Humans have a situated uniqueness on a unique Earth. They reflect the highest awareness of values only when they see that humans are not the sole locus of value. The human nobility warrants no arrogance.

So far from dominating nature on account of human superiority, we ought rather to follow nature, in the senses sketched in Chapter 1, though this includes commanding nature as nature is obeyed. And it is a strange paradox that when humans follow nature in an appreciative way, they excel over nature, since nothing else in nature has this capacity of appreciative respect for the system and for others in the system beyond itself. Humans are privileged resource users, but even more important, they are privileged respondents to the natural world.

Where humans move through the world ethically, cognitively, and critically, and deny or degrade animal values, they make of themselves a contradiction in terms. To take on the feelings of another is what humans can do and animals cannot, and what makes ethics possible. Aldo Leopold spoke of man as a "plain member and citizen" of the Earth, but he also spoke of him as "king." Recalling the extinction of the passenger pigeon, he located this superiority in responsibility. "But we, who have lost our pigeons, mourn the loss. Had the funeral been ours, the pigeons would hardly have mourned us. In this fact . . . lies objective evidence of our superiority over the beasts."[32]

Domestic and Hunted Animals

In the light of this empirical and normative claim to human superiority that also recognizes animal goods and welfare, we turn to three areas of application. None of these can be considered exhaustively, but general ethical strategies can be stated.

Domestic Food Animals

Animal agriculture is tangential to an environmental ethic, yet there is a carryover connecting the one to the other. Domestic animals are breeds, no longer natural kinds. They are "living artifacts,"[33] kept in culture for so long that it is often not known precisely what their natural progenitors were. They fit no environmental niche; the breeding of them for traits that humans desire has removed them from the forces of natural selection. Without human interest in these animals they would soon cease to exist. Most domestic breeds would go extinct; a few might revert to feral conditions; fewer still might resettle homeostatically into environmental niches. Most feral forms, unchecked by predators, competitors, and diseases, are misfits that cause heavy environmental degradation.

But domestic animals cannot enter the culture that maintains them. By all behavioral evidence, sheep, cows, and pigs are oblivious to the economy for which they are reared, much less to the cultural context of the persons who care for them. They cannot live in the world ethically, cognitively, and critically in those superior human ways. Pet dogs may join the life of the family, enthusiastically eating hot dogs at a picnic; nevertheless, pets are not in culture. Although food animals are taken out of nature and transformed by culture, they remain uncultured in their sentient life, cultural objects that cannot become cultural subjects. They live neither in nature nor in culture but in the peripheral rural world. Meanwhile, they can suffer.

This *is* the case, descriptive of their condition. What *ought* to be? Applying now the principle of value capture previously established, we recognize the wild condition from which such animals were once taken and recognize also that they can neither return to the wild nor enter cultural subjectivity. Although tamed, they can have horizons, interests, goods no higher than those of wild subjectivity, natural sentience. They ought to be treated, by the homologous, baseline principle, with no more suffering than might have been their lot in the wild, on average, adjusting for their modified capacities to care for themselves. In taking an interest in them, humans have assumed a responsibility for them. (Whether modern industrial farming introduces suffering in excess of ecological norms will have to be investigated elsewhere.)

By a weaker (but significant) hedonist principle, domestic animals ought to be spared pointless suffering, but they have no claim to be spared innocent suffering. The killing and the eating of animals, when they occur in culture, are still events in nature; they are ecological events, no matter how superimposed by culture. Humans are claiming no superiority or privilege exotic to nature. Analogous to predation, human consumption of animals is to be judged by the principles of environmental ethics, not those of interhuman ethics. We step back from culture into agriculture, toward the wild, and fit the ecological pattern. What *is* in nature may not always imply *ought* (and it may seldom do so in interhuman ethics), but *ought* in environmental ethics seldom negates what *is* in wild nature. Humans eat meat, and meat-eating is a natural component of ecosystems, one to which we do not object in nature nor try to eliminate from our cultural interactions with nature.

A troop of half a dozen chimpanzees, our nearest relatives, will kill and eat about a hundred medium-sized animals a year. Hunter-gatherer cultures are the earliest known, and when agricultural cultures replace them, humans have no duty to cease to be omnivores and become herbivores. They might elect to become vegetarians, perhaps on grounds of more efficient food production or better nutrition, but they have no duty to sentient life to do so.

A characteristic argument for vegetarianism runs as follows:

1. Pain is a bad thing, whether in humans or in animals.
2. Humans (at least most of them) can live nutritiously without causing animal pain.
3. It is immoral for humans to kill and eat humans, causing them pain.
4. Food animals suffer pain, similarly to the way humans do, if killed and eaten.
5. There are no morally relevant differences between humans and food animals.
6. It is immoral for humans to kill and eat animals, causing them pain.

Appealing to sentiment and logically attractive in its charitable egalitarianism, such argument fails to distinguish between nature and culture, between environmental ethics and interhuman ethics. We simply see ourselves in fur. But there are morally relevant differences that distinguish persons in culture from food animals in agriculture, where quasi-ecosystemic processes remain. Whether or not there are differences in pain thresholds between sheep and humans, the value destruction when a sheep is eaten is far less, especially since the sheep have been bred for this purpose and would not otherwise exist. Because animals cannot enter culture, they do not suffer the *affliction* (a heightened, cognitively based pain, distinct from physical pain) that humans would if bred to be eaten.

Chickens can live in ignorant bliss of their forthcoming slaughter (until the moment of execution); persons in such a position could not, because they are in the world culturally and critically. Even if such a fate could be kept secret from persons, the value destruction in their killing would still be greater. The fact that there are twilight zones (humans who are pre-persons or failed persons) does not challenge the existence of morally relevant class differences. In recognizing the human superiority, nothing should be subtracted from the natural condition of animals. But we have no strong duty to deny their original ecology, and only a weaker duty to make their lot better by avoiding pointless pain.

It is not "unfair" or "unjust" to eat a pig. Even an alligator that eats humans is not being unfair or unjust (although humans will be reprehensible if they do not try to prevent it). Humans in their eating habits follow nature; they can and ought to do so. But humans do not eat other humans because such events interrupt culture; they destroy those superior ways in which humans live in the world. The eating of other humans, even if this were shown to be an event in nature, would be overridden by its cultural destructiveness. Cannibalism destroys interpersonal relations. But in nature no such relations obtain, or can obtain. (Human cannibalism has been rare and virtually always a cultural event with religious overtones, not a natural event.)

It may be objected that the differences in rules for those with superior gifts means here that the only moral animals should refuse to participate in the meat-eating phase of their ecology, just as they refuse to play the game merely by the rules of natural selection. Humans do not look to the behavior of wild animals as an ethical guide in other matters (marriage, truth-telling, promise-keeping, justice, charity). Why should they justify their dietary habits by watching what animals do? But these other matters are affairs of culture. Marriage, truth-telling, promise-keeping, justice, charity—these are not events at all in spontaneous nature. They are person-to-person events. By contrast, eating is omnipresent in spontaneous nature; humans eat because they are in nature, not because they are in culture. Eating animals is not an event between persons but a human-to-animal event, and the rules for it come from the ecosystems in which humans evolved and which they have no duty to remake. Humans, then, can model their dietary habits on their ecosystems, but they cannot and should not model their interpersonal justice or charity on ecosystems.

It may seem that while animals are not to be treated like persons in all respects, both they and persons have about equally the capacity to feel pain, and so both ought to be treated equally in this relevant respect involving the pain-pleasure scale. But this is not the only relevant scale, because it does not catch the full scale of value destructions at stake. The eating of persons would destroy cultural values, which the eating of animals does not. The eating of animals, though it does destroy values, reallocates such values when humans gain nutrition and pleasure at the sacrifice of animal lives in a manner wholly consistent with the operation of the natural ecosystem in which such animals were once emplaced and are still quasi-placed in their agricultural stations. Different rules do apply to persons, to persons in exchange with persons, and even to persons in exchange with nature. These rules do require that animal lives count morally, but they do not require humans to deny their ecology and replace it with a charity or justice appropriate to culture.

Sentience in nature and sentience in culture are not really the same thing, despite their common physiology and origin. Sentience in nature belongs with food chains and natural selection; sentience in culture has been transformed into another gestalt, that of self-reflective personality and moral agency. Eating an animal implies no disrespect for animal life as set in a trophic pyramid; to the contrary, it respects that ecology. Eating a person would disrupt personal life as set in a cultural pattern; it would reduce personal life to the level of animal life in an ecology. It insults persons to treat them as food objects by the criteria of animal ecology; persons may and must treat nonhuman lives as food objects, but it respects animals to treat them so.

Pain is a bad thing in humans or in animals. But this fools us until we distinguish between intrinsic and instrumental pain. Instrumental pain has contributory reference to further goods; intrinsic pain has no such reference. Intrinsic pain is a bad thing, absolutely; but only instrumental pain is characteristic of nature, where intrinsic pain is a nonfunctional anomaly. Pain is routinely instrumental in ecological defenses, captures, and transfers of goods, and the pains imposed in agriculture are homologous. They are not intrinsic pains; they must be judged in their instrumentality and with no presumption against innocent suffering.

Enjoying pleasure and escaping pain are of value, and evolutionary ecosystems are full of devices for accomplishing both. But much pain remains, and much thwarted pleasure. In nature, the pain-pleasure axis is not the only spectrum of value; indeed, it is not the highest value in either human or nonhuman life. It might be said, for instance, that knowing the meaning of life is more important for humans than leading a painless life, that a life with courage and sacrificial charity in it, which requires the presence of some pain, is a richer life than one without it. Similarly, the evolution of a world with carnivorous mammals, primates, humans, and culture is a richer world than one without them, and the presence of pain seems to have been necessary for such evolution. In that sense, advanced values are frequently built on suffering.

Perhaps it is not merely the pain but the indignity of domestication that is deplorable. A gazelle is pure wild grace, but a cow is a meat factory, pure and simple; a cow might even suffer less than a gazelle but be greatly disgraced. Cows cannot know they are disgraced, of course, and the capture of values in nature is not undignified. A lioness destroys a gazelle, and there is nothing unworthy here. Likewise, in domestication, humans parallel ecosystems and capture agriculturally the values in a cow. There is nothing undignified in this event, even though the once-natural values in the cow, like those in the gazelle, have to be destroyed by the predator.

Although we have defended eating animals as a primary, natural event, we have also said, secondarily, that there is an obligation to avoid pointless pain. Consider, for instance, the following case. There are more than 2,000,000 Muslims in Britain; the Jewish community numbers nearly 400,000. Muslims still practice animal sacrifice; a sheep or goat is sacrificed during a feast concluding a month of fasting, and often at the birth of a child. The animal is sacrificed to Allah, and the meat is eaten and enjoyed. Though Jews no longer practice animal sacrifice as they did in former times, they require their meat to be kosher, slaughtered according to religious ritual. Modern secular abattoirs stun animals with a massive blow or an electric shock before butchering them, and this is thought to be more humane. But it makes the animal unacceptable to Jews and Muslims, who must sever the major blood vessels of an unblemished animal. About 1,500,000 sheep and goats and 100,000 cattle are slaughtered by Jews and Muslims each year.

Animal rights activists have pressed to require stunning, and a government report finds that religious methods of slaughter result in a degree of suffering and distress that does not occur in a properly stunned animal. Muslims and Jews have joined forces to defend their practices.[34] But the additional pain that their methods impose, no longer necessary, cannot be interpreted in the context of ecology; it is pain inflicted for culture-based reasons. Unblemished animals make better sacrifices to God; they enhance religious cleanliness. This pain is ecologically pointless; it has point only culturally and, by the account given here, is not justified. This pain is not homologous; it is superfluous. Perhaps both Jews and Muslims can reach reformed religious convictions, in which respect for animal life overrides their previous concepts of cleanliness, or where the mercy of God prohibits pointless suffering.

Wildlife Commerce and Management

Elephants are killed to make piano keys from their ivory; beaver are trapped for hats, rhinoceroses are speared in the superstition that their powdered horns are aphrodisiac. Over 20,000 birds of paradise, 40,000 hummingbirds, and 30,000 birds of other species were slaughtered to supply London ladies with feathers for fashion in 1914. Soon afterward the trade in feathers was judged to be unconscionable and largely ceased, and there is little evidence that London ladies were any the worse for the change. On the other hand, 635,000 Rhesus monkeys were used to test polio vaccine in the early years of its manufacture, and polio, once a scourge of childhood, has largely disappeared. There are thousands of nonfood, commercial uses of wildlife. What does an environmental ethic permit in wildlife commerce and management?

The alligator was once listed as an endangered species, but no longer; it is a success story in conservation. There are 400,000 in Louisiana, with 16,000 a year taken in a carefully regulated harvest, perhaps a sustainable harvest of 50,000. Most alligator hides are exported to France, where they are crafted into ultrachic, terribly expensive purses and shoes. Some of the meat is eaten. Over 100,000 alligators were sold from 1972 to 1983, worth $9.8 million.[35] Is alligator hunting ethical, providing income for Louisiana hunters ($10 to $15 per hide-foot) and fashionable decor for French ladies ($150 for a pocketbook)? Do the principles of universal benevolence or the Golden Rule have application here?

Part of the answer, remember, depends on whether the species is endangered, on keeping it a satisfactory fit in its ecosystem. Part of the answer depends on whether the alligator population needs to be cropped for its own good or to prevent its becoming a nuisance. The survival of the alligator may depend on its being economically valuable: seventeen of twenty-one crocodilian species worldwide are endangered, often in such economically productive areas as river drainage systems, and some think they can be saved only if it can be made economically advantageous to native peoples to keep them.

But part of an answer depends on the suffering inflicted and what is traded for the suffering.

The ecological model, following which we patterned domestication of livestock, involves a food pyramid. The use of animals to manufacture clothing or medicine is unknown in nature, but there seems no reason to prohibit those uses of animals to provide utilities which, like food, secure health and basic human well-being: leather for shoes, wool for jackets, insulin for diabetics. This stretches the homologous logic beyond that of food chains, but it recognizes that in culture there are necessities unknown in nature. At the same time the constraint continues to apply. Animals must suffer no more, on average, than might have been their lot in wild nature. Nor should humans inflict pointless pain.

As these uses of animals pass from the essential through the serious into the merely desirable and finally to the trivial, the ecological pattern rapidly fades, and the justification collapses. The use of fir for survival—a jacket on a frontiersman—is much closer to the natural, and the suffering is justified thereby. The use of fur for status—a jaguar coat on an actress—is highly artificial. Status is a cultural artifact, as is the status symbol. The suffering traded for it is not justified by any naturalistic principle.

A bumper sticker issued by the Defenders of Wildlife reads, "Real People Wear Fake Furs." A billboard in Denver shows a woman dragging a fur coat trailed by a swath of blood and reads, "It takes up to 40 dumb animals to make a fur coat. But only one to wear it." Such advice and censure could not be given to Eskimos, but perhaps it can to well-heeled Americans. If bobcats must be caught in leghold traps, mostly to flatter female vanities, and any superiority of fur over fiber is a rationalizing illusion, there is no justification for the practice. If alligators are killed mostly for chic decor and the superiority of alligator hide over synthetic vinyl is merely rationalizing, then the killing is pointless. Shoes for bare feet are one thing; anaconda cowboy boots worn to a pro football game in Texas are another. Domestic furbearers, which would not otherwise exist and are humanely treated, are an intermediate case, but even here the fur products are luxuries and cannot be made to fit the ecological model. Using fur and hide as status symbols is something different from using them as survival tools.

Commercial wildlife operations are subject to profit pressures, which introduce additional moral hazards. The forces that drive capitalism need moral watching. There are abundant rationalizations and temptations to compromise, pass the buck, shrug one's shoulders, do what the boss says or what customers want; to say that one is caught in the market, needs a living, and cannot do otherwise. This is true even where wildlife is traded for basic needs, but further pressures for economic growth tend to escalate supposed needs, to enlarge markets, and thereby to maximize profits to operators and minimize sensitivities to sentient life. Given that this sense of duty is already weak in Western society, it can be expected that commercial operations will pay no heed to it and that commerce will increase callousness. We want our ethical attitudes toward animal suffering to be consistent with ecology, not distorted by economics.

That may require some protest and consciousness raising. In 1979 in a Portuguese harbor, the 206-foot icebreaker trawler *Sea Shepherd* rammed a pirate whaling ship to put it out of business. "They had already killed 25,000 whales and I wanted to make sure it wouldn't kill any more," said Paul Watson, the ship's captain. The meat was sold to Japan for $9 million annually, where it formed a tiny fraction of the diet. The militant whale defenders also claimed that pirate whalers waste meat and kill more cruelly than legal whalers. The militants were not prosecuted, partly because of Portuguese media and public sympathy for their cause, partly because the whalers were operating illegally.

In the Gulf of St. Lawrence, the *Sea Shepherd*'s crew ventured onto the ice to paint thousands of infant harp seals with a harmless dye. This made their soft white fur useless, rendering them safe from seal clubbers. The Canadian government in 1983 jailed Watson, fined him $5,000, and seized his ship (worth $1,000,000). These penalties were imposed by courts in an economy that profits from seal hunting and where sentiment runs against the militants. The judge interpreted this as enforcing laws about legitimate resource use and protecting the rights of seal hunters. But the protestors, and many others, saw it as stifling moral dissent. It was, at a minimum, civil disobedience where laws must be broken to test their moral legitimacy.[36]

On the other hand, in wildlife management a certain callousness toward sentient life is demanded. One cannot be sentimental about the welfare and sufferings of individual animals in isolation from the inexorable limits of an ecosystem. The baseline concern is for species filling niches in ecosystems, for a satisfactory fitness.

In wild nature an invisible hand took care of these things; predators and diseases provided population controls. The nature now encountered is often semiwild or merely rural. The deer in the pasture, the antelope on the range have no predators and do compete, in part, with cattle there. No duty to sentient life overrides the carrying capacity of an ecosystem, whether wild or modified by agricultural changes.

Angel Island, a state park in the San Francisco Bay area, has a problem deer herd. It is unknown whether deer swam to the island originally; some were introduced to be hunted when the island was formerly under military control. Without predators or human hunters, the population fluctuated dramatically, rising to highs followed by sudden drops due to disease outbreak and starvation. Each high produced further environmental deterioration and erosion, with the natural vegetation invaded successively by more weeds. The California Departments of Fish and Game and of Parks and Recreation began to cull the deer but were stopped by a lawsuit from the San Francisco Society for the Prevention of Cruelty to Animals. The deer are popular with picnickers, and the SFSPCA fed the deer at times—opposed by state managers, who proposed introducing coyotes. But some said coyotes on the relatively small island, with no alternative prey, would eliminate the deer entirely, then starve themselves.

In a first attempt to resolve the issue, 215 deer were captured for relocation elsewhere, at a cost of $100,000 and with considerable media attention. The deer were in only fair condition when taken from the island; they had little fear of hunters, automobiles, or predators. Relocated, they survived poorly; only about 15 percent were alive a year later. Meanwhile, the island population rebounded. In a second attempt, SFSPCA put contraceptive implants into almost half the does (thirty of seventy), but the population multiplied nevertheless. State authorities have been quietly culling excess deer, though the issue is officially unresolved.[37]

If considerations of carrying capacity can show that culling deer or hunting alligators really is in the interest of these species, prior to considerations of human utility, then there is no reason not to kill. Though the killing is cruel, it saves deer and gators. In the latter case there is no reason not to combine both sorts of benefits—a limited population and hides (although in the case of predators overpopulation is less likely, since predator populations adjust to available prey—as ungulates often do not adjust to available forage). Such considerations can be ethical, but they also easily permit rationalizations, which are on the whole as great a danger as is excessive sentiment in forming a clear logic about duties to sentient life.

The test really ought to be whether the commerce and management are based on a philosophy that promotes a reverence for life, even when such life is sacrificed in the ecological pyramid. A biologist who shoots a deer can reverence life as much as a Humane Society member who feeds one. A woman who eats a chicken can reverence life; she can also if she wears leather shoes. But with a jaguar coat and ultra-chic purse she blasphemes life. Her vanity takes jaguar and alligator life in vain.

Hunting

Eating domestic animals cannot be good and eating wild ones bad. Nothing is more natural than hunting for food; the homologous logic of an environmental ethic is even more evident. It is not less wrong to kill a pig than a deer because the former is an artifact. Bullets inflict no more pain than do the fangs of a cougar but rather less. The fact that the hunter is a moral agent does not prohibit him from occupying a place in the ecosystemic food chain. But with the success of domestication, hunting for food has become steadily less important; it is replaced by sport hunting, where morally relevant differences appear. There is little analogue to sport hunting in nature, even if predators do sometimes enjoy their hunts. Joseph Wood Krutch writes:

> Killing "for sport" is the perfect type of that pure evil for which metaphysicians have sometimes sought. Most wicked deeds are done because the doer proposes some good to himself. The liar lies to gain some end; the swindler and the thief want things which, if honestly got, might be good in themselves. Even the murderer may be removing an impediment to normal desires or gaining possession of something which his victim keeps from him. None of these usually does evil for evil's sake. They are selfish or unscrupulous, but their deeds are not gratuitously evil. The killer for sport has no such comprehensible motive. He prefers death to life, darkness to light. He gets nothing except the satisfaction of saying, "Something which wanted to live is dead."[38]

A characteristic injunction in the sportsman's ethic is that meat must not be wasted. Its waste is indecent, if not morally wrong. This does not accidentally couple an ethic about waste with sport hunting; the concern is rather different from that about wasted bread. Mere killing for sport is not justified but must join its ancient function. The dislike of waste is set, unconsciously or consciously, in a larger gestalt; the quarry should not be sacrificed outside the paradigm of meat-hunting. In the last century, hundreds of thousands of buffalo were shot by sportsmen from the windows of trains; passenger pigeons were used like clay pigeons today. Most hunters disapprove of such killing. A varmint hunter needs the justification that crows steal corn, that woodchucks dig holes into which cattle stumble, or that porcupines kill trees. A trophy hunter may claim that he culls the herd. Such reasons, or rationalizations, reflect ethical disquiet with recreational killing. The killing cannot be senseless, but has become nearly so if merely recreational.

A survey by Stephen Kellert of American public attitudes toward types of hunting (nonendangered species) is graphed in Figure 2.1.[39] The graph shows averages; persons in cities disapprove more, in towns and rural areas less. The graph reveals a progressive disapproval of hunting as it is removed from an ecological context, also perhaps an elevated concern for sentient life (mammals over birds), presumably coupled to a feeling that more animal value is sacrificed more painfully but pointlessly in killing mammals than in killing birds. But most approve of hunting for food and are willing to couple it with sport.

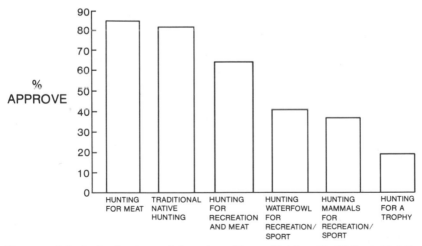

FIGURE 2.1 *Attitudes toward hunting. From Stephen R. Kellert,* Public Attitudes toward Critical Wildlife and Natural Habitat Issues, *U.S. Fish and Wildlife Service, 1979, fig. 29, p. 107.*

Keeping the exhilaration of the hunt in the context of ecological predation seems to justify the sport because it keeps up the
illusion that it is not (mere) sport. Since the hunt ends in a meal,
there is a fractional truth here, although not one hunter in several hundred needs the game in his diet. They eat what they kill;
they do not hunt to eat. Sport hunting uses nature as a playground
on which there is killing. On human playgrounds (gridirons, ball
diamonds, courts) the killing would be immoral. But the field
and stream are different playgrounds, which, as they recreate,
re-create an illusion of the primordial hunt, where the opponent
animals may legitimately be killed. Such a hunt was once necessary to life, but human predation has long since been made unnecessary by domestication, the latter requiring killing as well. The
old, honorable context regained remains genuinely set in an ecological pyramid, where a dominant animal stalks its prey. This is
play, but the play reenacts a deadly serious game, the archetypal
hunt. Since it remains an ecological event, there is here no duty to
impose interhuman ethics ("Thou shalt not kill"). Rather, "Every
moving thing that lives shall be food for you."[40]
     This is the principal motif, though there are always further
considerations pro and con. With predators gone, some animals
overpopulate (herbivores, usually not birds, usually not small animals, and not other predators). Humans may replace natural
predators, so that without hunters deer would suffer the more,
starving instead—assuming clean kills and few cripples. Sociologically, hunting interrelates with cultural ways of life. On the
other hand, it can degenerate into a machismo killing for thrills,
covering up inferiority complexes. Wildlife, surrounded as it is by
culture, does require some management, and compromises have
to be made between ideals and the real, between what is moral
and what is politically possible. Meanwhile, it is a strange sort of
federal or state wildlife conservation agency whose principal objective is to provide an annual crop of animals to kill. How much
more intelligent and less contradictory their goals if they can,
with or beyond the annual killing, teach an appreciation of fauna,
flora, ecosystems, natural history, a land ethic.
     The best case that can be made for sport hunting is that
it is not merely recreational but is a vicarious, therapeutic,
character-building, *re-creational* event, where a visceral urge is
vented in the sport hunt, carried forth in its ecological setting.
The sport hunt sublimates the drive for conquest, a drive without
which humans could not have survived, without which we cannot

be civilized. The hunter is as propelled as the bullets he or she shoots. Civilization has required the modified expression of this atavistic urge, but dimensions of it are still nowhere better expressed than in this reversion from civilization to nature. From this perspective, we can understand Ortega y Gasset's dictum that death is a "sign of reality" in hunting, where "one does not hunt in order to kill; on the contrary, one kills in order to have hunted."[41] In this sense, hunting is not *sport;* it is a *sacrament* of the fundamental, mandatory seeking and taking possession of value that characterizes an ecosystem and from which no culture ever escapes.

Is hunting blood lust, covered over with some ecological philosophy? Or is it an ecological morality that accepts the facts of a world humans did not make and have no duty to remake? Is it hardened hearts versus bleeding hearts? Or is it taking the world to heart? The ecological ethic, which kills in place, is really more advanced, more harmonious with nature, than the animal rights ethic, which, in utter disharmony with the way the world is made, kills no animals at all. Those who go out and kill for fun may have failed to grow up morally; sometimes those who object to any killing in nature and in human encounter with nature have not grown up either biologically or morally.

The human being is uniquely unspecialized, a species in whom aboriginal genetic drives can be sublimated and primitive ecologies modified. Perhaps the hunting drive, like the sexual urge, is dangerous to suppress and must be reckoned with. But this can sometimes be done without the pleasure in killing—on the gridiron or the tennis court, by the hunter who stalks with a camera or the mountaineer with his pitons. These other players also remain meat-eaters and hire professional slaughterers to insulate themselves from their kills, but they do not make a sport of killing or play a game kept honest only by the (trivial) meat-eating and the illusion of the archaic hunt.

A Maine referendum pitted an old ethic against a new one. Moose were not hunted there from 1935 until 1980, because of declining numbers. But recovery efforts were successful, and hunting was resumed. There are about 20,000 moose; 1,000 licenses are granted each season. About 400,000 pounds of meat is harvested; $400,000 in revenue is generated for the Department of Fisheries and Wildlife, with further income to those with whom hunters trade. Biologists follow the kills and monitor the condition of the herd.[42] Maine One is steeped in the traditions of hunting.

But there is Maine Two, affluent and educated, loving the country but disliking sport hunting. This "softer" ethic argues that moose hunting, even if once justified, is outmoded, essentially pleasure killing and no longer "real" hunting; "sportsmen" use four-wheel drives, high-powered rifles, walkie-talkies, all to blast away a kind of cow in the bushy marsh, a large conspicuous animal with little fear of humans. Further, the moose is the state animal, and watching moose is enjoyed by thousands. Hunting them is like shooting Yellowstone elk.

Whether the hunting should continue was put to a hotly contested referendum. The ban on hunting failed by a three-to-two margin. Although there is something to be said on both sides of the issue, this particular form of hunting does seem more to flatter male vanities, not unlike the way jaguar coats flatter female vanities, and does little to convey to Maine residents the tragic sense of life in an ecosystem.

Still, some hunters need to be immersed immediately in the bloodletting. The hunter feels not "perfect evil" (Krutch), but "perfect identification" with the tragic drama of creation, the blood sacrifice on which sentient life is founded, which both *is* and *ought to be*. In ways that mere watchers of nature can never know, hunters know their ecology. The hunter's success is not conquest but submission to the ecology. It is an acceptance of the way the world is made. In all this, nowhere should it be forgotten that there is also a nature to which humans by genetic disposition are attracted, and hence the congenital ambiguity toward a nature we need to slay and to love, surfacing in the contradictions of the hunt. The unease with which the good hunter inflicts death is an unease not merely with his conscience but with affirming his animality in the midst of his struggles toward humanity and charity, an unease about the dialectic of death with life. The authentic hunter knows suffering as a sacrament of the way the world is made.

Hunting is a complex phenomenon, and the limited justification of it allowed here mixes psychoanalysis with logical analysis, anthropology with ecology, human nature with wild nature. But this is sometimes required in environmental ethics, where there is an interplay of subtle dimensions in the human attitude toward nature. It was hunting that first forced man to produce tools, long before agriculture required them. The brain, the eyes, the hands evolved and were selected for success in savannas and forests as surely as for language, abstract thought, or morality. The satisfactions of skill at the hunt must run deep; they sometimes flatter male vanities, but we cannot always interpret them so. And the fact that men enjoy skilled hunting, mixed with unease about killing, is no embarrassment. After all, the tiger enjoys her kill, necessary as this is. Hunting is a form of what we earlier called a dialectical value, one where seeming evils (killing, pain, the ordeal of the hunt) are transformed into goods (pleasure in conquest, re-creation in recreation, the expression of primordial drives, food on the table, an ecology affirmed). This too is homologous to nature, a field of the coincidence of opposites and the complementarity of values and disvalues. The ambiguity with which we conclude this section is not merely faulty or incomplete analysis; it reflects the bloodstained world.

The question is not as simple as Bentham thought. It is not, Can they reason? or, Can they talk? or even, Can they suffer? The question is, Is nature at the level of sentient life a passion play? Ought humans to transform this nature into something else? or refuse to join in, having learned something better? One answer is that hunting, a seeming sport, has sacramental value because it unfolds the contradictions of the universe.

The pains, pleasures, interests, and welfares of individual animals are one, but only one, of the considerations in an environmental ethic. Human superiority is another, as is the degree to which our behavior can be modeled after ecosystemic patterns, which themselves figure into what ought to be. We have finished only the second chapter in an environmental ethic.

3 Organisms: Duties to Organic Life

 "A SOLITARY ANT, afield, cannot be considered to have much of anything on his mind; indeed, with only a few neurons strung together by fibers, he can't be imagined to have a mind at all, much less a thought. He is more like a ganglion on legs."[1] Lewis Thomas, an astute biologist, seems to imply that ethically we need never mind about a lowly ant because neurologically an ant has no mind. Peter Singer, a sensitive defender of duties to sentient life, stops "somewhere between a shrimp and an oyster" and finds all lower animals, insects, and plants beyond moral consideration. "A life with no conscious experiences at all . . . is a complete blank; I would not in the least regret the shortening of this subjectively barren form of existence. . . . The life of a being that has no conscious experiences is of no intrinsic value."[2] My young son enjoys kicking up anthills to watch the ants' frenzied scattering. I once found him using a magnifying glass to sizzle an ant's abdomen. This much animated the captured ant and ended with an amusing pop. There might seem nothing wrong with either activity, because ants are mere ganglia on legs, beyond moral concern. Reverence for life does not extend this far.

Jesus sent 2,000 swine crashing to their deaths, an event which has dismayed even the most conservative interpreters of scripture, for whom the destruction seems cruel. Jesus also cursed and blighted a fig tree. Magical elements aside, interpreters have asked whether this was intemperate in Jesus, but none has shown any sympathy for the fig tree. Sympathy for a tree is misplaced affection. On the other hand, in the Genesis myth, God created all things and pronounced them good, and, after the tragic flood in the legendary days of Noah, reestablished his covenant not only with humans but "with every living creature . . . the birds, the cattle, and every beast of the earth." Noah's ark was the first endangered species project! So the other organisms are in God's covenant as much as humans.[3]

In college zoology I did an experiment on nutrition in rats, to see how they grew with and without vitamins. When the experiment was completed, I was told to take the rats out and drown them. I felt squeamish but did it. In college botany I did an experiment on seedlings to test how they grew with this or that fertilizer. The experiment over, I threw out the seedlings without a second thought. While there can be an ethic about sentient animals, after that perhaps ethics is over, except as instrumental to sentient interests. (I cannot noticeably find that I am any smarter for having starved and drowned rats, and I think I could have taken it on good authority, as I do the vastest part of my science, that nitrogen, phosphorus, and potassium are all requisite for plant growth.)

We would not say that the needless destruction of a plant (or ant?) was *cruel*, but we might say that it was *callous*. Would this be an ethical judgment? We might be concerned not about what the *plant did feel* but about what the *agent did not feel*. That is not to value the plant's *sensitivity* but to disvalue the person's *insensitivity*. Sizzling ants for amusement, even though we think ants feel no pain, produces a sense of disgust. Kicking up anthills is juvenile vandalism. But that does not end the inquiry, because we are valuing sensitivity not *in* plants but in persons *to* something in plants. The question is not just about a missing feeling in the person but about a feeling that should be directed toward properties of the organisms, though the organisms feel nothing. Judgments of disgust and vandalism are parasitic on an admiration for something of value in the living organisms.

In the 1880s a tunnel was cut through a giant sequoia in what is now Yosemite National Park. Driving through the Wawona tree, formerly in horse and buggy and later by car, amused and impressed millions. The tree was perhaps the most photographed in the world. On holidays there was a waiting line. The giant blew over in the snowstorms of 1968–69, weakened by the tunnel, although it had long stood despite it. Some have proposed that the Park Service cut more drive-through sequoias, but the rangers have refused, saying that one was enough and that to do so is an indignity to a majestic sequoia. It is better to educate visitors about the enormous size and longevity of redwoods and their resistance to fire, diseases, insect pests; better to teach visitors to admire a durable, stalwart, marvelous tree, a sort of natural Ming classic. They will then wish to leave redwoods untouched. Is this valuing the redwoods intrinsically? Was the Wawona tree a mistake? Is it wrong (or just silly) to mutilate a sequoia to excite tourists? Does this pervert the tree or pervert persons? Is this a "management" question and not an "ethical" question?

We have reached a critical divide, crossing into the headwaters that lead into the unexplored territory of environmental ethics in a primary sense. Does vegetation (a sequoia) count morally? Do we have duties to endangered species (*Discus macclintocki*, the Iowa Pleistocene snail)?[4] duties to landscapes and ecosytems (the Great Smoky Mountains)? These will be the explorations in succeeding chapters. The less adventurous (thinking themselves to be more rational) will draw back and return to familiar duties to persons and kindred sentient animals. But ethically responsible though this is on better mapped terrain, such persons do not yet have a primary environmental ethic—only an animal ethic and a secondary ethic concerning the environment. Much can be said for protecting human interests as carried by natural things (the values defended in Chapter 1). But now the question is deeper. There is much to be said urging concern for animal sentience in conflict with human interests. But we have left that question too. The question is not, Can they suffer? but, Are they alive? Sentience aside, is there anything of value in organisms, and how does it figure in an ethic?

This is perhaps not what ethics normally is, but that protest is not enough, because the question is whether ethics as normally conceived covers the whole field that properly belongs to it. Appeal to normal or familiar usage does nothing to settle revolutionary claims. We may want to change the meaning and scope, the connotation and denotation, of ethics. Some of the duties and concerns raised in the pages that follow may seem farfetched. But then most farsighted concerns have first seemed farfetched.

This issue is sometimes approached by asking what has *moral standing*—distinguished from the question who is a *moral agent*. That notion is useful but parasitic on the cultural idea of *legal standing*. It comes out of the courts, not out of value theory. The better question is what has value—standing on its own. Whatever has such resident value lays a claim on those who have standing as moral agents when they encounter such autonomous value. Just as, halfway down the phylogenetic levels of sentience, we abandoned the rhetoric and symbolism of *rights* in favor of what is *right*, we will also abandon the analogy of *moral standing* as we descend through organismic levels. But what remains always is the conviction that there is value, standing on its own, to which appropriate (= *right*) behavior is owed when those capable of duty meet such free-standing value. Such value counts morally; there are right and wrong ways to act in encounter with it. (It does not follow that the discarded terms are useless in their appropriate ranges.)

Objective Value in Organisms

Just as it is difficult to specify some particular essence that distinguishes humans from other sentient animals, it is difficult to distinguish by any single characteristic a living organism from nonbiotic matter, from computing machines, or from the communities in which organisms live. Biologists have looked for but never found "entelechy," animating force or spirit; organisms contain nothing but common chemicals. Still, these are organized at distinctively biological levels.

Organisms are self-maintaining systems; they grow and are irritable in response to stimuli. They reproduce, and the developing embryo is especially impressive. They resist dying. They post a careful if also semipermeable boundary between themselves and the rest of nature; they assimilate environmental materials to their own needs. They gain and maintain internal order against the disordering tendencies of external nature. They keep winding up, recomposing themselves, while inanimate things run down, erode, and decompose. Life is a local countercurrent to entropy. Organisms suck order out of their environment, stage an energetic fight uphill in a world that overall moves thermodynamically downhill. They pump out disorder. They can be healthy or diseased.

The constellation of these characteristics is nowhere found outside living organisms, although some of them can be mimicked or analogically extended to products designed by living systems, and some are found in spontaneous abiotic nature. A crystal reproduces a pattern and may restore a damaged surface; a planetary system maintains an equilibrium; a volcano may grow in countercurrent to entropy. A lenticular altocumulus cloud, formed as a standing wave over a mountain range, is steadily recomposed by input and output of airflow. A target-seeking missile adjusts its course by environmental feedback. Computers are cognitive processors and can be running well or poorly. Nevertheless, just as the animal precursors of human life fail in nonhumans to constitute a personality, these mechanical precursors of life fail to integrate into the pattern that we call an organism. Or perhaps we should say that they did so over evolutionary time, and there emerged something greater than the precedents: life. The organism is a vital gestalt, notably more than mere physics and chemistry.

Organisms as Normative Systems

The "genius" of life is coded into genetic sets, which are missing in minerals, volcanoes, clouds, computers, and target-seeking missiles. An organism is thus a spontaneous cybernetic system, self-maintaining with a control center, sustaining and reproducing itself on the basis of information about how to make a way through the world. There is some internal representation that is symbolically mediated in the coded "program" of the goal that is held forth. There is motion toward the execution of this goal, a checking against performance in the world, by means of some sentient, perceptive, or other responsive capacities with which to compare match and mismatch. Organisms measure success. On the basis of information received, the cybernetic system can reckon with the vicissitudes, opportunities, and adversities that the world presents.

Something more than causes, if less than sentience, is operating within every organism. There is *information* superintending the causes; without it the organism would collapse into a sand heap. This information is a modern equivalent of what Aristotle called formal and final causes; it gives the organism a *telos*, "end," a kind of (nonfelt) purpose. Organisms have ends, although not always ends-in-view. All this cargo is carried by the DNA, essentially a linguistic molecule. Humans artificially impose an alphabet on ink and paper, but living things long before were employing a natural alphabet, imposing a code on four nucleotide bases strung as cross-links on a double helix. A triplet of bases stands for one of the twenty amino acids, and thus by a serial "reading" of the DNA, "translated" by messenger RNA, a long polypeptide chain is synthesized such that its sequential structure predetermines the bioform into which it will fold. Ever-lengthening chains, logical lines (like ever longer sentences) are organized into genes (like paragraphs and chapters), and so the story of life is told. Diverse proteins, lipids, carbohydrates, enzymes—all the life structures are "written into" the genetic library.

The genetic set is thus really a *propositional* set—to choose a deliberately provocative term—recalling how the Latin *proposi-*

tum is an assertion, a set task, a theme, a plan, a proposal, a project, as well as a cognitive statement. From this it is also a motivational set, unlike human written material, since these life motifs are set so as to drive the movement from genotypic potential to phenotypic expression. No book is self-actualizing. Given a chance, these molecules seek organic self-expression. They proclaim a life way, and with this they claim the other for self as needs may be, an assertive claim. An inert rock exists on its own, making no assertions over the environment and not needing it (although it did not come into being on its own). But the living organism cannot exist alone. It must claim the environment as source and sink, from which to abstract energy and materials and into which to excrete them. It "takes advantage" of its environment. Life thus arises out of earthen sources (as do rocks), but life turns back on its sources to make resources out of them (unlike rocks), because life is a propositional and motivational set.

The DNA representing life is thus a *logical set* not less than a biological set. Organisms use a sort of symbolic logic, use these molecular positions and shapes as symbols of life. In this sense, the genome is a set of conservation molecules. The novel resourcefulness lies in the epistemic content conserved, developed, and thrown forward to make biological resources out of the physicochemical sources. The presence of this executive steering core makes fitting the term "cybernetic," a word recalling a governor or helmsman. An open cybernetic system is partly a special kind of cause-and-effect system and partly something more: partly a historical information system discovering and evaluating ends so as to map and make a way through the world, partly a system of significances attached to operations, pursuits, resources.

The DNA codes the logic of a life carried on not merely at that level but at the environmental, phenotypical level. What occurs at the level of molecular biology mainfests itself, via a complicated translation and interaction from genotypic to phenotypic levels, at the native-range levels (macroscopic ranges for organisms larger than microbes), where such life is selected for or against as it is defended in its environment.

Even stronger still, the genetic set is a *normative set;* it distinguishes between what *is* and what *ought to be.* This does not mean that the organism is a moral system, for there are no moral agents in nature apart from persons, but that the organism is an axiological system, an evaluative system. So it grows, reproduces, repairs its wounds, and resists death. We can say that the physical state the organism seeks, idealized in its programmatic form, is a valued state. *Value* is present in this achievement. *Vital* seems a better word for it than *biological.* We will want to recognize that we are not dealing simply with another individual defending its solitary life but with an individual having situated fitness in an ecosystem it inhabits. Still, we want to affirm here that the living individual, taken as a "point experience" in the web of interconnected life, is per se an intrinsic value. A life is defended for what it is in itself, without necessary further contributory reference, although, given the structure of all ecosystems, such lives necessarily do have further contributory reference. The organism has something it is conserving, something for which it is standing: its life. This is "Value Ownership" (Chapter 1) at a new location.

A favorite campground in the Rawah Range of the Rocky Mountains is adjacent to subalpine meadows of wildflowers: profuse displays of daisies, lupines, columbines, delphiniums, bluebells, paintbrushes, penstemons, shooting stars, and violets. The trailside signs for years read, "Please leave the flowers for others to enjoy." When I returned to the campground recently, the wasted wooden signs had been replaced by newly cut ones that read, "Let the flowers live!" Will the new signs be more effective? Do they represent a shifting environmental ethic? Is this only an aesthetic appeal? "Let lovely things be!" Is it a psychological appeal? "Don't vandalize!" Are the new signs subtly trying to recommend an experience? "Appreciate beautiful things!" Or is there a respect for life, replacing what on the earlier signs was only a respect for persons? (Would you recommend replacing signs that read, "Don't crosscut switchbacks," with new signs: "Give Earth a chance!"?) Perhaps the signs mean, "Let the flowers have their own standing!"

There seems no reason why such own-standing normative organisms are not morally significant.[5] That is, a moral agent in deciding his or her behavior ought to take account of the consequences for other evaluative systems. This will be "Following Nature in an Axiological Sense" (Chapter 1). We are not yet addressing the question of how morally significant butterflies or trees are, nor what justifiable considerations may outweigh such value, only establishing in principle what sorts of things can command our moral attention. The answer at this point is that organisms as spontaneous evaluative systems can. Being an organism is sufficient to do so, though (as later chapters argue) being an organism is not necessary for the presence of value that constrains our conduct. Whether and how far such organismic goods may or must be sacrificed for the goods of others is a subsequent question. The competing, exchanging, and intermeshing of goods in every ecosystem means that the goods of organisms are contextually situated. Everything is what it is in relation to other things, but every organism is what it spontaneously seeks to be. Whether or not there is *Nature-as-a-whole*, there evidently are specific *natures* programmed into each species, exemplified in individual organisms, so that each organism has its own good. Such goods are values that claim our respect.

Good Kinds, Bad Kinds, and Good-of-Their-Kinds

Organisms have their own standards, fit into their niche though they must. They promote their own realization at the same time that they track an environment. They have a technique, a know-how. Every organism has a *good-of-its-kind;* it defends its own kind as a *good kind.* In that sense, as soon as one knows what a blue spruce is, one knows what a good blue spruce is. One knows the biological identity that is sought and conserved.

Among moral agents an actor may be *good-of-his-kind* and yet not a *good kind.* Jack the Ripper was a good murderer in the sense that he was clever and never caught, but being a murderer is reprehensible. Jack had a good of his own: as a normative system he sought to kill. But his norm was morally wrong. Among moral agents one has not merely to ask whether x is a normative system but to judge the norm. But organisms, sentient or not, are amoral normative systems, and there are no cases where an organism seeks a good of its own that is morally reprehensible. Neither wolves nor nettles are bad because they defend their kinds of good. In organisms, the distinction between having a good-of-its-kind and being a good kind vanishes, so far as any faulting of the organism is concerned. To this extent, everything with a good-of-its-kind is a good kind and thereby has value.

One might say, however, of an organism which, during the course of pressing its normative expression, upset the ecosystem or caused widespread disease that it was a bad organism. In this sense *Choristoneura fumiferana*, the spruce budworm that is ravaging northeastern boreal forests, or *Plasmodium vivax*, the malaria parasite, or *Chlamydia*, the microbe that causes conjunctivitis in the bighorns in Yellowstone, might meaningfully be judged bad kinds, though each has a good-of-its-kind. If one does say this, one means that, though considered as normative organismic systems that have goods-of-their-kind and are intrinsically good kinds, still they are bad kinds instrumentally in the roles they play. If this is so, their own-standing goods might be overridden by other goods. We have nowhere intended in this account that some values cannot be overridden by others, and comparisons will follow. The point here is to get the theory clear: who counts, not how much. Even in "bad" cases there is value present in the offending organisms—value which, though it clashes with ours, is morally significant merely because the organism is a spontaneous evaluative system.

Remember, though, that an organism cannot be a good kind without situated environmental fitness. With rare exceptions, organisms are well adapted to the niches they fill. By natural selection their ecosystemic roles must mesh with the kind of goods to which they are genetically programmed. Despite the ecosystem as a perpetual contest of goods in dialectic and exchange, it is difficult to say that any organism is a bad kind in this instrumental sense either. The misfits are extinct, or soon will be. In spontaneous nature any species that preys upon, parasitizes, competes with, or crowds another will be a bad kind from the narrow perspective of its victim or competitor. But if we enlarge that perspective, it typically becomes difficult to say that any species is a bad kind overall in the ecosystem. An "enemy" may even be good for the "victimized" species, though harmful to individual members of it, as when predation keeps the deer herd healthy. Beyond this, the "bad kinds" typically play useful roles in population control, in symbiotic relationships, or in providing opportunities for other species. The *Chlamydia* microbe is a bad kind from the perspective of the bighorns, but when one thing dies, something else lives. After the pinkeye outbreak, the golden eagle population in Yellowstone flourished as never observed in recent times, preying on the bighorn carcasses. For them *Chlamydia* is a good kind instrumentally, as is *Choristoneura* for the birds that feed on it. The Cape May warbler, a jewel in the tree tops and usually rare, thrives during budworm outbreaks; other birds that eat the worms can nest twice in a season when normally they would be hard-pressed to complete one nesting.

Someone might say that even though an organism evolves to have a situated environmental fitness, not all such situations are good arrangements; some can be clumsy or bad, involving bad organisms in bad evolutionary patterns. For instance, humans with the hemoglobin deformity known as the sickle-cell trait acquire resistance to malaria when they have one copy of the sickle cell gene but often die of anemia when they have two copies. This hemoglobin deformity persists in balanced polymorphism in a malarious environment because it is favorable to the heterozygotes, though often fatal to the homozygotes. It is rapidly selected against in a nonmalarious environment. So we could say that *Plasmodium vivax* (a mosquito-borne microbe that causes malaria) is a bad organism and that its situated environmental fitness in the human ecology is bad. Humans try to eliminate it by medical science.

This condition, however, is only partially a natural one. It seems to have appeared with the introduction of Malaysian agriculture into Africa about 2,000 years ago, a short-range feature on an evolutionary time scale. As a serious problem in Africa, malaria is a disease of civilization, as are most infectious diseases. Cultural innovations have often upset stable biological regimens, as in the current ecological crisis. Still, one might find examples of organisms with a situated environmental fitness that seem bad arrangements.

But the burden of proof is on a human evaluator to say why any natural kind is a bad kind and ought not to call forth admiring respect. Something may be a good kind intrinsically but a bad kind instrumentally in the system; these will be anomalous cases, however, soon edited out. There are also deformed organisms in nature, bad organisms of their kind, and even monstrosities that have no natural kind, unfitted for any habitat. Such individuals are immediately eliminated, although in the course of experimental mutation they are required if life is to continue. So even mutants and monsters play their roles in the trial and error by which the evolutionary ecosystem tracks changing environments and achieves new life forms. Earth may not be the best possible world, but it is the only one we know that has produced any life at all, and the life it has produced is, on the whole, a good thing. These claims about good kinds do not say that things are perfect kinds or that there can be no better ones, only that natural kinds are good kinds until proven otherwise.

We ought not to be misled by counterexamples such as a "good cancer cell." Unlike disease organisms, which do have a good of their own and which do have a function in the ecosystem, a good (healthy) cancer cell is not good of its kind. A cancer cell has no natural kind but is a good cell gone out of control, a misfit in the body. Further, the goodness of cells in the multicellular organism is as instrumental parts in a whole. The intrinsic goodness of kind comes at the level of the organism, as well as at the species level. From the perspective of cell or organism, a good cancer cell is a contradiction in terms. A vigorously growing cancer cell is enroute to its own destruction.

Meanwhile, one does have to make a place, both biologically and philosophically, for death in the system. Without death there can be no life. If nothing much had ever died, nothing much could have ever lived. Even the aging processes that break down life, of which cancer is an example, are goods when incorporated into the system, though they are evils for individual organisms.

What is almost invariably meant by a "bad" kind is that an organism is instrumentally bad when judged from the viewpoint of human interests, often with the further complication that human interests have disrupted natural systems. The spruce budworm threat results from overaged forests too long sprayed in order to bolster the timber industry. This was doubtfully good even from the perspective of the spruce species. Malaria became epidemic with the introduction of agriculture; it was little threat to hunter-gatherer peoples. In 99 percent of cases, a "bad" kind means an organism with a role such that humans judge their interests to override the good-of-its-kind/good kind in spontaneous nature.

According to this environmental ethic, what the injunction, "Let the flowers live!" means is "Daisies, marsh-marigolds, geraniums, larkspurs are evaluative systems that express goods-of-their-kind and, in the absence of evidence to the contrary, are good kinds. There are trails here by which you may enjoy these flowers. Is there any reason why your human interests justify destroying good kinds?" The old signs, "Leave the flowers for others to enjoy," were application signs using a humanistic ethic. The new ones invite a change of reference frame.

Organisms versus Human Machines

We ought not be led astray by comparisons with artifacts. An objector may say that an automobile has a good-of-its-kind; it has needs, as when my car needs spark plugs. A computer can be running well or poorly; it defends its program, responds to input, adjusts its output. Yet no one thinks that machines are morally considerable. So why should we think that "organic machines" count morally?

The objection fails to distinguish between organisms and artifacts, and unless this distinction is made, there will be hopeless confusion. A car has no nature of its own; it does not exist by nature. An automobile is a means to human good; spontaneous nature could not conceivably have produced an automobile. Or, to make the point by playing with language, nature's "automobiles"—its things with genuinely "autonomous motion"—are living organisms. Cars have no self-generating or self-defending tendencies; they are called automobiles only by historical accident, because they are horseless carriages. When a human steps out of a car, she takes all the purposes, needs, programs, interests of the car away with her, all of which she gave to the car in the first place.

But none of this is true when a human walks away from a deer or a delphinium. The car does not "need" spark plugs except as a locution for, "I need plugs for my car." The car is not an automobile except insofar as it needs no horses to draw it. It must have a driver. Nor is the computer automatic; its program was written for it by a person, even if it is a program with elements of learning in it. Machines have an end only mediately as the extrasomatic products of human systems. But the tree has a *telos* before the logger arrives, and the logger destroys it. It is *auto-telic;* it has a law (Greek: *nomos*) on its own (= *autonomos*). It is on autopilot.

A Montana loggers' slogan runs, "The only good tree is a stump." That may be so from the loggers' perspective, who desire to remake trees into artifacts. *Good* then means *useful*. But from the *telos* of the tree, a stump is a bad tree. Organisms are healthy, thrive and flourish; they have self-generating, self-defending tendencies. We do not speak in this way of artifacts.

The values that attach to machines are therefore entirely instrumental, derivative from the persons who have created these instruments. But the values that attach to organisms result from their nonderivative, genuine autonomy (though environmentally situated) as spontaneous natural systems. The standards of performance, of excellence, are in the organism itself, relative to its reference frame. These are not absolute standards, but they are objective standards in that they are not generated by subjective human preferences. These are relative standards in that, at a level surrounding the organism, there exist further, systemic requirements by which the organism is tested as fit or misfit.

We remain in the humanistic reference frame when we talk of artifacts, but we enter the naturalistic reference frame when we value organisms for their spontaneous, self-evaluative life. A machine is a good kind only because it is a good-of-my-kind; an organism can have a good-of-its-kind and be a good kind intrinsically, as well as be dialectically a short-range-bad-fitting-into-a-larger-good kind in an ecosystem. Machines are by us and for us; organisms live on their own. No machine is wild, but it is significantly the wildness of life that we treasure.

Objective Life versus Subjective Life

Perhaps it is not enough to say positively why organisms count morally. Something must be said against the prevailing view that moral significance enters and exits with sentient interests or, more specifically, with the capacity to suffer pain and enjoy pleasure. W. K. Frankena concludes, "I can see no reason, from the moral point of view, why we should respect something that is alive but has no conscious sentiency and so can experience no pleasure or pain, joy or suffering."[6] Peter Singer agrees: "If a being is not capable of suffering, or of experiencing enjoyment or happiness, there is nothing to be taken into account."[7] "As nonconscious beings have no interests, so nonconscious life lacks intrinsic value."[8] But, we are replying, they do "take account" of themselves; and we should take account of them. They "stand up" for themselves, and so (in a more legal phrase) they should "have standing" with us. An objector can say, "The tree doesn't care, so why should I?" But the tree does care, in the only form of caring available to it; and why should I take no account of that form of caring because it is not my form of caring?

Hiking a wilderness trail in New Hampshire in July 1981, I encountered this sign, neatly printed on cardboard and posted at a backcountry campsite:

DO NOT PEEL BARK FROM WHITE BIRCH TREES
WITHIN 200 FEET OF CAMPS, TRAILS, ROADS, HUTS, OR
OTHER PLACES WHERE PEOPLE CONGREGATE.
                                        White Mountain National Forest

I thought to myself, "Why the 200-foot limit?" The concern is not for the trees themselves, but only for their visibility by humans. If one mutilates white birch that are out of sight, who cares? Later, thinking that the sign would make a good discussion starter, I wrote and asked for a copy. In prompt, concerned reply I received a long-distance call from an official of the forest wanting to know where the sign was. He was anxious to remove it because it was an old one. Current regulations prohibit defacing birch trees anywhere in the forest, with a $25 fine for offenders. Peeling bark damages trees, leaves them vulnerable to insect and fungal infestation, and is vandalism. Among multiple factors in this change of regulation, one seems to result from or in—or at least to invite—a subtle shift of ethic. "Let the birch trees live!"

W. K. Frankena says, "Why, if leaves and trees have no capacity to feel pleasure or to suffer, should I tear no leaf from a tree?"[9] Or peel no bark from a birch, out of sight of others? Should I not discourage my son from practicing with his ax on living birch and encourage him to use a fallen log instead? Birch is one of the few woods that will burn green, and its papery bark provides excellent kindling. But another forest sign at the trail junction urged, "Burn down [i.e., fallen] wood!" Why?

Psychological and Genetic Preferences

Life is an objective process in the world. No one will deny this—short of solipsism, phenomenalism, or insanity! Only some forms of life sponsor the subjective process characterized by inwardness, by psychological experience. Panpsychists claim that an elementary or attenuated feeling characterizes even plants and microbes. Lacking clear evidence for this belief, most persons judge sentience to accompany approximately the central nervous system and thus to be absent in flora and protozoans, lower invertebrates, and probably those forms with nerves and ganglia but little or no brain. There is no particular cause to expect a sharp cutoff point here; sentience likely emerges across a twilight zone, although nature sometimes surprises us with radical changes of state at narrow thresholds (as when water freezes at zero degrees Celsius). An environmental ethic that distinguishes between sentient and nonsentient life does not depend on whether the boundary is sharp or fuzzy.

The question is rather, Is there some reason to value only subjective life intrinsically and objective life only instrumentally, if at all? The question, notice, is not, "Does subjective life count more than objective life?" but, "Does only subjective life count?" To say that the threshold of our moral sensitivity is just the same as the threshold of felt sensitivity is to say that moral concern is directed only toward inwardness; its scope does not include outwardness except relationally. That is, in a sense, to make morality *subjective*, to attach it to subjects and deny it to objects. Only subjects—indeed, on Earth only human subjects—can be moral *agents*. But who are their moral *patients?*

We here hope to defend an *objective* morality, one with a focus on objective life. Environmental ethics is not merely an affair of psychology but of biology. Further, although in principle diverse kinds of experience might be valued, in practice the language that ethicists (illustrated by Frankena and Singer) usually use is restricted to that of pains and pleasures, suggesting a hedonist theory of value, as though pain is nature's only disvalue and pleasure its only value. Our environmental ethic will be more holistic. Pains and pleasures will be part of a larger picture, derivative from and instrumental to further values at the ecosystemic level, where nature evolves a flourishing community in some indifference to the pains and pleasures of individuals, even though pain and pleasure in the higher forms is a major evolutionary achievement.

Already, dealing with the *goods* of sentient organisms, we found it necessary to distinguish between *psychological interests* and *biological interests*. The coyote takes no felt interest in poisons in her drinking water; the elk takes an interest in the salty Polaroid paper, tossed aside as tourist trash, although the toxic chemicals are detrimental to the biological interests of both animals (and in due course result in psychological suffering; see Chapter 2).

Below the threshold of sentience (assuming this to be roughly the threshold of suffering and satisfaction), there are only biological interests. It is sometimes said that plants can have *needs* (as when a tree needs water) but can have no *interests*, because the only sorts of interests allowed are psychological interests. Joel Feinberg says, "Mindless creatures have no interests of their own."[10] True, beneath the level of awareness the word "interest" becomes strained because we factor out all psychological desires, which are often active in our ordinary use of that word. But some meaning is left, caught by "need" or "biological interest." Some things are good for, goods for, plants and insects; some are not.

Plants and insects have a well-being, and they respond with a (nonfelt) interest in this well-being, as when a tree sends roots down deeper for water or an ant (though but a ganglion on legs) scurries off with a crumb. *Escherichia coli*, a common bacterium, placed in a food supply with both lactose and glucose, prefers glucose over lactose and eats the latter only after the former is gone. The microbe presumably does not have any options in this preference; the preset preference is hardwired into the genes. But this is the way genetic preferences operate, as opposed to the later-evolving neural and consciously expressed preferences.

Stentor roeselii, a trumpet-shaped, one-celled aquatic organism, has a mouth at the top and attaches itself by a foot to the substrate. If irritated, it may contract, or duck, bending first this way and then that, or reverse the ciliary movement of its peristome and sweep water currents away. It may withdraw into a mucous tube about the base, to return after a few minutes and, upon further irritation, repeat various avoidance reactions. But finally, with a jerk, it will break the attachment of its foot and swim away to attach itself elsewhere. *Difflugia urceolata*, a protozoan like a snail, builds a house of sand grains, carries it about, and retreats into it upon the approach of danger. Such organisms, though nerveless, are genuinely autonomous (= self-impelled) evaluative systems, even if it is also true that their behaviors work by genetic programs, biochemistries, instincts, or stimulus response mechanisms. They may have no autonomous options, but they defend a life as a good-of-its-kind.

There is an object-with-will, even though there is no subject-with-will. The organism is genetically programmed to argue, to probe, to fight, to run, to grow, to reproduce, to resist death. Some will protest that with words like these we sneak in a "closet awareness," as though the organisms were "trying," and elicit an ethical sympathy for a frustrated pathos that is not there. They have tendencies, but they intend nothing. But the point is that below the threshold of subjectivity life remains. It can yet flourish or be harmed. Life still has its commitments, something it values, a cybernetic program defended, goods of an objective kind, genetically based preferences. Such organisms have no envisaged goals, but why should we restrict value to mentally guided behavior when much behavior is guided by genes and instincts—and we do value this kind of behavior even in ourselves. Is there no reason to count this ethically, unless and until it is accompanied by sentience? Is not objective life too among the archetypes on which the world is built?

Subjective Experience and Objective Value

Fishermen in Atlantic coastal estuaries and bays toss beer bottles overboard, a convenient way to dispose of trash. On the bottom, small crabs, attracted by the residual beer, make their way inside the bottles and become trapped, unable to get enough foothold on the slick glass neck to work their way out. They starve slowly. Then one dead crab becomes bait for the next victim in an indefinitely resetting trap! Are those bottle traps of ethical concern, after fisherman have been warned about this effect? Or is the whole thing out of sight, out of mind, with crabs too mindless to care about? Should sensitive fisherman pack their bottle trash back to shore, whether or not crabs have much, or any, felt experience?

Although we may abandon the symbolism of *rights*, abandon even the appeal to some *moral* standing analogous to *legal* standing, we do not abandon the concept of *value* when we descend below sentience on the phylogenetic spectrum. To the contrary, *value* is a critical paradigm-indicator word. By value analysis differing paradigms can be detected. According to the reigning paradigm, there is no value without an experiencing valuer, just as there are no thoughts without a thinker, no percepts without a perceiver, no deeds without a doer, no targets without an aimer. Valuing is *felt* preferring; value is the product of this process.

Value is of two kinds, intrinsic and instrumental. Intrinsic values are psychological interest satisfactions desired without further contributory reference, pleasures good in themselves. Instrumental values contribute to further interest satisfactions. Objective things, living or not, may have instrumental value, contributing to subjective interest satisfactions. But they do not have intrinsic value. Intrinsic value requires a beholder, an experiencer. The beholder perhaps may not assign the value, but he at least admits and receives it. Such value is not (entirely) at his option. A redwood is thus valuable without his will but not without his awareness. Before his coming, there are only precursors of value; value does not emerge until these are thickened by the addition of human interests.

By this account, value exists only where a subject has an object of interest. David Prall concludes:

> The being liked, or disliked, of the object is its value. . . . Some sort of a subject is always requisite to there being value at all.[11]

Wilhelm Windelband agrees:

> Value . . . is never found in the object itself as a property. It consists in a relation to an appreciating mind, which satisfies the desires of

its will or reacts in feelings of pleasure upon the stimulation of the environment. Take away will and feeling, and there is no such thing as value.[12]

Ralph Barton Perry continues:

The silence of the desert is without value, until some wanderer finds it lonely and terrifying; the cataract, until some human sensibility finds it sublime, or until it is harnessed to satisfy human needs. Natural substances . . . are without value until a use is found for them, whereupon their value may increase to any desired degree of preciousness according to the eagerness with which they are coveted. . . . Any object, whatever it be, acquires value when any interest, whatever it be, is taken in it.[13]

W. M. Urban adds:

The value of an object consists . . . in its satisfaction of desire, or more broadly, fulfilment of interest.[14]

William James starkly portrays the utterly valueless world, suddenly transfigured as a gift of the human coming.

Conceive yourself, if possible, suddenly stripped of all the emotions with which your world now inspires you, and try to imagine it *as it exists*, purely by itself, without your favorable or unfavorable, hopeful or apprehensive comment. It will be almost impossible for you to realize such a condition of negativity and deadness. No one portion of the universe would then have importance beyond another; and the whole collection of its things and series of its events would be without significance, character, expression, or perspective. Whatever of value, interest, or meaning our respective worlds may appear endued with are thus pure gifts of the spectator's mind.[15]

In contrast, we here claim that in an objective gestalt some value is already present in nonsentient organisms, normative evaluative systems, prior to the emergence of further dimensions of value with sentience. Biology has steadily demonstrated how subjective life is a consequence of objective life, the one always the necessary sponsor of the other (so far as we know it on Earth). Objective life, when reaching sufficient levels of neural complexity, is often sufficient for subjective life. Why not value the whole process with all its product organisms, rather than restrict valuing to the subjective aspect of the process? When we exclaim, "Let flowers, birch trees, crabs, ants, live!" there is excitement in the beholder; but what is valued is what is beheld. Insentient organisms are the *holders* of value although not the *beholders* of value. With such a prolife injunction in environmental ethics, humans are not so much lighting up value in a merely potentially valuable world as they are psychologically joining an ongoing defense of biological value. (We develop this value theory at the ecosystem level in Chapter 5.)

By this account some values are dependent on conscious preferences; others are not. Some portion of the value in a particular event may be preference-dependent and the rest of it not. Whether I value lettuce partly depends on my felt preferences (I may opt for cauliflower instead), but it partly depends on my biochemistry, to which my felt preferences are irrelevant. My biochemistry is genetically preset to value the vitamins and amino acids in nutrients, as *Escherichia coli* is hardwired to prefer glucose over lactose.

Projecting Intrinsic Value?

There is an intermediate position. Noticing that humans value most natural things by making them over resourcefully but value a limited number of wild things as they are in themselves, we say that humans are making instrumental uses of the former type of resource but are valuing the latter type intrinsically. That is, humans may value sequoias as timber but may also value them as natural classics for their age, strength, size, beauty, resilience, majesty.

Let-the-flowers-live valuing is of this kind; humans make no instrumental, consumptive use of the flowers. They do not pick them. But they do view them, a nonconsumptive use. This viewing constitutes the flowers' value, a value not previously present in the flowers independent of the human presence. Still, it is a value that, when it appears as a product of subjective awareness, is attached objectively to the flowers flourishing in the meadow, not attached instrumentally in relation to some resource use humans may make of them—for instance, as a bouquet. Value thus requires subjectivity, since only subjectivity can coagulate it in the world. But the value so coagulated, we will claim, is objectively intrinsic to the nonsentient life and not merely instrumental.

On these occasions natural things are not used, at least not used up, to satisfy human needs. Rather, they are valued, when humans encounter them, for what they are in themselves, and not just for the sake of human appreciation. That "*x* is valuable" does mean "interest is taken in x,"[16] but it need not mean "x satisfies my desire," since I may take an interest in the wildflowers for what they are in themselves, not merely to satisfy my desires. Still there is no value until consciousness comes on scene, because consciousness is required for interest be taken in x. (In a way, however, that interest is "taken" in x very nearly means that interest in x is "satisfied," found worthwhile, satisfying. One "takes" an interest only to "satisfy" it.)

J. Baird Callicott, a keen advocate of the proper appreciation of nature, says that all intrinsic value is "grounded in human feelings" but is "projected" onto the natural object that "excites" the value. "Intrinsic value ultimately depends upon human valuers." "Value depends upon human sentiments."[17]

> The *source* of all value is human consciousness, but it by no means follows that the *locus* of all value is consciousness itself. . . . An intrinsically valuable thing on this reading is valuable *for* its own sake, *for* itself, but it is not valuable *in* itself, i.e. completely independently of any consciousness, since no value can in principle . . . be altogether independent of a valuing consciousness. . . . Value is, as it were, projected onto natural objects or events by the subjective feelings of observers. If all consciousness were annihilated at a stroke, there would be no good and evil, no beauty and ugliness, no right and wrong; only impassive phenomena would remain.[18]

This, Callicott says, is a "truncated sense" of value where "'intrinsic value' retains only half its traditional meaning." At the same time, "value is, to be sure, humanly conferred, but not necessarily homocentric."[19]

The word "project" here needs analysis. Motion picture projectors project an image when light travels from the projector to the screen, but we are not here to think of a value-bestowing ray. Nothing travels from the human valuer to the natural object. Rather, humans value trees somewhat as they color them green. The greenness of the tree is in my head, but it looks as though the tree is green. Out there are only electromagnetic waves of 550 nanometers. The greenness is projected, manufactured in my head and apparently hung onto the tree. Dogs, with black and white vision, project no greenness onto the same tree. I have no options about the greenness; I do have options about the valuing—to some extent. I can see the tree as board-feet of timber or as a poem (Joyce Kilmer). I can value it as an instrument to satisfy my desires, or I can see it as having intrinsic value.

In all this nothing travels from the human to the tree. The

"projection" is better called a "translation." The "value confer-
ring" does not transmit anything to the tree, and in that sense
the value never really gets outside the human head. The tree is
sending, and the human is *receiving*. The human is not really doing any sending, nor the tree any receiving. The incoming signals
from the tree are "translated" as green, and so the tree appears
green. In one sense this is an illusion; in another it is not. There is
no experience of green in the tree, but there is ample reality (radiation) out there, behind and exciting my experience. My coloring
the tree green is mapping what is really there, though my mind is
translating as it maps. My finding of intrinsic value in nature is
to be modeled after my finding green. (Green insects, camouflaged
on the leaves, are protected from predators who, though they have
no experience of green, have other sense modalities that catch
electromagnetic signals and distinguish wavelengths.)

To say that something is valuable means that it is able to be
valued, if and when (human) valuers come along, but it has this
property whether or not humans (or other valuers) ever arrive.
To say that something is intrinsically valuable means that it is of
such kind that were valuers to arrive they might value it intrinsically rather than instrumentally. The trilobites that went extinct
before humans evolved were (potentially) intrinsically valuable.
Undiscovered species on Earth now or on uninhabited planets are
intrinsically valuable in this potential sense.

By this account there is no actual value ownership autonomous
to the valued and valuable flower; there is a value ignition when
humans come. Intrinsic value in the realized sense is subjectively generated, emerging relationally with the appearance of
the subject-generator, although nothing is generated except under
the field of force of the objective item valued. The object plays its
necessary part, though this is not sufficient without the subject.
Also, humans err: they can (and often do) value flowers insufficiently; they fail to appreciate what flowers are in themselves.

This theory of *anthropogenic intrinsic* value differs from the
theory of *autonomous intrinsic* value that we are defending.[20] Notice that, although anthropogenic, it is not anthropocentric. Value
is not self-regarding or even human-regarding, merely, though it
is human-generated (anthropogenic). It is not centered on human
well-being, though it is still tethered to human experience.

This compromise account is certainly to be welcomed over
less enlightened humanistic accounts. It affords enormously more
environmental respect and protection than weaker theories. It

is not yet a genuinely biological or ecological theory of value, however, but residually a psychological one, which refuses to burn all humanistic bridges behind as it enters the wilderness of environmental ethics.

Despite the language of value projection and conferral, if we try to take the term *intrinsic* seriously, it cannot refer to anything the object gains, to something *within* ("intra") the object, for the human subject does not really project anything to the natural object. We have only a "truncated sense" of *intrinsic*. All the *attributes* under consideration are objectively there before humans come, but the *attribution* of value is subjective. The object causally affects the subject, who is excited by the incoming data and translates this as value, after which the object appears as having value (and color). But nothing is really added *intrinsically* to the object at all; everything in the object remains what it was before. Despite the language that humans are the *source* of value which they *locate* in the natural object, no value is really located there at all. The only new event is that these properties are registered in—translated into felt values by—the perceptual apparatus of the beholder.

The features are all there in the object itself, which is why I value it for what it is in itself. But the value arises with my awareness. This is said to be the ignition (projection) of value, hitherto only potentially present. But is not this like looking for time in the clock that measures it, looking for a birthday party in the camera that photographs it? I seem to be assuming that, among all the phenomena in the universe, only one sort of thing, psychological interest, produces actual value intrinsically, although I recognize that myriads of things present in the world before, during, or after the presence of (human) valuers can excite such value. Actual value was not lost when the various species of trilobites went extinct, nor is value lost now when unknown species in tropical forests go extinct, bulldozed away unbeknown to humans.

Now, however, it appears that the term *intrinsic*, though claimed in a truncated sense for this view, is misleading. What is really meant is better specified by the term *extrinsic*,[21] the *ex* indicating the external, anthropogenic coagulation of the value, which is not *in—intrinsic*, internal to—the nonsentient organism, even though this value, once generated, is apparently conferred on the organism. The value is noncontributory in the sense that it is not utilized in some human reference frame: that is, not possessed in a rebuilt environment. The value is accepted, reflected, enjoyed just as it is. Still, human consciousness realizes this value in the organism, which the organism did not have before but which, on encounter with humans, it does come to have extrinsically. We humans carry the lamp that lights up value, although we require the fuel that nature provides.

The value-generating event is something like the light in a refrigerator—only on when the door is opened. Values in flora and nonsentient fauna are only "on" when humans are perceiving them, and otherwise "off." That is, actual value is an event in consciousness, though of course natural items while still in the dark have potential intrinsic value.

But by now we begin to suspect that the anthropogenic account of intrinsic value is a strained saving of what is really an inadequate paradigm, that of the subjectivity of value conferral. For all the kindly language about intrinsic value in nature, the cash value is that, "Let the flowers live!" really means, "Leave the flowers for humans to enjoy" after all, because the flowers are valuable—able to be valued—only by humans even though when properly sensitive humans come along they do value these flowers for what they are in themselves.

A thoroughgoing value theory in environmental ethics is more radical than this; it fully values the objective roots of value with or without their fruits in subjectivity. Sometimes to be radical is also to be simpler. The anthropogenic theory of intrinsic value strains to insist on the subjectivity of value conferral while straining to preserve the object with all its properties. It admits that the exciting object is necessary for generating value. Surely this is a paradigm beset by anomalies, ready for overthrowing. A simpler, less anthropically based, more biocentric theory holds that some values are objectively there—discovered, not generated, by the valuer. A fully objective environmental ethics can quite enjoy a "translator" when subjective appreciators of value appear. It can value such appreciation (experienced respect) more highly than untranslated objective value. Value appreciates (increases) with humans. But such an ethic does not insist upon a translator for value to be present at all, else it commits a fallacy of the misplaced location of values.

Trees may not be colored without a perceiver, but they do exist per se. Is their value like their color or their existence? Trees have their norms and needs, defenses, programs; these are factors in their existence, and so value, coupling with existence defended, is not an analogue of color after all. Trees do appear to be green, and perhaps we do not want to call the electromagnetic waves that are actually there "greenness." Trees are also valuable in themselves, able to value themselves; they stand on their own. By contrast with "greenness," we do want to say that "treeness" is objectively there, the tree with its life project defended. We want to call this valuable regardless of what "seems" to us. We shall be saying (in Chapter 5) that some values are already there, discovered, not generated, by the valuer because the first project here is really the natural object, nature's project; the principal *projecting* is nature creating formed integrity. Beside this, the human *projecting* of value is an epiphenomenon.

Protecting Human Excellences?

A still weaker account of value, yet one that much desires to protect the environment, interprets human encounters with nature in terms of human excellences.[22] Intrinsic values exist only in human subjects; natural objects never have intrinsic value at all either before or after humans come. But certain excellences of human character arise only with appropriate sensitivity toward natural things. Nature is like fine art, literature, music. It elevates character. This makes it a resource of a finer type (as well as, on everyday occasions, of a utilitarian type).

A morally mature person will say, "I do not want to be the type of person who values everything by cost-benefit analysis, nor by a what's-the-pleasure-in-it-for-me-and-my-kind analysis. One admirable trait in persons is being able to appreciate things outside themselves. The more at distance from their daily concerns, the finer this is. If I let whooping cranes go extinct, my grandchildren will say that their grandfather was callous, just as I now deplore my great-grandfathers who shot up the buffalo and passenger pigeons. I do not want such disrespect. There is something philistine, obnoxious, tacky about the mere consumer of nature—not to mention cutting drive-through sequoias or sizzling ants for amusement. Humans who lord it over nature do not lead fully worthwhile lives (see Chapter 6, pp. 227–28). Such actions are uncalled for. I want to be a bigger person than that. It is a condition of human flourishing that humans enjoy natural things, at least at times, as they flourish in themselves."

But why are such insensitive actions "uncalled for" unless there is something in the natural object that "calls for" a more appropriate attitude? We do not love wildflowers *for the pleasure they bring us*. They themselves *are* our pleasure; their flourishing is that in which we take pleasure. But likewise it seems "unexcellent" to say that the excellence of human character is what valuing wildflowers is all about. Our excellence of character comes as the wildflowers give us pleasure, but they are strong to do this because they have value in themselves, which we humans are sensitive enough to track onto with subjective experiences. If the excellence of character really comes from appreciating *otherness*, then why not attach *value* to this otherness? Why praise only the *virtue* in the beholder? How can it be an ideal of human excellence to treasure for what it is in itself something that has no value in itself? We seem incoherently to be trying to value for its own sake and for our sake what has no sake! Why take a wildflower into account unless there is something there to take into account?

We do indeed want from nature high-quality scientific, recreational, aesthetic, character-building, and religious experiences. We want to learn frugality, simplicity, honesty, our place under the sun. We want to learn to respect life, to admire evolutionary speciation, ecosystem interdependence, to be sensitive to the natural world. But to say that the values here are nothing but concerns for human excellences reduces the admonition "Keep life wonderful" (Chapter 1, p. 26) to "Keep human life excellent," which misperceives the basic location of value ownership, even though it is correct that humans come to own these values. We covertly replace the question, "What is its good?" with "What is it good for?" and answer, "It is good for human excellences." We are not disinterested in a wild life but interested in our own interests. That hardly seems ethical. We may owe it to ourselves not to destroy the Rosetta Stone, but letting the wildflowers live is something we owe to the flowers, not merely to ourselves.

Perhaps one can value a fossil for its otherness, although it has no value in itself, and receive some excellence of character; the fossil is a memento of natural history, and I am enriched by respecting it. Perhaps one can value a wild river in its otherness, although the river has no value in itself; it is an event in geophysical nature, and I am stretched by contacting it. Neither fossil nor river has a self. But with organisms—the part of the environment considered in this chapter—there is a defended integrity, a life owned, which is objectively of value whether or not my excellent character is present. Living things do take account of themselves, and in that sense even nonpsychological lives have a somatic "self." The only sober account of treasuring such lives is that virtue in the beholder fundamentally reflects value in the beheld. My inward excellence of character appropriates excellent characteristics in the wildflower, and this is why respectful behavior is appropriate. Art, literature, music are our human doing, but here we wish to value what does not depend on human consciousness, else we are not yet valuing living otherness.

Human Interests and Organismic Values

Perhaps objectively valuing organisms, even if ethically and metaphysically plausible, is hopeless unless it can be made operational. Plants, insects, snails, crustaceans, though in principle to be counted morally, would in practice have no moral significance. R. D. Guthrie, who rejects the principle, rejects also the practice: "A human's act toward other organisms is, in and of itself, an amoral one. It becomes a moral act only when humans are affected. . . . The inclusion of other organisms as primary participants in our ethical system is both logically unsound and operationally unfeasible."[23] At the other extreme, Paul Taylor accepts the biocentric principle and says that the interests of plants and persons should have equal consideration. He claims that it can be as wrong to kill a plant as a person. "The killing of a wildflower, then, when taken in and of itself, is just as much a wrong, other-things-being-equal, as the killing of a human."[24] That seems incredible, and one wonders, if all organisms are to be equally counted morally (= to be counted equals?), how to escape a kind of paralysis of moral judgment—sometimes called Schweitzer's dilemma—in which we are unable to weigh competing claims. There are no criteria for judgment. Again, including other organisms seems operationally unfeasible.

Perhaps the intrinsic value of plants lies on the attenuating slope of a curve somewhat like those encountered in physics, where an actual field of force, measurably present at some location, falls off rapidly with distance and soon in practice vanishes, although it never in theory reaches zero. A small magnet has in theory an infinite field; in practice, the field is insignificant twenty centimeters away. Combining such curves for several groups would produce descending differential value curves along gradients, gradual or steep, with the general picture that the intrinsic value of sentient animals would be lower than that of humans, that of insects still less. The value of plants would be practically nil, a barely usable idea in ethics. Nature crosses various thresholds of emergent values.

Having refused (in Chapter 2) to be sentimental about sentient animals, sacrificing them to humans needs within the general patterns of an ecosystem, we do not want here to be sentimental about insects or plants. As in hunting, there is no reason for humans to deny their ecology. We eat plants, as we eat animals. But there is every reason for humans to affirm their ecology, and this means nonsentimentally and objectively to affirm the standing of the member components of Earth's biological communities. We want to affirm all life, not just sentient life. Being nonsentimental means valuing life that flourishes without sentiments, as do the wildflowers.

In making judgments at this level, however, the principle of the nonaddition of suffering will not work, since there is no suffering. We can substitute a principle of *the nonloss of goods*. The goods preserved by the human destruction of plants must outweigh the goods of the organisms destroyed; thus, to be justified in picking flowers for a bouquet one would have to judge correctly that the aesthetic appreciation of the bouquet outweighed the goods of the flowers destroyed. One might pluck flowers for a bouquet but refuse to uproot the whole plant, or pick common flowers (daisies) and refuse to pick rare ones (trailing arbutus) or those that reproduce slowly (wild orchids).

True, intrinsic values in plants are attenuated compared with those manifested in persons, but it does not follow that they can never enter an environmental ethic. The gradient of descending intrinsic values may seem like a slippery slope where we will get lost trying to stabilize any judgments of value, but the seeming downslopes may also be the incremental upslopes over which evolutionary nature has built up value—the upslope achievements of evolutionary history. And it is vital to remember that we are here speaking only of intrinsic worth, not instrumental worth functionally in an ecosystem, not what we will later call systemic value. In the latter values, plants exceed humans!

One should honor "well-being," but at various levels that can be an affair of individuals, of species, and even of ecosystems. We will be turning to the integration of species into ecosystems in chapters to follow. For the present, when only considerations of intrinsic value (well-being) obtain, value magnitudes will be something like this: highest in humans, descending across animal life in rough proportion to phylogenetic or neural complexity, lower in plant life, and least in microbes. That is only an intuitive scale; it will need to be corrected by the detailed descriptions of biological science.

To see how the biological interests of plants or lower animals can on occasion outweigh those of humans, let us approach the issue from two directions—either aggregating the values of plants and animals, or trivializing the interests of humans. Consider the following cases, which involve one or both of these strategies. Are these cases where humans *should* lose?

- Chapman's rhododendron, *Rhododendron chapmanii*, is an attractive evergreen, federally listed as endangered. It is naturally rare, but made much more rare by clear-cutting its habitat for paper production, draining its bog habitat to replant pines, and digging clumps for the nursery trade. It now exists in only three locations in the deep South, a few hundred plants. Do human interests—a few more acres of pines, a few more rolls of newsprint, a few more ads—justify destroying the remaining plants? Does it make a difference whether there are human interests (or "excellences") on the side of conserving the species?
- Ginseng, *Panax quinquefolius*, once common, is much sought in the mistaken belief that its powdered roots prolong virility and vitality. It has been nearly exterminated in the Appalachian mountains, its only locality, with the roots sold mainly in China. The Orientals, prizing a similar ginseng, had virtually eradicated it when a Jesuit priest in Canada in the early 1700s found that the Appalachian plant was similar. Many tons were shipped to Asia, and ginseng became known as Appalachian gold. Ginseng sold in the 1970s for about $70 a pound of roots. Ought one to gather ginseng? Does the price make a difference? Suppose the belief were true that ginseng increases an aging man's fertility—either dramatically or slightly, either as a psychosomatic or a physiological effect. Would exterminating a species to produce a few more humans be justified?
- Should the Park Service cut more drive-through sequoias? (p. 95).
- Formerly, Boy Scout handbooks showed how to make temporary camp beds from evergreens. A tree was felled and springy boughs from the branches arranged as a mattress. Suppose that a backcountry canoeist in a remote Canadian

forest is spending a week at localities unlikely to be visited by others. Ought he to cut firs for more comfortable nights rather than take along a foam pad?

■ Do your Christmas festivities, lasting about ten days, justify cutting a wild Colorado blue spruce, which if left uncut would have a life span of 150 years? Should real people use artificial Christmas trees, in addition to wearing fake furs? About thirty million trees are used in the United States each year, with ninety million seedlings replanted. Does it matter whether the trees are farmed or wild? Does a family gain more than the tree loses? What would the Christmas spirit be like in a family that thought too much of a blue spruce to sacrifice it for their festivities?

■ Mike Borkowski, a Roosevelt University student, won an especially large old lobster in a charity raffle. Sandy Claws II weighed twenty-eight pounds and was estimated to be 105 years old. After the drawing, Mike announced, "I'm going to give it to the Shedd Aquarium (in Chicago), rather than to eat it. I figure it's got a few good kicks left in it. So let it live out the rest of its life in peace."[25] Do the age and size of the lobster make any difference, so that one might eat ordinary lobsters but spare this especially large one?

■ You and your girl are on a picnic, having slipped away and found a meadow, and she has just said yes to your proposal. Is this an appropriate occasion to carve your initials together into the beech tree under which you have picnicked, a lasting souvenir of the memorable occasion?

■ "Give a hoot, don't pollute!" One version of this National Park Service slogan is, "The birds, animals, and flowers are dying to tell us, 'Give a hoot, don't pollute!'" Are additional moral considerations introduced in the variant form? Is the slogan (with its "wise old owl") really a psychological device, a Bambi-type appeal, to get tourists to mind their trash? Or can there be some consideration of the flourishing of plants in pollution questions?

■ Southeastern deciduous forests are often converted to pine-woods for timber production. Hardwoods, though also valuable for timber, take too long to mature; pine brings a quicker cash crop, used for pulp and newsprint. But the more environmentally oriented forestry officials urge, "Leave the hardwoods along the stream courses" in a strip a quarter-mile wide. Hardwoods reach their best development there and provide a good mast crop for wildlife, whereas their removal destroys the precocious wildflower ground story, especially luxuriant in the spring before the leaves emerge. Additionally, the wildlife population is less affected, streams less polluted by soil erosion, and their temperatures better regulated if the streamside buffer zones are left. Should the justifications for all this be entirely humanistic—good public relations between paper companies and the local hunters? Does there lurk in such decisions some moral consideration, some appropriate appreciation of the vegetation, the ecosystem? Given a combination of humanistic and naturalistic reasons, would it be unjustifiable government intervention in business to require commercial timber operators to save belts of hardwoods along some streams?

■ Horse packers in alpine wildernesses in the Rockies may be urged, or even required, by permit-granting agencies to carry feed rather than to picket their horses in the alpine meadows. Further, they may sometimes be urged or required to carry pellet feed, not hay, since weed seed mixed with the hay introduces dandelions, thistles, and the like, which become established initially along the disturbed trailsides or in grazed meadows, eventually to disrupt the vegetation elsewhere. (In ecological terms, weeds are r-selected species; especially in disturbed sites they outcompete the natives, likely to be k-selected species.) Is this only a matter of leaving the flowers for others to enjoy? Ought there to be any consideration for letting the native flowers live, at least in wilderness areas, as uninterrupted as possible by human activities?

■ Certain rare species of butterflies occur in African hummocks (slightly elevated forested ground) on the grasslands. It was formerly the practice of unscrupulous collectors to go in, collect a few hundred specimens, and then burn out the hummock with the intention of destroying the species, thereby driving up the price of their collections. Is the wrong here only a failing in human excellence, or is there a butterfly good-of-its-kind that constrains permissible human action?

The answers to such questions are admittedly rough. Answers to ethical (and legal and political) questions, indeed to most value

questions, are often rough in the sense that they resist calcula-
tion and logical proof. "Did his silence really count as deception?"
"Was the actress's reputation much damaged by that sensational-
ist article, considering how attendance doubled afterward at the
play?" But it does not follow that the answers are subjective because they are rough. The deception or damage being discovered
is not in the ethicists' or jurists' minds; they seek to estimate what
actually took place in the world.

Answers in environmental ethics can be even more rough because the questions are novel. They involve immeasurable and
seemingly incommensurable values. An answer must be approximate, but approximation ought not to be confused with mere opinion. Damage to wildflowers, trees, butterflies is real; it actually
takes place in the world. We must not assume that there can be
no objectivity without commensurability and quantification. To
the contrary, what the ethical subject is trying to do, especially
in environmental ethics, is to make an objective appraisal of values manifest in the natural world, of what is at stake there, and
to place human experiences on that scene as one kind—perhaps
the richest but not the only kind—of value that counts morally. In
that sense we sometimes have to evaluate (appraise the value of)
what we do not personally value (have any preference for, any attraction to). We discover duties, past preferences. That requires
a considerable objectivity in ethics and value judgment.

The answers to such questions are also impure. It is frequently
impossible to isolate human interests from the interests of sentient
animals and organic goods. Mixed motives are always present,
and we find it difficult to be sure which elements are—or ought
to be—there and in what proportion. Considering their instrumental and systemic importance in ecosystems, it is usually possible to ally preserving plants or lower animals on the side of
some humanistic gain that counterbalances, more or less, other
humanistic gains to be obtained through destroying such plants
or lower animals. But the interdependencies of goods in an ecosystem are like that. Even in traditional ethics, motives are mixed.
"Buy a raffle ticket to the charity ball!" "Honesty is the best policy." In environmental ethics the intermixing of human, animal,
and plant interests is even more confusing than is that between
humans within culture. Humans and the natural world have entwined destinies, as does so much else in an ecosystem. But the
fact that components are mixed does not mean that they are not
significantly present.

The task of environmental ethics is to identify and adjudicate all these components. Little theory and no formulas exist for doing that now, and we must rely largely on intuitions, trying to judge these critically as best we can in the light of what we are learning in the biological and ecological sciences, improving judgments by what we are coming to experience in more sensitive, less anthropocentric encounters with the natural world. We are doing more objective evaluating, less subjective valuing. Decisions will be made. Because they are borderline decisions, it is better to make them thoughtfully than thoughtlessly.

4   *Life in Jeopardy:* *Duties to Endangered Species*

"CERTAINLY ... THE DESTRUCTION of a whole species can be a great evil." John Rawls, however, advocating his most perceptive contemporary theory of justice, admits that in his theory "no account is given of right conduct in regard to animals and the rest of nature."[1] The explorations of the preceding chapters have taken us into progressively less familiar ethical territory, and now we reach almost wholly unexplored terrain. One searches in vain through several thousand years of philosophy (back at least to Noah!) for any serious reference to endangered species. Previously, humans were seldom able to destroy species; this "great evil" did not threaten, so there are few resources in our heritage with which to confront it. Even the ethics we have so far developed for sentient animals and other organisms has not yet directly addressed obligations concerning species.

But the *Global 2000 Report* projects a massive loss of Earth's species (up to 20 percent) within a few decades if present trends go unreversed.[2] These losses will be about evenly distributed through major groups of plants and animals in the United States and in the world. Congress has lamented, in the Endangered Species Act, the lack of "adequate concern (for) and conservation (of)" species.[3] The act was tougher than was realized by most of those who passed it. The Supreme Court, interpreting the law, said that species are to be conserved with "no exception" at "whatever the cost," their protection overriding even the "primary missions" of federal agencies.[4] That seemed extreme, and the act has been modified. Still, that many do not wish to weaken it much has been shown by its repeated renewal. Articulating an ethic here involves an unprecedented mix of science and conscience.

Duties to Persons Concerning Species

Some say there are no duties to endangered species, only duties to persons. "The preservation of species," by the usual utili-

126

tarian account, reported by Stuart Hampshire, is "to be aimed at and commended only in so far as human beings are, or will be, emotionally and sentimentally interested."[5] Joel Feinberg says, "We do have duties to protect threatened species, not duties to the species themselves as such, but rather duties to future human beings, duties derived from our housekeeping role as temporary inhabitants of this planet."[6] The relation is three-place. Person A has a duty *to* person B which *concerns* species C, but is not *to* C. Using traditional ethics, we can reapply familiar duties to persons and see whether this exhausts our moral intuitions or leaves a residue of concern. Such a line of argument can be impressive but seems to leave deeper reasons untouched.

Species as Stabilizers and Resources

Persons have a strong duty of nonmaleficence not to harm others and a weaker, though important, duty of beneficence to help others. Arguing the threat of harm, Paul and Anne Ehrlich maintain, in a blunt metaphor, that the myriad species are rivets in the airplane in which humans are flying. Extinctions are maleficent rivet-popping. On the Earthship in which we ride there is considerable redundancy, but humans cannot safely lose 1.5 million species-rivets, and any loss of redundancy is to be deplored. Species, including endangered ones, are stabilizers.[7]

In this model, nonrivet species, if there are any, have no value. Nor is any particular species the object of care. Humans desire only the diversity that prevents a crash. No single thread, but the strength of the fabric is the issue. The care is not for species, not for a breeding population of each kind, but (in Norman Myers's variant metaphor picturing the failing Earthship) for the "sinking ark."[8] To worry about a sinking ark seems a strange twist on the Noah story. Noah built the ark to preserve each species, brought on board carefully, two of each kind. In the Ehrlich/Myers account, the species-rivets are preserved to keep the ark from sinking! The reversed justification is revealing.

On the benefits side, species that are not rivets may have resource value. Wild species can have agricultural, medical, industrial, and scientific uses. Thomas Eisner testified to Congress that only about 2 percent of the flowering plants have been tested for alkaloids, which often have medical uses.[9] North Americans regularly eat almost nothing native to their ecosystem. Elsewhere in the world, loss of the wild stocks of the cultivars leaves Americans genetically vulnerable, so it is prudent to save the native materials. The International Union for the Conservation of Nature and Natural Resources (IUCN) says, "The ultimate protection of nature, . . . and all its endangered forms of life, demands . . . an enlightened exploitation of its wild resources."[10] Myers further urges "conserving our global stock."[11] At first that seems wise, yet later somewhat demeaning for humans to regard all other species as *stock*.

Ingenious biologists and ethicists can stretch the meaning of rivet and resource. On the harm side, the loss of a few species may have no evident results now, but this has destabilizing lag effects generations later. When an extremely cold winter hits, the ecosystem will be thrown into a degenerating spiral. Rare species do not now function significantly in the ecosystem, but they lie in wait as part of the backup resilience. The extinction of nonrivet and nonresource species will affect rivet and resource species. Getting by with a few extinctions lulls humans into thinking that they can get by with more, when in fact the danger increases exponentially with subtractions from the ecosystem. Humans will stumble over the disaster threshold because of bad habits formed when these extinctions were not yet harmful. Concern for all species puts up guard rails and provides a margin of safety on a slippery slope.

Species, Science, and Natural History

One should count as resources all those species that generate recreational, aesthetic, and scientific experiences. The rare species fascinate enthusiastic naturalists and are often key scientific study species. They provide entertainments and new knowledge of spaceship Earth, regardless of their stabilizing or economic benefits. One whooping crane in a flock of sandhills perks up a bird watcher's day. A National Science Foundation report advocated saving the Devil's Hole pupfish, *Cyprinodon diabolis*, in a case that went to the Supreme Court, because it and its relatives thrive in hot or salty water.

> Such extreme conditions tell us something about the creatures' extraordinary thermoregulatory system and kidney function—but not enough as yet. . . . They can serve as useful biological models for future research on the human kidney—and on survival in a seemingly hostile environment. . . . Man, in the opinion of many ecologists, will need all the help he can get in understanding and adapting to the expansion of arid areas over the Earth.[12]

The Socorro isopod, *Exosphaeroma thermophilum*, has lost its natural habitat and lives only in the drain of an abandoned bathhouse at a New Mexico hot springs site. Nevertheless the U.S. Fish and Wildlife Service claims that it "is of particular interest and importance. . . . How this species arrived at its present state of evolutionary adaptation is of concern to isopod specialists, and the concept of landlocked fauna is of concern to biologists as a whole."[13] *Eriogonum gypsophilum* is worth saving for a Ph.D. candidate to find out its adaptation to gypsum, even though this could restrict the proposed lake that would threaten its habitat and despite the fact that nothing practical may come from the dissertation. *Shortia galacifolia* is worth saving as a historical souvenir of the excitement of the early American botanists who traded specimens at $50 each.

Destroying species is like tearing pages out of an unread book, written in a language humans hardly know how to read, about the place where they live. We do not know, for instance, whether there are five or ten million species on Earth. We know little about the processes of *ecosystem* evolution as something more than organismic evolution. We do not know whether or how natural selection operates at that level. Biologists are divided over whether interspecific competition is a minimal or a major force in evolution, and sizable natural systems with all their species preserved intact are the likeliest places to settle this debate.

No sensible person would destroy the Rosetta Stone, and no self-respecting humans will destroy the mouse lemur, endangered in Madagascar and thought to be the modern animal nearest to the relatively unspecialized primates from which the human line evolved. Nor should we destroy *Zoonosaurus hazofotsi*, the Madagascar lizard with a third eye atop its head, the pineal eyespot, from which humans might learn about the parallel evolution of sight. Still, following this logic, humans have duties not to the book, the stone, or the species but to ourselves, duties both of prudence and education. Humans need insight into the full text of natural history. They need to understand the evolving world in which they are placed. It is not endangered species but an endangered human future that is of concern.

Such reasons are pragmatic and impressive. They are also moral, since persons are benefited or hurt. But are they exhaustive? Can all duties concerning species be analyzed as duties to persons? Do we simply want to protect these endangered forms of life *for* exploitation, or do we sometimes want to protect them *from* exploitation? Answering these questions involves issues partly scientific and partly ethical.

Nonfunctional and Nonresource Species

One problem is that pragmatic reasons get overstated. Peter Raven testified before Congress that a dozen dependent species of insects, animals, or other plants become extinct with each plant that goes extinct; cascading chain reactions amplify disaster (amplify diminution) through the ecosystem.[14] But Raven knows that cascading extinction is true only on statistical average, since a plant named for him, Raven's manzanita, *Arctostaphylos hookeri* ssp. *ravenii*, is known from a single wild specimen, and its extinction is unlikely to trigger others.

The small whorled pogonia, *Isotria medeoloides*, is known to occur at only seventeen sites, and three account for half the population. Since its discovery in 1814 it has been found at only forty-five sites and has been extinct in Missouri for nearly a century without adverse effect; it is difficult to think that the Appalachian woods would miss it. *Thismia americana*, an odd orchidlike plant, was known for only two years (1912–14) from a single station in the prairie Midwest, disjunct several thousand miles from its nearest tropical relative. Some species are locally ephemeral, perhaps nothing more than unsuccessful mutations. Some stations of rare plants are unimportant, perhaps the quirky germination of a few seeds carried in the guts of migrating birds and never long established. If all ninety-three plants now on the endangered species list disappeared, it is doubtful that the ecosystems involved would measurably shift their stability. Few cases can be cited where the removal of a rare species damaged an ecosystem.

Let's be frank. A substantial number of endangered species have no resource value. Beggar's ticks (*Bidens* spp.), with their stick-tight seeds, are a common nuisance through much of the United States. One species, tidal shore beggar's tick (*Bidens bidentoides*), which differs little from the others in appearance, is increasingly endangered. It seems unlikely that it is either a rivet or potential resource. So far as humans are concerned, its extinction might be good riddance.

With some species even the softer kinds of humanistic reasons vanish. With the deaths of a handful of now elderly bryologists, specialists in difficult taxa, taxonomists competent to name certain endangered species could become extinct before the mosses do. Surely if no one cares enough to learn to distinguish these species, there cannot be any great human loss. But then again, ethics is not merely about what humans love and enjoy, find profitable to study, rewarding, wonderful, or want as souvenirs. It is sometimes a matter of what humans *ought* to do, like it or not, and these *oughts* may not always rest on the likes of other humans. This may be a case where we ought to evaluate (appraise the worth of) what we ourselves do not value (have a personal preference for).

We might say that humans ought to preserve an environment adequate to match their capacity to wonder. All species might be resources for wonder. But this is to value the *experience* of wonder, rather than the *objects* of wonder. Valuing merely the experience seems to commit a fallacy of misplaced wonder, for speciation is itself among the wonderful things on Earth. Our own human excitement is a latecoming phenomenon; what we are excited about is this long-continuing, vital excitement of matter, irradiated by solar energy, spontaneously assembling itself into millions of species. Earth's five to ten million auto-evolved species must be among the marvels of the universe. And a hundred million more species lie behind us in history. Valuing speciation directly, however, seems to attach value to the evolutionary process (the wonderland), not merely to subjective experiences that arise when humans reflect over it (the wonder).

We might say that humans of decent character will refrain from needless destruction of all kinds, including destruction of any species. Vandals destroying art objects do not so much hurt statues as cheapen their own character. Is the American shame at having destroyed the passenger pigeon *only* a matter of self-respect? of "Protecting Human Excellences"? (see Chapter 3). Or is it shame at our ignorant insensitivity to a form of life that (unlike a statue) had an intrinsic value that placed some claim on us? We might say that the prohibition of extinction does not rest on rights that species have but (so to speak) on rights that humans do not have. A species has no right to exist, but humans have no right (license) to destroy species either. But such a prohibition seems to depend on some value in the species as such, for there need be no prohibition against destroying a valueless thing.

Human Prudence and Moral Principles

The deeper problem with the anthropocentric rationale, beyond overstatement, is that its justifications are submoral and fundamentally exploitive and self-serving, even if subtly so. This is not true intraspecifically among humans, when out of a sense of duty an individual defers to the values of fellows. But it is true interspecifically, since *Homo sapiens* treats all other species as rivets, resources, study materials, or entertainments. Ethics has always been about partners with entwined destinies. But it has never been very convincing when pleaded as enlightened self-interest (that one ought always to do what is in one's intelligent self-interest), including class self-interest, even though in practice altruistic ethics often needs to be reinforced by self-interest. To value all other species only for human interests is rather like a nation's arguing all its foreign policy in terms of national self-interest. Neither seems fully moral.

Perhaps an exploitive attitude, and the tendency to justify it ethically, has been naturally selected in *Homo sapiens*, at least in the population that has become dominant in the West.[15] But some humans—scientists who have learned to be disinterested, ethicists who have learned to consider the interests of others—ought to be able to see further. If the beliefs and ethical attitudes of highly educated scientists and ethicists are still swayed by subtle genetic influences, it will be hard rationally to justify any ethic.

Humans have learned some intraspecific altruism. The challenge now is to learn interspecific altruism. The practical conservationist will warn that if humans sacrifice these species to purported, immediate needs, they may blindly dehumanize themselves, robbing their race later of raw materials or rich experiences. It is better to preach that than to lose 100,000 species. Sometimes we must move through our fears to learn what we ought to love. But it would be better still, beyond our strategies and our loves, to know the full truth of the human obligation, to have the best reasons as well as the good ones. This could humanize our race all the more. That truth could make us moral overseers, appreciating with a global view the Earth on which we dwell, and not just managers conserving our global stock (see Chapter 2, "Humans as . . . Overseers"; Chapter 9). This would be an ethic about sources beyond resources.

It is safe to say that in the decades ahead the quality of life will decline in proportion to the loss of biotic diversity, though it is usually thought that we are sacrificing biotic diversity in order to improve human life. So there is a sense in which humans will not be losers if we save endangered species. There is a sense in which those who do the right thing never lose, even when they respect values other than their own. Slaveowners do not really lose when they free their slaves, since the slaveowners become better persons by freeing their slaves, to whom they can thereafter relate person-to-person. Subsequently, human relationships will be richer. In morality, only the immoral lose—ultimately. Similarly, humans who protect endangered species will, if and when they change their value priorities, be better persons for their admiring respect for other forms of life.

But this should not obscure the fact that humans can be short-term losers. Sometimes we do have to make sacrifices, at least in terms of what we presently value, to preserve species. Moreover, the claim that we are better humans if we protect species is an empirical, statistical claim—true on average, true unless shown otherwise. There might be cases where the worth of a species, coupled with human benefits from respecting it, do not override the human benefits to be gained by sacrificing it. Then humans might be duty-bound to be losers in the sense that they sacrifice values, although they would still be winners for doing the right thing.

Dealing with a problem correctly requires an appropriate way of thinking about it. On the scale of evolutionary time, humans appear late and suddenly. Even more lately and suddenly, they dramatically increase the extinction rate. About 500 species, sub-species, and varieties have been lost in the United States since 1600; the natural rate of extinction would have resulted in about ten.[16] In Hawaii, a bellwether state, half the 2,200 native plants are endangered or threatened; of sixty-eight species of birds unique to the islands, forty-one are extinct or virtually so. In the near future, humans threaten to approach and even exceed the catastrophic rates of the geological past, if indeed we are not doing this already.[17] What is offensive in such conduct is not merely senseless destabilizing, not merely the loss of resources and rivets, but the maelstrom of killing and insensitivity to forms of life and the sources producing them. What is required is not prudence but principled responsibility to the biospheric Earth.[18]

Specific Forms of Life

Species as Arbitrary Conventions?

There are many barriers to thinking of duties to species, however, and scientific ones precede ethical ones. It is difficult enough to argue from an *is* (that a species exists) to an *ought* (that a species ought to exist). Matters grow worse if the concept of species is rotten to begin with. Perhaps the concept is arbitrary, conventional, a mapping device that is only theoretical. Perhaps it is unsatisfactory theoretically in an evolutionary ecosystem. Perhaps species do not exist. If not, duties to them would be as imaginary as duties to contour lines or to lines of latitude and longitude. Is there enough factual reality in species to base duty there?

Betula lenta uber, round-leaf birch, is known in only two locations on neighboring Virginia creeks and differs from the common *B. lenta* only in having rounded leaf tips. For thirty years after its discovery it was described as a subspecies or merely a mutation. But M. L. Fernald pronounced it a species, *B. uber*, and for forty years it has been considered one. High fences have been built around all known specimens, about twenty. If a greater botanist were to designate it a subspecies again, would this change in alleged facts affect our alleged duties? Botanists are divided as to whether *Iliamna remota* (Kankakee mallow) in Illinois and *Iliamna corei* in Virginia—both rare—are distinct species. Must environmental ethicists then hesitate between two duties and one? Ornithologists recently reassessed the endangered Mexican duck, *Anas diazi*, and lumped it with the common mallard, *A. platyrhynchos*, as subspecies *diazi;* U.S. Fish and Wildlife authorities took it off the endangered species list partly as a result. Did a duty cease? Was there never one at all?

If a species is only a category or class, then boundary lines may be arbitrarily drawn, and the class is nothing more than a convenient grouping of its members. Darwin wrote, "I look at the term species, as one arbitrarily given for the sake of convenience to a set of individuals closely resembling each other."[19] Some natural properties are used to draw the lines—reproductive structures, bones, teeth—but which properties are selected and where the lines are drawn are decisions that vary with taxonomists. When A. J. Shaw recently "discovered" a new species of moss, *Pohlia tundrae*, in the alpine Rocky Mountains, he did not find any hitherto unknown plants; he just regrouped herbarium material that had been known for decades under other names.[20] Indeed, biologists routinely put after a species the name of the "author" who, they say, "erected" the taxon.

Individual organisms exist, but if species are merely classes, they are inventions that aggregate member organisms in this fashion or that. A. B. Shaw claims, "The species concept is entirely subjective"; concluding a presidential address to paleontologists, he even exclaims, "Help stamp out species!"[21] He refers, of course, to the artifacts of taxonomists, not to living organisms. Still, if species do not exist except as embedded in a theory in the minds of classifiers, it is hard to see how there can be duties to save them. No one proposes duties to genera, families, orders, phyla; everyone concedes that these do not exist in nature.

Species as Historical Lineages

But a biological "species" is not just a class. A species is a living historical form (Latin *species*), propagated in individual organisms, that flows dynamically over generations. G. G. Simpson concludes:

> An evolutionary species is a lineage (an ancestral-descendant sequence of populations) evolving separately from others and with its own unitary evolutionary role and tendencies.[22]

Ernst Mayr holds:

> Species are groups of interbreeding natural populations that are reproductively isolated from other such groups.

He can even emphasize, though many biologists today would deny this, that *"species are the real units of evolution*, they are the entities which specialize, which become adapted, or which shift their adaptation."[23] Mayr sympathizes with Michael Ghiselin and David Hull, who hold that species are integrated individuals and that species names are proper names, with organisms related to their species as part is to whole.[24] Niles Eldredge and Joel Cracraft find:

> A species is a diagnosable cluster of individuals within which there is a parental pattern of ancestry and descent, beyond which there is not, and which exhibits a pattern of phylogenetic ancestry and descent among units of like kind.

Species, they insist, are *"discrete entities in time as well as space."*[25]

It is admittedly difficult to pinpoint precisely what a species is, and there may be no single, quintessential way to define species; a polythetic or polytypic gestalt of features may be required. All we need in order to raise the issue of duty, however, is that species objectively exist as living processes in the evolutionary ecosystem; the varied criteria for defining them (descent, reproductive isolation, morphology, gene pool) come together at least in providing evidence that species are really there. In this sense, species are dynamic natural kinds, if not corporate individuals. A species is a coherent, ongoing form of life expressed in organisms, encoded in gene flow, and shaped by the environment.

The claim that there are specific forms of life historically maintained in their environments over time does not seem arbitrary or fictitious at all but, rather, as certain as anything else we believe about the empirical world, even though at times scientists revise the theories and taxa with which they map these forms. Species are not so much like lines of latitude and longitude as like mountains and rivers, phenomena objectively there to be mapped. The edges of all these natural kinds will be sometimes fuzzy, to some extent discretionary. We can expect that one species will slide into another over evolutionary time. But it does not follow from the fact that speciation is sometimes in progress that species are merely made up instead of found as evolutionary lines articulated into diverse forms, each with its more or less distinct integrity, breeding population, gene pool, and role in its ecosystem.

Many species are closely related to others in their genera, and the loss of a particular species is less tragic if, so to speak, 85 percent of that form of life continues elsewhere in the genus. Nevertheless, each species has elements of uniqueness. Each brings to realization some potential in nature unreached by others.

It is sometimes suggested that mammals and birds should be saved at the species level but that for nongame and noncommercial fish and many plants (unless of special interest to humans), saving at the level of genus would be enough. Those natural kinds that do not differ much even as genera (some insects, nematodes, microbes) might be saved at the family level—or at least this is all the law should require. We have earlier found that there is increased intrinsic value as one goes up the ecosystemic pyramid, and so there is more point in saving advanced forms in more detail. Lower down, fauna and flora should be saved mostly for their instrumentality, and saved in specific detail only if this is critical for roles in the ecosystem.

There are several troubles with this proposal. To begin with, species are real historical entities, interbreeding populations; families, orders, and genera are not. If one tried to save *Branchinecta coloradensis* (a fairy shrimp in alpine Rocky Mountain ponds) as a representative of and thereby to save family Branchinectidae, or order Anostraca, division Eubranchiopoda, subclass Branchiopoda, or class Crustacea, this would only misplace what is intended to be saved; one would be trying to save a real entity as a token of a nonreal class.

Further, what ought to be saved would largely be lost, for two reasons. First, species are most similar where the speciation process is dynamic and fecund; there the dynamic lineages are profuse and procreative. There are 200 species of fairy shrimp, and one has to look closely to tell them apart. This speciating fertility would be reduced to nothing if but one such species were preserved. Though supposedly representing the nonreal family, order, or division, it could not represent—re-present, really keep present—the dynamic speciation of which it is an instance.

Second, to try to preserve representatives of families or orders in isolated fragments of habitats would preserve puzzle pieces taken out of the whole gestalt, and a species would soon no longer work as it formerly did in the biotic community, removed from the full set of interactions with its competitors and neighbors. The level of species (and subspecies) is the level where the production and reproduction of life occurs. This is no longer the focus if one saves only representatives of families, orders, classes, or when one saves representative mountains, rivers, landscapes. With species one must alike and equally save the ecosystems that are the context of such speciation. Otherwise, the token species will collapse in the reduced fretwork, no longer an ecosystemic network.

At this point, we can anticipate how there can be duties to species. What humans ought to respect are dynamic life forms preserved in historical lines, vital informational processes that persist genetically over millions of years, overleaping short-lived individuals. It is not *form* (species) as mere morphology, but the *formative* (speciating) process that humans ought to preserve, although the process cannot be preserved without its products. Neither should humans want to protect the labels they use but rather the living process in the environment. "Endangered species" is a convenient and realistic way of tagging this process, but protection can be interpreted (as the Endangered Species Act permits) in terms of subspecies, variety, or other taxa or categories that point out the diverse forms of life.

Duties to Species

Humans value their environment and have duties to fellow humans. But these duties yield an ethic concerning the environment that, from an interspecific viewpoint, is submoral, although it is moral intraspecifically within *Homo sapiens*. Even those duties that we have been advancing to extend ethics into the nonhuman environment—duties to sentient animals and to plants and other organisms—are not duties to species. Can we make any sense of the idea of duties to species? Especially with regard to endangered species, such duties might supplement or challenge—even override—our duties to persons or to individual animals and plants.

Humans versus Endangered Species

Based on the claims of human superiority, made in Chapter 2, the obligation to protect humans trumps the obligation to protect *individual* animals and plants, short of extenuating circumstances and even if critical animal and plant goods sometimes outweigh nonbasic humans goods. But it does not follow that the obligation to protect one or even a group of humans trumps the obligation to protect whole *species*. Further, our obligation to protect *existing* lives can be greater than our obligation to bring into existence yet *unborn* lives, and this may offset the otherwise greater obligation to protect humans over animals and plants. It could be more important to protect one million existing species than to bring into existence an additional one million persons—a choice not as farfetched as it may first appear in view of the present pace of tropical deforestation.

The mountain gorilla (*Gorilla gorilla beringei*) survives in a population of about 240 animals, with most hope of survival in a group of 150 in the Parc des Volcans, a 30,000-acre national park in Rwanda. This small African country has the highest human population density in Africa, a population expected to double by the end of the century. About 95 percent of the people subsist on small farms that average 2.5 acres per family. The park has already been shrunk by 40 percent to bring land into cultivation; there are pressures to reduce it more. Elimination of the park could support perhaps 36,000 persons at a subsistence level, only 25 percent of one year's population growth. Most persons in Rwanda have little interest in wildlife. Some poach gorillas to make the skulls and hands into souvenirs for tourists or to use certain organs—testicles, tongues, ears—for their magical powers over enemies.[26] One gorilla, Digit, who had been seen by millions on a National Geographic television feature, was speared and his head and hands sold for $20. Gorillas in the zoo trade sell for over $10,000. In captivity they reproduce poorly.

Do the human values here—land for an exploding population, souvenirs, magical charms, zoo sales—justify exterminating the gorilla? There would be many negative effects: clearing the high ground would bring erosion and reduced income from tourism; moreover, given the existing social institutions, the benefits of cattle grazing and zoo sales are unlikely to reach many of the poor. There is really no evidence that the Rwandans would, on average, be any better off a decade hence, since nothing would have been done about the real sources of poverty and injustice. Extinction of the gorilla would provide only momentary relief space for a fraction of an annually enlarging population of subsistence farmers. It would not solve any of the deeper problems.

Though humans are superior to gorillas, gorillas are a majestic life form. Often they are placed in family Pongidae, but many think they should be placed in family Hominidae, the same family as humans. (Recall the intelligence and affection shown by Koko.) Humans are an overpopulating species; mountain gorillas are on the verge of extinction due to human encroachments. The benefits to be gained by the humans doubtfully exceed the losses to be suffered, even from the human point of view; they are often doubtful benefits to existing humans (magical charms, income inequitably distributed, the short-term relief of moving onto new lands) and real but marginal benefits to a small group of not yet existing humans (a future generation of subsistence farmers who would live on the new land, perhaps only until erosion made it useless). For this is traded extinction for the gorillas—forever. Here it seems that if in fact they have anything to lose, humans ought to lose.

A Florida panther, one of about thirty surviving in an endangered subspecies, was mangled when hit by a car. Named Big Guy, he was flown by helicopter to the state university veterinary medical school. Steel plates were inserted in both legs, and the right foot rebuilt. Is this appropriate treatment? Is it something humans ought to do out of justice or benevolence? Because of concern for the individual animal or for the subspecies? Big Guy's story mostly served to bring to focus a bigger issue. He cannot be released into the wild but is being bred and his offspring will be used for experiments to protect his species.

Protecting the panther, Florida's state animal, could cost $112.5 million. The subspecies is peculiarly adapted to the Florida swamps, in contrast with the dry, mountainous areas inhabited by the West's cougars. The panther is nearly extinct because of dwindling habitat, and the last critical habitat—the Big Cypress Swamp, adjacent to the Everglades—is being cut in half by Interstate 75. Florida has argued for spending $27 million (about $1 million per panther) to build forty bridges that will allow the panthers to pass under the high-fenced interstate: both "animal crossings," bridges over dry land, and "extended bridges," bridges over water with spans over land at each end. Otherwise, as Big Guy illustrates, many will be killed by the fast, increasing traffic. Critics—including some federal authorities, who bear 90 percent of the costs—say this is too expensive and won't work. Wildlife biologists claim that it will (as the Alaska pipeline was redesigned to permit caribou migration); they have tracked radio-collared cats and located their routes. The ten-foot-high fence, combined with an outrigger and a drainage canal beside it, will discourage the cats from entering the highway. Most of the remaining costs are to compensate several dozen landowners for isolating their land and for the purchase of buffer zones. It will also be necessary to restrict deer hunters (deer are the panther's principal prey) and to curb 4,000 offroad vehicle recreationists who disturb the area.[27] Although federal authorities were unable to release any money for this project, the state of Florida is building thirty-seven of the bridges at state expense.

Again, though humans are superior to panthers, the human costs here (about $10 per Floridian, about fifty cents per U.S. citizen) hardly seem high enough to justify the extinction of a subspecies. The loss of limited recreation and sport hunting would be offset by renewed respect for life. Wildlands acquired or protected in an already overcrowded state are valuable with or without the panther. Corridors and crossings that connect otherwise isolated reserves are important for many mammals. The bridges may prove futile, but Americans regularly risk those amounts of money in lotteries. To be gained is the continued existence of an animal handsome enough to be chosen as the state symbol, highly evolved on the top trophic rung of a rare Everglades ecosystem, thought by many to be the most aesthetically exciting animal on the North American continent. In this case too, if in fact humans can be shown to lose, they ought to be the losers in favor of the cat.

Sentient Life versus Endangered Species

A concern for species is not just a way of protecting sentient lives or even individual organisms. The National Park Service allows hundreds of elk to starve in Yellowstone each year, but the starving of an equal number of grizzly bears, which would involve about the same loss in felt experience, would be of much greater concern. Only about 100 whooping cranes remain; to kill and eat them would result in jail sentences. But we kill and eat 100 turkeys without a thought. Something more is at stake ethically than a concern for individual lives. Humans have no duty to deny their ecology and thus do not interrupt spontaneous nature (assume no duty to feed the elk), and humans do sacrifice individual animals and plants to meet their needs. But humans have at least some duty not to cause ecological disruption, a duty not to waste species. If we can identify this concern more precisely, we can formulate our duties to species and complete this chapter in an environmental ethic.

On San Clemente Island, the U.S. Fish and Wildlife Service and the California Department of Fish and Game asked the Navy to shoot 2,000 feral goats to save three endangered plant species: *Malacothamnus clementinus, Castilleja grisea, Delphinium kinkiense*. That would mean killing several goats for each known surviving plant. Isolated from the mainland, the island had evolved a number of unique species. Goats, introduced in the early 1800s, thrived even after humans abandoned them but adversely affected the ecosystem. They have probably already eradicated several never-known species. Following renewed interest in endangered species, officials decided to eliminate the goats. By herding and trapping, 21,000 were removed, but the remaining goats were in inaccessible canyons, which required their being shot from helicopters.

The Fund for Animals filed suit to prevent this, and the court ordered all goats removed. After the shooting of 600 goats, the Fund put political pressure on the Department of the Navy to secure a moratorium on further shooting. Happily, workers for the Fund rescued most of the goats with novel trapping techniques; unhappily, neither they nor others have been able to live-trap them all. The goats reproduce rapidly during any delay, and there are still more than 1,000 on the island.[28]

Despite the Fund's objections, the Park Service did kill hundreds of rabbits on Santa Barbara Island to protect a few plants of *Dudleya traskiae*, once thought extinct and curiously called the Santa Barbara live-forever. This island endemic was once common. But New Zealand red rabbits, introduced about 1900, fed on it; by 1970 no *Dudleya* could be found. With the discovery in 1975 of five plants, a decision was made to eradicate the rabbits.

Does protecting endangered species justify causing suffering and death? Does the fact that the animals were exotic make a difference? An ethic based on animal rights will come to one answer, but a more broadly based environmental ethic will prefer plant species, especially species in their ecosystems, over sentient animals that are exotic misfits.

Following the theory worked out in Chapter 3, a goat does have more intrinsic value than a plant, although plants have more instrumental value in ecosystems than goats. So if the tradeoff were merely 1,000 goats for 100 plants, regardless of instrumental, ecosystemic, and species considerations, the goats would override the plants. But the picture is more complex. Out of place from their original ecosystems, goats are degrading the ecosystems in which they currently exist, producing the extinctions of species that are otherwise well fitted and of instrumental value in those ecosystems. At this point the well-being of plants outweighs the welfare of the goats.

The golden trout, state fish of California, evolved in three California creeks—the South Fork of the Kern River, Golden Trout Creek, and the Little Kern River—and is restricted to three drainages. It is an attractive, "flashy" fish, and anglers highly prize it; because it is now threatened, however, the catch is quite limited. The brown trout, introduced into California in the late 1800s and now widespread throughout the state, encroached on the golden trout, coming to outnumber it 100 to 1 in the golden's own range. The California Department of Fish and Game decided to eliminate the brown trout in golden trout habitat and for eighteen years (1966–84) waged a campaign to accomplish this. Three downstream barriers were built, and upstream golden trout were rescued, while brown trout were poisoned by the tens of thousands. After the poison was neutralized, the golden trout were returned to the streams. About $300,000 was spent on this effort.[29]

The justification for this was partly aesthetic, partly for quality fishing, partly out of respect for the state fish. It was also out of considerable respect for an endangered species, historically evolved to fit a particular ecosystem, even though the introduced species was outcompeting it in its native ecosystem. If we simply aggregated individual fish lives, oblivious to differences of species, the larger population would be preferred. But we do not, because respect for species makes a difference. Assuming that fish suffer somewhat when they are killed, we even think that the killing of brown trout in order that golden trout may live is justified on a differential basis of 100 to 1.

Speciation and Superkilling Species

A consideration of species is both revealing and challenging because it offers a biologically based counterexample to the focus on individuals—typically sentient and usually persons—so characteristic of Western ethics. In an evolutionary ecosystem it is not mere individuality that counts; the species is also significant because it is a dynamic life form maintained over time by an informed genetic flow. The individual represents (re-presents) a species in each new generation. It is a token of a type, and the type is more important than the token.

It is as logical to say that the individual is the species' way of propagating itself as to say that the embryo or egg is the individual's way of propagating itself. We can think of the cognitive processing as taking place not merely in the individual (either in the brain or in the genetic set) but in the populational gene pool. Genetically, though not neurally, a species over generations "learns" (discovers) pathways previously unknown. A form of life reforms itself, tracks its environment, and sometimes passes over to a new species. There is a specific groping for a valued *ought-to-be* beyond what now *is* in any individual. Though species are not moral agents, a biological identity—a kind of value—is here defended. The dignity resides in the dynamic form; the individual inherits this, exemplifies it, and passes it on. To borrow a metaphor from physics, life is both a particle (the individual) and a wave (the specific form).

Because a species lacks moral agency, reflective self-awareness, sentience, or organic individuality, we may be tempted to say that specific-level processes cannot count morally. But each ongoing species defends a form of life—on the whole, good things; prolife impulses that have achieved all the planetary richness of life. All ethicists say that in *Homo sapiens* one species has appeared that not only exists but ought to exist. But why say this exclusively of a latecoming, highly developed form? Why not extend this duty more broadly to the other species (though not with equal intensity over them all, in view of varied levels of development)? These kinds too defend their forms of life. We humans are the product of such defenses during long eons past. Only the human species contains moral agents, but perhaps conscience *ought not* be used to exempt every other form of life from consideration, with the resulting paradox that the sole moral species acts only in its collective self-interest toward all the rest.

The main thing wrong is that extinction shuts down the generative processes. The wrong that humans are doing, or allowing to happen through carelessness, is stopping the historical gene flow in which the vitality of life is laid and which, viewed at another level, is the same as the flow of natural kinds. The story at the microlevel (in the genes) is really the same story as that at the macrolevel (the phenotypes fitting into a biotic community); the molecular biology records and tracks the molar level. The ecosystem determines the biochemistry as much as the other way round. The shape that the microscopic genetic molecules take is controlled "from above" as information discovered about how to make a way through the macroscopic, terrestrial-range world (or marine world) is stored in the molecules. In a species we cannot say which level is prior and which is subordinate; the story of life is told at multiple levels. One thing is obvious: the singular individual is neither the only level at which the flow of life is to be understood nor at which its stopping is cause for concern.

Every extinction is an incremental decay in this stopping of the flow of life, no small thing. Every extinction is a kind of superkilling. It kills forms (*species*), beyond individuals. It kills "essences" beyond "existences," the "soul" as well as the "body." It kills collectively, not just distributively. A duty to a species is more like being responsible to a cause than to a person. It is commitment to an *idea* (Greek, *idea*, "form," sometimes a synonym for the Latin *species*). This duty is a categorical imperative to living categories. It is not merely the loss of potential human information that we lament but the loss of biological information that is present independent of instrumental human uses of it. At stake is something vital, past something biological, and all this is something more than an anthropocentric concern. We are called on, again, objectively to evaluate (appraise the worth of) what we may or may not subjectively value (have a personal preference for).

Much is conserved in Earth's subroutines and cycles (matter, energy, materials); much can be recycled and renewed (water, energy, nutrients); there are many equilibria (food chains, species turnover, natural extinctions with respeciation). But in human-caused extinctions there is the loss of unique biological information, with no conservation by respeciation. A shutdown of the life stream is the most destructive event possible. "Ought species x to exist?" is a distributive increment in the collective question, "Ought life on Earth to exist?" Life on Earth cannot exist without its individuals either, but a lost individual is always reproducible; a lost species is never reproducible. The answer to the species question is not always the same as the answer to the collective question, but since life on Earth is an aggregate of many species, the two are sufficiently related that the burden of proof lies with those who wish deliberately to extinguish a species and simultaneously to care for life on Earth.

Every species is a "display" or "show" (also a meaning of the Latin *species*) in the natural history book. These stories are plural, diverse, erratic, but they are not wholly fragmented episodes. The pressures of natural selection pull them into roles into their communities, fit them into niches, give continuity to the stories, and make more unified ecosystemic stories of the many stories. Always, there are themes in their settings, characters moving through space and time, problems and their resolutions, the plotting of life paths. Exceeding the births and deaths of individual members, a specific form of life unfolds an intergenerational narrative. What humans are bound to respect in natural history is not one another's scientific, recreational, or reading material, not rivets in their Earthship, but the living drama, continuing with all its actors. To kill a species is to shut down a unique story, and although all specific stories must eventually end, we seldom want unnatural ends. Humans ought not to play the role of murderers. The duty to species can be overridden—for example, in the case of pests or disease organisms—but a prima facie duty stands nevertheless.

One form of life has never endangered so many others. Never before has this level of question—superkilling by a superkiller—been deliberately faced. Humans have more understanding than ever of the natural world they inhabit and of the speciating processes, more predictive power to foresee the intended and unintended results of their actions, and more power to reverse the undesirable consequences. The duties that such power and vision generate no longer attach simply to individuals or persons but are emerging duties to specific forms of life. If, in this world of uncertain moral convictions, it makes any sense to claim that one ought not to kill individuals without justification, it makes more sense to claim that one ought not to superkill the species without superjustification.

Individuals and Species

Many will be uncomfortable with claims about duties to species because their ethical theory does not allow duty to a collection, only to individuals. Only individuals can inject preferences into the system. As Joel Feinberg writes, "A whole collection, as such, cannot have beliefs, expectations, wants, or desires. . . . Individual elephants can have interests, but the species elephant cannot."[30] That premise underlies Feinberg's conclusion, cited earlier, that duties cannot be to species but must be to future humans, who will have beliefs, desires, and so on. Singer asserts, "Species as such are not conscious entities and so do not have interests above and beyond the interests of the individual animals that are members of the species." That premise supports Singer's conclusion that all our duties must be to sentient beings.[31]

Tom Regan defines the "rights view" as "a view about the moral rights of individuals. Species are not individuals, and the rights view does not recognize the moral rights of species to anything, including survival."[32] Nicholas Rescher says, "Moral obligation is thus always interest-oriented. But only individuals can be said to have interests; one only has moral obligations to particular individuals or particular groups thereof. Accordingly, the duty to save a species is not a matter of moral duty toward it, because moral duties are only oriented to individuals. A species as such is the wrong sort of target for a moral obligation."[33] But beliefs, desires, conscious awareness, rights, individuality, and so forth, are not the only relevant criteria in an emerging environmental ethic.

Individual Goods and the Good of the Species

Even those who recognize that organisms, nonsentient as well as sentient, can have goods, owing to their *telos,* may see the good of a species as the sum of, and reducible to, the goods of individuals. The species is well off when and because its members are; species well-being is just aggregated individual well-being. The "interest of a species" constitutes only a convenient device— something like a "center of gravity" in physics or a "mean" in statistics (neither of which actually exists in the real natural world)—for speaking of an aggregated focus of many contributing individual member units.

But duties to a species are not to a class or category, not to an aggregation or average of sentient interests, but to a life line. An ethic about species needs to see how the species *is* a bigger event than the individual interests or sentience. Making this clearer can support a conviction that a species *ought* to continue.

Events can be good for the well-being of the species, considered collectively, even though they are harmful if considered as distributed to individuals. This is one way to interpret what is often called genetic load, genes that somewhat reduce health, efficiency, or fertility in most individuals but introduce enough variation to permit improvement of the specific form.[34] Not all variation is load; much of it is harmless. And much load may never prove beneficial. But some load, carried detrimentally through generations, on later occasion proves to be beneficial. Less of this variation and better repetition in reproduction would, on average, benefit more individuals in any one next generation, since individuals would have less "load." But in the longer view, variation, including the load, can confer stability in a changing world. A greater experimenting with individuals, although this typically makes individuals less fit and is a disadvantage from that perspective, benefits rare and lucky individuals selected in each generation, with a resulting improvement in the species. Most individuals in any particular generation carry some (usually slightly) detrimental genes, but the variation is good for the species. Note that this does not imply species selection; selection perhaps operates only on individuals. But it does mean that we can distinguish between the goods of individuals and the larger good of the species.

Predation on individual elk conserves and improves the species *Cervus canadensis*.[35] The species survives by its individual elk being eaten! When a wolf is tearing up an elk, the individual elk is in distress, but the species is in no distress. The species is being improved, as is shown by the fact that wolves will subsequently find elk harder to catch. If the predators are removed and the carrying capacity is exceeded, wildlife managers may have to benefit a species by culling half its member individuals. A forest fire harms individual aspen trees, but it helps *Populus tremuloides* by restarting forest succession, without which the species would go extinct.

Even the individuals that escape external demise die of old age;

and their deaths, always to the disadvantage of individuals, are a necessity for the species. A finite life span makes room for those replacements that enable development, allowing the population to improve in fitness or to adapt to a shifting environment. The surplus of young, with most born to perish prematurely, is disadvantageous to such individuals but advantageous to the species. Without the "flawed" reproduction that incorporates mutation and permits variation, without the surplus of young, without predation and death, which all harm individuals, the species would soon go extinct in a changing environment, as all environments eventually are. The individual is a receptacle of the form, and the receptacles are broken while the form survives, but the form cannot otherwise survive.

When a biologist remarks that a breeding population of a rare species is at a dangerously low level, who or what is the danger to? To humans, in view of their impending loss? To individual members of the species? Rather, the remark seems to imply a specific-level, point-of-no-return threat to the continuing of that form of life. No individual crosses the extinction threshold; the species does. Reproduction is typically assumed to be a need of individuals, but since any particular individual can flourish somatically without reproducing at all, indeed may be put through duress and risk or spend much energy reproducing, by another logic we can interpret reproduction as the species keeping up its own kind by reenacting itself again and again, individual after individual. It stays in place by its replacements.

In this sense a female grizzly does not bear cubs to be healthy herself, any more than a woman needs children to be healthy. Rather, her cubs are *Ursus arctos*, threatened by nonbeing, recreating itself by continuous performance. A species in reproduction defends its own kind from other species, and this seems to be some form of "caring." The locus of the intrinsic value—the value that is really defended over generations—seems as much in the form of life, the species, as in the individuals, since the individuals are genetically impelled to sacrifice themselves in the interests of reproducing their kind.

Conservation biologists recommend that adjacent nature preserves should be designated in a triangular rather than a linear pattern, preferably with adequate corridors preserved between them. This increases crossbreeding between seedbed colonies, which benefits species even though it steps up the genetic experimentation and may sacrifice numerous individuals that serve as probes to produce still more healthy later individuals. Vitality is a property of the population as readily as of the individuals within it. An insistent individualist can claim that species-level phenomena (vitality in a population, danger to a species, reproduction of a life form, tracking a changing environment) are only epiphenomena, byproducts of aggregated individuals in their interrelationships, and that the phenomena really center on individual organisms. But our more comprehensive account, interpreting the species itself as a kind of individual, historic lineage over time, is just as plausible. We want individuality, too, but also at the species level. And we want individuality within community, the one as real as the other.

Biologists have often and understandably focused on individual organisms, and some recent trends interpret biological processes from the perspective of genes. A consideration of species reminds us that many events can be interpreted at this level too. As noted already, properly understood, the story at the microscopic genetic level reflects the story at the ecosystemic specific level, with the individual a macroscopic midlevel. The genome is a kind of map coding the species; the individual is an instance incarnating it.

The biological individual is certainly a cybernetic achievement. An individual organism maintains its negentropy by metabolic defenses. On the basis of genetic information it runs a telic course through the environment, taking in environmental materials, using these resourcefully, discharging wastes. But much of what we said (in Chapter 3, "Organisms as Normative Systems") about individual organisms as nonmoral normative systems can now be resaid, *mutatis mutandis*, of species. The single, organismic directed course is part of a bigger picture in which a species too runs a telic course through the environment, using individuals resourcefully to maintain its course over much longer periods of time.

In this way of thinking, the life that the individual has is something passing through the individual as much as something it intrinsically possesses. The individual is subordinate to the species, not the other way around. The species too is a cybernetic achievement. The genetic set, in which is coded the *telos*, is as evidently the property of the species as of the individual through which it passes. Some will object that a species does not act on needs or with interests because there is no "it" to act. But the specific type, no less than individual tokens, is an "it." A specific form of life urges survival of "its" kind, defends "its" life form. The "it" is a historic process with vital individuality, though it is not a single organism. This helps us to see that the *telos* of a species is not a fixed end but rather one evolving over the propagation of the gene linkage, an endless end, although some lines go extinct and others so transform that taxonomists recognize successive species.

Value at the Species Level

There is no value without an evaluator. So runs a well-entrenched dogma in value theory. Humans clearly evaluate their world; sentient animals may do so also. Less clearly, any organism "evaluates" its environment, as when an *Escherichia coli* bacterium prefers glucose over lactose (even though it is programmed to do this genetically). But (some say) no species—whatever "species" exactly is—can evaluate anything, and therefore nothing called "species" can be the holder of intrinsic value, although a collection may be of instrumental value to ("valuable," able to be valued by) bona fide evaluators. Hence, any duties that humans have cannot be to species (though they may concern them) but must be to those evaluators (normally other humans) in whom sooner or later values come to birth.

But we need to revise this logic. Biologists and linguists have learned to accept the concept of information without any subject who speaks or understands. Can environmental ethicists learn to accept value in, and duty to, an informed process in which centered individuality or sentience is absent? Here events can be of value at the specific level, an additional consideration to whether they are beneficial to individuals. The species-in-environment is an interactive complex, a selective system where individuals are pawns on a chessboard. When human conduct endangers these specific games of life, destroying the habitats in which they are played, duties may appear.

The older ethic will say that duties attach to singular lives, most evidently those with a self or some analogue to a self. In an individual organism the organs report to a center; the good of a whole is defended. But the members of a species report to no center. A species has no self. It is not a bounded singular. Each individual has its own centeredness, but the species has no specific analogue to the nervous hookups or circulatory flows that characterize the organism. Like the market in economics, however, an organized system does not have to have a controlling center to have identity. Perhaps singularity, centeredness, selfhood, individuality are not the only processes to which duty attaches.

Having a biological identity reasserted genetically over time is as true of the species as of the individual. In fact, taxonomists can often distinguish two species more readily than two individuals within a species. Uniqueness attaches to the dynamic historical lineage, even if the members also are, in their own ways, idiographic. Individual organisms come and go; the marks of the individual species collectively remain much longer. Biological identity need not attach to the centered organism; it can persist as a discrete, vital pattern over time.

A consideration of species strains any ethic fixed on individual organisms, much less on sentience or persons. But the result can be biologically sounder, though it revises what was formerly thought logically permissible or ethically binding. When ethics is informed by this kind of biology, it is appropriate to attach duty dynamically to the specific form of life. The species line is the more fundamental living system, the whole of which individual organisms are the essential parts. The species too has its integrity, its individuality, its "right to life" (if we must use the rhetoric of rights), and it is more important to protect this than to protect individual integrity. Again and again, processes of value found first in an organic individual reappear at the specific level: defending a particular form of life, pursuing a pathway through the world, resisting death (extinction), regeneration maintaining a normative identity over time, storied achievements, creative resilience learning survival skills. If, at the specific level, these processes are just as evident or even more so, what prevents duties from arising at that level? The appropriate survival unit is the appropriate level of moral concern.

Protecting Species versus Protecting Individual Organisms

Should sportsmen forgo shooting ducks at twilight, when it is difficult to distinguish common ducks from endangered species? Migratory game birds are hunted on national forest lands; regulations ordinarily permit shooting from a half-hour before sunrise to a half-hour after sunset. The Defenders of Wildlife sued the Department of the Interior and its secretary, Cecil Andrus, to prohibit shooting at dawn and dusk and thus reduce the accidental shooting of endangered species.[36] The court found that the impact of twilight shooting might be considerable, that the Interior Department had not sufficiently studied the question, that it must adjust hunting hours to keep the killing of endangered species at a minimum, consistent with the other responsibilities assigned by Congress to the department.

In this case there was little concern for individual ducks sacrificed in the hunt; sportsmen were asked to reduce their recreational pleasures (twilight shooting is prime time) in deference to endangered duck species. This seems to value a form of life over these hunters' recreational interests. One could weigh in the recreational pleasures of bird watchers, who enjoy seeing rare ducks, and perhaps argue that on overall balance humans lose nothing. And there is always the sense in which those who do the right thing never lose. Yet there remains in this decision some respect for species that overrides human preferences, a respect that operates at a different level from respect for individual ducks—in contrast, for instance, to the moral concern that seeks to prohibit the use of lead shot (Chapter 2).

Should fishermen suffer reduced fishing privileges to protect the endangered crocodile? Everglades National Park authorities have restricted fishing to protect the American crocodile, in jeopardy throughout southern Florida and the Caribbean. The crocodile, while nesting, is quite sensitive to human disturbances especially from motorboats. Commercial fishing, involving about $1.2 million annually, is to be prohibited entirely, and recreational fishing forbidden in 18,000 of the total 660,000 estuarine acres of the park. The Organized Fishermen of Florida sued the Department of the Interior (and Secretary Andrus again!) to relax the restriction. But the court found undisputed evidence that the stricter regulations would benefit the species.[37]

Here again, consideration for an endangered species, beyond the concern for individuals, seems to override the interests of the fishermen. In Louisiana, where the alligator is no longer threatened, there are no comparable restrictions, though the life of an individual alligator is presumably the approximate equal of the life of an individual crocodile. Many thousands of alligators are killed every year (see Chapter 2).

Again too, one could introduce the recreational interests of crocodile watchers and say that humans on overall balance have nothing to lose. Yet meanwhile, we have an ethic, enforced by law, that restricts human preferences in favor of a crocodile species, without any particular regard to the welfare of individuals.

The legislation establishing Everglades National Park provides that "the said area or areas shall be permanently reserved as a wilderness, and no development of the project or plan for the entertainment of visitors shall be undertaken which will interfere with the preservation intact of the unique flora and fauna and the essential primitive natural conditions now prevailing in the area."[38] The tone of that legislation is oriented as much to ecosystem and to species ("unique flora and fauna") as to individuals. The principal intent of the Endangered Species Act is to protect species—with their individuals—but nothing in the act takes individuals as such to be the object of particular concern. (See also the Hawaiian palila case and the Supreme Court interpretation of the act, Chapter 7.)

Species and Ecosystem

A species is what it is inseparably from the environmental niche into which it fits. Although a creative response within it, the species has the form of the niche. Particular species may not be essential—in the sense that the ecosystem can survive the loss of individual species without adverse effect—but habitats are essential to species, and an endangered species typically means an endangered habitat. Species play lesser or greater roles in their habitats, which is not denied by noticing that often there are available substitutes. A specific identity is polar to a communal ecosystem, both in tandem balance.

The species stands off the world; at the same time it interacts with its environment, functions in the ecosystem, and is supported and shaped by it. Humans value a species for its contribution of richness to the system, but its richness exceeds its role effectiveness. Integrity in the species fits into integrity in the ecosystem. The species and the community are not identical goods but complementary goods in synthesis, parallel to but a level above the way the species and the individual have distinguishable but entwined goods. It is not preservation of *species* that we wish but the preservation of *species in the system*. It is not merely *what* they are but *where* they are that we must value correctly. (This is the main concern in the next chapter.)

In Situ *and* Ex Situ *Preservation*

The species *can* only be preserved *in situ;* the species *ought* to be preserved *in situ.* Zoos and botanical gardens can lock up a collection of individuals, but they cannot begin to simulate the ongoing dynamism of gene flow over time under the selection pressures in a wild biome. They amputate the species from its habitat. The full integrity of the species must be integrated into the ecosystem. This species-environment complex ought to be preserved because it is the generative context of value. *Ex situ* preservation, while it may save resources and souvenirs, does not preserve the generative process intact. Besides missing half the beauty of what is taking place, it misses the burden of the human duties. Again, the appropriate survival unit is the appropriate level of moral concern.

Pere David's deer, extinct in the wild for 2,000–3,000 years, was preserved by Chinese royalty. In the last century Pere Armand David brought some deer to Europe from the Imperial Garden in Peking, and there are now about 800 in zoos throughout the world. The deer in China were killed during the Boxer Rebellion, but some have been returned to Chinese zoos. The original habitat of the deer is unknown and, so far as it can be guessed, is gone. The deer do well in captivity. Should they be preserved? By any duty to species, they need not be. In an important sense they cannot be, for the deer have already become domestic animals, no longer subject to natural selection. One has only the product, not the process. But they might be preserved as relics, souvenirs, entertainment for persons. Since the extinction was artificial, one might argue that if the natural habitat were known and available, they should be restored to the wild.

Anthropogenic versus Natural Extinctions

It might seem that ending the history of a species now and again is not far out of line with the routines of the universe. But artificial extinction, caused by human encroachments, is radically different from natural extinction. Relevant differences make the two as morally distinct as death by natural causes is from murder. Though harmful to a species, extinction in nature is no evil in the system; it is rather the key to tomorrow. The species is employed in but abandoned to the general currents of life much as the individual is employed in but abandoned to the specific currents of life. Such extinction is normal turnover in ongoing speciation.

But anthropogenic extinction has nothing to do with evolutionary speciation. Hundreds of thousands of species will perish because of culturally altered environments that are radically different from the spontaneous environments in which such species were naturally selected and in which they sometimes go extinct. In natural extinction, nature takes away life—when it has become unfit in habitat or when the habitat alters—and supplies other life in its place. Artificial extinction shuts down tomorrow because it shuts down speciation. Natural extinction typically occurs with transformation either of the extinct line or related or competing lines. Artificial extinction is without issue. One opens doors; the other closes them. In artificial extinctions, humans generate and regenerate nothing; they only dead-end these lines.

From this perspective, humans have no duty of benevolence to preserve rare species from natural extinction, although they may have a duty to other humans to save such species as resources or museum pieces. No species has a "right to life" apart from the continued existence of the ecosystem with which it cofits. But humans do have a duty of nonmaleficence to avoid artificial extinction, which superkills the species in the formative process in which it stands. This prima facie duty can on occasion be overridden: for example with the extinction (which we have almost achieved) of *Orthopoxvirus variola*, the smallpox virus or (could we ever achieve it) of *Plasmodium vivax*, a malaria parasite. But a prima facie duty stands nevertheless. Humans cannot and need not save the product without the process.

Through evolutionary time nature has provided new species at a higher rate than the extinction rate: hence the accumulated diversity. In one of the best-documented studies of the marine fossil record, D. W. Raup and J. J. Sepkoski find that in Cambrian times there were perhaps 100 marine families, in Pennsylvanian times 400, in Triassic times 700. The general increase over time in standing diversity is summarized for marine fossils in Figure 4.1. Regardless of differing details on land or biases in the fossil record, a graph of the increase of diversity on Earth must look something like this.[39]

There have been four or five catastrophic extinctions, anomalies in the record, each succeeded by a recovery of previous diversity. The late Permian and late Cretaceous extinctions are the most startling, with still more remarkable regenerations. Although natural events, these extinctions so deviate from the trends that many paleontologists look for causes external to the evolutionary ecosystem. If caused by supernovae, collisions with asteroids, oscillations of the solar system above and below the plane of the galaxy, or other extraterrestrial upsets, such events are accidental to the evolutionary ecosystem. Thousands of species perished at the impingement of otherwise unrelated causal lines. The disasters were irrelevant to the kinds of ecosystems in which such species had been selected. If the causes were more

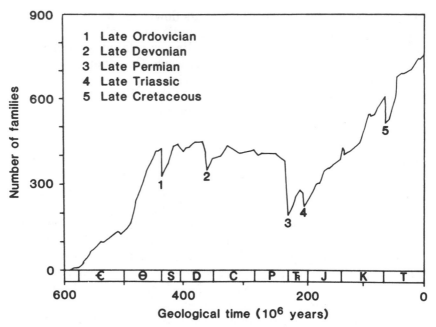

FIGURE 4.1 Standing diversity through time for families of marine vertebrates and invertebrates, with the standard geological symbols, and catastrophic extinctions numbered. From D. M. Raup and J. J. Sepkoski, Jr., "Mass Extinctions in the Marine Fossil Record," Science 215 (1982): 1501–03. ©1982 AAAS.

terrestrial—cyclic changes in climates or continental drift—the biological processes that characterize Earth are still to be admired for their powers of recovery. Uninterrupted by accident, or even interrupted so, they steadily increase the numbers of species.

Raup and Sepkoski further find that the normal extinction rate declines over evolutionary time from 4.6 families per million years in the Early Cambrian to 2.0 families in recent times, even though the number of families (and species) enormously increases. The general increase in diversity results from increased speciation and decreased extinction rates. The reduced extinction rate from Early Cambrian to recent times means that approximately 710 family extinctions did not occur that would have if the Cambrian rate had been sustained. This seems to mean that optimization of fitness increases through evolutionary time.

An ethicist has to be circumspect. An argument might commit what logicians call the genetic fallacy to suppose that present value depends upon origins. Species judged today to have intrinsic value may have arisen anciently and anomalously from a valueless context, akin to the way in which life arose mysteriously from nonliving materials. But in an ecosystem, what a thing is differentiates poorly from the generating and sustaining matrix. In a historical story that sweeps over time, the individual and the species have what value they have to some extent inevitably in the context of the forces that beget them.

Imagine that Figure 4.1 is the graph of the performance of a business 600 million years old. Is it not a healthy one? But this record is of the business of life, and as such the long-term performance deserves ethical respect. There is something awesome about an Earth that begins with zero and runs up toward five to ten million species in several billion years, setbacks notwithstanding.

What is valuable about species is not merely to be located in them for what they are in themselves; rather, the dynamic account evaluates species set as process, product, and instrument in the larger drama, toward which humans have duties instanced in duties to species. R. H. Whittaker finds, despite "island" and other local saturations and equilibria, that on continental scales and for most groups "increase of species diversity . . . is a self-augmenting evolutionary process without any evident limit." There is a natural tendency toward increased "species packing."[40] Nature seems to produce as many species as it can, certainly not just enough to stabilize an ecosystem, much less only species that can directly or indirectly serve human needs. Humans ought not to inhibit this exuberant lust for kinds. That process, with its products, is about as near to ultimacy as humans come in their relationship with the natural world. The human limiting of this limitless process seems wrong intuitively, although we are straining to develop an ethic that clearly specifies why.

Several billion years' worth of creative toil, several million species of teeming life, have been handed over to the care of this latecoming species in which mind has flowered and morals have emerged. Ought not this sole moral species do something less self-interested than count all the products of an evolutionary ecosystem as rivets in their spaceship, resources in their larder, laboratory materials, recreation for their ride? Such an attitude hardly seems biologically informed, much less ethically adequate. It is too provincial for superior humanity. Or, in a biologist's term, it is ridiculously territorial. If true to their specific epithet, ought not *Homo sapiens* value this host of species as something with a claim to their care in its own right? A reverence for life seems "called for."

An Endangered Ethic?

When an ethicist compares this description of Earth's biological history with the threatened human disruption of Earth's adventure, human activities seem misfit in the system. Although humans are maximizing their own species interests, and in this respect behaving as does each of the other species, they do not have any adaptive fitness. They are not really fitting into the evolutionary processes of ongoing biological conservation and elaboration. They are not really dynamically stable in their ecosystems. Humans do not transcend their own interests to become moral overseers (see Chapter 9). They do not follow nature, evaluating what is going on. Yet contemporary ethical systems limp when they try to prescribe right conduct here. They too seem misfits in the roles most recently demanded of them.

The most common cause of extinction in spontaneous nature is for a species to fall into the ever deepening ruts of overspecialization. *Homo sapiens* has proved remarkably unspecialized and seems in no danger of extinction. Still, there is something overspecialized about an ethic, held by the dominant class of *Homo sapiens*, that regards the welfare of only one of several million species as an object and beneficiary of duty.

There is nothing wrong with humans exploiting their environment, resourcefully using it. Nature requires this of every species, humans not excepted. What *is* the case—that humans must consume their environment—*ought to be* so: humans ought to consume their environment. But humans have options about the extent to which they do so; they also have, or ought to have, a conscience about it. The consumption of individual animals and plants is one thing; it can be routinely justified. But the consumption of species is something else; it cannot be routinely justified. To the contrary, each species made extinct is forever slain, and each extinction incrementally erodes the regenerative powers on our planet.

If this requires a paradigm change about the sorts of things to which duty can attach, so much the worse for those humanistic ethics no longer functioning in, or suited to, their changing environment. The anthropocentrism associated with them was fiction anyway. There is something Newtonian, not yet Einsteinian, as well as something morally naive, about living in a reference frame where one species takes itself as absolute and values everything else relative to its utility. Such limited theories can become true only when they learn their limits.

Concluding a survey of paleontology, D. V. Ager writes, "The history of any one part of the earth, like the life of a soldier, consists of long periods of boredom and short periods of terror."[41] Boredom is not the most apt description of the long routines of evolutionary speciation, but the mass extinctions were certainly periods of terror. Of late, in the most recent chapter in the story, humankind is the great terror—but a terror with a conscience. Turned in on itself to value the human species alone, this conscience makes humankind only a greater terror. Turned outward to accept duties to species and to the ecosystemic Earth, this conscience could make humans the noblest species and give them a more inclusive environmental fitness.

5 Life in Community: Duties to Ecosystems

 WE HAVE BEEN TRAVELING into progressively less familiar ethical terrain, starting with humans—to whom humans have familiar duties (duties within the *family*)—and moving to consider higher animals, lower animal and plant organisms, and species. Duties to species began to open out toward duties to the speciating process and the supporting ecosystem in which species live and move and have their being. Now we have to explore the ecosystemic level of biological organization more fully. This is ultimately—at least on the earthen scene—our home; hence the derivation of *ecology* (Greek: *oikos*, house). We need a logic and ethic for Earth with its *family* of life.

Aldo Leopold, one of the prophets of environmental ethics, called the living landscape "the land" and concluded, "A thing is right when it tends to preserve the integrity, stability, and beauty of the biotic community. It is wrong when it tends otherwise."[1] "That land is a community is the basic concept of ecology, but that land is to be loved and respected is an extension of ethics."[2] Can there be duties to ecosystems? To Earth and its communities of life?

"The plant formation is an organic unit . . . a complex organism."[3] So Frederic Clements, a founder of ecology, concluded from his studies of plant associations in the Nebraska grasslands. Henry Gleason, a botanist of equal rank, protested, "Far from being an organism, an association is merely the fortuitous juxtaposition of plants."[4] Leopold takes a middle route between these extremes.[5] The ecosystem is a "biotic community." Moreover, moving from what *is* the case to what *ought* to be, Leopold argues a land ethic, duties toward ecosystems.

Clements's description has seemed implausible to most ecologists, but if correct, duties to a superorganism could plausibly follow, since ethics has classically felt some respect for organismic lives. Gleason's description has seemed as simplistic as Clements's is overdone, but if correct, duties to ecosystems would vanish.

160

There can be no obligations to an accidental jumble. That would be even more absurd than duties to species as arbitrary conventions. But what of Leopold's biotic community? Duties to communities might be more important than duties to individuals; they might be aggregated or indirect duties to individuals, or duties generated in encounter with prolife forces that transcend individuals. Most ecologists think that an ecosystem is a real natural unit, a level of organization above its individual member organisms.[6] An ecosystem may not be a superorganism, but it is some other kind of coordinated organic ("organized") system, a "biotic community." Is the description plausible? Do prescriptions follow?

John Passmore, a philosopher entering the argument, thinks that only paradigmatic human communities generate obligations:

> Ecologically, no doubt, men form a community with plants, animals, soil, in the sense that a particular life-cycle will involve all four of them. But if it is essential to a community that the members of it have common interests and recognise mutual obligations, then men, plants, animals, and soil do *not* form a community. Bacteria and men do not recognise mutual obligations nor do they have common interests. In the only sense in which belonging to a community generates ethical obligation, they do not belong to the same community.[7]

Donald H. Regan, another philosopher, agrees:

> Community—in the only sense in which it can possibly have any moral significance—requires at least the potential for shared beliefs and values. The universe of living creatures simply does not amount to a community in any morally relevant sense.[8]

Passmore and Regan are assuming that the members of a morally bound community must recognize reciprocal obligations. If the *only* communal belonging that generates obligations is this social sense, involving mutual recognition of interests, then the human community is the sole matrix of morality, and the case is closed. Gorillas, much less bacteria, cannot recognize mutual obligations. So humans owe nothing to nonhumans, much less to ecosystems. But Leopold wants to open the question these philosophers think closed. Extending the logic of ethics beyond culture, can mutually recognized obligations and interests be replaced by respect and love for ecosystemic integrity, stability, and beauty? Can a community per se count morally?

Cooperation and Struggle

A first consideration is that the organism is a model of co-operation, while the alleged ecosystemic "community" seems a jungle where the fittest survive. Fully functioning persons can be expected to cooperate in the deliberate sense, and interhuman ethics has admired being kind to one another, doing as you would have others do to you, mutually recognizing rights, calculating the greatest good for the greatest number. But symmetrical reciprocity drops out when moral agents encounter amoral plants and animals. To look for considerate cooperation in the biotic community is a category mistake, expecting there what is only a characteristic of culture.

We might think, however, that at least nondeliberate *cooperation* is an admirable feature in organisms, which seem to command ethical respect because, from the skin in, they are models of coaction. The heart cooperates with the liver, muscles with the brain, leaves with the cambium, mitochondria with the nucleus. Life is contained within individualized organisms, notwithstanding colonial species, slime molds, and other minor exceptions. Respect for life, therefore, ought to attach to individuals, which is where the "integrity, stability, and beauty" are.

From the skin out, everything is different. Interactions between individuals are nothing but *struggle*. Each is out for itself, pitted against others in predation and competition. Carnivores kill herbivores, who consume the grasses and forbs. Every living thing pushes itself through the world and grabs resources. Young pines smother each other out. Black walnuts and *Salvia* shrubs secrete allelopathic agents that poison other plants. Apparent harmony in ecosystems is superficial. Chokecherries benefit redwing blackbirds, but the fruits are bait and a gamble in reproductive struggle. Neither plants nor animals are moral agents, and to regard carnivore or *Salvia* behavior as "selfishness" is as much a mistake as to expect deliberate cooperation. We are not faulting organisms. Still, the organism is parts admirably integrated into a whole. The ecosystem is pulling and hauling between rivals, no admirable community. To adapt Garrett Hardin's phrase, there is tragedy on the commons.[9]

From Conflict to Situated Fitness

Such a picture accentuates the skin-in cooperation and the skin-out conflict. Ecology refocuses both the description and the resulting prescription. The requirement that parts in wholes "help each other"—charitably in culture and functionally in nature—makes another category mistake, trying to find in nature what we admire in civilization rather than judging nature for what it is in itself. Were cooperation the sole criterion for admirable events, we would admire the elephant's heart and liver and even admire the integrated whole elephant, only to despise the elephant's behavior, since the integrated elephant-unit consumes all the bamboo and acacia it can and tramples the rest of the gallery forest in majestic indifference. The elephant is coordinated within to struggle without, and would-be admirers are left ambivalent about individuals. The individual is an aggrandizing unit as much as a cooperative one. Such units propel the ecosystem.

The deeper problem seems to lie in the axiom that everything is pushing to maximize itself, with no further determining forces. In fact, although aggrandizing units propel the ecosystem, the system limits such behavior; there is a sufficient but contained place for all the members. Imposed on organisms from the upper organizational level (if indeed each species increases toward a world-encompassing maximum, until "stopped"), this containment can seem more admirable than the aggressive individual units. The system forces what cooperation there is, embedding every individual deeply in coaction.

What we want to admire in nature, whether in individuals or ecosystems, are the vital productive processes, not cooperation as against conflict; ethicists will go astray if they require in nature precursors or analogues of what later proves admirable in culture. We want to value the lush life that ecosystems maintain—their diversity, unity, dynamic stability, spontaneity; the dialectic of environmental resistance and conductance; the generating life forces (Chapter 1, pp. 17-25)—and the question of "helping each other out" is at most going to be a subset of these more significant issues, if "helping" is an appropriate category at all.

Painting a new picture on the conflict side, even before the rise of ecology, biologists concluded that to portray a gladiatorial survival of the fittest was a distorted account; they prefer a model of the better adapted. Although conflict is part of the picture, the organism has a situated environmental fitness. The plants in a forest may adapt to each other in ways that reduce competition. Plant growth seasons and flowering are staggered; plants evolve differing degrees of tolerance to light, moisture, and soil conditions.

Animals eat different foods, or use a food resource in sequential stages. All share energy pathways. Fitness includes many characteristics that are not competitive for resources or detrimental to neighbors, as when some elephants survive heat or drought better than others.

The elephant fits the savannas just as much as its heart fits its liver; within and without there is equal fitness in amount but not in kind. There are differences. The heart and the liver are close-coupled; remove either and the elephant dies. Elephants and savannas are immediately weak-coupled. Elephants do migrate from savannas to forests; they can also be removed to zoos—but again, *Loxodonta africana*, removed from the selection pressures where the species evolved and its vigor is retained, soon dies. Savannas and forests are as necessary to elephants as hearts and livers. In the complete picture, the outside is as *vital* as the inside. The more satisfactory picture is of elephants pushing to fit into a system that provides and imposes sufficient containment. In that communitarian sense, elephant and savanna are as coordinated (orders that couple together) as heart and liver are coordinated organismically. Shifting the metaphor, the ecosystem supplies the coordinates through which the elephant moves. The elephant cannot really be mapped or located outside these coordinates.

The *environmental necessity* (the requirement that an organism reside in a biotic community) involves conflicts, selection pressures, niche fitness, environmental support, a web of life; the *organic necessity* (the required maintaining of organismic processes) involves cooperation, functional efficiency, metabolically integrated parts. The skin-in processes could never have evolved, nor can they remain what they are, apart from the skin-out processes. Elephants are *what* they are because they are *where* they are. What we mean by a *community* as a different systemic level from an *organism* includes these weaker, though not less valued or fertile, couplings. The two levels are equally essential. Adaptedness covers both. This invites respect for the ecosystemic processes quite as much as for organismic processes. There seems no reason to admire the inside and depreciate the outside; to do so is to include only half the truth about life. In result we will mislocate our sense of duty.

Even in human society, conflict is not always taken as evil. Every academic pledges to keep the critical process open, wishing for the "attacks" of those who can constructively (if first destructively) spot his or her flaws. Like business, politics, and sports, ecosystems too thrive on competition. In natural community the cougars are the critics (if we may put it so) that catch the flawed deer and thereby build better ones, as well as gain a meal. Alternately, the fleet-footed deer test out any cougars slow enough to starve. There is violence in the one process, and the other ought to be civil. Ideas die in the one realm, while individuals die in the other. Justice and charity may be relevant in culture and not in nature. But in both communities, helping is subtly entwined with competition. There is a biological, though not a cultural, sense—a dialectical sense—in which deer and cougar cooperate, and the integrity, beauty, and stability of each is bound up with their coactions. Ecosystems are not of disvalue because contending forces are in dynamic process there, any more than cultures are.

Predator and prey or parasite and host require a coevolution where both flourish, since the health of the predator or parasite is locked into the continuing existence, even the welfare, of prey and host. The one must gain maximum benefit with minimum disturbance of the other; it is to the advantage of predator and parasite to disturb prey and host species minimally. Although individuals are weakened or destroyed, if the disturbance is too great, the prey will evolve to throw off the predator, the host the parasite; or host and prey will become rare, or extinct, to the disadvantage of predator and parasite. Certainly ichneumon wasps destroy the individual butterfly caterpillars they parasitize. Mosquitoes and nose-botflies can torment caribou, who seek windy areas and shake their heads to escape them. Nevertheless all these kinds together flourish in their ecosystems. Parasitism often remains just that, but it also tends to evolve into mutualism (cellulose-digesting bacteria in the ungulate rumen, algae and fungi synthesizing lichens, or *Chlorella* alga within the green hydra, *Hydra viridis*).

It seems doubtful that "plant defenses" are that and nothing more. Plants regulate but do not eliminate the insects and animals that have coevolved with them. Pollinators and fruit eaters benefit, and benefit from, the plants they serve; different species of plants sometimes evolve sequential flowering and fruiting with the result that they sustain beneficial insect and animal populations throughout the season, where no one species of plant could do so alone. Insect consumers eat less than 10 percent of the terrestrial biomass upon which they graze (certain outbreaks excepted), and insects (even outbreaks of them) often seem to provide benefits of which we are yet little aware. It is difficult to think that insects, pressed for survival as they are, are not marginally sensitive to the vigor of the plants on which they graze (or the animals they "torment"); they do better nutritionally if their hosts do better nutritionally. Aphids secrete sugars that stimulate nitrogen-fixing bacteria in the soil, and short-lived insect grazers permit rapid nutrient recycling in long-lived plants, something like that accomplished more slowly by seasonal leaf fall and decay.

When a forest stand is aging and senile, insects may overtake it, and there will be an outbreak; in this sense insect vigor is inversely correlated with forest vigor. But that is a short-scope phenomenon on the scale of succession. The insects depend on the continued existence of these forests, and if the forests are not rejuvenated by, or at least following, the outbreak, the tree species goes extinct. The benefits of insects, even insect outbreaks, can be something like the benefits of fire, of which we were long unaware. Some species of grasses have coevolved with grazing ungulates; neither can flourish (or even survive) without the other. Herbivory is, as seems obvious, routinely detrimental to plants; herbivores capture nutritional value and the plants are the losers. But there is increasing evidence that gain/loss is not the whole story. Many plants coevolve with their grazers so as to lessen deleterious effects, by compensation to neutralize them, or even to benefit from grazing. There is characteristically significant coaction, whether antagonistic or mutualistic; in these ecological relationships sometimes the selection pressures can result in double benefits, a gain on both sides.[10] Here too, as with predators and prey, being eaten is not always a bad thing.

Assessing Satisfactory Ecosystems

Selection pressures will routinely drive adaptation and counteradaptation toward minimum disturbance, that is, to check competitions by forced cooperations. If we take optimization theory seriously in evolutionary ecology (which is only to say that those mutations which prove beneficial to members of a species are selected for, resulting in situated environmental fitness), then disadvantageous arrangements will be extinguished and advantageous ones selected for. This will usually or at least initially be to the benefit of the predator/parasite and at cost to the prey/host, to the benefit of the grazer and at cost to the plant, but any mutations tending in the direction of symbiosis will be selected. Among the possible interactions, as diagrammed in Figure 5.1, selection will drive the arrows in the directions shown. Any mutation with negative effects will be selected against; mutations with zero effect

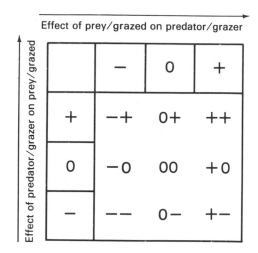

FIGURE 5.1 *Nine possible interactions between predator/grazer and prey/grazed. Adapted from W. J. Mattson and N. D. Addy, "Phytophagous Insects as Regulators of Forest Primary Production,"* Science *190 (1975): 515-22. ©1975 AAAS.*

will drift without selection, but mutations with positive benefits will accumulate over time.

That can yield positive effects for one partner and negative effects for the other (perhaps the usual case with parasitism), but there will be still further selection pressures for the double-positive benefits. If by random mutation the consumer happens on any behavior that benefits its host at no cost to itself, a feedback loop will be set up by which the directly benefited host indirectly benefits the consumer. There will be trial and error, and such solutions may seldom be found. But the directions of selection move this way statistically, and those that do will accumulate over evolutionary time.

An ecosystem is an imposing critical system, with a dialectic that keeps selection pressures high, enriches situated fitness, evolves congruent kinds in their places with sufficient containment. The ecologist finds that ecosystems *objectively* are *satisfactory communities* in the sense that, though not all organismic needs are gratified, enough are for species long to survive, and the critical ethicist finds (in a *subjective* judgment matching the *objective* process) that such ecosystems are imposing and *satisfactory communities* to which to attach duty.

Centered and Loose Organization

It may be objected that an organism is a highly centered system; in contrast, an ecosystem has no centeredness at all. The one is a marvel; the other is a muddle. The "inside" coactions routinely look teleologically constructed. Before Darwin, that fooled people into believing in design, and whatever we think now of creation, when we come to judge the present results, humans ought to value organisms as negentropic evolutionary achievements that simulate intelligent purpose. The cooperation praised earlier can be put more precisely; *integrated cybernetic autonomy* ought to be respected.

The struggle disliked earlier can be put more simply: ecosystems are primarily *stochastic process*. A seashore or a tundra is a loose collection of externally related parts. Even after biologists soften conflict with adaptive fitness, a forest is mostly a game played with loaded dice. With measurable probability, red maple trees replace gray birch, and beech trees replace maples; each on average outcompetes the other in the deepening shade. In a network of invasions there is minimal integrated process. The fox, its heart, and liver together need meat and water. But the members of a biotic community have no shared needs; there is only shoving. Or there is indifference and haphazard juxtaposition.

Much of the environment is not organic at all (rain, groundwater, rocks, nonbiotic soil particles, air). Some is dead and decaying debris (fallen trees, scat, humus). These things have no organized needs at all. The biotic sector runs by need-driven individuals interacting with other such individuals and with the abiotic and exbiotic materials and forces. Everywhere the system is full of "noise." The mathematics becomes complex; often the interactions are too messy to find regularities at all. Still, the issues are those of the distribution and abundance of organisms, how they get dispersed here and not there, birthrates and deathrates, population densities, moisture regimes, parasitism and predation, checks and balances. There is really not enough centered process to be called common unity, which is why ecology has so few paradigms and why duty directed here seems misplaced. There is only catch-as-catch-can scrimmage for nutrients and energy.

The parts (foxes, sedges) are more complex than the wholes (forests, grasslands). Individual organisms are not decomposable; their parts (livers, hearts, culms, roots) crumple into waste outside their wholes. They cannot be divided without death, this attests to their heightened individuality. But in an ecosystem the parts (so-called) are transients. A vixen can move her den from forest to grassland and switch prey. Migrating birds inhabit no one community but range over dozens. Ecosystems are a continuum of variation, a patchy mosaic with fuzzy edges. Some interactions are persistent, others occasional; some drive coevolution; some do not. Species in any particular ecosystem do not have the same limits to their geographical distribution; their tolerance regimes differ. There are few obligate associations. There may be strongly coupled subsystems, these weakly coupled to one another in the big system. A *Juncus* species can suffer a blight and its "place" be taken by a *Carex*. An ecosystem is often transitional and unstructured; that makes it (some say) doubtfully a natural kind at all. That boundaries are sometimes marginal gradients supposedly leads to a conclusion that central interconnections within the system are less significant, less valuable. So far from being a satisfactory community, an ecosystem is rather sloppy.

From this perspective, the units counted as ecosystemic "parts" have more integrity than the system in which they reside. To attach duty to the loose-coupled system would misplace duty, like valuing a social institution (a business firm, a state legislature) or even a casual collection (college alumni on tour) more than the individual persons who constitute these groups. The centers of autonomy, meaningful response, satisfaction, intrinsic value all lie in the persons. However much society supplies a context of support and identity, it is *egos* that count in human ethics. By parity of reasoning, though there are no egos in nonhuman nature, we should count the nearest thing: *selves*—somatic if not psychological selves. The focal point for cultural value is the high point of individuality: the *person*. The moral focus in ecosystems should be the high point of integrated complexity: the *organism*.

Organismic Development in Demanding Environments

This too is a picture that ecological science refocuses. Admiring concentrated unity and stumbling over environmental looseness is like valuing mountains and despising valleys. One fails again to understand the dialectic between organism and environment. Unity is admirable in the organism, but the requisite matrix of its generation is the open, plural ecology. Internal complexity arises to deal with a complex, tricky environment. Had there been either simplicity or lockstep unity in the surroundings, no creative unity could have been composed internally. There would have been less elegance in life.

Rapid and diverse insect speciation, resulting in highly specialized forms, is a response to increasing niches in varied topographies. Complex plant biochemistries arise to produce and to offset allelopathic agents, increasing heterogeneity. The primate brain, integrated with hands and legs, is a survival tool in a "jungle." Using instinct and conditioned behavior, lemurs "figure out" probabilities; there is that much order, and contingency enough to churn the evolution of skills. The environment is not capricious, but neither is it regular enough to relax in. One always needs better detectors and strategies. When lions are kept in cages, their brains degenerate within a decade; their jungle has been taken away and replaced with boring order. Simple, little-changing environments usually result in stagnation across millennia. Dialectic with the loose environment (rich in opportunity, demanding in know-how) invites and requires creativity. The individual and the environment seem like *opposites;* they are really *apposites;* the individual is set in opposition to its world but is also appropriate to it. That is why terrestrial life is more complex than marine life.

Further, a lack of centeredness or sharp edges does not mean a lack of relational complexity. Leopold is right to insist, against Gleason's fortuitous juxtaposition, that "the individual is a member of a community of interdependent parts."[11] Ecosystems are not as coherent as organisms but are not randomly fortuitous either; they fit together with a characteristic systems structure. Situated environmental fitness for organisms often yields a complicated life together.

Sometimes this is in symbiosis. Spotted salamander (*Ambystoma maculatum*) eggs are invaded by a green alga that thrives on the nutrients excreted by the developing embryo, the embryo benefiting as the alga removes its wastes and provides oxygen. The tadpoles eat the algae but not before the algae produce motile cells that swim off to invade other egg masses.[12]

Sometimes this is in competitive coevolution. The latex in milkweed is toxic to many potential grazers. Monarch caterpillars have evolved a metabolism that tolerates the latex and depend on the toxin to prevent being eaten. Blue jays eat caterpillars that graze on other plants but not those that feed on *Asclepias*. When caterpillars metamorphose, the toxin is concentrated in wings and legs, so that a jay that grabs a butterfly by the wings will get a bad taste and drop it. Smart jays learn to strip off the wings and legs and eat only the butterfly thoraxes. Juvenile jays do not do this instinctively and are tested for their capacity to learn it.[13]

Complexity is an organism-in-environment phenomenon, from the mutations that result in *Asclepias* toxins to the demand for smarter jays. Each kind is molded by the survival pressures of its environment; each kind has to have an adaptive fit. But each kind is creatively pushing to wedge itself in, and this pushes the creativity uphill—producing smarter jays, milkweeds with novel chemistries, butterflies with novel metabolisms. And all three—milkweeds, butterflies, and jays—find the system satisfactory enough to flourish in.

Sometimes the interdependence is in predation. A herbivore must move to its stationary food, but that requirement alone does not yield much alertness. The herbivore is a food for others, however, and since a carnivore's food moves, the excitement increases by an order of magnitude. Sight, hearing, smelling, speed, and integrative consciousness—all of which contribute to concentrated unity—grow intense just because there is a decentralized interdependence.

Animals high in the food chain (carnivores) may range over many habitats. Bears and panthers roam over 400 square miles. In one sense this means that they have no habitat; they inhabit a landscape. In another sense, they are using and integrating more communities than are animals lower in the food chain (herbivores). Deer may move only a mile or two. Plants do not move at all. This does not mean that there is no community; it only means that the upper-level, more mobile species establish community cross-links of wider scope, across a biome. Depending as they do on what lies below in the ecosystemic pyramid, these species prove the systemic organization rather than demonstrating some freedom from community. A cougar moves through its environment with a freedom not available to a grass plant; a single grass plant can live on its own in a handful of soil, while the cougar requires a landscape of 400 square miles. In a way, these are different kinds of autonomy: the grass plant an autotroph in a bit of soil; the cougar on the loose, free to roam. But there is no lack of community. Though the grass has no dependence on the cougar; the cougar, in its freedom, depends on the grass, since without herbivores the cougar will perish. The concentrated unity in the cougar is superposed on the community it inhabits. Both grass and cougar find their environments satisfactory.

Order and Openness in Biotic Communities

An ecosystem has no genome, no brain, no self-identification. It does not defend itself against injury or death as do blue jays, milkweeds, cougars. It is not irritable. An oak-hickory forest has no telos, no unified program it is set to execute. But to find such characteristics missing and then to judge that ecosystems do not count morally is to make another category mistake. To look at one level for what is appropriate at another faults *communities* as though they ought to be organismic *individuals*. One should look for a matrix of interconnections between centers, not for a single center; for creative stimulus and open-ended potential, not for a fixed telos and executive program. Everything will be connected to many other things, sometimes by obligate associations, more often by partial and pliable dependencies; among still other things there will be no significant interactions. There will be shunts and criss-crossing pathways, cybernetic subsystems and feedback loops, functions in a communal sense. One looks for selection pressures and adaptive fit, not for irritability or repair of injury; for speciation and life support, not for resisting death.

There is freedom in the interdependencies. The connections are lax; some show up only in statistics. But we do not want to see in the statistics relationships so *casual* that there is no community at all but rather relationships so *causal* as to permit genuine (loose) community, not (tight) organism. Statistics can be quite revealing. Causal links are not less significant because they are probabilistic (as one learns in physics), though they may no longer be determinate. This will be disliked by conservative ecologists and ethicists who, like Einstein, think that dice-throwing is irrational. But others find that the looseness is not "noise" in the community; it is a liberal sign of beauty, integrity, and dynamic stability.

Not every collection of interacting constituents is a community. Planets form no community; plants do. The latter have an *ecology*, a home (*oikos*) with its logic (*logos*) of biofunctions and resources. Molecules in a gas or moons around Jupiter have no fitness there, but caterpillars on milkweeds and cougars in landscapes do. The logic of the resident home is as significant as the logic of any ephemeral inhabitant. To praise the individuals (as the creative actors) and to disparage the system (as mere stochastic, inert stage) is to misunderstand the context of creativity.

There is weak organic holism—communitarian holism—not strong organismic holism, though the "weakness" (if we must use that term) is a strength in the system. The looseness abets community; too much tightness would abort it. The looseness is not simplicity but is itself a form of environmental complexity that generates organismic complexity.

It is unlikely that there is any one defining characteristic of, or correct approach to, such a community. Complex and merging phenomena may be seen from numerous perspectives. Ecology may have to remain (like sociology, with its several models of culture) a multiple-paradigm science. Because we are dealing with a community, its laws will be fewer and more statistical than those in organismic biology, chemistry, or physics. In another sense, we do not need multiple paradigms *for* the community; *the paradigm is community.* Ecology discovers simultaneously (1) what is taking place in ecosystems and (2) what *biotic community* means as an organizational mode enveloping organisms. Crossing over from science to ethics, we can discover (3) the values in such a community-system and (4) our duties toward it. Interdependence does not always deliver duty, but biological obligation is a relevant consideration in determining moral obligation.

There is a kind of order that arises spontaneously and systematically when many self-concerned units jostle and seek their own programs, each doing its own thing and forced into informed interaction with other units. In culture, the logic of language and the integrated efficiency of the market are examples. Science and Christianity are community enterprises too vast to be comprehended by any one mind; many minds contribute to the building of each. No one individual orders language, markets, science, religion. Individuals pursue their interests in all four, but none of these processes is fully to be explained merely as aggregated individual interests. The communities constructed are sometimes wayward; there are false starts, trials and errors, but there is much fitting together of rationality and positive value.

In nature, an ecosystem systematically generates spontaneous order, an order that exceeds in richness, beauty, integrity, and dynamic stability the order of any of the component parts, an order that feeds (and is fed by) the richness, beauty, and integrity of these component parts. The organismic kind of creativity (regenerating a species, pushing to increase to a world-encompassing maximum) is used to produce, and is checked by, another kind of creativity (speciating that produces new kinds, interlocking kinds with adaptive fit plus individuality and looseness). We get diversity, unity, dynamic stability, spontaneity, a life-support system, a fortunate place, the wonderland of natural history, the miracle of creation (values recognized in Chapter 1).

When humans evaluate such a display, we have an initial tendency to think that decentralized order is of low quality because it is uncentered and not purposive; there is no center of experience or control. We do need to be circumspect about "invisible hand" explanations, especially in culture, where there is immorality. But science, religion, markets, and language are not irrational because they are decentralized; some decentralizing permits more rationality than would otherwise be possible. A culture is richer, more diverse, more beautiful because it is the product of tens of thousands of minds; it would be quite poor under the centralized control of one mind or if all thought alike. One mind can provide or appreciate only a fraction of the wealth of a culture.

Analogously in ecosystems—and with more objectivity, compared with the intersubjectivity of science or religion—such order may be a comprehensive, complex, fertile order just because it integrates (with some looseness) the know-how of many diverse organisms and species; it is not an order built on the achievements of any one kind of thing. Ecosystems are in some respects more to be admired than any of their component organisms because they have generated, continue to support, and integrate tens of thousands of member organisms. The ecosystem is as wonderful as anything it contains. In nature there may sometimes be clumsy, makeshift solutions. Still, everything is tested for adaptive fitness. Producing adaptive fits and eliminating misfits, the ecosystem is the satisfactory matrix, the projective source of all it contains. It takes a great world to breed great lives, great minds.

The seeming disorder (really loose, communitarian, organic order) present at upper, ecosystem levels generates at middle levels the tight organismic order of individual plants and animals. Also, the sometimes seeming disorder at still lower, microscopic levels—random mutations in genes—generates this middle-level organismic order. The organism with its holistic integration is sandwiched between and produced by these embracing levels, the one an environment, the other a substratum. The system has built the world with a resulting tradeoff between individuality and an environment loose enough for individuality to evolve and function in. Individuality and looseness have to be jointly optimized; the two are not accidentally related. In this communitarian sense, elephant and savanna are even more coordinated than we earlier realized. The level of the organism seems almost both empirically and logically to imply community, and vice versa. Each phenomenal level requires the others.

Further, we cannot admire ecosystems until we see them as places of value capture, which is an aspect of this value integration. One can admire a peregrine falcon's flight or the gait of a cheetah, but locomotion takes high energy funding. Muscles, nerves, and brains depend—several trophic rungs down the pyramid—on plants (99.9 percent of the biomass) that soak up the sunlight. By their concentration on capturing solar energy, stationary plants make possible the concentrated unity of the zoological world. A result is that animals, the more so the more mobile, select the communities that select them—looseness, if you like, but also freedom in communities, not freedom from community.

Plants do not intend to help falcons and cheetahs, nor does any ecosystemic program direct this coaction. But the system is nevertheless a transformer that interlocks dispersed achievements. Falcons feed on warblers, which feed on insects, which feed on plants; there is a food chain from cheetah through gazelle to Bermuda grass. It is the protein in warblers that falcons can use and the protein in insects that warblers can use; the energy that plants have fixed is recycled by insects. The kills are the capture of skills. Upper-level organisms use other organisms' vital products, organic resources that they cannot produce themselves. All these metabolisms are as linked as are liver and heart. The equilibrating system is not merely a matter of push-pull forces; it is an equilibrating of values. Once again, the dissonance is related to the consonance. What seems like environmental resistance (and is so from a limited perspective) plays its part in forming the channels of environmental conductance.

The system is a game with loaded dice, but the loading is a prolife tendency, not mere stochastic process. Though there is no *Nature* in the singular, the system has a nature, a loading that pluralizes, putting *natures* into diverse kinds, $nature_1$, $nature_2$, $nature_3$ . . . $nature_n$. It does so using random elements (in both organisms and communities), but this is a secret of its fertility, producing steadily intensified interdependencies and options. An ecosystem has no head, but it has a "heading" for species diversification, support, and richness. Though not a superorganism, it is a kind of vital "field."

We do not want to extrapolate from organism to biotic community, any more than we extrapolate from culture to nature. Rather, we want criteria appropriate to this level. A monocentered organism is a tautology. A monocentered community is a contradiction in terms, though a holistic community is not. Given the logic of ecosystems, there is no reason to shut off value judgments at the skin. We want to love "the land," as Leopold terms it, "the natural processes by which the land and the living things upon it have achieved their characteristic forms (evolution) and by which they maintain their existence (ecology)."[14] The appropriate unit for moral concern is the fundamental unit of development and survival. Loving lions and hating jungles is misplaced affection. An ecologically informed society must love lions-in-jungles, organisms-in-ecosystems, or else fail in vision and courage.

Succession and Natural History

Ecosystemic Succession and Its Resetting

On the scale of decades and centuries, ecosystems undergo succession; on the scale of centuries and millennia, they evolve. Cyclic systems in the short range, they are historical systems in the long range. Fires, floods, disease epidemics, windstorms, volcanic eruptions, and glaciation episodically reset succession, whether in process or at climax. One seldom travels far in a forest without evidence of fire. A majority of the resident species will find niches in the nonclimax stages. On regional scales, succession is always somewhere being upset, and the nonclimax species migrate accordingly. As a result, all phases of succession and associated species are somewhere present. This can seem loose and merely "fortunate" (lucky). It is also a statistical "law" of ecology, an evolved characteristic of ecosystems, interruptions included, and in that sense not fortunate but highly probable. As in genetics—only now at a different level—elements of randomness are incorporated in a dynamic life system. A stochastic process is loaded toward richness of life.

In succession, one species pushes out another; the competitions seem noncooperative. But there is another way of looking at this. The pioneering species gain ground, only to make way for later invaders that replace them. The gray birch succumb to the red maple; the beech later depend on shade provided by the maple. If, in disrupted areas (as all areas eventually are), there are no earlier species that reproduce in the sun, there can be no later species that reproduce only in shade. Water-loving plants invade the margins of a lake; as detritus collects, marsh-loving plants replace them; afterward the bog fills, and broad-leaved trees can enter. On Lake Michigan shores a sand dune starts after an unusually strong wind blowout and thereafter migrates inland. Marram grass can stabilize a dune in a few years; after another decade the grass dies out. Jack pine and white pine invade the dune for about a century, and after that black oak replace the pines.

"Each stage reacts upon the habitat in such a way as to produce physical conditions more or less unfavorable to its permanence, but advantageous to the invaders of the next stage."[15] Species work themselves out of a home and leave a place for what comes after. This is not always true; there are perpetually self-regenerating stands, and some species enter communities in spite of, not because of, their predecessors. But one thing that often drives succession is this remarkable competition where winners by their very success alter their environment and become losers; it is a "fortunate" aspect of the "law" of succession, an odd natural selection, and a strange situated environmental fitness!

Some contend that there is nothing admirable about succession or its periodic upset, nor about beeches depending on the maples whose ground they invade. Yet after one has become ecologically sensitive, the system is a kaleidoscope: it turns around with the accidental tumbling of bits and pieces, each with its own flash and color, and yet the whole pattern is also of interdependent parts coacting, patterns repeated over time and topography, endlessly variable and yet regular, buzzing with life.

And there is much more. Succession is a subroutine in a dramatic story.

Historical Evolutionary Ecosystems

It is sometimes said that ecosystems are Markov processes: that is, stochastic systems without long-term memory.[16] The succession from state A (subclimax) to state B (climax) can be specified without attention to history. Whether dice thrown today will come up deuce is independent of what the throws last month were. Whether the maples push out the birches on the east side of the Wisconsin River in the next decade is independent of whether they did this on the west side in the last decade. By contrast, higher organisms and especially persons in cultures are historical entities. Whether the coyote falls for the trap depends on its earlier experiences. Whether a nation passes from state A (peace) to state B (war) depends on lessons learned in the past. As a person matures, the quality of life depends upon cumulative reaction patterns. Ecosystems have no analogous "character." Unlike coyotes or blue jays, they learn nothing. They simply undergo succession, episodically reset. This can seem to give ecosystems less identity and worth than persons and intelligent organisms. Noncognitive systems deserve little respect—none at all if clumsy and inelegant.

But over evolutionary time ecosystems are quite historical, although decentralized. There is an enormous amount of history in a handful of earthen humus (contrasted with a handful of lunar soil) in the sense that what goes on there bears the memory (cognitive information coded in DNA) of discoveries in previous millennia of Earth's history. This makes biology different from chemistry. Geologists extrapolate from mineralogy on Earth to that on Jupiter and Mars, but biologists extrapolate nothing extraterrestrially from the birch-maple-beech succession, because earthbound successions are historically evolved phenomena. The birches have "memories," "experiences," strategies accumulated over tens of thousands of years. Black walnuts and *Salvia* shrubs "remember" how to inhibit their competitors. Some of the biochemistries (like photosynthesis) are a billion years old. The behavior of the marmot, hibernating at the onset of winter, is not a probabilistic reaction to cold but a historically conditioned instinct. An ecosystem has a "heritage," a "tradition," in which lie the principal causes of what is taking place.

Yet there are surprises. No ecologist can predict successions a thousand years hence, nor are paleobiogeographers surprised when pollen analysis reveals that successions were something else than they are now a thousand years ago. New historical developments take place.[17] Ecosystems have weak laws and few "constants," only statistical mathematics, and no comprehensive theories—all of which can dismay a scientist anxious about predictions. But it can delight the philosopher who finds the laws sufficient constantly to generate history and who finds historical communities satisfying. This liberal environment proves both empirically necessary and sufficient (requisite and satisfying) for producing life, and yet it fails to be logically necessary and sufficient (yielding hard deterministic laws). A closed necessary and sufficient environment (a deterministic one) would logically and empirically prevent both the historicity and the individuality we admire within ecosystems. It would block potential and openness.

The "weak" laws, the few "constants" are a strength generating story in the system. The ecosystem is contingently sufficient for what takes place in it. The ethicist finds this satisfying, contingently sufficient for generating duty.

The species of the community are something like the genes of an organism, said A. G. Tansley.[18] Despite differences between organisms and communities, the analogy correctly teaches that just as the organism is not its genes but has its history stored there, the community history is not merely that of its species, although the history is written there. The context of history is not all privately in individuals, though the sectors relevant to individuals are coded in their DNA strands. The stories recorded in the biomolecular events are stories particular to individual organisms but substories of a bigger story. Everything is what it is in relation to other things, and the genetic stories are as much of relational roles as of individual integrities.

History is smeared out across the system. Some is concentrated in the DNA sequences of the birch tree, some in the individual coyote's career, and the history diffused in the biotic community as a matrix of coevolved historical centers is equally remarkable. All the transmissible memory is somewhere in the genetic pool, but to think that history is all pinpointed in individuals because the DNA that stores it is within organisms would be as mistaken as to think that human history is all in the books that record it. The impetus for history is as much the system-place as it is the member inhabitants.

A technical way of summarizing this is that communities, not less than individuals, are as idiographic (historically particular) as they are nomothetic (regular and lawlike).

Individuals in Communities

The Reality of Communities: Appropriate Levels of Control and Concern

Perhaps the good of the community, spoken of collectively, is just the goods of individuals distributively, conveniently aggregated—rather like the way a center of gravity in physics focuses at a point the masses of myriads of particles, or a mean in statistics averages as a single number the contributions of many data points. Perhaps the "community" is a metaphor for the goods of individuals, much as the goods of U.S. citizens are summed up as "the nation." When a hiker who has seen all the trees asks next, "Show me the forest," he has not understood that the forest is nothing more than the trees. Some community-level epiphenomena appear—communities have trophic patterns and organisms do not—but these are merely byproducts of interacting individuals. There is complicated life together, but without emergent system-level properties. The system is an ontological fiction. Only the organisms are real.

On the other hand, all nominalists soon learn to fear a slippery slope: communities are fictions, their organisms are real; organisms are fictions, their organs are real; organs are fictions, their cells are real—and so on down to atoms and quarks. But then we discover that quarks are just wave patterns, and then nothing seems real. Again, perhaps all these things are real, each at a different level. Trees seem as real as atoms.

After one has discarded category mistakes and associated prejudices for skin-in cooperation, centeredness, and so forth, there seems little reason to count one pattern (the organism) as real and another (the ecosystem) as unreal. Any level is real if there is significant downward causation. Thus the atom is real because that pattern shapes the behavior of electrons; the cell because that pattern shapes the behavior of amino acids; the organism because that pattern coordinates the behavior of hearts and lungs; the community because the niche shapes the morphology and behavior of the foxes within it. Being real at the level of community does not require sharp edges or complex centeredness, much less permanence; it requires only organization that shapes, perhaps freely so, the behavior of member/parts.

Humans may not have duties at every such level of organization. But humans have duties at appropriate survival-unit levels. The organism is one kind of survival unit, as the liver is not. The ecosystem is another: a comprehensive, critical survival unit without which organisms cannot survive. The patterns (energy flow, nutrient cycles, succession, historical trends) to which an organism must "tune in" are set "upstairs," though there are feedback and feedforward loops, and system-level patterns are altered by creativity arising from individual-level mutations and innovations. (We might also want to say that any level is real if there is upward causation.) Selection and support come "from outside" the skin boundary, "from above" the level of the organism. The community forces are prolific, though they are also stressful forces from the perspective of the individual.

Cultural versus Biotic Communities: Avoiding Confusion

Has the community priority over the individual? Individuals are ephemeral and dispensable, role players in a historical drama where even ecosystems—indispensable and perennial in native-range time frames—enter and exit on geological time scales. The prescription that seems to follow such a description is that communities are more important than individuals because they are relatively much longer-lasting. Giving more significance to communities than individuals is the (supposedly admirable) way that nature operates. But, moving from *is* to *ought*, this priority counters the respect for individual autonomy that has become the trademark of liberalism. Community dominance becomes a totalitarian juggernaut. Ethicists would at once censure a social community crushing individuals. Ethicists have fought to protect individuals from the tyrannies of culture. Must environmental ethicists reverse hard-won victories and give the community priority? To trump the individual seems retrogressive.

This fear is a confusion. For instance, returning to the quotation with which we began this chapter, had Leopold said, "A thing is right when it tends to preserve the integrity of the human *social* community," he would have on his hands most of the arguments between utilitarian and rights theorists, as well as disputes between liberal and conservative social theorists. A considerable case can be made for the descriptive fact that social forces do shape persons; they induce behavior more than liberals like to admit, and a less considerable case can be made that this ought to be so. Individuals who test whether personal preferences are right by asking what these preferences do to advance the good of nation, church, or heritage do not always have their priorities reversed. Leopold does think that ethics "tries to integrate the individual to society,"[19] and limits freedom in order to favor cooperative social conduct. Any social contract theorist would endorse as much.

But Leopold is making no serious claims about interhuman ethics. Nothing really follows from what *is* or *ought to be* in culture to what *is* or *ought to be* in nature. Sociologists, their studies of society in hand, would not tell ecologists what they must find descriptively about ecosystems; that would be a category mistake. Cultures are an organizational mode radically different from biotic communities. Social philosophers, with justice and charity praised in moral society, cannot tell environmental ethicists what is good and bad in amoral ecosystems, nor what is right and wrong when humans deal with ecosystems. That is another category mistake.

When humans gain a description of how ecosystems work, Leopold believes that a prescription arises to respect the beauty, integrity, and stability of such systems. That is not all of ethics, only an extension of it. Duties to other humans remain all they have ever been, but "the land" now counts too. Duties to humans (feeding the starving) that conflict with duties to ecosystems (preserving tropical forests) remain a quite unfinished agenda, but Leopold only wanted to start a dialogue that could not even begin when the land had no "biotic right" at all.[20]

Relations between individual and community have to be analyzed separately in the two communities. To know what a bee is in a beehive is to know what a good (functional) bee is in bee society, but (*pace* sociobiologists) nothing follows about how citizens function in nation-states or how they ought to. And vice versa. So, when humans confront beehives, complaints about a totalitarian society are confusions. Likewise, whether humans have duties to ecosystems must be asked without bias from human society. It may be proper to let Montana deer starve during a rough winter, following a bonanza summer when the population has edged over the carrying capacity. It would be monstrous to be so callous about African peoples caught in a drought. Even if their problems are ecologically aggravated, there are cultural dimensions and duties in any solution that are not considerations in deer management.

Priorities: Ecosystems over Individuals in Individualizing Ecosystems

In biotic communities, the community is the relevant survival unit; its beauty, integrity, and stability come first. Feral goats on San Clemente Island are degrading the ecosystem, and authorities who eliminate the goats are overriding individual goat welfare out of respect for the ecosystem (see Chapter 4). When park officials refused to treat pinkeye in Yellowstone's bighorn sheep, although half the herd became blind and died through starvation and injury (see Chapter 2), officials argued that the Yellowstone ecosystem should be preserved as untampered with as possible and that its processes included the struggle between mammals and their natural parasites. Foresters may let wildfires burn, destroying individual plants and animals, because fires rejuvenate the system.

But we need to bring back into focus the looseness, decentralized order, and pluralism of biotic communities. Within an individual organism the organs are so tightly integrated that we do not term the organism a community at all. No one complains that the goods of heart and liver are only instrumental to the good of the organism. But communities, social or biotic, never have this kind of organization. Biotic communities leave individuals "on their own" as autonomous centers, spontaneous somatic selves defending their life program. Thus, Yellowstone bighorns should be left "on their own" to combat the *Chlamydia* microbe; San Clemente plants should be left "on their own" in their island ecosystem, even though this requires that they be protected against feral goats that humans have introduced, disrupting the system.

Ecosystems bind life up into discrete individuals and cast them forth to make a way resourcefully through their environment. So far from being a regimented community, the wilderness has seemed anarchy to many observers, who, viewing the pulling and hauling, are more likely to complain that there is no community at all than to complain that the individual is subordinated to the community. The picture we need, however, is of community that packages everything up into individual lives and binds them together loosely (= freely) enough that individuals remain gems in a setting, yet tightly enough that the generating, maintaining system is prior to individual life.

Evolutionary ecosystems maximize individuality in several ways. First, the stochastic contingencies and idiographic historicity that beset each particular organism in its environment make its characteristics and fortunes more or less different. There is a wildness in ecosystems that resists being completely specified in geology, botany, zoology, and ecology textbooks, even when principles set forth in theories are coupled with initial conditions. Scientific laws never catch in individual detail all that goes on in a particular place—Okefenokee Swamp or Bryce Canyon—and each new lake and canyon will have some differences. No matter how well one knows a particular place, tomorrow and next year will bring surprises. This fact is logically and empirically entwined with the heightened individuality of each inhabitant. Each life is given a unique genetic set and lived in a unique place. Some unrelated causal lines and even indeterminate lines meet and make every individual a one-time event. No two coyotes in Bryce Canyon or even two maple trees in the Okefenokee Swamp are alike. Sometimes the differences are insignificant, but sometimes they yield significant individuality. Any organization that removed the diversity, the looseness, the "disorder," the historical particularity of place and individual would impoverish the ecosystem and the individuality of its member individuals.

Second, over geological time evolutionary ecosystems have steadily increased the numbers of species on Earth from zero to five million or more. Extinction and respeciation have increasingly differentiated more natural kinds. As Leopold wrote, "Science has given us many doubts, but it has given us at least one certainty: the trend of evolution is to elaborate and diversify the biota."[21] G. G. Simpson, after surveying the fossil record and noticing that there are exceptions, concluded:

> The evidence warrants considering general in the course of evolution . . . a tendency for life to expand, to fill in all available spaces in the liveable environments, including those created by the process of that expansion itself. . . . The total number and variety of organisms existing in the world has shown a tendency to increase markedly during the history of life.[22]

Although locally poor in a desert or on a polar ice cap, Earth's ecosystems in the aggregate are many-splendored things. Elton found that 5,000 species of animals inhabited two square miles of Wytham Wood in Britain.[23]

Third, superimposed on this increase of quantity, the quality of individual lives in the upper trophic rungs of the ecological pyramid has risen. One-celled organisms evolved into many-celled, highly integrated organisms. Photosynthesis supports locomotion—swimming, walking, running, flight. Stimulus-response mechanisms become complex instinctive acts. Warm-blooded animals follow cold-blooded ones. Neural complexity, conditioned behavior, and learning emerge. Sentience appears— sight, smell, hearing, taste, pleasure, pain. Brains couple with hands. Consciousness and self-consciousness arise. Subjective life is superposed on objective life. Persons appear with intense concentrated unity, and nature transcends itself in culture. These are liberating developments in the ecosystem; they free individuals. A falcon is more liberated in its ecosystem than is the grass downward in its food chain (even though the grass is an autotroph, and relatively more self-sufficient); the falcon can overlook a territory, migrate, switch prey. This is community looseness now interpreted positively as nourishing individuality.

These developments do not take place in all ecosystems or at every level. Microbes continue, as do plants and lower animals.

These kinds serve continuing roles. All the understories remain occupied. If they did not, the quantity of life and its diverse qualities would diminish. Most creatures are cryptogams, dicots, monocots, fungi, bacteria, protozoans, beetles, mollusks, crustaceans, and the like. Simpson finds:

> Few, if any, of the broadest and most basic types have ever become extinct. . . . All main types represent abilities to follow broadly distinctive ways of life, and the earlier or lower persist along with the later and higher because these latter represent not competitors doing the same sorts of things as their lower ancestors but groups developing distinctively new ways of life.[24]

Sometimes there is retrograde evolution, as in tapeworms or viruses, when once free-living organisms lose eyes, legs, metabolisms, or even brains—although retrograde evolution requires that such organisms live in an environment more complex than they are themselves, so that they can borrow their lost skills from their hosts.

Meanwhile, the quality of individuality generated at the top rises; both the quantity and the quality of individuality intensify. There is a sort of push-up, lock-up, ratchet effect that conserves the upstrokes and the outreaches. The accelerations and elaborations are selected—not all life forms are accelerated or elaborated, but the later we go in time the more accelerated are the forms at the top of the tropic pyramids, the more elaborated are the multiple tropic pyramids of Earth. There are upward arrows over evolutionary time.

This has continued despite at least five catastrophic extinctions, so anomalous that many scientists look to extraterrestrial causes: supernovae, collisions with asteroids, or oscillations of the solar system above and below the plane of the galaxy. Regardless of their causes, the crashes were followed by swift resurrections, often with novel and advanced forms (this trend is shown in Figure 4.1). Optimization of fitness seems to increase through evolutionary time. As a result of what Whittaker called species packing (Chapter 4), there are vastly more individuals and species and they are better fits in their communities.

These developments in natural history are not just a random walk, not just drift. They reveal the rationality of the system, including trial and error. Spasmodic on short ranges, rather like the episodic upset of succession, these prolific trends are a recurrent tendency on long-range scales. Sometimes the evolutionary (like the ecosystemic) processes seem wandering and wayward, loose, but the results are considerable. There is dice-throwing, but the dice are loaded. The probabilities show causal connections, "weak" laws in that they are not deterministic but stochastic, historical trends that reveal the prolific strength of the system. Though it can seem indifferent to life, this system in which all individuals are perpetually perishing is the system that creates life and exemplifies it in individuals of increasing number, kind, and quality over several billion years of evolutionary time. The journey from zero to five million species, from microbes to men, can hardly be an accidental result of lifeless physicochemical forces, or even the byproduct of individual organisms pursuing their several and separate life programs. The story seems some kind of steady, if statistical, heading of the system.

The community beauty, integrity, and constancy includes a persistent selecting for individuality. That is a strange, liberating "priority" or "heading" of the system: escalation of individuals in kind and complexity, in quantity and quality, never producing two of a kind exactly alike—yet accomplished without extinguishing many, or any, of the broad, basic "lower" ancestral types. That process is as much to be defended as any of its products. The goods and "rights" of individuals (their flourishing and freedom) belong in such a system; the ecosystem itself promotes them in its own way. When humans enter the scene, they should in this respect follow nature. Individual welfare is both promoted by and subordinated to the generating communal forces.

Intrinsic, Instrumental, and Systemic Values

Instrumental value uses something as a means to an end; *intrinsic value* is found worthwhile in itself without necessary contributory reference. Leopold laments that nature has previously been considered to have only instrumental value for humans, who are regarded as the sole holders of intrinsic value. Those sensitive to ecology will revise their axiology (toward which we are headed in Chapter 6). An immediate conclusion is that apart from any human presence, organisms value other organisms and earthen resources instrumentally. Organisms are selective systems. Plants make resourceful use of water and sunshine. Insects value the energy that plants have fixed by photosynthesis; warblers value insect protein; falcons value warblers. Value capture and transformation propel an ecosystem. An organism is an aggrandizing unit on the hunt for instrumental values.

In a continuation of this logic, organisms value these resources instrumentally because they value something intrinsically: their selves, their form of life. No warbler eats insects in order to become food for a falcon; the warbler defends her own life as an end in itself and makes more warblers as she can. From the perspective of a warbler, being a warbler is a good thing. A blackpoll warbler is a good kind; a blackpoll tries to be good-of-its-kind. A life is defended intrinsically, without further contributory reference—unless to defend the species and that still is to defend a form of life as an end in itself. Such defenses go on before humans are present; and thus both instrumental and intrinsic values are objectively present in ecosystems. The system is a web where loci of intrinsic value are meshed in a network of instrumental value (see Figure 6.6).

Neither of these traditional terms is completely satisfactory at the level of the holistic ecosystem. Member components serve the system, as when warblers regulate insect populations; perhaps that is systemic instrumental value. But—if we reconsider this terminology—the decentered system, despite its successions and headings, has no integrated program, nothing it is defending, and to say that an ecosystem makes instrumental use of warblers to regulate insect populations seems awkward. We might say that the system itself has intrinsic value; it is, after all, the womb of life. Yet again, the "loose" system, though it has value *in* itself, does not seem to have any value *for* itself, as organisms do seem to have. It is not a value owner, though it is a value producer. It is not a value beholder; it is a value holder in the sense that it projects, conserves, elaborates value holders (organisms).

Nevertheless the system-field has characteristics that are as vital for life as any property contained within particular organisms. Organisms defend only their own selves or kinds, but the system spins a bigger story. Organisms defend their continuing survival; ecosystems promote new arrivals. Species *increase their kind;* but ecosystems *increase kinds,* superposing the latter increase onto the former. *Ecosystems are selective systems, as surely as organisms are selective systems.* The natural selection comes out of the system and is imposed on the individual. The individual is programmed to make more of its kind, but more is going on systemically than that; the system is making more kinds. This extends natural selection theory beyond the merely tautological formulation that the system selects the best adapted to survive. Ecosystems select for those features that appear over the long ranges, for individuality, for diversification, for sufficient containment, for quality supervening quantity of life. They do this, appropriately to the community level, by employing conflict, decenteredness, probability, succession, spontaneous generation of order, and historicity.

We are no longer confronting instrumental value, as though the system were of value instrumentally as a fountain of life. Nor is the question one of intrinsic value, as though the system defended some unified form of life for itself. We have reached something for which we need a third term: *systemic value*. This cardinal value, like the history, is not all encapsulated in individuals; it too is smeared out into the system. The value in this system is not just the sum of the part-values. No part values increase of kinds, but the system promotes such increase. Systemic value is the productive process; its products are intrinsic values woven into instrumental relationships. Systemic value is what we will call in Chapter 6 *projective nature*. When humans awaken to their presence in such a biosphere, finding themselves to be products of this process—whatever they make of their cultures and anthropocentric preferences, their duties to other humans or to individual animals and plants—they owe something to this beauty, integrity, and persistence in the biotic community. Ethics is not complete until extended to the land.

Duties arise to the individual animals and plants that are produced as loci of intrinsic value within the system; these were the duties defined in Chapters 2 and 3. Duties also arise to the species that overleap individual lives; these were the duties defined in Chapter 4. But that is not all. Now we place the preceding duties in their environment. Duties arise in encounter with the system that projects and protects, regenerates and reforms all these member components in biotic community. These duties to individuals and species, so far from being in conflict with duties to ecosystems, are duties toward its products and headings. The levels differ, but, seen at depth, they integrate. Perhaps on some occasions duties to the products will override duties to the system that produced them, but—apart from humans who live in culture as well as in nature—this will seldom be true.

Perhaps we can even go the system one better. Life needs its habitats, and certain ocean bottoms can be relatively barren of life because there are no refuges there. By sinking derelict freighters or abandoned cars, humans are creating reeflike oases on the ocean floor. These artificial reefs are havens for underwater life: colorful corals and sponges, anemones, algae and other marine plants, barnacles, mussels, crustaceans, schools of fish. They do not simply concentrate life previously present; they multiply up to twelve times what was there before. This flourishing of marine life is also often a good thing for humans, who can increase their catch of fish or enjoy the reefs as scuba divers. About 400 such man-made reefs have been established off United States coasts; Japan has set aside $1 billion to create 2,500 of them.[25]

Such encouragement of additional life, though the reefs are artificial, seems in a way to be following nature while also exceeding what nature has produced at these localities. It projects further the historic tendency of the prolife system to multiply niches and fill them up with kinds, even though this tendency has been little realized on the degraded ocean floor. Nature can be locally barren, however globally dominant the productive tendencies we have been analyzing. It need not follow that deserts and tundras ought to be watered and heated until they teem with life; desert and polar ecosystems are admirable communities just because of the special tenacity and intensity of the struggle for life there. The duty to produce further life may be optional in a way that the duty to protect existing life is not. We will seldom want to add exotic plants and animals to existing ecosystems, even when we are sure the exotics can be fitted in without upsetting the natives. But in a dynamic ecosystem, we cannot assume that the optimum beauty, stability, and fertility of the landscape, though a heading of the system, has already been reached.

Subjective Experience and Evolutionary Ecosystems

Some will still object: cooperation versus conflict, centered cybernetic autonomy versus loose stochastic process, succession and natural history, systemic values—none of this has touched the nerve of the matter. The final, fundamental problem is that ecosystems have no subjectivity, no felt experiences. Organisms with central nervous systems have psychological life, manifestly present by introspection in human lives and easy to extend to some nonhumans—more so to chimpanzees, less so to birds. Plants are objects with life but not subjects of a life. But ecosystems are doubtfully objects at all; rather they are communities mostly of living objects and sparsely of living subjects. No such collection can of itself count morally; any duties must attach to the few subjects who inhabit such places.

An ecosystem cannot be satisfied when given wilderness status; a person can be satisfied when a wilderness is designated. Even coyotes can be satisfied within such a wilderness. Such psychological satisfaction is what the inside/outside issue should have been identifying. The skin is not a morally relevant boundary; rather the boundary is subjective inwardness versus objective metabolisms and ecologies. Duties may *concern* ecosystems but must be *to* subjects. With similar reasoning, we earlier heard some ethicists object to duties to plants and species.

The attractiveness of the duties-to-subjects-only position is that the duties we first know in interhuman ethics are indeed to subjects. An ethicist can always stipulate that duties must always be directed toward subjects and that a mere object, even one with life, is a misplaced target for duty. This can seem right because it is so familiar (within the family!). Any duties that involve living or nonliving objects must be reduced to duties to subjects. No doubt some duties do attach only to subjects; some make sense only with human subjects. Persons ought not to be insulted, but squirrels do not suffer much from verbal insults. To subjects of a psychological life one may have a duty not to cause needless pain, perhaps not to interfere with their pleasures without justification. We have duties to persons to preserve the integrity, beauty, and stability in whatever biotic communities these persons enjoy and resourcefully use.

But from the ecological point of view the subjectivist position takes a part for the whole. It has a subjective bias. It values a late product of the system, psychological life, and subordinates everything else to this. It mistakes a fruit for the whole plant, the last chapter for the whole story. It orders all duty around an extended pleasure/pain axis, from richer down through poorer experiences. Such an ethic is really a kind of psychological hedonism, often quite enlightened. Still, ecosystems are not merely affairs of psychological pains and pleasures. They are life, flourishing in interdependencies pressed for creative evolution. The satisfaction defended at this level is not subjective preference but the sufficient containment of species.

Here we do not want a subjective morality but an objective one, even though we find that subjectivity is the most valuable output of the objective system. Is there any reason for ethical subjects to discount the vital systemic processes unless and until accompanied by sentience? Perhaps to evaluate the entire biological world on the basis of sentience is as much a category mistake as to assess it according to the justice and charity found there. The one mistake judges biological places by extension from psychology, the other from culture. What is "right" about the biological world is not just the production of pleasures and positive experiences. What is "right" includes ecosystemic patterns: organisms in their generating, sustaining environments.

True, the highest value attained in the system is lofty individuality with its subjectivity, present in vertebrates, mammals, primates, and preeminently in persons. This is where the most significant of evolutionary arrows tends. But such products are not the sole loci of value, concentrate value though they do. Even the most valuable of the parts is of less value than the whole. The objective, systemic process is an overriding value, not because it is indifferent to individuals but because the process is both prior to and productive of individuality.

Subjects count, but they do not count so much that they can degrade or shut down the system, though they count enough to have the right to flourish within the system. Subjective self-satisfactions are, and ought to be, sufficiently contained within the objectively satisfactory system. The system creates life, selects for adaptive fit, constructs increasingly richer life in quantity and quality, supports myriads of species, escalates individuality, autonomy, and even subjectivity within the limits of decentralized community. If such land is not an admirable, satisfactory biotic community, why not?

6   The Concept of Natural Value: A Theory for Environmental Ethics

 "YOU SEE, I am fond of learning. Now the country places and trees won't teach me anything, and the people in the city do."[1] Socrates loved the city with its politics and culture but avoided nature as profitless and boring. On the other hand, when John Muir finished his formal education and went to live in the Sierra Nevadas, he wrote, "I was only leaving one University for another, the Wisconsin University for the University of the Wilderness."[2] No education is complete until one has a concept of nature, and no ethics is complete until one has an appropriate respect for fauna, flora, landscapes, and ecosystems. This involves following nature in what we have called axiological and tutorial senses (Chapter 1).

The preceding chapters have asked about duties to animals, plants, species, and ecosystems. We have reached the point for an overview of the concept of natural value, resurveying the ground over which we have been traveling, now from the perspective of value theory. The previous chapter explored ecosystems and their values; we next need an account of humans valuing within ecosystems. A further question we explore is whether and how abiotic nature, as well as biotic nature, can have value.

Valuing Projective Nature

From earth to Earth

The belief that dirt could have intrinsic value is sometimes taken as a kind of ultimate foolishness, a *reductio ad absurdum* in environmental philosophy. Dirt is instrumentally valuable but not the sort of thing that has value by itself, certainly not any value that could make a claim on humans. Putting it like that, we agree. An isolated clod defends no intrinsic value, and it is difficult to say that it has much value in itself. But that is not the end of the matter, because a handful of dirt is integrated into an ecosystem;

192

earth is a part, Earth the whole. Dirt is product and process in a systemic nature that we do respect.

Edward O. Wilson writes:

> Think of scooping up a handful of soil and leaf litter and placing it on a white cloth—as a field biologist would do—for closer examination. This unprepossessing lump contains more order and richness of structure, and particularly of history, than the entire surface of all the other (lifeless) planets. It is a miniature wilderness that would take almost forever to explore, should we choose to make the organisms in it the objects of serious biological study. Every species living there is the product of millions of years of history, having evolved under the harshest conditions of competition and survival. Each organism is the repository of an immense amount of genetic information.
>
> The abundance of the organisms increases downward, according to size, like layers in a pyramid. The handful of soil and litter is home for dozens of insects, mites, nematode worms, and other small invertebrates, most of which are just visible to the naked eye. There are also about a million fungi and ten billion bacteria, mostly microscopic. Each of the species has a distinct life cycle fitted to a portion of the micro-environment in which it thrives and reproduces. The individuality of each is programmed by an exact sequence of nucleotides, the ultimate molecular units of the genes. These species have evolved as independent elements for thousands of generations.[3]

In the language of computer science, a single bacterium possesses about ten million bits of genetic information, a fungus one billion, and an insect up to ten billion bits. The amount of information in an insect, printed in ordinary English, would stretch over a thousand miles. The information in a typical clump of dirt would fill numerous public libraries. So more is buried in dirt than first seems; dirt is part of a global natural history. Socrates could have unearthed from dirt far more than he suspected; Muir would have been wise indeed had he known all the goings on in the humus, let alone what the Sierras had to teach. An ethic needs an appropriate way of valuing the systemic, historic nature in which dirt figures so prominently.

Even Wilson's concern for a handful of soil seems largely directed to the life in it, so we should try next to get the global picture by switching from a lump of dirt to the Earth system in which it has been created. Located at a felicitous distance from the sun, Earth has liquid water, atmosphere, a suitable mix of elements, compounds, minerals, and an ample supply of energy.

Radioactivity deep within the Earth produces enough heat to keep its crust constantly mobile in counteraction with erosional forces, and the interplay of such forces generates and regenerates landscapes and seas—mountains, canyons, rivers, plains, islands, volcanoes, estuaries, continental shelves.

The Earth and its solar system are perhaps five billion years old. About three billion years ago, life evolved. In the chemical evolution of life, the first stage is relatively unproblematic; amino acids were constructed by energy radiated over inorganic materials. The second stage is more difficult. Many amino acids had to be assembled into long polypeptide chains, with no previous templates or enzymes for their hooking up, with no information to steer the process. Nevertheless, this somehow managed to happen, and these polypeptide chains folded into complex functional structures, preproteins. In a third stage, when the polypeptide sequence was suitable, there was a self-folding intrinsic to the chemical structures.

Coincident with this, in a fourth stage, other molecules formed which, under the electrostatic pressures of water, organized into hollow microspheres, the empty prototypes of cells. These spheres came to envelop the preproteins, protecting the about-to-be-life chemistries from degradation by the outside environment and providing a semipermeable membrane across which the necessary nutrient inputs and waste outputs could take place. Metabolism and life got underway. What was before merely a landscape or seascape became an ecosystem. What was only a place became a home.

Somehow too, in a fifth stage, in ways only dimly understood, life learned to replicate itself. Part of the genius of replication is that there is also variation and development. At this point biological evolution and natural selection arose, with the differential survival of the better adapted. Again in ways for which biology has little theory, the pressures for survival proved to be pressures for complex development, not in all but in some lines of descent (ascent). Evolution has steadily introduced new forms, some replacements merely comparable to those gone extinct but some with newly acquired skills—metazoans with specialized cells, photosynthetic forms, sexuality, neurons, muscles, sentience, instincts, brains, behavior, the capacity to acquire information through experience, to live on land or fly through the air.

In result we have ecosystemic nature set in its landscapes and seas. The whole storied natural history is little short of a series of "miracles," wondrous, fortuitous events, unfolding of potential; and when Earth's most complex product, *Homo sapiens*, becomes intelligent enough to reflect over this cosmic wonderland, we are left stuttering about the mixtures of accident and necessity out of which we have come.

From Earth to Universe

If we look further than our Earth environment, the heavens at first seem a vast, hostile wasteland as much as a wonderland. Nothing seems more valueless than a distant asteroid or a lifeless star. But this picture too has been refocused by recent science. Nature on the cosmic scale is a vast energetic system, beginning some fifteen to twenty billion years ago in an incredible explosion and ever since expanding, cooling, developing. From this primordial energy, matter was formed—mostly hydrogen and helium.

A striking property is that the universe is prone to form pacts of energetic matter, stars assembled in galaxies, and these stars have served as furnaces in which all the higher elements have been forged, with a cooking time of many millions of years. The products have included carbon, oxygen, nitrogen, iron, silicon, and other elements in proportions that later proved propitious for evolving dirt and, out of the dirt, life. Certain of the stars exploded as supernovae and scattered their elements in space, but gravitational forces recollected these into clumps called planets, at least in our own solar system and presumably elsewhere. So the dirt that is the precursor of life is really fossil stardust.

Astronomy has become sufficiently mathematical to calculate that there are many physical constants and processes, both at microphysical and astronomical levels, that strikingly fit together to result in what has happened. B. J. Carr and M. J. Rees, cosmologists, explain:

> The basic features of galaxies, stars, planets and the everyday world are essentially determined by a few microphysical constants and by the effects of gravitation. Many interrelations between different scales that at first sight seem surprising are straightforward consequences of simple physical arguments. But several aspects of our Universe—some of which seem to be prerequisites for the evolution of any form of life—depend rather delicately on apparent "coincidences" among the physical constants. . . . The Universe must be as big and diffuse as it is to last long enough to give rise to life.[4]

Bernard Lovell, an astronomer, finds it an "astonishing reflection" that

> a remarkable and intimate relationship between man, the fundamental constants of nature and the initial moments of space and time seems to be an inescapable condition of our existence. . . . Human existence is itself entwined with the primeval state of the universe."[5]

Mike Corwin, a physicist, concludes:

> This 20-billion-year journey seems at first glance tortuous and convoluted, and our very existence appears to be the merest happenstance. On closer examination, however, we will see that quite the opposite is true—intelligent life seems predestined from the very beginning. . . . Life and consciousness are not only the direct result of the initial conditions, but could only have resulted from a narrow range of initial conditions. . . . Any significant change in the initial conditions would have ruled out the possibility of life evolving later. . . . The universe would have evolved as a lifeless, unconscious entity. Yet here we are, alive and aware, in a universe with just the right ingredients for our existence.[6]

P. C. W. Davies, a theoretical physicst, finds numerous properties in microphysics, astronomy, and chemistry "fine-tuned to such stunning accuracy" that "had this exceedingly delicate tuning of values been even slightly upset, the subsequent structure of the universe would have been totally different" and life impossible. "A hidden principle seems to be at work, organizing the cosmos in a coherent way."[7]

"This universe breeds life inevitably," asserts George Wald, an evolutionary biochemist.[8] After a long study of the possibility of the evolution of biological molecules capable of self-organization, Manfred Eigen, a thermodynamicist, concludes "that the evolution of life . . . must be considered an *inevitable* process despite its indeterminate course."[9] But we hardly know whether to put it that strongly, since nothing suggests much coding for life in the microscopic particles as such, and life is presumably quite rare in the universe. Still, life does seem to be some sort of accident waiting to happen. Astronomers speak with excitement of the "anthropic principle," which holds that the universe is constructed with a tendency to evolve life and mind. At the same time, evolutionary biologists can be adamant that nothing in evolutionary theory guarantees the ascent of ever more complex forms.

For environmental ethics, "anthropic principle" is an unfortunately chosen term, one that no ecologist would have selected. We wish to avoid associating anthropocentrism with the process, especially any suggestion that everything in the universe is arranged to produce and serve humans. But what the anthropic principle points to is important—a rich, fertile nature that is energetic and creative, so much so that at length nature evolves life and mind. That may involve some accident, but it cannot be all accident; it is in some sense a property, a potential of systemic nature that it projects natural history.

David Hume claimed that nature "has no more regard to good above ill than to heat above cold, or to drought above moisture, or to light above heavy."[10] Or to life above nonlife, he probably would have added. That indifference can seem true in the short range, though day-to-day nature is an impressive life-support system. Sometimes it even seems true in the long range: every organism dies; species go extinct. Nature doesn't care.

Yet nature has spun quite a story, first in the heavens and later on Earth, making this planet with its landscapes, seascapes, and going from zero to five million species in five billion years. Perhaps to say that nature "has regard" for life is the wrong way of phrasing it; we do not want to ascribe purpose to nature. At the same time something is going on—systematically, historically. We live in what K. G. Denbigh calls "an inventive universe."[11] We confront a *projective nature*, one restlessly full of projects— stars, comets, planets, moons, and also rocks, crystals, rivers, canyons, seas. The life in which these astronomical and geological processes culminate is still more impressive, but it is of a piece with the whole projective system. Everything is made out of dirt and water, stellar stuff, and funded with stellar energy. One cannot be impressed with life in isolation from its originating matrix. Nature is a fountain of life, and the whole fountain—not just the life that issues from it—is of value. Nature is genesis, Genesis.

Values in Projective, Systemic Nature

Environmental ethics asks: What is an appropriate attitude toward such a projective system? Has it any value? any claim on human behavior? Ethics begins in interactions between persons, and at this scope nature is a *resource*. At first it seems right to say that our duties are to persons, and that dirt, water, air, minerals, rivers, landscapes are instrumental in such duty. But there comes a point in environmental ethics when we ask about our *sources*, not just our *resources*. The natural environment is discovered to be the womb in which we are generated and which we really never leave. That is the original meaning of *nature*, from the Latin *natans*, giving birth, Mother Earth.

From a short-range, subjective perspective we can say that the value of nature lies in its generation and support of human life and is therefore only instrumental. But from a longer-range, objective perspective systemic nature is valuable intrinsically as a projective system, with humans only one sort of its projects, though perhaps the highest. The system is of value for its capacity to throw forward (pro-ject) all the storied natural history. On that scale humans come late and it seems shortsighted and arrogant for such latecomers to say that the system is only of instrumental value for humans, who alone possess intrinsic value, or who "project" intrinsic value back to nature. Both of these are inappropriate responses. The only fully responsible behavior is to seek an appreciative relationship to the parental environment, which is projecting all this display of value.

It is likewise shortsighted to say that the only value in the system is its production of life, although this is of greatest moment within it. True, the astronomical and geological phases are precursors to life, but that does not reduce them to mere instrumental value. Nature is not inert and passive until acted upon resourcefully by life and mind. Neither sentience nor consciousness are necessary for inventive processes to occur. The inventiveness of systemic nature is the root of all value, and all nature's created products have value so far as they are inventive achievements.

Nonbiotic things have no information in them, no genome, much less sentience or experience. There are no cells, no organs, no skin, no metabolisms. Impressed with the display of life and personality on Earth, we correctly attach most of our ethical concern to persons and to organisms; but we may incorrectly assume that mere things are beyond appropriate and inappropriate consideration.

A "mere thing" can, however, be something to be respected, the project of projective nature. Crystals, volcanoes, geysers, headlands, rivers, springs, moons, cirques, paternoster lakes, buttes, mesas, canyons—these also are among the natural kinds. They do not have organic integrity or individuality; they are constantly being built, altered, their identity in flux. But they are recognizably different from their background and surroundings. They may have striking particularity, symmetry, harmony, grace, story, spatiotemporal unity and continuity, even though they are also diffuse, partial, broken. They do not have wills or interests but rather headings, trajectories, traits, successions, beginnings, endings, cycles, which give them a tectonic integrity. They can be projects (products) of quality. The question now is not "Can they suffer?" or "Is it alive?" but "What deserves appreciation?"

In nature there is a negentropic constructiveness in dialectic with an entropic teardown, a model of working for which we hardly yet have an adequate scientific, much less a valuational, theory. Yet this is nature's most striking feature, one that ultimately must be valued and of value. In one sense we say (with Hume) that nature is indifferent to planets, mountains, rivers, and trilliums. But in a more profound sense nature has bent toward making and remaking these objects (= projects), and millions of other kinds, for several billion years. These performances are worth noticing—remarkable, memorable—and they are worth noticing not just because of their tendencies to produce something else, certainly not merely because of their tendency to produce this noticing in certain recent subjects, our human selves. They are loci of value so far as they are products of systemic nature in its formative processes. The opening movements of a symphony contribute to the power of the finale, but they are not merely of instrumental value; they are of value for what they are in themselves. The splendors of the heavens and the marvels of Earth do not lie simply in their roles as a fertilizer for life or a stimulator of experience. There is value wherever there is positive creativity.

In Mammoth Cave, in a section named Turner Avenue, there are rooms laden with gypsum crystals spun as fine threads, a rare formation known as "angel hair." So fragile are these needles that humans passing through and disturbing the air destroy the hair-thin filaments. This part of the cave is closed, never visited by tourists and only on exceptional occasions by mineralogists. A nonbiotic work of nature (a kind of dirt!) is here protected at the cost of depriving humans of access to it. This park policy is partly for humanistic reasons: to preserve angel hair for scientific research. But it also involves an appreciation of angel hair as a project of systemic nature. Angel hair counts morally in the sense that natural value here lays a claim on human behavior.

It was once the practice in Yellowstone National Park to put soap into certain geysers (altering the surface tension of the water) in order to time the eruptions conveniently for tourists. For almost a century the Park Service at Yosemite built an enormous fire on the lip of Glacier Point at dusk. "Indian Love Call" was played, and the fire pushed over the cliff to the ahs! of spectators. But the spectacle has now been discontinued as inappropriate. Bridges, simply for amusement, have been built defacing Royal Gorge in Colorado and Grandfather Mountain in North Carolina, and highways constructed to the 14,000-foot summits of Colorado's Mount Evans and Pike's Peak. George Washington carved his initials in rock on Virginia's Natural Bridge and left his signature in Madison's Cave at Grand Caverns, as did hundreds of others, including Thomas Jefferson and James Madison.

Mount Rushmore, South Dakota, has been carved into a monument to national pride with the faces of four presidents and has provoked a response at nearby Crazy Horse, a (partially completed) mountain-sized Indian on his horse. Stone Mountain, Georgia, is a monument to the Old South. Christo built of white fabric a twenty-five-mile-long, eighteen-foot-high, artistic *Running Fence* over California ranchland, range, cliffs, and seashore, ending in the sea. The cost was $3 million, and the fence was taken down after a few weeks. His *Valley Curtain* across a Colorado canyon was an orange sheet 1,300 feet long and 300 feet high; it cost $700,000 and was ripped apart by winds as soon as it was completed. (Poetic justice?) His *Surrounded Islands* enveloped eleven islands with 5.5 million square feet of pink plastic. Walter De Maria used a bulldozer to cut *The Circumflex*, a shallow trench eight feet wide and more than a mile long in a desert wilderness (privately owned), cut in the shape of a loop in a rope. Michael Heizer built *Complex One*, a rectangular mound twenty-three feet high, 140 feet long, of concrete and earth in an otherwise untouched, extremely remote high desert plateau. His *Double Negative* is a fifty-foot by thirty-foot double cut that is 1,500 feet long, displacing 240,000 tons of rhyolote and sandstone in Virgin River Mesa, Nevada.[12]

Some claim that such environmental artworks provide positive aesthetic experience in stark polarity with virgin nature. Any damage to the environment, whether to ecosystems, wildlife, or scenery, is justified by the positive drama of big-scale art in antithesis/synthesis with nature. These artists may not be claiming that virgin nature is aesthetically bad or neutral; to the contrary, they want the natural scene as a support and contrast for their works. Where these works are ephemeral, they can perhaps be tolerated. Their environmental impact is thereby reduced, although they may still be an aesthetic affront to nature. But where they mar landscapes, mountains, deserts, what they do is of moral concern because destruction of value is wrong. At least the burden of proof lies with the artists to show that their complex of art and nature augments values present.

We may not want any more summit roads up fourteeners, or fun-bridges over gorges, or carved-up mountains, firefalls, valley curtains, soap in geysers, or names written over rock cliffs or stalagmites, because a developing environmental ethics insists that there is a better way to behave at these places, one that recognizes their site integrity and accepts them as givens of projective nature. We will leave the pyramids on the sands of Egypt for historic reasons but oppose carving a president's face on Yosemite's Half Dome. These are questions of right conduct. We will say that humans can have no duties to clouds or dust devils, even though these are temporary aggregations with enough identity for us to say where they start and stop. They have little integrated process in them. But toward other projects in nature there is irresponsible (inappropriately responsive) behavior.

The Mount of the Holy Cross is another of Colorado's fifty-four fourteeners, famous for the giant snow cross formed by whim of nature in couloirs and ledges on its north face. The ascent requires a fourteen-mile hike through spectacular alpine wilderness, with an arduous gain, loss, and regain of elevation. A ranger on patrol met a group of climbers, one of whom bragged (unaware who the ranger was) that he was going to celebrate reaching the summit by throwing rolls of toilet paper off the top. The ranger replied that this was "uncalled for." His reasons included humanistic ones (trashing up the place irritates later climbers), but they also involved a naturalistic respect for place. A shallow ethics will say that such appropriate behavior is only a matter of cultivating human excellences (Chapter 3, pp. 117–19). A deeper ethics finds a natural project out there that "calls for" respect. It is as reasonable to say that such objective (projective) achievements are of value in themselves as to say that the only value is subjective human excellence generated in the presence of nature's wonders.

Valuing in Ecosystems

We next present an explanation sketch of valuing consistent with natural history.[13] Our inquiry is about natural value of the kind met in unlabored contexts, as in pure rather than applied

science, in contemplative outdoor recreation rather than in industry, in ecology rather than in economics, in thinking of nature as
a source past its being a resource. We are not considering, for instance, how molybdenum has value as an alloy of steel, a use that
it does not have in spontaneous nature. Further, we should be cautioned against thinking that nature has a single kind or few kinds
of value, or no disvalues. Nature is a plural system with values
unevenly distributed and counterthrusting. Like the meanings in
life, values too may come piecemeal and occasionally. Still, they
come regularly enough for us to wonder whether we are coping
with some value-tending in the system.

From Dialectical to Evolutionary Value

Consider a causal sequence (A, B, C, D) leading to the production of an event associated with natural value (E_{nv}) that produces
an event of experienced value (E_{xv}), perhaps of the beauty in a
waterfall or the wealth of life in a tidal zone (Figure 6.1). A human consciousness responds to the waterfall or estuary, so that we
need a reverse arrow (↓) making the encounter relational. One is
first tempted to say that value does not lie in either polar part, but
is generated in their relations. Like science or recreation, valuing
before nature is an interactive event.

But with this, more has been allocated to the natural world
than may at first be recognized. The act of responding (response-
ability) has been ecologically grounded. The subjective self is not a
polar opposite to objective nature, not in the dyadic relation suggested by the paired arrows set at right angles to the ongoing,
objective causal chain. Rather, the self is enclosed by its environment so that the person values in environmental exchange, in the
diagrammed case and in myriads of others (E'_{nv}, E''_{nv}) only suggested in Figure 6.2. The self has a semipermeable membrane.

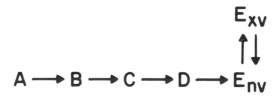

$$E_{xv}$$
$$\uparrow\downarrow$$
$$A \longrightarrow B \longrightarrow C \longrightarrow D \longrightarrow E_{nv}$$

FIGURE 6.1 *A causal sequence producing a valued event.*

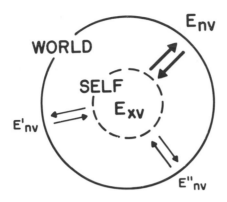

FIGURE 6.2 *A self evaluating the world.*

The setting is a given, a datum of nature, even though the subject must respond in imaginatively resourceful ways. I see things out there in the "field" which I choose to value or disvalue. But on deeper examination I find myself, a valuing agent, located within that circumscribing field. I as subject do not have the valued object in "my field" but find myself emplaced in a concentric field for valuing. The whole possibility is among natural events, including the openness in my appraising. John Dewey remarked that "experience is *of* as well as *in* nature."[14] We say that valuing is *in* as well as *of* nature. What seems a dialectical relationship is an ecological one. The whole happening, subject and its valued object, occurs in a natural ambience (Figure 6.3).

When an ecologist remarks, "There goes a badger," he thinks not merely of morphology, as might a skin-in taxonomist. He

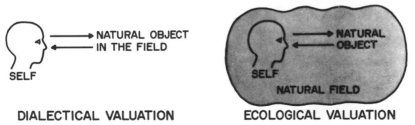

FIGURE 6.3 *Dialectical and ecological valuation.*

has in mind a whole mosaic of functions, interconnections, food chains, a way of being resident in a niche where the badger is what it is environmentally. When a sociologist remarks, "There goes a vicar," she is not so much identifying a human as seeing a role in the community. The being of a vicar, like that of a badger, is a contextual affair. When a philosopher says, "There goes a valuer," he should not think of a happening inside the human in such a way as to forget how this is also an ecological event. The responsibility here is a response-ability in our natural setting.

Add the fact that the valuing subject has itself evolved out of these surroundings. The organs and feelings mediating value—body, senses, hands, brain, will, emotion—are all natural products. Nature has thrown forward (pro-jected) the subjective experiencer quite as much as that world which is objectively experienced. On the route behind us, at least, nature has been a personifying system. We are where this track has been heading; we are perhaps its head, but we are in some sense tail. So we next sketch a further productive sequence that generates the self (S) out of ancestral precedents (O, P, Q, R)—natural events in causal sequence—and here also place reverse, valuational arrows (←) indicating reactive elements that cultural and personal responses superadd to the natural basis of personality. We add an evolutionary time line to the holistic, ecological sketch (Figure 6.4).

Seen in broad historical scale, these lines go back to common biological beginnings, from which they become richer eventually to reach the experiencing self embraced by its environment. Diverse, simple, complex forms are all maintained in and by

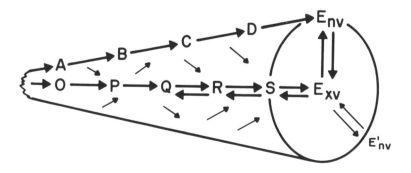

FIGURE 6.4 *Evaluating in an evolutionary ecosystem.*

the ecosystemic pyramid, and there are many coordinating connections that we only suggest (\). In such a picture, even though keeping the phenomenon of human valuing central, it is increasingly difficult to see valuing in isolation or even in dialectic. Values do not exist in a natural void but rather in a natural womb.

The sudden switch in Figure 6.1 from horizontal, merely causal arrows (→), to a vertical, valuational arrow (↑) now seems too angular a contrast. How far experienced value is a novel emergent we need yet to inquire, but there has been the historical buildup toward value, and there is presently surrounding us the invitation to value. The first series would have been better sketched in as it appears in Figure 6.5.

The reason for the new sketch is that it is difficult to say why the arrows of valuational response should value only the immediately productive natural event and not include at least some of the precedents, with unshown coordinates as well. The last event is at hand, and we may have had no consciousness of value during former events. But in an evolutionary ecosystem nothing happens just all at once and per se; everything is enveloped, developed in process.

A critic might complain, and perhaps fiercely, that we have diagrammatically sketched out single sweep lines while the real world is a much more tumultuous affair, where the valuational and constructive lines are not vectors but a near chaos of causes and happenstance, luck and struggle, serendipity and emergence, with much waste and little worth. The diagram screens off the heterogeneous and alien character of the ingredients of value. We have straightened out strands that do not lie straight in

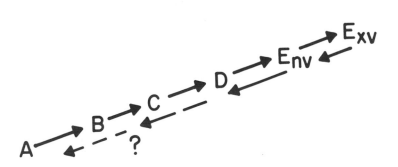

FIGURE 6.5 *A revised model of evaluating.*

the actual world, as though we never heard of Darwin and his junglelike world.

There is truth in the complaint, and in the next section we will return to the hostility in nature. We may wish conservatively to keep our judgments short-scope claims. Values immediately experienced might run back to some nonvaluable base out of which they have emerged. Analogously, living organisms once emerged out of lifeless nature. A present good might have come out of historically mixed values and disvalues, as when a little good comes from much evil. Natural values might be oddly occasional, though the causal sequence is continuous. Nature is not homogenized but unevenly located, and so too are its values.

Recall also that we found (in Chapter 5) that a strength of the system is its weak holism, its looseness, its openness, by which the community system promotes individuality, in which conflict is as constructive as is cooperation. The nature of the community is logically and empirically related to the nature of the valuing organisms that develop within it; organism and community are coordinated orders. Prolific diversity, species packing, testing for situated adapted fitness—such forces are objectively satisfactory in that many forms of life are satisfied in many resident environments. An environmental ethics can find this subjectively satisfactory.

It is reigning doctrine among prominent interpreters of paleontology that both the diversity and the advancement have been produced at random. Jacques Monod insists:

> Chance *alone* is at the source of every innovation, of all creation in the biosphere. Pure chance, absolutely free but blind, at the very root of the stupendous edifice of evolution: this central concept of modern biology is . . . today the *sole* conceivable hypothesis. . . . The tremendous journey of evolution over the past three billion years or so, the prodigious wealth of structures it has engendered, and the extraordinarily effective telenomic performances of living beings, from bacteria to man . . . [are] the product of an enormous lottery presided over by natural selection, blindly picking the rare winners from among numbers drawn at utter random.[15]

If that is all there is to be said, then there is no systemic projection of value. The wealth of species, the arrival of mammals, primates, and humans are only "chance riches," concludes Stephen Jay Gould. "We are the accidental result of an unplanned process . . . the fragile result of an enormous concatenation of improbabilities, not the predictable product of any definite process."[16] A person may value what he has—or has become—by chance, but it is hard to see how one can value systemically a nature whose output is nothing but chance.

It is certainly true that there is randomness in evolutionary nature, but it is not random that there is diversity. Four billion species do not appear by accident. Rather, *randomness is a diversity generator*, mixed as it is with principles of the spontaneous generation of order. Nor is it random that there is advancement. The story from microbes to persons is not just a random walk. Rather, *randomness is an advancement generator*, supported, as advancement comes to be, by the trophic pyramid in which lower ways of life are also conserved. We do not here wish to cast out the randomness (or the conflict); we want to recast it in a bigger picture. Randomness is not valueless noise in the system. Rather, embedded within systemic principles of order, it is a value generator, a value transformer. What emerges, what is projected, seems to be some kind of implication, unfolding, of the system, even though randomness is one of the searching mechanisms by which the system achieves this result. Randomness guarantees the trial-and-error exploration of the potentialities of the system. Randomness sifts through new options for both diversity and advancement. What systemic nature achieves over evolutionary time is made possible by randomness, but the headings are shown by the statistical results—not the lack of heading shown by randomness in the innovative process. This long-term, statistical production of values is what Figure 6.4 suggests. (Randomness can also contribute to looseness in the biotic community, which we admired in Chapter 5.)

In upshot, value is sometimes there before us, strikingly so, and we will sometimes be valuing contributors toward value, past or present, seen at whatever level. If ever we do extrapolate to try a systemic overview, the likeliest account will find some programmatic evolution toward value, and this not because it ignores Darwin but just because it heeds his principle of natural selection and deploys it into a selection exploring new niches and elaborating kinds, and even a selection upslope toward higher values—at least along some trends within some ecosystems.

How do we humans come to be charged up with values if there was and is nothing in nature charging us up so? We prefer not to believe in the special creation of values, or in their dumbfounding epigenesis. We let them evolve. Nor is our account merely a selection from the chaotic data of nature. Rather our interpretation notices how there is a world selection of events over evolutionary time (without denying other neutral or disvalued events), which builds toward the ecological valuing in which we now participate. Perhaps we will not want to say that this had to happen. But it did happen.

Many evolutionary and ecological connections are shared between ourselves as experiencers and the natural events we appraise. These bring a new orientation toward the presence of photosynthesis, the appearance of hemoglobin, or the genetic keying of information. We discover that decomposers and predators have value objectively in the ecosystem and then realize that our own standing as subjective valuers atop the biotic pyramid is impossible except in consequence of decomposition and predation. An interlocking kinship suggests that values are not merely in the mind but at hand in the world. We start out valuing nature like land appraisers figuring out what it is worth to us, only to discover that we are part and parcel of this nature we appraise. The earthen landscape has upraised this landscape appraiser. We do not simply bestow value on nature; nature also conveys value to us.

From Epiphenomenal to Educational Value

Let us work toward this same conclusion from another direction, by finding partial but inadequate some lesser accounts.

Natural value as an epiphenomenon. Pollen is not an allergen "by nature," for nasal irritation is no part of its reproductive role. But certain pollens "by accident" evoke mistakes in susceptible immunological systems. The allergy reaction is thus a disvalue that bears no meaningful connection with the natural operation. Analogously, some natural events can (to coin a term) be "valugens," evoking positive responses without meaningful basis in spontaneous nature. We react with a sense of beauty before the swirled flow in a pegmatite exposed in a rock cut. Aesthetic experience is sparked off when humans strike the rock. Again, we are enchanted by the mist sweeping in over the dell. But this is a kind of mis-taking of what is essentially there. Value is adventitious to nature, more fiction than fact, more dream than description; poetry, not prose; real in consciousness, unreal in the world.

But while partially useful, this account, if taken for the whole, leaves the human valuing subject eccentric to his world. Causal connections obtain, and the relational context is required, but value is a fluke without intelligible support in its stimulus.[17] Dealing with causes, one may be content with any kind of *how* explanation that hooks up antecedent and subsequent events. But in the case of value one would hope for an explanation more or less logically adequate to the effect. Yet so far from enlightening us about *why* value appears, this is in fact a nonexplanation. Value is an epigenetic anomaly.

Natural value as an echo. Strolling on the beach, I examine dozens of pieces of driftwood, discarding all but one. This I varnish and frame for its pleasing curvature. I value this piece because it happened to mirror the sweep and line of my subjective preference; the rest did not. Nature once in a while chances to echo my tastes. We still have an element of accident, but we can make more sense of origins. Value does not come in pleasantly allergic reaction but rather as a reflection of my own composition. This led Samuel Alexander to claim that we, not nature, are the artists.

> The nature we find beautiful is not bare nature as she exists apart from us but nature as seen by the artistic eye. . . . We find nature beautiful not because she is beautiful herself but because we select from nature and combine, as the artist does more plainly when he works with pigments. . . . Nature does live for herself without us to share her life. But she is not beautiful without us to unpiece her and repiece. . . . Small wonder that we do not know that we are artists unawares. For the appreciation of nature's beauty is unreflective; and even when we reflect, it is not so easy to recognise that the beauty of a sunset or a pure colour is a construction on our part and an interpretation.[18]

But the more we reflect, the less easy it becomes to see value as nothing but a reflection. Doubtless this is sometimes so, but in a general theoretical account we have to reckon with the felicitous echoing capacity of nature, and also with its stimulus and surprise when we are struck by what we are not looking for. Both the epiphenomenon and echo models are unecological, not sufficiently interactive. To say that humans enjoying blackberries or the spring sun are participating in anomalous value seems biologically odd. The cardinal on the wing and the trillium in bloom have grace, coloration, symmetry that are structurally related to flight, flowering, and life cycles. Is the beauty here nothing but a mirroring of our arbitrary selecting? Does it not involve our responding to overtones that go with biological function? If I am choosing shells rather than driftwood, the color, sweep, and vault are better realized in one than in another but seem a nisus in them all. Each attempt (project) is an architecture under genetic control. If I collect crystals, the development of each appears superficial and accidental; this specimen has better developed faces than that one, resulting from environmental contingencies. But the crystalline structure runs deep and is fundamental; the symmetries, faces, colors, refractions are mathematically governed projects inherent in the mineral chemistries and physics. The earthen geology, Earth's logic, has crystals and crystalline matter among its ever repeated projects.

Humans are endowed with naturally selected capacities to value such projects. Is the whole evolution of human valuing an anomalous, serendipitous afterglow? one without rational basis in the structures of nature? Perhaps our immunological system makes mistakes, but its development is incredible except as a protection against hurts in the world. The human valuational system may luck into some benefits, but its generic presence can best be accounted for in terms of an inclusive fitness to helps in the world. A valuing system would be an odd benefit indeed unless it better fitted us to our home niche. The echoing is most often working the other way around; the human valuer is reflecting what is actually there.

Natural value as an emergent. Emergent phenomena occur strikingly in nature, as when first life and afterward learning appeared where none before existed. Perhaps the valuing capacity emerges to create value out of mere potential? Value is a kind of fiery excitement; no natural scene, however complex and splendid, can have value until the precursors of value are supplemented and thickened by the arrival of human interest. Value cannot be said to have happened until it is present as an event in consciousness. There must be the delivery of some kind of "charge" into the valued experience. Humans may have little sense of manufacture or decision, but still we furnish the required awareness. Like knowing, the process of valuing goes on in the conscious mind. Like knowledge, the product—value—exists only there.

We can now give an intelligible account of the objective precedents. They are not flukes but fuel. The valuing experience, like combustion, does indeed feed on natural properties and proceeds in keeping with their potential. Though emergent, it is not adventitious. The waterfall, the cardinal, the columbine, the crystal, the shell, the blackberry, the warming sun, glycolysis, photosynthesis—all have indeed their stimulating properties and thus are rightly valued when they are valued, but not until then does value appear. Perhaps, too, valuing can fail. But everything is potential until clinched in experience. Consciousness ignites what before were only combustible materials, and value lights up. The precondition for value need not itself be a value.

To say that wood is combustible means that wood will burn if ignited even though it never nears fire. This is a predicate of objective potential: wood might ignite in the spontaneous course of nature. But to say that wood is valuable is a predicate of subjective potential. If a human subject appears in relation, wood can be valued. This sort of dispositional predicate can be realized only in human experience. Some exception can here be made for subhuman experience. Animals may not have aesthetic, moral, philosophical, or religious sensibilities. They may be incapable of normative discourse. But they can undergo pain and pleasure; they have interested concerns. To this extent, they own values. Sugar is not sweet all by itself, but it is sweet both to humans and to ants. Valuing dilutes across the simplifying of the central nervous system, but if we rely entirely on the emergent account, value is never extraneural. Where there are no centers of experience, valuing ceases and value vanishes.

But neither will this account explain the main body of natural values. While it may be true that some ranges of value emerge, such as the capacity for joy or aesthetic experience, these are capstone goods; they are built on valuable substructures. Some values come only with consciousness, but it does not follow that consciousness, when it brings its new values, confers all value and discovers none. The nutritional value of sugar is independent of experience in either human or ant. The cane or the beet that produced the sugar already valued it, storing it for future use.

Natural value as an entrance. We can best appraise the emergent account in the light of another account where value is more generously allocated to the natural world. The arriving beholder enters into a surrounding scene; it enters him. There is a two-way entrance and resulting fulfillment. Subjective experience emerges to appreciate what was before unappreciated. But such valuing is a partnership, and the freestanding objective partner cannot enjoin value upon the subjective partner if it has nothing to offer. Emergence is not the whole story; there is a joining of situational value. If emergence is a *dispositional* account, we can call this a more ecological, *positional* account.

An ecologist might say that the eater realizes the potential in blackberries (and incidentally enjoys their sweetness), but he will equally say that the eater captures nutrients embedded functionally into the ecosystem. The experienced taste is an overlay on objective food chains. The eater is waking up in the midst of events that precede and exceed his awareness. The eating of the berries, like the burning of the wood, is really a matter of formed energy throughput, a physical energy onto which life has been modulated. Initially received as solar input, nature has by photosynthesis locked this energy into cellulose and carbohydrates. When humans overtake it, energy previously there is transformed in the eating and ignition.

This flow-through model is a more basic one than the model of emergence. The potential is to be conceived of as a kind of capital on which we can draw a check. But the check-cashing does not entirely constitute the value, even though it may reconstitute it. Seen this way, it is not merely life that is of value, much less sentience or consciousness, but the whole of projective nature. Value does not begin with blackberries, cellulose, photosynthesis—with biology—but also lies in nitrates, phosphates, water, energy, minerals: in dirt, in the landscape, in geosystemic nature.

We ought not to forget the uppermost steps, but we ought not to mistake the last steps for the whole history. Valuing is not apart from the whole; it is a part in the whole. Value is not isolable into a miraculous epiphenomenon or echo, even though some valued events may be happenstance. It is systemically grounded in major constructive thrusts in nature. The most satisfactory account is an ecocentric model, one that recognizes the emergence of consciousness as a novel value but also finds this consciousness entering a realm of objective natural value.

This accounts works equally well where humans value things that we do not consume. When we value a thrush singing in the wild, we have a sense of entrance into events ongoing independently of our subjective presence. We cannot genuinely care here unless we care what happens after we are gone.

Natural value as an education. A natural object has no frame or pedestal; much depends on how I take it. The hawk flies past, and I can follow to admire his strength and speed or let him pass and gaze into the blue expanse, pondering his fleeting smallness in the vast emptiness. When I lie on my back, resting trailside, the stalwart ponderosa pine strikes me with its strength. It has stood the wintry storms. But then a hummingbird flits on scene, and how am I to interpret this interruption? By the contrast of great and small, mobile and immobile? or by comparison of different strengths? The bird has stood the winter by flight from it and arrives after 5,000 miles over land and sea. I remark to my companion that this is a strong flight for so tiny a creature. But she has seen nothing. With eyes closed, she has been wondering whether the Swainson's or the hermit thrush is the better singer.

The Fibonacci series in the spiral galaxy in Andromeda can be drawn into association with that spiral in the chambered nautilus, in weather cyclones, and waterfall whirlpools. I can dwell on the galaxy's size and age, on the nautilus's age and smallness, on the local whirlpool's being driven by the global Coriolis force. Natural objects trigger imaginative musings of discovery and theoretical recombination, depending upon an active following of the show, on cultural preconditioning, and an adventurous openness.

Natural events thus educate us, leading out the beholder into self-expression. But it would be a mistake to conclude that all values derive entirely from our *composition* and none from our *position*. There are valued states of consciousness, but some are directed from the outside in essential though not absolute ways by the natural objects of consciousness. The situation remains a providing ground and catalyst, and also a check on experience. We can be deceived, as we could not if we were only composing. If, through the floating mists at evening, I am appreciating the moon hanging over the summit, only to discover with a bit of clearing that this was the disc of a microwave antenna, I judge the experience to have been false and cannot afterward regain it. I may be deceived about strength in the ponderosa or the hummingbird. Human value judgments have to be more or less adequate to the natural facts.

Nature presents us with superposed possibilities of valuing, only some of which we realize. It is both provocative source of and resource for value. Here fertility is demanded of us as subjects but is also found in the objects that fertilize our experience. Nature does indeed challenge us to respond as artists, poets, philosophers, evaluators. But rather than devaluing nature, this educational ferment deepens its valued dimensions. The self has its options as to where to take the experience nature launches—but only interactively, with nature carrying the show forward. There is trailblazing by the conscious self, but we also go in the track of our surroundings, with consciousness a trailer of what lies around.

Nature as a Value Carrier

The notion that nature is a value carrier is ambiguous. A great deal depends on a thing being more or less structurally congenial for the carriage. Promiscuous items—logs, rocks, horses—support the body and serve as seats. Other values require rather specific carriers, for one cannot enjoy symmetry, display of color, or adventure everywhere in nature. Still others require pregnancy with exactly that natural kind, as when only the female body can carry a child. Nature both offers and constrains values, often surprising us. We value a thing to discover that we are under the sway of its *valence*, inducing our behavior. It has among its "strengths" (Latin: *valeo*, be strong) this capacity to carry value to us, if also to carry values we assign to it. This "potential" cannot always be of the empty sort that a glass has for carrying water. It is often pregnant fullness. In the energy throughput model, nature is indeed a carrier of value but just as it is also objectively a carrier of energy and of life.

In climax, the values that nature is assigned are up to us. But fundamentally, there are powers in nature that move to us and through us. America became great, remarked Alfred North Whitehead, when the pioneers entered "an empty continent, peculiarly well suited for European races."[19] That suggests a vast, valueless continent waiting to carry our imported values, although even this is belied by its being a "peculiarly well suited" emptiness. Wild America, said John Locke, was a "waste": "Nature and the earth furnished only the almost worthless materials as in themselves," the Europeans' labors added 999 parts of the value; hardly one part in a thousand is natural.[20]

But under our model we ought to think of a majestic and fertile ecosystem, the natural values of which could blend with those of the immigrants. Only the ecologically naive would see the energy flow, the work done, the value mix on a farm in Locke's proportions. The farmer mostly redirects natural sources—soil fertility, sun and rain, genetic information—to his own advantage. Even the settlers could call it (borrowing a biblical phrase) a land of promise. Indeed, Americans have sometimes found values so intensely delivered that we have saved them wild, as in Yellowstone, the Sierras, and the Smokies. The cathedrals were the gems of Europe, left behind; but the national parks are the gems of America, left untouched and positively treasured for their natural value.

Subjective and Objective Values

How shall we judge our theory that value is (in part) provided objectively in nature (T_o), against the counterbelief that value arises only as a product of subjective experience (T_s), albeit relationally with nature? Even in scientific theories, hard proof is impossible. All we can hope for is a theory from which we can logically infer certain experiences (E). If T, then E. Given these, our theory is corroborated by a kind of weak, backtracking verification. Given counterevidence (not E), we have to estimate whether the anomaly is serious. No big theory even in science, much less in value theory, is trouble-free, and the theory of objective value can be stung by our seeming incapacity to know anything whatsoever in naked objectivity. But value is not the sort of thing one would expect to know without excitement. If there is objective value in nature (T_o), then one would predict it to stir up experience (E). This does not always mean that we value (have preferences satisfied) in what we evaluate (judge to be of worth). Still, there must be a positive experience of value, alien though this value sometimes is. Sometimes too that experience fails (not E), and we must presume a faulty registration and/or valueless parts of nature.

If value arrives only with consciousness (T_s), we have no problem with its absence in nature (not E). But experiences where we do find value (E) have to be dealt with as "appearances" of various sorts. The value has to be relocated in the valuing subject's creativity as he meets a valueless world, or even a valuable one—one *able* to be *valued* but one which, before the human bringing of value ability, contains only possibility and not any actual value. This troubles the logic by hiding too much in such words as epiphenomenon, echo, emergent, potential, projection. They occasionally help but in the end give us the valuing subject in an otherwise (yet) valueless world, an insufficient premise for our experienced conclusion.

Resolute subjectivists cannot, however, be defeated by argument, although they can perhaps be driven toward analyticity. One can always hang on to the claim that value, like a tickle or remorse, must be felt to be there. Its *esse* is *percipi*. Nonsensed value is nonsense. It is impossible by argument to dislodge anyone firmly entrenched in this belief. That theirs is a retreat to definition is difficult to expose, because here they seem to cling so closely to inner experience. They are reporting, on this hand, how values always touch us. They are giving, on that hand, a stipulative definition. That is how they choose to use the word value.

Meanwhile, the conversion to our view seems truer to world experience and more logically compelling. Here the order of knowing reverses—and also enhances—the order of being. This too is a perspective, but it is ecologically better informed. Science has been steadily showing how the consequents (life, mind) are built on their precedents (energy, matter), however much they overleap them. We find no reason to say that all value is an irreducible emergent at the human (or upper animal) level. We reallocate value across the whole continuum. It increases in the emergent climax but is continuously present in the composing precedents.

A Model of Intrinsic, Instrumental, and Systemic Value

The diagram we need now (Figure 6.6) portrays levels in projective nature. There is increasing richness of value upward in the pyramid, and some value does depend on subjectivity, yet all value is generated within the geosystemic and ecosystemic pyramid. Systemically, value fades from subjective to objective value but also fans out from the individual to its role and matrix.

Things do not have their separate natures merely in and for themselves, but they face outward and co-fit into broader natures. Value-in-itself is smeared out to become value-in-togetherness. Value seeps out into the system, and we lose our capacity to identify the individual as the sole locus of value. A diagram can only suggest these diverse and complex relationships in their major zones. The boundaries need to be semipermeable surfaces, and

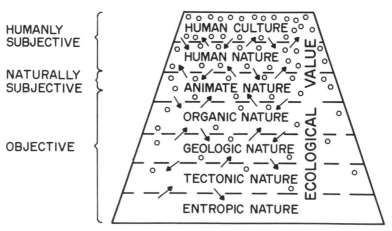

FIGURE 6.6 *Levels of value in projective nature.*

arrows of instrumental value ($\nearrow$, $\searrow$) will be found throughout, connecting occasions of individual intrinsic value (o). Each of the upper levels includes and requires much in those below it. The upper levels exist not independently or in isolation but only as supported and maintained by the lower levels, though the diagram, while showing this, inadequately conveys how the higher levels are perfused by the lower ones. We have also to remember that a sketch is not a story; the model is not historical enough for the environment in which we reside.

Intrinsic value, the value of an individual "for what it is in itself," becomes problematic in a holistic web. True, the system projects such values more and more with its evolution of individuality and freedom. Yet to decouple this from the biotic, communal system is to make value too internal and elementary, to forget relatedness and externality. The humus and the brooklet are valuable (able for value) and are of value (carry values objectively) because in that matrix the trillium springs up. They supply nutrients and water for the lake on which the loons call. Concern about populations, species, gene pools, habitats requires a corporate sense where value can also mean "good in community." Every intrinsic value has leading and trailing *ands* pointing to value from which it comes and toward which it moves. Natural fitness and positioning make individualistic value too system-independent. Intrinsic value is a part in a whole, not to be fragmented by valuing it in isolation.

Everything is good in a role, in a whole, although we can speak of objective, intrinsic goodness wherever a point event—a trillium—is defended as a good in itself, when trilliums project and protect their own kind. We can speak of subjective intrinsic goodness when such an event registers as a point experience, at which point humans pronounce both their experience and what it is of good without need to enlarge their focus. Neither the trilliums nor the human judges of it require for their respective valuings any further contributory reference.

The trillium eaten by foragers or in death resorbed into the humus has its value destroyed, which is to say transformed into instrumentality. Relations between entities are just as real as the entities themselves. In their interrelations things become and remain what they are. The system is an integrated manifold in which form and being, process and reality, individual and environment, fact and value are inseparably joined. Intrinsic and instrumental values shuttle back and forth, parts-in-wholes and

wholes-in-parts, local details of value embedded in global structures, gems in their settings, and their setting-situation a ma-
ternal matrix. To change the figure, intrinsic values are particles that are also waves, and instrumental values are waves that
are also particles, as one shifts valuing perspective or coagulates
events this way or that.

Conflict and Complementarity: The Transformation of Value

Now we are in a position to interpret the seeming conflict in
nature as, at more depth, interdependence in projective nature,
deepening themes that were introduced in the previous chapter.

When we first become acquainted with ecosystems and try to
interpret them axiologically, we may find only a survival value
whose operation hurts too much for us to value it more. Everything is making a resource of something else so far as it can, except when it is resisting being made a resource of. The jumping
spider eats the fly, the roundworms the opossum, the coyote the
ground squirrel, which eats the grass and its seeds, which grow
in the rotting humus. Once again everything is a resource, really. We have lamented an attitude regarding nature as "nothing
but resource" when that attitude is found in humans (a subjective
experience), but now we seem to find that nature is objectively
nothing but a system of resource use.

Wildness is a gigantic food pyramid, and this sets value in a
grim, deathbound jungle. Earth is a slaughterhouse, with life a
miasma rising over the stench. Nothing is done for the benefit
of another, much less for my human benefit, and all this is remote from what society ideally should value. Nothing recognizes
anything else's rights; each individual defends itself as an end in
itself, even in reproduction merely defending its own genes. Blind
and ever urgent exploitation is nature's driving theme.

An ecosystem contains only the thousandth part of creatures
that sought to be but rather became seeds eaten, young fallen to
prey or parasites or disease. The Darwinian revolution has revealed that the governing principle is survival in a world thrown
forward (projected) in chaotic contest, with much randomness and
waste besides. The wilderness teems with its kinds but is a vast
graveyard with hundreds of species laid waste for one or two that
survive. Four billion species have gone extinct; five million remain. Nature, lamented John Stuart Mill, is "an odious scene of
violence."[21] Can we stabilize a positive orientation in such a negative picture?

The cutthroat portrait of nature does not mean there are no

valuers in the wild; it portrays too many claimants contesting scarce worth. A life is never self-contained but incessantly moves through its environment, ingesting and eliminating it. Rocks attach no value to the environment, but coyotes must eat. Where anything is being made a resource of, just this claiming of the environment as nutrient source and sink reveals valuational systems in interaction.

The wilderness can seem a great scene of disorder, but it is also a great scene of the pumping-out of disorder. Indeed, all this resourcefulness has to be so understood. The phenomenon of life struggles on but has achieved much, pumped up out of the soil, persisting by ever novel arrivals. The marvel is how dirt spontaneously assembled itself into Cambrian worms, later into Cretaceous opossums, and still later into wondering persons. The degradation of things in the wild is followed by nature's orderly self-assembling of new creatures amidst this perpetual perishing. Earth slays her children, a seeming great disvalue, but bears an annual crop in their stead. This prolife, generative impulse is the most startling and valuable miracle of all.

To keep our bearings, we must locate individual lives on larger horizons as goods of their kind, good kinds, in an ecosystem greater than they know. We saw in the preceding chapter that we can subsume struggle under the notion of a comprehensive situated fitness. Forms live on that more efficiently use food resources, take better care of their young, learn to form societies, fill niches not exploited by others. The survival of the fittest shapes the ever more fit in their habitats. Each is for itself, but none is by itself; each is tested for optimal compliance in an intricately disciplined community. Every organism is an opportunist in the system but without opportunity except in the ongoing system. The parasitic worms may not cripple their hosts too successfully lest they destroy themselves. But free-living forms are just as contextually situated and just as "parasitic" (dependent) on other organisms whose values they must capture.

What survives is never mere individuals or species but the system containing them, a dynamic system that takes on storied form. Each is against the others, but each locus of value is tied into a corporation where values are preserved even as they are exchanged. From that point of view, we see conversions of resources from one life stream to another—the anastomosing of life threads that weaves an ecosystem. Now it becomes difficult to say whether anything of value is lost at all.

Of course, there are many disvalues in the sense that

individuals are losers; they become diseased, get eaten, die. But what seems waste in the rabbit life stream is nutrient within the coyote stream, and even the rabbit population benefits by the ongoing selection over mutants. The surplus of offspring is cut back by premature death, but this cutback is executed unawares by the coyotes so as to leave, on statistical average, the smarter, faster, more fertile, efficient, and wary. The rabbits suffer for the coyotes—but not entirely; they collectively gain from their pains. The surplus of young permits both mutational advance and the synthesis of biotic materials with higher forms at the top of the pyramid. This produces further demands on coyotes, and the coevolutionary race goes on.

Predation is a value-shunting device. Feeding is part of a feedback loop, and we saw in the preceding chapter how, by means of such value capture, all the higher values (sentience, locomotion, mentality, conditioned behavior, learning) depend on the value support in the lower rungs of the pyramid (photosynthesis, decomposition). Thus organisms are seen to inherit value not only in their genes but from their competitors, enemies, and prey. On the short scale, values may seem hopelessly relative and impossible to evaluate, but in the whole, for all the borrowing and spending, biomass and energy are transformed and recycled so that wilderness is a no-waste world, frugal in its economies. We need a theory of value-transporting something like a theory of energy-transporting. We begin to get a new picture painted over the old, although some of the old picture still shows through. Wildness seemed a great struggle, and so it is; but it is also a great flowing of opposites into each other; a redeeming and transforming of values. Wildness is a complex tapestry of values on the one side, though it can seem a jumble of values on the other. The seeming chaos is really a richness in alternatives and possibilities for value circulation, a projecting and trading of form/energy/information/pleasure.

The Systemic Evolution of Values

Over evolutionary time, the defenses of life and kind by individual organisms yield systemic advancements. Nature builds life up across perpetuated millennia. The cycling of values becomes the spiraling of stories. Once there were simple things; later, complicated things. Fins become flippers, then feet, then fingers. Once there was no smelling, swimming, hiding, gambling, making mistakes, or outsmarting a competitor, but all these appear by trial and error. Through attempting and discarding, nature learns to build eyes, wings, photosynthesis, hemoglobin, muscles, fat, nerves, and brains.

Nothing knows what it is becoming, so much transcends the individual. The selective system must be capable of producing additional values beyond those entertained by any individual organism, because it has long done so. More diverse and higher forms appear, replacing earlier species—though broadly speaking, the basic ways of life seldom if ever go extinct. Natural selection edits to leave those forms that are justified in at least a right-for-life sense, and perhaps partly in some increasing right-to-life sense. This need not mean that such creatures have a right to life in a moral sense that is derived (extrapolated) from culture-based rights; rather, they embody evolutionary achievements that have been tested over time and result from long struggles for life. These kinds are winners and deserve admiring respect.

Wildness as a jungle of exploitation becomes a theater of adventure and improvisation. Some forms merely track through stable environments, but others grow more clever in the same, changing, or new environments. Mixed with a lust for life is a lure that elaborates higher values. Nature treats any particular individual with a momentary life, but life is a propagating wave over time. Located in individuals, value is also consigned to a stream. Even species regularly come and go, over millions of years. The half-life of a species is typically upward of ten million years.[22] Some become extinct without issue, but nature's long-standing trends transform others and increase the numbers of species present in each later epoch, as well as their richness.

Even the few crashes and mass extinctions, though setbacks, have reset life's directions, as happened at the ends of the Permian and Cretaceous Periods (Figure 4.1). Retrenchments in the quantity of life were followed by explosive inventiveness in its quality. The mammals came into their own, triggered by the wiping out of the dinosaurs, even while reptiles and amphibians—and their descendants, the birds—remain important in our ecosytems.

Wild nature is an unquenchable prolife force in this respect, however groping, blind, and unmerciful it may otherwise seem. Ongoing survival is not all that is going on; new arrivals are moving in, moving up. All this happens in a dialectic of environmental conductance and resistance, almost in the paradox that out of seeming disorder, order comes the more. There flows this great river of life, strange and valuable because it flows (projects) uphill, negentropically from nonbeing to being, from nonlife to objective life and on to subjective life. Nature is full of crooked, winding paths. Some are wayward lines; some prove routes to interesting places; some are ascents to summits.

An individual's life is a defense of its value set, a concrete attempt at problem-solving, exemplifying an intrinsic value. But an individual's death, by which such value collapses, contributes to values being defended by others who recycle its materials, energy, and information. Overall, the myriad individual passages through life and death upgrade the system. Value has often to be something more, something opposed to what any individual organism likes or selects, since even struggle and death—which are never approved—are used instrumentally to produce still higher intrinsic values. Things good in themselves, good of their kind, are not permitted to have such integrity alone but are required to be good in their niche, good corporately. This can seem to devalue their individuality, treating each as a means to an end. But the systemic community in turn generates more and higher individuality (Chapter 5, pp. 182–86).

Problem-solving is a function of the spontaneous system (as it is of organisms) when the community recycles, recovers from setbacks, speciates, increases sentience and complexity, pulls conflicts into harmony, and redeems life from an ever pressing death. The systemic source interblends intrinsic and instrumental values. As we earlier used the term, value is what makes a favorable difference to an organism's life. But as we now enlarge it, value is what makes a favorable difference to an ecosystem, enriching it, making it more beautiful, diverse, harmonious, intricate. Here a disvalue to an individual may be a value in the system and will result in values carried to other individuals. Intrinsic value exists embedded in instrumental value. No organism is a mere instrument, for each has its integral intrinsic value. But each can also be sacrificed in behalf of another life course; then its intrinsic value collapses, becomes extrinsic, and is in part instrumentally transported to another organism.

When we interpret this transfer between individuals systemically, the life stream flows up an ecological pyramid over evolutionary time. The incessant making-use of resources unifies the intrinsic and instrumental distinctions (the small circles and arrows of Figure 6.6) and the result is the storied achievements of natural history. Value as storied achievement is a property alike of organisms and the evolutionary ecosystem. Against the standard view that all value requires a beholder; we now claim that some value requires only a holder, which can be an individual but can be also the historic system that carries value to and through individuals.

There is nothing secondary about instrumental value. When resource use is found omnipresent in the system, it loses its sting. Although there is something wrong with making everything else a resource for humans, there is nothing wrong with something being an instrumental resource for others. We think that a person is narrow and selfish who cultivates intrinsic worth and withdraws from seeking any instrumental value in the community. A person's intrinsic worth—for example, creative ability—is not separable from the power to confer a benefit on others. Excellence does not consist in what a thing is merely for itself, but in what it is for others. This is true of persons, animals, and plants. Excellence is not a matter of encapsulated being, but of fitness in a pervasive whole.

Nevertheless, instrumental and intrinsic values are not homogeneously distributed throughout the ecosystem. We can summarize with some rough distinctions in their proportion:

- Nonbiotic things (rivers, rocks, mountains) have minimal though foundational intrinsic value and are more importantly elevated in instrumental value in the communities in which they become incorporated.
- Flora and insentient fauna (grass, amoebas) individually have more, yet still weak, intrinsic value as compared with their crucial instrumental value collectively in the communities in which they are incorporated.
- Sentient fauna (squirrels, baboons) have increasingly stronger intrinsic value individually and (typically) weaker instrumental value collectively in the communities in which they are incorporated. Ecosystems suffer less disruption with disturbances in their upper trophic levels.
- Humans are of maximal value intrinsically as individuals and of minimal value instrumentally in the biotic community. Although humans in technological culture have massive disruptive powers, few or no ecosystems depend on humans at the top of the pyramid. (The value of persons instrumentally in culture is not here addressed.)

■ The instrumental/intrinsic value ratio shifts as the level of being rises, although both are always present in some proportion. As the power for mobile autonomy evolves— always embedded within an ecological context—individualistic value overtakes communitarian value and eventually, with humans, sometimes overrides it. Thus grass (though an autotroph) is of value largely instrumentally; humans (though heterotrophs), largely intrinsically.

■ Although humans are not valued for what they contribute to the ecosystem, their value gain is constrained by whether they degrade the ecosystems where they reside. Without overriding justification, humans ought not to impoverish the biotic pyramid on the top of which they live, which will adversely affect everything below, both individuals and systems, all the interfitting intrinsic/instrumental/organismic/communitarian values. (This shifting proportion has been suggested in Figure 6.6.)

■ The eminent human values (individuality, autonomy, intrinsic values that are displayed in personality and culture) are purchased through dependence on those with instrumental roles lower down the ecosystemic pyramid (organisms that photosynthesize, digest cellulose, or decompose the dead). There is independence only in dependence, a dialectical value.

■ Humans in culture will often capture and transform natural values—organismic, specific, ecosystemic. This is both permissible and required, but it requires justification proportionately to value loss in the natural world as this is traded for value gain in culture.

■ Primitive wild value (relict wilderness ecosystems, endangered species) gains in proportion to its rarity and to the threat of irreversible change in encounter with human cultural value that is already abundantly present (overpopulated, overdeveloped human societies). One whooping crane has less intrinsic value than one human, but in a world with only a hundred whooping cranes and four billion humans, we ought not replace whooping cranes with humans. Humans ought not destroy a million species in tropical forests to replace them with a million humans. Humans ought not destroy the humpback chub to gain more water for Denver lawns.

■ The projective system is fundamentally the most valuable phenomenon of all, though humans are its most valuable products. A shallow reading of "valuable" here means that *humans*, when they arrive, are *able to value* the system out of which they have emerged. A deeper reading means that the *system* is *able to project values*, among which are humans.

"Nature," exclaimed Loren Eiseley, "is one vast miracle transcending the reality of night and nothingness!"[23] How that contrasts with Mill's shrinking from nature as an odious scene of violence—nothing but night and darkness! But the brighter outlook is a truer perspective; it sees that nature is not chaos but a projective system that creatively overcomes chaos.

Ethics in Ecosystems

In an environmental ethic, what humans want to value is not compassion, charity, rights, personality, justice, fairness or even pleasure and the pursuit of happiness. Those values belong in interhuman ethics—in culture, not nature—and to look for them here is to make a category mistake. What humans value in nature is an ecology, a pregnant Earth, a projective and prolife system in which (considering biology alone, not culture) individuals can prosper but are also sacrificed indifferently to their pains and pleasures, individual well-being a lofty but passing role in a storied natural history. From the perspective of individuals there is violence, struggle, death; but from a systems perspective, there is also harmony, interdependence, and ever-continuing life.

The beauty, integrity, stability of an ecosystem can put constraints on appropriate human conduct in both small and larger ways. This is what is wrong, at the deepest ethical level, with such seemingly trivial behavior as putting soap in geysers, carving names on trees and boulders, carving mountains into monuments to human pride, tossing toilet paper off the Mount of the Holy Cross, or bulldozing a giant fire off the lip of Glacier Point. Mere sport hunting is wrong on this count alone, even if those killed feel no pain. To make of nature a mere plaything is to profane it, just as to make playthings of persons is to misunderstand them. We humans ought to have our parks and pleasuring places, but we ought to check the types of enjoyments there with an appropriate appreciation of those places.

An Indiana Dunes National Lakeshore poster depicts a clump of marram grass, sand, a lake, with the injunction *"Let it be!"*[24]

The Indiana sand dunes are adjacent to Chicago on the shores
of Lake Michigan; they are valuable industrial and residential
property as well as ecosystems of biological and historical interest. The science of ecology was, in significant part, founded by
Henry Cowles as a result of his studies there, discovering dune
succession. Preserving areas of the dunes was achieved only after
one of the longest, bitterest fights in environmental conservation,
a century of struggle against powerful industrial and development interests.[25] A major reason was to preserve a playground
for Chicagoans. But in the imperative "Let it be!" there seems an
element also of respect for ecosystems; at least some token of the
ecosystem type that natural history placed on the Lake Michigan
shore ought to remain in the midst of the Chicago culture.

When humans make their living off the land, this ethic asks a
gentle presence rather than a domineering and thoughtless one.
Humans are permitted to make many wild areas rural and some
areas urban, and they do rebuild the environment dramatically.
But this ethic requires that rural places be kept as full of nature
as is consistent with their being agricultural places as well. It
thinks of nature as a community, not just a commodity. It limits
road-building to minimize the impact on wildlife. It likes brushy
fencerows and dislikes clean (and barren) ones. It protects all
species, not just the "game." It leaves the hardwoods along the
stream courses when converting the uplands to pinewoods for
paper pulp. It appreciates a forest, not just board feet of timber.
It sees water first as the lifeblood of an ecosystem, secondly as
acre-feet in a reservoir. It sees humans as biotic citizens (if also
kings) who belong to the land, not man as conqueror to whom
the land belongs. This ethic urges multiple appreciations of the
landscape, not just multiple uses. It says that humans ought to let
sand dune ecosystems be—sometimes, at least. Humans are not
free to make whatever uses of nature suit their fancy, amusement,
need, or profit.

It has been necessary in the course of human history to sacrifice most of the wildlands, converting them to rural and urban
settlements, and this is both good and ecological; nevertheless,
when humans prey on nature to build culture and make the land
yield its wealth, these "moral predators"—who can have a view of
the whole and a conscience about their presence—have some duties to the ecosystems of which they are part. This demands that
places of especially striking site integrity be left untrammeled by
humans. These are named national parks, wildernesses, wildlife

refuges. But not only do the highly distinctive places present values that count morally. Representatives of once common ecosystems (hemlock forests, tall-grass prairies, sand dunes) also have their integrity, now threatened by advancing agriculture and culture, and ought to be preserved.

Perhaps it was necessary for the plainsmen to reduce the buffalo herds so that they could put cattle on the range; the plains states could hardly have been settled any other way. But it was not right to destroy the bison; respect for those bison in their plains ecosystems should have preserved ample grasslands wilderness and national parks in every plains state. Alas, the United States has not a single grasslands national park or grasslands wilderness with free-ranging buffalo.

The extension of an ethic to the land gives humans a comprehensive situated fitness in the global ecosystems. Such fitness, more than predatory success, makes the human behavior here right—right because humans respectfully appreciate the integrity of the places they inhabit.

Consider the following argument for the preservation of wilderness.

1. Seeking the unchecked domination of others is self-defeating.
2. Persons who (only) dominate other persons are not free to appreciate them.
3. Persons who (only) dominate other persons lead inferior lives. Slaveowners, for example, lead better lives after the slaves are freed, when human relationships are more just and generous.
4. Persons who (only) dominate nature are not free to appreciate nature.
5. Persons who (only) dominate nature lead inferior lives.
6. Ours is a society that (only) seeks to dominate nature.
7. Ours is an inferior society—to the extent that it seeks unchecked domination of nature.
8. Wilderness is a region undominated by persons. A wilderness is "an area where the earth and its community of life are untrammeled by man, where man himself is a visitor who does not remain."[26]
9. Designating wilderness by deliberate resolve checks the human domination of nature. (Congress and government agencies resolve to "let it be!")

10. Maintaining wilderness by citizen cooperation checks the human domination of nature. (Visitors observe wilderness regulations, walking gently, leaving little or no trace. They "let it be!")
11. In wilderness, nature may be appreciated for what it is in itself. Wilderness serves as a living symbol or representative of pristine nature.
12. Persons who appreciate nature live better lives than those who seek (only) to dominate nature. Be a better person! Let wilderness be! Is this a self-serving argument? (Compare the discussion of human excellences, Chapter 3, pp. 117–19.)
13. Wilderness is essential to a better society. "In Wildness is the preservation of the World" (Thoreau).[27]

Civilization needs to be tamed as well as nature. American society in earlier centuries tamed nature, but in this century civilization needs to tame itself and recognize the integrity of wild places.

Would it be better, as a symbolic gesture of nondomination, to leave some wilderness areas unmapped, at least on small scales? Is mapping the last acre of wilderness necessary for, or might it prevent, positive human appreciation of wild nature?

The land ethic rests upon the discovery of certain values— integrity, projective creativity, life support, community—already present in ecosystems, and it imposes an obligation to act so as to maintain these. This is not, we have repeatedly warned, an ethic concerning culture, not an interhuman ethic. We will continue to need the Ten Commandments, categorical imperatives, the Golden Rule, concepts of justice, and the utilitarian calculus. But we are developing an extension of ethics into environmental attitudes, a new commandment about landscapes and ecosystems.

This ethic, although amply functional, is not merely functional. The dialectic of instrumental and intrinsic values, embedded in systemic value, is communitarian without subtracting anything organismic because it integrates organic parts in a community whole. Earthworms are of value because they aerate the soil for grasses and supply food for catbirds, but also because they have an inherent good of their own. Neither their instrumental value to grasses and catbirds or to the system, nor their intrinsic value in themselves—no single thing alone but the fusion of all contributes to integrity, stability, and beauty in the community.

We are dealing with the kind of system where gems sparkle in their setting and are made the more beautiful by it. The intrinsic values contribute just as much as do the instrumental values to the richness of the community. Subtract panthers from the south Florida ecosystem, no matter how minimal the function of the few remaining panthers in the Everglades, and that system will be less integral and beautiful, owing to the loss of the "sparkle" supplied by the panther's intrinsic value. That wetlands ecosystem once shaped a subspecies of panther peculiarly adapted to it, and the system will have a dull void when the panther is gone. It will heal itself with systemic readjustments (stability thereby remaining), but the system will have less luster with the loss of the lithe, handsome cat.

Our duties to persons in culture will at times bring us into conflict with this land ethic, and we will have to adjudicate such conflicts. We may even take a clue from the sorts of values here defended. What if humans simplify the native ecosystems of Iowa and Kansas, planting monocultures of corn and wheat as Americans have done, in order to feed a growing nation? What if the plainsmen reduce the bison herds so that they can put cattle on the range? They will have done harm to the original ecosystems in the sense that farming and ranching has reduced natural values there, even though this may be justified by the increased value produced in society. Beauty, integrity, stability, community (which, when found in culture, moralists usually call justice and utility) are increased in American society when persons are better fed; but the increase is purchased by the sacrifice of beauty, integrity, stability, community in the native grasslands. There is in one sense nothing unecological about this transformation of value, for we have just been describing how in all ecosystems there is the sacrifice and capture of values on a landscape of contest and conflict. Higher trophic levels always "eat up" the lower ones—although well-adapted species can do this only within the limits of renewability—and culture is the highest trophic level (Figure 6.6).

But we have also been saying that there is, and should be, systems-wide interdependence, stability, cohesiveness. These have been achieved amorally in nature, where the community is found, not made. But when humans, who are moral agents, enter such a scene and make their communities, rebuilding those found naturally, they may and should capture such values in their own behalf, but they also have an obligation to do so with a view over the whole (which also, derivatively, involves considering individual pains, pleasures, and welfares). The obligation remains a prima facie one: humans ought to preserve so far as they can the richness of the biological community. This too is among human obligations. It is not the only one. In a capstone sense it is not the ultimate one, since the cultural values supervening on nature are more eminent. But in a foundational sense it is ultimate, since it is out of projective nature that everything is created and maintained. Such duty must be heeded or reasons given why not. The global ecosystem too counts morally because it is inclusive and productive of all the individual landscapes, plants, animals, and persons within it.

From Is to Ought: Ecosystem Descriptions and Ethical Prescriptions

In environmental ethics one's beliefs about nature, which are based upon but exceed biological and ecological science, have everything to do with beliefs about duty. The way the world *is* informs the way it *ought to be*. In interhuman ethics it is sometimes held that world views are (more or less) logically independent of ethics. Thus a Christian, who believes that God created a good world that has fallen into evil; and a Buddhist, who, enroute to nirvana, denies God but has taken the *bodhisattva*'s vow of compassion upon all; and a naturalist, who denies supernature and believes that nature is all there is; and an agnostic, who does not know what to believe—all these can nevertheless agree to censure murder, stealing, marital infidelity, and so on. Their ethics has no close connection with their metaphysics.

Regardless of how far this is true in interpersonal ethics, however (and it is debatable there), it is not true in environmental ethics. Sometimes, of course, environmentalists can agree on policy though they differ in their concepts of nature. But we always shape our values in significant measure in accord with our notion of the kind of universe we live in. What we believe about the nature of nature, how we evaluate nature, drives our sense of duty. Our model of reality implies a model of conduct. Differing models of reality may sometimes imply similar conduct, but they more often do not. A model in which nature has no value apart from human preferences will imply different conduct from one where nature projects all values, some of them objective and others that further require human subjectivity superposed on objective nature.

There is here a prior assumption that one ought to protect values—life, creativity, community—wherever these are found. But like the injunction that one ought to promote the good or that one ought to keep promises, the obligation to protect value is so high-level as to be, if not definitional or analytic, so general as to be virtually unarguable and therefore without any real theoretical content. Substantive values emerge only when something empirical is specified as the locus of value. Here humans make judgments about what is going on in nature, judgments coached by ecology, affecting value judgments. To some extent, the natural course we choose to preserve is filtered through our concepts of beauty, stability, and integrity, concepts whose origins are not wholly clear and which are perhaps culturally biased. But perspectival though this is, what counts as value in nature is not just brought to and imposed on the ecosystem; it is discovered there.

This evaluation is not scientific description; hence not ecology per se but metaecology. No amount of research can verify that the right is the optimum biotic community. Yet ecological description generates this valuing of nature, endorsing the systemic rightness. The transition from *is* to *good* and thence to *ought* occurs here; we leave science to enter the domain of evaluation, from which an ethic follows. The injunction to maximize the ecosystemic excellence is ecologically derived but is an evaluative transition.

This account initially suggests that ecological description is logically (if not chronologically) prior to the ecosystemic evaluation, the former generating the latter. But the connection of description with evaluation is more complex, for description and evaluation to some extent arise together and it is often difficult to say which is prior and which is subordinate. Ecological description finds unity, harmony, interdependence, creativity, life support, conflict and complement in dialectic, stability, richness, community—and these are valuationally endorsed, yet they are found, to some extent, because we search with a disposition to value these things. We find in nature a mirror of what is in our minds. Still, the ecological description does not merely confirm these values; it informs them, and we find that the character, the empirical content, of order, harmony, stability, richness, community is drawn from no less than brought to nature. What is in our minds mirrors nature.

In post-Darwinian nature, for instance, in the odious scene of violence deplored by Mill, many looked for these values in vain. With ecological redescriptions we now find them. Yet the earlier data are not denied, only redescribed or set in a larger ecological context. Somewhere en route our notions of harmony, stability, creativity, community, and so on, have shifted too, and we see value now where we could not see it before.

What is ethically puzzling, and exciting, in the marriage and mutual transformation of ecological description and evaluation is that here an *ought* is not so much *derived* from an *is* as discovered simultaneously with it. As we progress from descriptions of fauna and flora, of cycles and pyramids, of autotrophs coordinated with heterotrophs, of stability and dynamism, and move on to intricacy, to planetary opulence and interdependence, to unity and harmony with oppositions in counterpoint and synthesis, to organisms evolved within and satisfactorily fitting their communities, arriving at length at beauty and goodness, it is difficult to say where the natural facts leave off and where the natural values appear. For some, at least, the sharp *is/ought* dichotomy is gone; the values seem to be there as soon as the facts are fully in and both alike seem properties of the system. We do now find a trend in nature—its projecting of life, stability, integrity, culminating in a sense of beauty when humans enter the scene—that we ought to follow (in the axiological sense), although there are no moral agents other than ourselves in nature.

Valuing Aesthetic Nature

A sign at Lake Manyara National Park in Tanzania reads:

> Let no one say and say it to your shame
> That all was beauty here until you came.[28]

This sign raises two interesting issues. A first critic will respond that the sign is a confusion: there was no beauty at all in the wilderness before humans came; beauty is an experience in the eye of the beholder. This critic will consider proper, however cute, the reply:

> I must say, and say it with some fame,
> There was no beauty here, until I came!

A second critic will respond that regardless of whether beauty arrives with humans *all* that goes on there apart from human disturbances is not to be judged beautiful. Wild nature is a mixed scene: some things there can be judged aesthetically positive, but many things are ugly; others are neutral. Perhaps beauty is in the eye of the beholder, but a beholder will often find nature aesthetically displeasing or indifferent. Humans bring the celebration of beauty, but sometimes there is nothing to celebrate.

Is There No Beauty at All in Nature?

"A thing is right," said Leopold, "when it tends to preserve the integrity, stability, and beauty of the biotic community." Immanuel Kant cautioned that in appreciating natural beauty we ought not to assume that nature has fashioned its forms for human delight; instead, "it is we who receive nature with favor, not nature which shows us favor."[29] So perhaps, to be accurate, we ought to say that a thing is right when it preserves in nature what humans receive with favor aesthetically. Stability and even integrity (wholeness) are objectively present in biotic communities, but not beauty. Only by accident (*epiphenomenon*) does nature excite the subjective, human experience of beauty. We humans are the artists, as Alexander said. Nature is not an artist; it only sometimes chances to *echo* our aesthetic tastes.

Phenomena such as life and life support, nutrition, resource capture and recycling, photosynthesis, oxygen transport by hemoglobin, warblers regulating insect populations, genetic mutations producing varying phenotypes in novel niches, speciation—all these and many of the values they carry we may concede to be objectively present in nature before humans come. But beauty? With beauty we cross a threshold into a realm of higher value; the experience of beauty is something humans bring into the world. Just as there is no creature with a world view and an ethic before humans arrive, nothing has any sense of beauty. Humans ignite beauty, rather as they ignite ethics in the world.

Environmental value theory does need to split aesthetic value off from many other values carried by nature. Aesthetic value is a transitional type. For some interpreters, beauty is the paradigm case of value, and, finding aesthetic experience to be inevitably subjective, they extrapolate to find all value subjective. Aesthetic experience is indeed a capstone value, but that does not make it a model for all underlying value. Rather, environmental value theory builds a more foundational, biologically based account like the one we developed in the preceding sections. An understanding of aesthetic experience now needs to be superposed on this more objective account.

The experience of beauty emerges to become well developed in humans. Some will say that aesthetic experience is entirely absent in nonhumans. That is too swift a judgment. Aesthetic experience comes in diverse forms. Stimulation by scenic beauty and the sublime are high forms; other ("lower"?) forms accompany such physical satisfactions as eating a tasty meal or enjoying the warm sun, which may be shared with some animals. A human may admire the muscular strength and power of a full-curl bighorn ram. Dare we say that the ewe, attracted to him, experiences nothing of this as she permits mating? Though we do not think she self-consciously makes judgments about her aesthetic experience, it is entirely consistent with natural selection theory that she is positively attracted to the ram's strength and power and that this registers in some way in her experience.

When the male bowerbird decorates a bower with shells and feathers, the female "likes it"—with whatever experiential capacities she has. The peahen must have some delight in the colorful tail of the peacock, spread high; otherwise the tail is a liability that natural selection would never have preserved. Unless we think that birds and beasts have no experience at all, it is difficult to deny them the precursors of aesthetic experience.

Nevertheless, the capacity for aesthetic experience sparkles in humans, and animal precursors, if any, are still subjective. So we might conclude that beauty is not objectively present in nature; it is in the eye of the beholder—mostly in human eyes, perhaps nascent in the eyes and experiences of birds and beasts.

At this point we have to distinguish two sorts of aesthetic qualities: *aesthetic capacities*, capacities for experience that are only in beholders; and *aesthetic properties*, which lie objectively in natural things. The experience of beauty does arise in the beholder, but what is this experience of? It is of form, structure, integrity, order, competence, muscular strength, endurance, dynamic movement, symmetry, diversity, unity, spontaneity, interdependence, lives defended or coded in genomes, creative and regenerative power, evolutionary speciation, and so on. These events are there before humans arrive, the products of projective nature; when we value them aesthetically, our experience is being superposed on natural properties.

In a sense, systemic nature even has an *aesthetic power*, since it is able to produce aesthetic properties, even though nature does not have—until it produces it in humans—the capacity for aesthetic experience. When humans arrive and value wild nature, we are sometimes valuing a projective nature that we are discovering, more than we are projecting our values onto nature. Nature carries aesthetic properties objectively, and these are ignited in the subjective experience of the arriving beholder. There is aesthetic stimulation, for instance, in the sense of abyss when one overlooks a canyon or stares into space. Similarly, the experience of the fury of a hurricane at sea is in the beholder. But the abyss and the fury (the aesthetic properties) are not in the mind; they are in nature. Human emotions track the motions of nature.

The world is beautiful in something like the way it is mathematical: neither aesthetic experience (in the "high" sense) nor mathematical experience exists prior to the coming of humans. Mathematics and aesthetics are human constructs; they come out of the human head and are used to map the world. This is also true of theories in the natural sciences, of lines of latitude and longitude, or of contours on maps. Regression lines (averaging out trends in data and correlating variables) and centers of gravity do not exist in nature. But these inventions succeed in helping humans to find their way around in the world because they map form, symmetry, harmony, distribution patterns, causal interrelationships, order, unity, diversity, and so on, that are discovered to be actually there.

It is true to say that the world is objectively mathematical and at the same time to say that mathematics is a subjective creation of the human mind. Mathematical properties are really there, though mathematical experience awaits the human coming—and, analogously, aesthetic properties and capacities. It is thus no accident that mathematicians are invariably among those who find the world aesthetically delightful in its symmetries, curves, patterns. What we are further claiming now is that a biological appreciation of the world finds it beautiful.

The wildness of a place, in which we sometimes delight, is not in the mind. "Wild" means "apart from the hand (or mind) of humans." The sense of beauty may be in the mind, but the wildness that is sensed and that generates the experience of beauty is not. The constructive and erosional forces that have formed the Montana landscapes, the West Virginia hills, the Maine tidal basin are out there in the world. When landscapes regularly produce a sense of beauty, we begin to suspect that more needs to be said than that humans are receiving nature with favor. Perhaps nature is not doing us a favor either, for that way of expressing it is too intentional. Natural things are not made for the purpose of aesthetic appreciation; they are not artworks, and in that sense nature is not an artist. But projective nature regularly creates landscapes and ecosystems—mountains, seas, grasslands, swamps—whose properties include overtones of beauty. These aesthetic properties (though not aesthetic experiences) attach to nature objectively. Humans with an ecosystem approach will discover that beauty is a mysterious product of projective nature, an aura of objective aesthetic properties. This aura may require an experiencer with aesthetic capacities for its consummation but requires still more the forces of nature for its production.

When I am enjoying the fall colors of a New England landscape, I may (having taken a philosophy class) check my enjoyment with the thought, "I am just projecting this display of colors onto these trees—the red onto the maples, gold onto the aspen, scarlet and brown onto the oaks, green onto the spruce. There is no color out there, apart from my presence." In a sense that is true; the experience of color is in the eye of the beholder. But the eye is translating into the experience of colored form something that *is* out there (electromagnetic waves reflected from molecular structural planes; leaf, branch, and crown shapes). This is not being made up; it is being discovered (and translated). The color experience is the means of discovery.

The display out there might be translated via some other sense modality; it might, for instance, be translated by a system of equations that maps the landscape and electromagnetic waves mathematically, rather like a score mapping music. That mathematics would also be in the mind of the beholder, yet it would be mapping the same events out there in the world that color maps. In any method by which the fall display could be adequately mapped and translated—catching in this way or that what is taking place in the rich world—the result would be aesthetically stimulating because the form, symmetry, tonal complexity objectively there in the world is aesthetically worthy, variously caught by alternative modes of detection.

Two dimensions here are noteworthy: the display objectively in the world, and the detection device resulting from eye coupled with brain. Both are natural products, the result of projective nature.

In further truth as well, there is a great deal more going on in the New England fall landscape than our sense modalities ordinarily catch, much of which would be additionally aesthetically pleasing, could we know it. One of the things that science does is extend our sense modalities so that we contact these further dimensions of nature. We sometimes use computer images enhanced with colors to increase our sensitivity to events in the world (infrared waves at night; turbulence in gases on Jupiter) that our eyes are incompetent to detect. We may find the spiral symmetries of a DNA molecule aesthetically pleasing when these are mapped by computer simulation.[30]

Is All Beauty in Nature?

John Muir exclaimed, "None of Nature's landscapes are ugly so long as they are wild."[31] William Morris agrees: "Surely there is no square mile of earth's inhabitable surface that is not beautiful in its own way, if we men will only abstain from wilfully destroying that beauty."[32] While not logically incompatible with Kant's claim, in the unlikely case that humans invariably received all landscapes with favor, Muir's claim is of a different temper. Kant will advise us to take as much of nature as we can with aesthetic pleasure (sunsets, spring flowers, bird songs, waterfalls), and to discard the rest (parasites, burned forests), considering ourselves to be lucky or skilled as we do so.

But Muir claims that landscapes always supply beauty, never ugliness. They should unfailingly generate in us favorable experiences if we are suitably perceptive. Anyone who says that a desert or the tundra or a volcanic eruption is ugly is making a false statement and behaving inappropriately. Ecosystems, at least as scenes, contain only positive aesthetic properties. Rather like clouds, which are never ugly, only more or less beautiful, so too are mountains, forests, seashores, grasslands, cliffs, canyons, cascades, rivers. (Astronomical scenes, too—stars, galaxies, moons—are always more or less beautiful.)

This view does not find all places equally or perfectly beautiful; it maps them on a scale that runs from zero upward but has no negative numbers. It will be possible in some cases to increase natural beauty—by building artificial reefs, for instance. Further, this claim is an area-level judgment. It does not deny that some items in nature are ugly viewed from certain perspectives, only that in a landscape perspective—that is, in locale and ecosystemic perspective—there are only positive qualities. It would seem implausible to say of human works of art that they are never badly done, yet here the positive thesis claims that virgin landscapes are always (more or less) well formed aesthetically.

It is appropriate to say of various landforms and seascapes

that they are graceful, intense, unified, rich, contoured, fertile, expansive, awesome, sublime, even desolate, turbulent, severe, rugged. This list mixes terms that describe aesthetic experiences with terms that describe aesthetic properties, but that mix is no longer the issue. Here we are concerned only with whether the aesthetic response is, or ought to be, positive. Montanans enjoy their "big sky country," and Down-Easters stroll over a tidal basin at neap tide to sense a vast emptiness. Aesthetic properties "call for" appropriate aesthetic experiences, and it is never "called for" to say that such places are bland, dull, boring, incoherent, chaotic.

"Wild" is often thought to be a negative predicate, as when we say that a field or a child has gone wild. That is so from the perspective of culture, where an untamed wildness is a disvalue. From such a perspective, of course, humans will find many lands—tropical forests, tundras, deserts, moons, other planets—displeasing: that is, inhospitable to culture. But we are here considering not utility but beauty. If we come to a landscape on its own terms, sensitive to its integrity, wild is always a positive predicate. This wildness can produce in us a sense of beauty—"wild, wonderful West Virginia."

Are nature's aesthetic properties always positive? Allen Carlson claims, "All virgin nature . . . is essentially aesthetically good."[33] Initially, this claim seems evidently false; one can hold it only by shamelessly picking the evidence. In one sense, there can be no failures in nature because nothing is to be judged in the light of aesthetic intention. Evaluating works of human art involves judging them in the light of an artist's intention, but nature has no intentions; thus, nature cannot fail, not having tried.

But in another sense, it seems that there are frequent, even omnipresent failures in nature. Both organisms and ecosystems can be ruined. Let us first cite as counterexamples to the positive thesis various *items*, organisms, in the landscape and, second, consider *systemic processes*, which will lead us, third, to *scenic wholes*.

If hikers come upon the rotting carcass of an elk, full of maggots, they find it revolting. Here is a bad example of its kind, disharmony, a putrid elk. Any landscape looked at in detail is as filled with dying as with flourishing things. Everything is in some degree marred and ragged—a tree with broken limbs, a crushed wildflower, an insect-eaten leaf. An eagle chick plagued with ticks is not a pretty thing. Sometimes there are disfigured, even monstrous animals. So why is this not ugliness in the landscape? It is!

We do not enjoy such experiences. Tourists take no photographs of these eyesores.

Ugliness Transformed in Ecosystemic Perspective

If we enlarge our scope in retrospect and prospect (as ecology greatly helps us do), we get further categories for interpretation. The rotting elk returns to the humus, its nutrients recycled; the maggots become flies, which become food for the birds; natural selection results in better-adapted elk for the next generation. The monstrous mutants, unless by luck better fitted for some new niche, are edited out of the system, and the system continues to track new environments by casting forth further mutants. Every item must be seen not in framed isolation but framed by its environment, and this frame in turn becomes part of the bigger picture we have to appreciate—not a "frame" but a dramatic play. The momentary ugliness is only a still shot in an ongoing motion picture.

Life is a dynamic contest in which an organism struggles to express its genotype in a phenotype, with the phenotype supported and limited by the environment, helped and hurt by contingencies in it. With a more sophisticated critical sense the aesthetician comes to judge that the clash of values, pulled into symbiosis, is not an ugly but a beautiful thing. The world is not a jolly place, not a Walt Disney world, but one of struggling, somber beauty. The dying is the shadow side of the flourishing.

One has to appreciate what is not evident. There are lots of marvelous things going on in dead wood, or underground, or in the dark; they are not scenic at all, but an appreciation of them is aesthetic. The usefulness of a tree in the ecosystem is only half over at its death; as an old snag or a rotting hulk it provides nesting cavities, perches, insect larvae, food for birds, nutrients for the soil, and on and on. To say that decay or predation is bad is as incomplete as to say that rain is bad because it falls on my picnic. These things are local disvalues to individuals, but they are systemic values. A system without decay or rain would soon lock up and dry up; without predation the systemic processes could not build up life very far, with resulting benefits for later-coming individuals. To dislike the interlocking value capture is something like looking at a jigsaw puzzle and complaining that the pieces are misshapen. A human does not say that his apple is ugly after biting off a piece, so why should he think a leaf ugly because a worm has eaten some of it?

Lewis Carroll thought he had found something evil in nature:

> How doth the little crocodile
> Improve his shining tail,
> And pour the waters of the Nile
> On every golden scale!
>
> How cheerfully he seems to grin,
> How neatly spreads his claws,
> And welcomes little fishes in,
> With gently smiling jaws![34]

But there is nothing sinister or evil about the crocodile/fish food chain. Any ugliness here is in the eye of the beholder, any disvalue in fact only a projection—like the big, bad wolf. The objective events in the world, good for crocodiles and bad for individual fish, are a systemic good in an ecosystem in which both crocodiles and fish have a satisfactory place. So far from eliminating the crocodile to help the fish, humans ought rather, when the crocodile is endangered, reduce recreational and commercial fishing privileges in order that crocodiles can fish with more success. (See the Organized Fishermen of Florida versus Andrus case, Chapter 4.)

During his treks through Florida swamps, and after expressing repeated fear of stumbling unawares upon alligators, John Muir wrote:

> Many good people believe that alligators were created by the Devil, thus accounting for their all-consuming appetite and ugliness. But doubtless these creatures are happy and fill the place assigned them by the great Creator of us all. Fierce and cruel they appear to us, but beautiful in the eyes of God.[35]

Doubtless that beauty figured into Muir's claim that every landscape is beautiful so long as it is wild.

Still, there is itemized, individual ugliness in nature; virgin nature is not at every concrete locus aesthetically good: consider a crippled fish that has escaped an alligator. Those who are not programmatic nature romantics will admit this and go on to recover what beauty they can. But ugliness, though present at times in particulars, is not the last word. Realists with a "depth" past a "flat" vision can "see" the *time line* as well as the *ugly space* immediately present; they know that regenerative forces are already present, that over time nature will bring beauty out of this ugliness, and that this tendency is already present and aesthetically stimulating now. Such aestheticians can see longitudinally as well as cross-sectionally. When the point event, which is intrinsically ugly, is stretched out instrumentally in the process, the ugliness mellows—though it does not disappear—and makes its contribution to systemic beauty and to beauty in later-coming individuals, whether of the same or of other species.

We can expect that humans, like other animals, will have been naturally selected to find certain things repulsive, those things (rotting carcasses, excrement) that they as individuals need to avoid in order to survive. But these processes, abhorrent from the perspective of my individuality, may not be ugly at all in the system, where they are the recycling of resources. Environmental ethics stretches us out from our individualistic, self-centered perspectives into a consideration of systemic beauty. A cultural ethic might find it disrespectful to bury one's mother without embalming and preserving her body; an environmental ethic might oppose embalming on grounds that it locks up resources and that her body's decay is, systemically, a beautiful thing.

There is ugliness, but, even more, there are transformative forces that sweep toward beauty in the midst of this perpetual perishing. There are destructive forces of entropic teardown, and these work against the positive constructive, negentropic forces. When the negative temporarily overcome the positive forces, the result can be local ugliness. Sooner or later every life is so ruined. But the end of the individual is never the end of the story. The individual may be sacrificed for the life of its predator; one way or another its elements will be recomposed as surely as they are decomposed. There is always the resurrection of new life past the destruction of old life. This disorder and corruption are the prelude to creation, and in this perpetual re-creation there is high beauty.

Nature's beauty can be costly and tragic, yet nature is a scene of beauty ever reasserting itself in the face of destruction. When the various items in the landscape are integrated into a dynamic evolutionary ecosystem, the ugly parts do not subtract from but rather enrich the whole. The ugliness is contained, overcome, and integrates into positive, complex beauty. Yet this is not so much *viewed* as *experienced* after one reaches ecologically tutored understanding. It is not so much a matter of *sight* as of *insight* into the drama of life. In many of life's richest aesthetic experiences there is nothing to put on canvas, nothing to take snapshots of.

Are there ugly landscapes? Think of a beach destroyed by a tidal wave, a valley inundated by a lava flow. A windstorm in Idaho in April 1986 destroyed 1,500 acres of forest. The scorched earth after a fire would be thought ugly if it had resulted from a carelessly abandoned campfire. What is the difference if the fire was a result of a bolt of lightning instead? Must one know the origin of the flames to judge whether the scene is ugly or beautiful? Sometimes there are natural catastrophes that alter landscapes for the worse. Has not nature then produced ugly places? Again, in a way this is so. No one would feature these places in landscape paintings; they are not picturesque. But we are dealing not with paintings but with happenings in a living system, and deeper aesthetic sensibilities are required.

Consider how our attitudes toward fire have changed since being informed by ecology. Fire sanitizes and thins a forest, releasing nutrients from the humus back into the soil. It resets succession, opens up edging, initially destroys but subsequently benefits wildlife. It regenerates shade-intolerant trees. Fire is bad for a culture that wishes to exploit a forest or even to view it scenically this year and next; fire is bad for a hiker caught in the flames; but we no longer think that fire is bad for a forest. Rather, it is part of the formative process. Even from the perspective of culture, present management problems (such as insect blights) often result from decades of fire suppression. Soon it becomes difficult to say of a naturally burned forest that it is ugly. It is temporarily ugly, as is the elk carcass, in that the normal growth trends have been halted. But the temporary upset is integral to the larger systemic health.

Some violent forces in nature such as tidal waves and lava flows, are so massive and rare that ecosystems have no adaptations to them. The system cannot "remember" long enough to select strategies for coping with infrequent catastrophes. There may even be periodic extinctions due to astronomical causes, though we poorly understand these (Chapter 4). As disruptions are proportionately common (on the scale of decades up to a century or so), they become integrated into the successional cycles and are no longer bad events for grasslands or forests. Further, our understanding of long-term evolutionary and successional changes at the regional ecosystemic level is incomplete, perhaps the least understood phase of biology; it may be that scientists do not yet have the appropriate ecological categories to understand these events (as earlier we did not understand the place of fire).

Meanwhile, aestheticians may have to accept these ugly events as anomalies challenging the general paradigm that nature's landscapes almost without fail have an essential beauty. Even lava flows and tidal waves in their power and fury are not without aesthetic properties, destructive though they are of life, and there is dramatic beauty in the struggle of plant and animal communities to reestablish themselves after catastrophe. Life comes back, and the return is beautiful; but somehow the going out of life, once it is seen as a preface to its return, is less ugly than before.

Beyond Beauty to the Sublime

Aesthetic properties in nature push the beholder toward the experience of the sublime, something larger than beauty. At the beginning, we search for something pretty or colorful, for scenic beauty, for the picturesque. Landscapes regularly provide that, but when they do not, we must not think that they have no aesthetic properties. James McNeill Whistler complained: "Nature is usually wrong: that is to say, the condition of things that shall bring about the perfection of harmony worthy of a picture is rare, and not common at all. . . . Seldom does Nature succeed in producing a picture."[36] And when it does succeed, R. B. Litton, a forest planner, refers to this gathering of the scenic beauty that nature has produced as the "visual harvesting of scenic resources."[37]

But nature is not always to be treated as though it were material to be harvested for a picture postcard. "Harvest" is a word that belongs with agriculture; "picture" is a word that belongs with art; neither is adequate for interpreting spontaneous nature, landscapes, ecosystems. To try to understand the beauty of wildness with a resource model or with pictorial criteria is inevitably to misunderstand it. It is trying to interpret a sunset as a kind of crop, or a gazelle and its grace as a kind of cow, or an ecosystem as a kind of postcard. These are dreadful category mistakes.

We ought not to tour Glacier National Park interested only in a view—stopping at overlooks and examining rugged mountains as though the parts of nature that cannot serve us ought at least to please us. We rather discover that nature can throw us off balance, overwhelm us with the howling wind, the shifting sand, the frozen tundra, the vertigo of time and struggle. We find ourselves exhausted before the inexhaustible. One should find landscapes "wild" (Muir) and let each be "beautiful in its own way" (Morris). This is the "form" that one has to appreciate, not some form that fits a camera frame. The experience of beauty that we seek is not a recreational finding of something one can frame in a snapshot (that might be only a projection from the eye of the beholder) but a locating of oneself in and reconciling of oneself with the forces of creation that are objectively there. One ought not to look at nature expecting pictures; one should rather thrill over projective nature, where Earthen nature is regularly splendid. One should thrill over ecosystems, at the production of which Nature seldom fails. The scene is the projective system; until we see that, we miss what is sublimely there, and those who seek to harvest sublime resources are doomed to fail.

A criticism of the preceding argument—reinterpreting localized, intrinsic ugliness as systemic, instrumental beauty—is that we save a claim—"All virgin nature . . . is essentially aesthetically good" (Carlson)—by switching categories and levels, that we win by redefining beauty as the sublime and transforming the scope of events under consideration. Any victory is success by equivocation. One stretches and twists "beauty" to fit all the available evidence, some of which would by usual criteria be interpreted as repulsive. The rotting carcass, the monstrosity, the scorched earth, the lava-ruined ecosystem—not found to be beautiful—are pronounced sublime.

Perhaps one can admit that although evolutionary ecology makes all these events intelligible, it does not make them beautiful. Anyone who argues so accentuates the beauty, ignores the ugly (though as omnipresent as beauty), shifts reference frames to accommodate anomalies, dodges particulars with statistics, and believes the trends to be "essentially sublime." Nature romanticism becomes an aesthetic blindfold. The main claim becomes immune to refutation by evidence.

Our reply is that here there is no equivocation but rather an insistence on context. Good aesthetics knows what good science knows, that we catch beauty, as we catch facts, with a paradigm; and the struggle for truth in either field is always the struggle to gain a big enough paradigm, an Einsteinian past a Newtonian one, a holistic past a partial one. The aesthetician here is trying to experience all the facts, not limited and local ones only. This is not blind nature romanticism; it is open-eyed realism that wants to see beyond individualistic and humanistic perspectives, and it sees sublime beauty in the evolutionary and ecosystemic struggle for life.

The upshot is not that virgin nature is invariably aesthetically positive in immediate detail but that it is *essentially* so when even the ugliness is embraced by the sublime. As always with trends, one needs not only to evaluate the particulars in space and time but also to see the system. Within the histories of species, individuals are perpetually perishing, but species are prolonged until no longer fit in their environments—whereupon they evolve into something else or go extinct and are replaced. Beauty does not require permanence. Within landscapes there is ugliness in the detail, but at the systemic level, at the scope of the dynamic scene, softened by perspective from a distance, there is sublime beauty. This can be true even where the (rare) violence of nature is so massive that ecosystems have been unable to adapt their successions to such interruptions. Even here, life will reassert itself and regain its beauty. Great beauty, like great music, is often in a minor key.

This essential motif, the conquest of constructive over destructive forces, is the key to the aesthetic capacity in this storied natural history, producing aesthetic properties to which humans, when they arrive and discover where they are, respond with positive aesthetic experience—one that often leads toward religious experience. An appreciation of this essence in projective nature is what Muir could teach Socrates from the University of the Wilderness.

7 Environmental Policy: An Ethic of the Commons

 NO SUCH THING as policy exists in nature; the environment has no policy, although there may be trends such as species packing in ecosystems. Policy arises when humans corporately and deliberately confront their environment. The environment is crucially a "commons," that is, a public good. In the United States there have historically been fights over what to do with public domain lands, how much to reserve as commons and how much to pass into private ownership. Policies on such commons have been uncertainly related to capitalism, ownership of the means of production, and the property rights of individuals. Admire the private entrepreneur though we may, the forces of capitalism and individualism may not attend to the public good automatically.

Although there is a spontaneous order generated when many such citizen and economic units interact (a cultural analogue of the order spontaneously generated in ecosystems), we cannot conclude in society and its markets that an "invisible hand" guarantees an optimal harmony between a people and their landscape; or that the right things are done in encounter with fauna, flora, ecosystems, or regarding future generations. This is partly because short-term self-interest gets out of hand, especially when coupled with power and where one cannot count on the long-term cooperation of others. Thus there is a need for laws to regulate self-interest, private use, and business; such regulations are imposed in the public interest by the forces of democracy.

A test of a democracy is whether its citizens can learn to practice enlightened restraint, developing an ethic about the environment, as Americans have been doing over the last 100 years. But this is still a civil ethics. A further test, one for the next century, is whether a people can see the whole commonwealth of a human society set in its ecosystems, developing an environmental ethics in the primary sense. This will require a wild ethic. It is not simply what a society does to its slaves, women, blacks, minorities,

246

handicapped, children, or future generations but what it does to its fauna, flora, species, ecosystems, and landscapes that reveals the character of that society.

We have often distinguished between nature and culture in the chapters preceding; now we must relate culture to nature—first in governmental policy, second in business (Chapter 8), and finally (Chapter 9) in personal biography.

Collective Choice in an Environmental Ethic

This chapter and the next deal with collective choice. Some ethical choices are made by individuals, but in other cases we must choose together. We will be reassessing ground earlier covered, now from the perspective of what a culture chooses—first in its policy, then in its industry and labor. Government and business are large influences in our lives; both have vast amounts of power to affect the environment for good or ill; both influence our behavior greatly. Unless an ethic gives persons a place to encourage and constrain their governments and businesses, it will be incomplete and ineffective.

In setting policy, we can—by "mutual coercion, mutually agreed upon"—do in concert what no individual, interest group, or business can successfully do alone.[1] This is true in many areas of social responsibility but especially in environmental affairs. We sometimes "legislate morality," at least in minimum essential or common-denominator areas. There must be a management ethic for the commons—about soil, air, water, pollution, environmental quality, the ozone layer, mutagens, wildlife, the eagle as a national symbol, endangered species, future generations. This ethic will be voluntary in the sense that it is an enlightened and democratically achieved consensus, willingly supported by millions of citizens. But it will also be written into law and therefore be mandatory.

No laws can be enforced without the widespread voluntary compliance of citizens; there are never enough enforcement officers to compel everybody. But voluntary compliance depends on the expectation that even those who do not wish to obey will be required to do so. Unless such an ethic is enforced as well as encouraged, it is largely useless. No merely private, voluntary environmental ethics can be effective. Of course, minority rights and the right to dissent have also to be considered—and enforced. But no one has the right to harm others without justified cause. Where breaking an environmental ethic—especially one that has a democratic consensus behind it—harms others by destroying a public good (as well as goods in a biotic community), enforcement can be justified.

Though an ethic needs to be largely voluntary, a societal ethic cannot be stable if it is entirely voluntary. Even if 99 percent of citizens are glad to behave in a certain way provided that all others do, the 1 percent who freeload will trigger bad faith. One rotten apple spoils a bushel. What policy and regulation can do is enable citizens to act in concert. This does not mean that we expect large-scale social institutions to have moral commitments in the robust way that individuals and small groups can sometimes have them. Governments and big business firms are, strictly speaking, not moral agents at all, although as instruments of the persons within them they can do large amounts of right and wrong. Nevertheless, governments and businesses can have policies in which moral considerations are a factor. Often what citizens do must be done in concert if it is to be done at all. Concerted action can be taken with full or only partial agreement about reasons for so acting; it can sometimes involve agreeing about behavior while disagreeing about rationale. This is especially true regarding certain minimum standards (for example, permissible pollution levels, critical habitats for endangered species, or reclamation criteria for mined lands).

Not only is the environment a public good, but further, most remaining wildlands are public lands—national forests, parks, wilderness areas, seashores, grasslands, wildlife refuges, lands under the Bureau of Land Management, state or county parks and forests. These areas are largely managed for multiple use and remain only semiwild; still, they constitute a major component of the natural environment. They also contain most of the relict pristine wildlands, as nearly as these anywhere remain. One cannot look to the market to produce or protect the multiple values that citizens enjoy in general on public lands, much less in wilderness areas, because many of the values sought here are not, or not simply, economic ones.

A nation needs collective choices producing a public land ethic. Decisions here must be political decisions; but they are also taking place in the midst of a philosophical reassessment coupled with ecological concerns and moral concerns about how humans should value nature. They are political decisions entwined with reforming world views.

There is a long tradition about rights and restrictions of access to public goods such as water, grazing, and timber, as well as a history of regulation in the public interest in and multiple uses of public lands. But "ecological values" had little history in policy until about 1960. Though there is significant public sentiment concerning intrinsic values in nature, policy has only begun to address such issues as the right to exist of endangered species or ecosystems, the preservation of biotic diversity, rights and wrongs in the treatment of wildlife, and so on.

In the last quarter-century, however, there has been steady enactment of environmentally oriented legislation. A representative list is instructive:

Clean Air Act (1955), Amendments (1963, 1965, 1969, 1977)
Outdoor Recreation Resources Review Act (1958)
Public Land Administration Act (1960)
Cape Cod National Seashore Act (1961)
Golden Eagle Protection Act (1962)
Wilderness Act (1964)
Water Resources Planning Act (1965)
Water Quality Act (1965)
Water Pollution Control Act Amendments (1965)
Anadromous Fish Conservation Act (1965)
National Wildlife Refuge System Administration Act (1966),
    Amendments (1976, 1978)
Fur Seal Act (1966)
Air Quality Act (1967)
San Rafael Wilderness, California, Act (1968)
San Gabriel Wilderness, California, Act (1968)
Great Swamp National Wildlife Refuge Wilderness, New Jersey,
    Act 1968)
Wild and Scenic Rivers Act (1968)
National Trails System Act (1968)
Redwood National Park Act (1968), Expansion (1978)
North Cascades National Park Act (1968), with Pasayten Wilderness
Mount Jefferson Wilderness, Oregon, Act (1968)
National Environmental Policy Act (1969)
Ventana Wilderness, California, Act (1969)
Desolation Wilderness, California, Act (1969)
Sleeping Bear Dunes National Lakeshore, Michigan, Act (1970)
Omnibus Wilderness Act (1970), designating twenty-three
    wilderness areas in seven states
Gulf Islands National Seashore, Florida, Mississippi, Act (1971)
Voyageurs National Park, Minnesota, Act (1971)
Canyonlands National Park, Utah, Enlargement Act (1971)

Arches National Park, Utah, Act (1971)
Capitol Reef National Park Utah, Act (1971)
Wild Free-Roaming Horses and Burros Act (1971)
Pine Mountain Wilderness, Arizona, Act (1972)
Buffalo National River, Arkansas, Act (1972)
Sycamore Canyon Wilderness, Arizona, Act (1972)
Oregon Dunes National Recreation Area Act (1972)
Cedar Keys Wilderness, Florida, Act (1972)
Scapegoat Wilderness, Montana, Act (1972)
Sawtooth National Recreation Area, Idaho, Act (1972)
Washakie Wilderness, Wyoming, Act (1972)
Lava Beds Wilderness, California, Act (1972)
Federal Water Pollution Control Act Amendments (1972)
Lassen Volcanic Wilderness, California, Act (1972)
Eagle Cap Wilderness, Oregon, Act (1972), Additions
Marine Mammal Protection Act (1972)
Marine Protection, Research, and Sanctuaries Act (1972)
Bald Eagle Protection Act (1940), Amendments (1972, 1978)
Cumberland Island National Seashore, Georgia, Act (1972)
Coastal Zone Management Act (1972)
Glen Canyon National Recreation Area, Arizona, Utah, Act
    (1972)
Endangered Species Act (1973, 1982), Amendments (1976, 1977,
    1978, 1979, 1980)
Forest and Rangeland Renewable Resources Planning Act (1974)
Okefenokee Wilderness, Georgia, Act (1974)
Big Thicket National Preserve, Texas, Act (1974)
Big Cypress National Preserve, Florida, Act (1974)
National Park System, Appropriation Ceilings Increase Act (1974)
Farallon Wilderness, California, Act (1974), with Point Reyes
    National Seashore, California, Additions
Eastern Wilderness Act (1974), designating fifteen wilderness
    areas in thirteen eastern states
Omnibus Wilderness Act (1974), designating seventeen areas in
    thirteen states
Canaveral National Seashore, Florida, Act (1975)
Grand Canyon National Park Englargement Act (1975)
Flat Tops Wilderness, Colorado, Act (1975)
Hells Canyon National Recreation Area, Oregon and Idaho, Act
    (1975)
Fishery Conservation and Management Act (1976), Amendments
    (1978, 1982)
Bristol Cliffs Wilderness, Vermont, Act (1976), boundary modifi-
    cations
Alpine Lakes Area Management Act (1976)
Eagles Nest Wilderness, Colorado, Act (1976)

Toxic Substances Control Act (1976)

Point Reyes Wilderness, California, Act (1976)

Whale Conservation and Protection Study Act (1976)

Congaree Swamp National Monument, South Carolina, Act (1976)

Omnibus Wilderness Act (1976), designating nineteen wilderness areas in thirteen states

National Park Wilderness Act (1976), designating thirteen wilderness areas in eight states

Federal Land Policy and Management Act (1976)

Resource Conservation and Recovery Act (1976)

Bureau of Land Management Wilderness Study Act (1976)

National Forest Management Act (1976)

Montana Wilderness Study Act (1977)

Soil and Water Resources Conservation Act (1977)

Endangered American Wilderness Act (1978), designating fifteen wilderness areas in eight states

Absaroka–Beartooth Wilderness, Montana, Act (1978)

National Ocean Pollution Research and Development and Monitoring Planning Act (1978)

Forest and Rangeland Renewable Resources Research Act (1978)

Cooperative Forestry Assistance Act (1978)

Humane Methods of Slaughter Act (1978)

Indian Peaks Wilderness, Colorado, and Oregon Islands, Oregon, Act (1978)

Blackjack Springs Wilderness and Whisker Lake Wilderness, Wisconsin, Act (1978)

Boundary Waters Canoe Area Wilderness Act (1978)

Public Rangelands Improvement Act (1978)

Antarctic Conservation Act (1978)

Great Bear Wilderness and Bob Marshall Wilderness Enlargement Act, Montana (1978)

National Parks and Recreation Act (1978), including designating eight wilderness areas in nine states

Fish and Wildlife Improvement Act (1978)

Sandina Mountain Wilderness, New Mexico, Enlargement Act (1980)

Central Idaho Wilderness Act (1980)

Fish and Wildlife Conservation Act (Nongame Act) (1980)

Rattlesnake National Recreation Area and Wilderness, Montana, Act (1980)

Alaska National Interest Lands Conservation Act (1980), designating thirty-five wilderness areas

Comprehensive Environmental Response, Compensation, and Liability Act (Superfund, 1980), Amendments (1986)

Salmon and Steelhead Conservation and Enhancement Act (1980)

New Mexico Wilderness Act (1980)

Omnibus Wilderness Act (1980), designating twenty-one wilderness areas in five states

Fire Island High Dune Wilderness, New York, Act (1980)

Florida Keys Wilderness Enlargement Act (1982)

Coastal Barrier Resources Act (1982)

Charles C. Deam Wilderness, Indiana, Wilderness Act (1982)

Paddy Creek Wilderness, Missouri, Act (1983)

Cheaha Wilderness, Alabama, Act (1983)

Nuclear Waste Policy Act (1982)

West Virginia Wilderness Act (1982)

Lee Metcalf Wilderness, Montana, Act (1983)

International Environmental Protection Act (1983)

Wallop–Breaux Amendments to the Federal Aid in Fish Restoration Act (1984)

Irish Wilderness, Missouri, Act (1984)

Wisconsin Wilderness Act (1984)

Vermont Wilderness Act (1984), designating five wilderness areas

New Hampshire Wilderness Act (1984), designating three wilderness areas

North Carolina Wilderness Act (1984), designating eleven wilderness areas

Oregon Wilderness Act (1984), designating twenty-nine wilderness areas and additions

Washington State Wilderness Act (1984), designating twenty-two wilderness areas and additions

Arizona Wilderness Act (1984), designating thirty-nine wilderness areas and additions

California Wilderness Act (1984), designating thirty-nine wilderness areas and additions, and other designations

Utah Wilderness Act (1984), designating twelve wilderness areas

Florida Wilderness Act (1984), designating seven wilderness areas

Arkansas Wilderness Act (1984), designating nine wilderness areas and additions

Georgia Wilderness Act (1984)

Mississippi National Forest Wilderness Act (1984)

Wyoming Wilderness Act (1984), designating thirteen wilderness areas and additions

Texas Wilderness Act (1984), designating five wilderness areas

Tennessee Wilderness Act (1984), designating three wilderness areas, Amendments (1986)

Pennsylvania Wilderness Act (1984), designating two wilderness areas and Allegheny National Recreation Area

Virginia Wilderness Act (1984), designating eleven wilderness areas

San Juan Wilderness, New Mexico, Protection Act (1984)

Kentucky Wilderness Act (1985)

Tennessee Wilderness Act (1986), designating six wilderness
areas and additions

Nebraska Wilderness Act (1985)

Food Security Act (1985), with provisions to discourage swamp-
busters and sodbusters and to encourage conservation reserves
and easements

Georgia Wilderness Act (1986), designating five wilderness areas
and additions

Clean Water Act (1987)

The Congressional Office of Technology Assessment, after a
major study of policy options in the face of threatened loss of biological diversity, has recommended that Congress pass a National
Biological Diversity Act and a National Conservation Education
Act.[2] Others have recommended an Endangered Ecosystems Act.

The tone of these acts in recent decades characteristically differs
from that of earlier eras, reflecting a concern about environmental
quality, environmental values, endangered species, biotic diversity,
and wilderness; or unimpaired productivity or diversity of the land;
or retaining a natural or primitive character of wildlands; or
preservation rather than conservation. There is increased persuasion that the national treasures include natural givens—both
amenities and necessities—that are not always merely commodities.
The National Environmental Policy Act requires for major federal
projects with significant effect a detailed statement of expected
environmental impact and of alternatives to the proposed action.
There has been greatly increased environmental regulation and
litigation, and much controversy over agency decisions about public
land use.

It is also worth noticing that these drastic changes in the political system were for the most part not initiated by the political
leaders but began in value changes in the grassroots public, spear-
headed by environmental activists and citizens' groups. The policy
changes have reflected citizen reassessments in ethics and values
associated with the natural environment.

A Value Analysis for Environmental Policy

In Chapter 1 we itemized fourteen types of value associated with
the natural environment: life-support, economic, recreational,
scientific, aesthetic, genetic-diversity, historical, cultural-symbol-

ization, character-building, diversity-unity, spontaneity and stability, dialectical, life, and religious. In order to consider philosophically a collective policy designed to protect these values, we need to dissect the concept of value another way, this time to identify the personal and the social, the human and nonhuman, the individual and the systemic dimensions. In doing so, we find seven levels of value. Then we can consider an axiological model for policy. A number of guidelines will expand and accompany this model.

A Taxonomy of Value Levels

In the value levels narrated here, there is no reason to think of exclusive categories. But there is every reason to think of identifiable dimensions of value that citizens and their representatives need to factor into policy analysis.

$Value_{ip}$ = *individual preference value*. $Value_{ip}$ is what individuals prefer in contexts of choice. Here valuing and its product, value, lie in the experience of interest satisfaction. In this sense valuing is subjective; valuing brings value into being within subject-owners, who are persons in their relationship to the world. Mere objects, including organisms that have no pyschological life and no felt preferences can have no individual preference values, though they may be resources for preferences. In our private cases, for normal adults, what we ourselves prefer is reasonably evident from introspection coupled with action. The $values_{ip}$ of other humans can be known from verbal preferences and behaviors, although some situations compel discrepancies between attitude and action. Where there are constraints, it may be difficult to ferret out true values. We also have to separate goals from failed performances, latent from manifest preferences, and the like. $Value_{ip}$ has seemed to many to be the motor force of all value, from which all the rest are derived.

$Value_{mp}$ = *market price value*. Often, an illuminating way out of the subjectivity of $value_{ip}$ is to look to the market, which, though produced by $value_{ip}$, has empirical objectivity. Articles and services are regularly exchanged on the market, which in nonbarter societies invests them with a going price, a public and observable quantity resulting from many individuals' estimation of the worth of having these commodities. $Value_{mp}$ is a derivative of usefulness, rarity, labor, advertising, government regulation, and so on, but in the end things are traded instrumentally to satisfy human interests, and their price must reflect preferences. If no one desired these things, the market would collapse. In wild nature no monetary or barter economy exists. But humans buy and sell natural things incessantly. They labor, trade, and own property, using nature for interest satisfactions, and this brings wild nature into the economic sphere.

We value many things in nature that never reach markets directly (air, photosynthesis, scenic beauty) but make an important though unpriced contribution to things that are traded in markets. Sometimes it is possible to make an estimate in dollars of what this economic but nonmarket value is; often we have no very convincing method of doing this.

$Value_{ig}$ = *individual good value.* If valuing is just preferring, one can hardly make mistakes about what one has valued, any more than about having made a target of something, though mistakes abound in whether what is preferred brings satisfaction. We can make choices and purchases that are not in our best interests, not really; they bring momentary goods, or none at all, and soon leave us worse off than before. $Value_{ig}$ is what is in a person's interests, whether or not the individual chooses it, and preferences need to be constantly revised accordingly. There is something raw about untutored preferences; the individual needs education (even perfect knowledge) before she can competently say what (all) her goods are. Many things (such as the rain) are of value whether we welcome them or not. Biological processes (such as nitrogen fixation) are vital even in our ignorance of them. $Values_{ig}$ may not involve exercising preferences, much less marketing.

$Value_{sp}$ = *social preference value.* Through politics, ethics, religion, and so forth, individuals express a social will, often conflicting with some particular wills. $Value_{sp}$ is what a society prefers by collective choices among options allocating its time, resources, skills, energy, and money. Values characterize groups, not just individuals. $Value_{sp}$, a social trait, represents some amalgamating of $value_{ip}$, a psychological trait, though it is not clear how this does, or should, take place.

The cumulative effect is never merely additive (one person, one vote). Some (scientists, politicians, poets, philosophers, the wealthy, media people, and other "experts") hold their values more intensely than others, or hold more power, or are more clever; they affect the aggregating process disproportionately. The will of the establishment may not be the will of the people, and some of the social will never gets written into policy. Nevertheless, humans do make, for better or worse, collective choices.

Sociologists debate whether there is any social whole above the individual person-parts who compose it. Society itself has no center of experience; only individuals do. Society is not capable of interest satisfactions; it enjoys no pleasure, suffers no pain. Unlike a person, society has no skin or self, no continuous biological or psychological identity; a society has a loose, diffuse, changing membership, with some cooperation and much conflict—pulling and hauling—between individuals and interest groups.

Such considerations lead many to claim that value$_{sp}$ is some kind of fiction, a pragmatic operational concept (like a center of gravity) that is only apparent. By that account all social values would be instrumental, directly or indirectly, to intrinsic individual values. Still, some social preferences seem to serve society at large, beyond the fact that or regardless of whether they satisfy individual interests. Social preferences, unless oppressive, seem to command more importance than particular individual preferences. Perhaps this is only because they are massively aggregated individual preferences. But perhaps society has an importance that transcends the individual. At least, collective preferences are relatively more enduring.

Value$_{sg}$ = social good value. Society can err about what contributes to its well-being. Social choices too can be out of touch with reality. Further, given the prevailing pluralism in the United States, a negotiated consensus of values$_{sp}$ is likely not to be consistent. Separate individual values, itemized one by one, may be singly attractive but pernicious in combinations that nobody much foresees. Even if only individuals have a well-being (with society merely an aggregate of related individuals), society at least functions and dysfunctions. The vague, beguiling slogan "the greatest good for the greatest number" can mean "what most prefer on average" (value $_{sp}$) but usually means "what is on average functional in society" (value$_{sg}$). Part of the worth of a practice is whether it keeps society functioning smoothly, regardless of whether this agrees with the corporate will.

The Indian Peaks Wilderness "open space" serves as a pressure release valve for the Denver-Boulder metropolitan area, and it might be most functional for Colorado society to maintain it so, even though the legislature had voiced a preference, reflecting polls, that federal managers log the area to provide jobs and firewood. The Colorado Senate passed Bill 5 in 1985 changing state water law to give landowners the right to mine underground water for irrigation, industrial, and residential development where surface water development is unavailable or expensive. (Underground water was previously a public good to be parceled out by the state.) When, several decades hence, the bedrock water in the Denver Basin is gone and the economy crumbles, leaving dry fields in thistles and many empty factories and houses, the collective decision may prove to have been a bad one. That water might have been better used as backup in periods of major drought.

$Value_{or}$ = *organismic value.* Value is not just an economic, psychological, social, and political word but also a biological one. $Value_{or}$ is what is good for an organism, and all preferences and goods of humans are really subsets of this more comprehensive notion. Various instrumental organic and environmental goods contribute to an organism's well-being, and this well-being is for the organism a telic end-state, an intrinsic value, not always a felt preference. Survival value lies at the core of evolutionary adaptation. Genetic information is of high organismic value but has no necessary connection with sentience, experience, preference satisfactions, elections, legislatures, or markets. Wild creatures defend their lives as if they had goods of their own. An organism grows, repairs its wounds, resists death, and reproduces. Every genetic set is in this sense a (nonmoral) normative set, proposing what *ought to be* beyond what *is.* All this we have argued in preceding chapters.

At this level, wild nature is a place of values prior to human decisions, and one thing the reforming world view asks is whether any concern for wild organismic value limits human decisions about land use. This seems to have happened, at least in part, in policy concerning endangered species or in the setting aside of wildlife refuges. Perhaps, at a minimum, policy can protect the interests of citizens who wish to follow nature in the axiological and tutorial senses (Chapter 1), combining human $value_{ip}$, gained in encountering nature, with $value_{or}$, discovered and protected there.

$Value_{es}$ = *ecosystemic value.* Like persons in society, organisms live in ecosystems, where there is a parallel between the good of the system and that of the individual. Persons are good in their roles—mothers, wildlife biologists. Organisms fill niches and sustain a flourishing system, though not intentionally and perhaps unwillingly. Songbirds, which have intrinsic $value_{or}$ in themselves, have instrumental value regulating insect populations. Ecologists too (coached by sociologists?) have doubted whether ecosystems exist as anything over their component parts. To some, value$_{es}$ is even more convincingly a kind of fiction than value$_{sg}$, because in ecosystems there are no policymakers, no social wills, no goals. Though the ecosystem can seem more biologically real than the social system, it has less evidently any locus of value.

Nevertheless, we have argued that ecosystems too have their well-being and that value attaches to the whole as well as to the parts. There are duties to, appropriate behaviors toward, ecosystems as biotic communities. In any event, even for those who stop with a secondary environmental ethics, much concern remains with keeping these ecosystems running as they do. Some events can be better, some worse for the integrity of a biological community, as in the choice of a biodegradable pesticide or to let a wildfire burn. At a minimum, on wild and even rural lands, policy can protect what we called the homeostatic sense of following nature (Chapter 1): that is, intelligently fitting human collective choices in with the natural operations.

An Axiological Model for Environmental Policy

A diagrammatic sketch (Figure 7.1) should guide policy decisions in environmental affairs, with the humanistic sequence (horizontal, above the solid bar) applicable to all kinds of environmental issues, the naturalistic sequence (vertical, below the bar) to be added (1) on relict wildlands, or (2) concerning endangered species, or (3) where irreversible ecosystem alterations are involved. The model here described is restricted to the United States, though the humanistic sequence is globally applicable, and the full model is generally applicable to developed countries.

Social goods ordinarily override ($>$) social preferences, although the latter routinely produce ($\leftarrow$) such goods. In turn, this combination overrides individual goods, though these feed and determine social preferences, which reciprocally also promote ($\rightleftharpoons$) individual goods. A caveat (the small wedge checking the larger one: $>\!\!<$) specifies that some individual goods, few but crucial, veto some social preferences. Murder is not justified to obtain wilderness, even supposing society preferred this method of obtaining it. Individual goods trump those individual preferences that commonly produce them. Individual preferences are what produce ($\rightarrow$) market prices, and the existence of a market produces in turn ($\leftarrow$) the satisfaction of individual preferences, so there is a two-way arrow ($\rightleftharpoons$). The humanistic sequence applies across the public environmental commons, including those goods that may

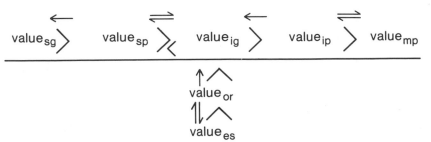

FIGURE 7.1 *An axiological model for environmental policy.*

implicate private properties. In the humanistic sequence, on the commons, we are advocating a corporate, holistic principle whereby the good of the whole is more to be valued than individual goods, subject to limiting injustices.

The naturalistic sequence suggests the greatly shrunken wild domain, and comes into force proportionately as wildness (species or ecosystems) is threatened either with extinction or with irreversible alteration. Here ecosystemic value is more basic than the life-form level, though biosystems are naturally selected to interfit (⇅) the two. Both contribute to the serial human goods.

Notice that the model incorporates a remnant priority of intrinsic natural value, one consistent with the theory and ethics of the preceding chapters. But an environmental policy in a pluralist society cannot presume complete philosophical agreement, and many citizens who have less naturalistic and more humanistic presuppositions will still be able to subscribe to this model, or some variant of it, since it is always in the public interest to have some minimum wildlands preserved. There will then be agreement about policy, despite differences in value theory. Nevertheless, the model, though social—as any model for policy must be—does have naturalistic constraints to which those that endorse this ethic must subscribe, either for further social or for naturalistic reasons.

About 2 percent of the contiguous United States is wilderness (1.2 percent designated; 1 percent under study); 98 percent is developed, farmed, grazed, timbered, or designated for multiple use. Another 2 percent might be suitable for wilderness or semiwild status—cutover forests that have reverted to the wild, or areas as yet little developed.[3] On these wildlands the naturalistic values override what (mostly minor) social or personal goods compete with them, though organisms and ecosystems usually contribute additional social values. Endangered species (those facing anthropogenic extinctions), on wildlands or not, are another instance of the shrunken wild domain; they override both social and private goods.

The hierarchical ordering here advocated prevents further reduction of environmental goods to economic or market values. From here on, such values—though present and considerable—come last in an ethic of the commons. There is some disposition among policymakers and citizens to think that the most useful principles and strategies in environmental issues are likely to be economic; the nearest thing to an adequate theory of "resource use" is going to involve an estimate of benefits over costs in dollars. Wise use will be "efficient" use.

Decisions ought to be democratic, since they are political and about public lands. But pitfalls in the democratic process are many. Those with political clout and savvy, those with concentrated high-order interests—a lot to gain or lose—outshout or outmanipulate the disorganized majority whose interests are diffuse and low level. Organized small groups typically outact large latent groups; legislators react to pressure groups and defend their own interests. Agencies grow bureaucratic and sluggish; citizen preferences are difficult to register and aggregate; voters never have the options they prefer presented at the ballot box, and so on.

One way to minimize these pitfalls is to insist on a decision analysis that is more systematic, more scientific—which often means more economic. So it is tempting to think that a cost-benefit analysis will introduce some sense of order into an otherwise sprawling dispute over values. Legislators and government professionals are always sensitive to the charge of misusing public funds and resources, and if they can make economically based environmental decisions, this will be as nearly scientific and democratic as can be. One sure route into human caring is by pricing—not in all cases, but routinely in matters of resource use. There will need to be, additionally, consideration of the just distribution of such benefits and costs, but that can come later. Initially, one needs an assessment of what environmental goods are worth in monetary terms.

Against this view, the main point of the axiological model, coupled with the spectrum of value types, is to display a richer value series than we have reason to believe can be caught by economic valuation, and to claim that on the commons—especially the common wildlands—a great many other values override economic ones.

In the naturalistic sequence, we are advocating a kind of *maxi-min* principle in something like the ratio of continental domestication to wildness. A minimum level (2 percent, 4 percent) of wildland values (intrinsic and human instrumental) need maximizing (at 98-to-2, 96-to-4 odds), opposing a *maxi-max* principle (maximum consumption increasing from 96 percent to 98 percent to 100 percent our available acreage to raise our already high standards of living). That 2 to 4 percent surfeit is a few more pounds on already fat people, who need the rigorous leanness that disciplined exposure to wilderness can give. Considering probable economic productivity rather than acreage, there is no reason to think that, on average, U.S. citizens would be even 1 percent better off if all the wildlands were sacrificed. From this viewpoint the odds are 99 to 1 that the sacrifice of wildness makes sense in terms of economic gain at the cost of the other values lost. From here on, any loss of wilderness is likely to be a tragedy.

The areas richest in resources have long since been domesticated, and sacrificing the remaining wildlands is scraping the bottom of the barrel, a matter of diminishing marginal returns (notwithstanding newly developed technologies), although from other points of view the value destruction would be enormous. Public lands, often left over from the public domain in the West or reacquired after marginal use in the East, tend not to be economically productive in agriculture, timber, or minerals.

The diagram yields prima facie rules. For exceptions, the burden of proof is on the dissenter. On remnant wildlands the odds are that the sacrifice of wild values will not both contribute to long-term human goods and be justified. The wilder and rarer the land, the lower the probability that any consumptive economic use will override other values. Virgin forests will stay intact. The demand for wilderness is increasing quite as rapidly as the demand for timber. The latter can be satisfied on private lands; the former cannot.

On particular occasions the saving of an endangered species (the California condor) might provide insufficient social and personal benefits and such high costs that one could plead an exception ($3.2 million annually: $2 million in oil and gas left underground and $1 million in phosphate left unmined—but all retrievable later; $0.2 million spent in research and management).[4] Nevertheless, the policy sets the presumptions, as in the Endangered Species Act, which mandates the preservation of species and permits only rare exceptions. To abandon a life form because of the economic costs, or in order to secure market goods, or to satisfy personal or social preferences will be exceptional. (Consider again the crocodile and the twilight duck-shooting cases from Chapter 4.)

Environmental Principles and Strategies

The rules that follow couple with the axiological model; the combined account will orient, like a compass, general directions of travel. Specific paths will have to be figured out locally. Like many rules in ethics and policy, these are middle-level rules: that is, neither precise ("Do not lower the dissolved oxygen content of that stream below 5 parts per million") nor primary ("Love your neighbor"), but they are operational at policy level. For the undergirding principles, they depend on the preceding chapters, although differing presuppositions can sometimes yield the same guidelines. In specific applications, decisionmakers will have to assess the various strengths of particular cases, which can only be suggested here by examples.

Maximize noncompeting value types. The fourteen types of natural value (Chapter 1) are incommensurable but also largely noncompeting in all cases except consumptive economic uses. They cannot be commensurated, but they do not have to be. There is no translation unit by which $A + B - C = D$. Genetic diversity (indicated by species counts, low extinction rates) cannot meaningfully be added to or subtracted from recreational benefits (visitor days). But we can easily add together and simultaneously enjoy multiple noncompeting incommensurables. Historical, character-building, or therapeutic uses of wildlands will seldom interfere with scientific and religious uses, and never were science and religion more congenial than here. The cultural value carried by eagles requires the preservation of a flourishing wild population. Aesthetic uses (measured on preference scales) do not upset the life-support value (indexed by energy flow?) in an ecosystem. So we are not forced to prefer only one value. The commensurability of values is, thus far, a pseudoproblem because these nonconsumptive values reinforce and need not be traded off against one another. They do not use the commons up.

On the commons, regulate for environmental values that are nonrival. Force consumptive use into the private sector. This is not to say that there should be no consumptive use of the commons, only that it carries a low priority when competing with noncompeting uses. Among consumptive uses, favor those that are soonest renewable because these are only temporarily competing. Wildlife photography will be favored over hunting, because the photographer leaves the buck there for others to enjoy; the hunter brings the buck back with him. Still, the buck will be replaced the following year. A large clear-cut may destroy hunting, photography (and many other values) for decades; a cut by selection may not adversely affect hunting; a patch-cut may even increase edging and improve hunting.

This may seem to give preferential treatment to noneconomic users or to bias against certain sorts of economic users, but on the commons the nearest that policy can come to nonpreferential treatment is by nonconsumptive use. Everyone can use the commons, but no one is allowed to use it up; and the more "use up" activity is involved, the lower the priority.

On relict wildlands, the bias against consumptive use is still greater. The question faced here is not whether the past economic reduction of the continent was justified. But is it enough? How much more of the goods (values $_{ip, sg}$) we already amply have (fiber, timber, energy) can we obtain by consuming the surviving wildlands, and do we want these as economic benefits (value$_{mp}$), trading the nonconsumptive set of values? That pits value to be gained by putting nature on the market against some or all of the other fourteen values, but for a wider public it pits only a little more extracted from the 2 percent wild (4 percent half wild) past what we have already extracted from the 98 percent (96 percent) in impressive amounts. This "more" could as easily and efficiently be extracted from nonwild lands, which are far and away already the richest ones economically. If we ask who are the chief beneficiaries (a few operators, perhaps more workers) and who the trickle-down beneficiaries (the public), we may find that the gains are a few concentrated, short-term values$_{ip,ig}$ (profits, jobs perhaps unobtainable elsewhere?) traded against values$_{sg}$ and diluted but extremely widespread, long-term values$_{ip}$ (recreational benefits, religious experiences). Do we have enough consumption? If more is needed, need it come by sacrificing wildlands?

Sometimes disparagingly called a "lock-up" use, preservation treats all users alike, even though (indeed, just because) the would-be economic or consumptive user is prohibited from "take-over" use. "Lock-up" only prevents "take-over." It is more likely to result in gradually unlocking an equal distribution of benefits of the other types over time. If basic needs were at stake, or if the country were not already 98 percent developed and developable, this might be unjustly prohibitive. But it is not unjust on the last 2 percent, where only more of already abundantly possessed goods is at stake.

This much is true considering merely the humanistic sequence in our model, but on relict wildlands value$_{or}$ and values$_{es}$ override individual preferences and market uses and would even override social goods and preferences, were these to compete with them, although they can usually be added to the social values and non-competing individual values in their bias against "take-over" use.

In an endangered species case, the palila, a Hawaiian bird species, was named as a plaintiff, along with some human environmentalists (Palila versus Hawaii Department of Land and Natural Resources).[5] The Hawaii Department of Land and Natural Resources was maintaining a population of feral sheep and goats in the mamane forest, providing sport hunting and income for the state and others but destroying the critical habitat of the bird. The court ordered the feral animals eradicated.

The Supreme Court once said that in "language, history, and structure" the Endangered Species Act "indicates beyond doubt that Congress intended endangered species to be afforded the highest of priorities." This seems to recognize both some good or interest of the species, an intent to protect them from danger and threat, and that to do so also coincides with "esthetic, ecological, educational, historical, recreational, and scientific value to the Nation and its people."[6] "Economic" is not on this list; it is certainly not the priority value that overrides all else. Rather, the palila case seems to combine the protection of a species in its native ecosystem with various goods to a nation and its people, all noncompeting, and to override a use that, though recreational, is consumptive and economic in such a way as to compete with, take over, and destroy the palila-based values. Against such threat, the court ordered the palila and the mamane forest to be "locked up," preserved in its natural state.

Sometimes, even the noneconomic uses of wildlands compete with each other. U.S. Forest Service policy permits scientific research in wilderness (1) if it cannot reasonably be done in non-wilderness areas, (2) if the study is in the interests of wilderness, and (3) if the tools used are the minimum necessary to do the research. The Environmental Protection Agency has proposed to conduct an acid rain study in alpine lakes in the West, often in wilderness areas, and to use helicopters to take water samples and to monitor instruments. Motorized equipment is generally prohibited in wilderness areas, and the American Wilderness Alliance has objected that the use of helicopters will disrupt the wilderness experiences of recreators in the area. It asserts that pack horses are quite adequate and as economical to accomplish the job; they are simply less convenient for scientists.[7] This is an example of conflict between scientific and recreational values.

Do not underestimate the diffused values. Although many persons may be hurt by a decision in favor of consumptive use, they are not hurt very much (a diminished vacation vista), while a few (the mill operators who clear-cut) have a lot to gain. We can expect the latter to lobby full force, but the former will be disorganized, slow to realize what is at stake, and ill-represented in the public participation process. Yet the aggregate loss of value to the majority can be much larger than the gain to the minority. The scenery is marred for a century. Even when the amenity values are accurately represented, they are intangible.

Sometimes the agenda can determine the result. The hard values, considered first, are thoroughly assessed in a stylized procedure; the soft values, held in abeyance to be considered last, are only loosely (and wearily) thrown in after the hard values are already massively in place. If the agenda is the other way round, with as much attention given to specifying the soft values and only afterward considering whether economic benefits override these, the results can be different. The path by which the collective choice is made can bias the choice. All this tends to stunt the attention given to soft values; that is, to underrepresent the widespread, low-level intangibles and overestimate the concentrated, intense tangibles.

Some contend that a preservationist policy imposes concentrated costs (on the few, local timber companies who lose a lot) and provides diffuse benefits (to the public, who gain slight recreational benefits). Such policy is rarely implemented, not only because it is difficult to maintain legislatively but even more because it is ethically unsatisfactory. But the better gestalt is to turn the picture around and say that a development policy, at least on relict wildlands, permits concentrated benefits (for the timber sellers and buyers) and imposes diffuse costs (in intangibles, to a larger public). The latter is the more logical and ethical gestalt because the public, which is the present owner and has its benefits of wildness taken away, is the loser. The timber operators, who do not now own the timber but who buy it for profit, are the gainers.

Further, if the timber companies do not pay the full costs,

or if they destroy what money cannot buy, then they (and their customers) are subsidized by public loss, a situation that is even more ethically unsatisfactory. The ideal in a democracy is for the majority to have their well-considered way, provided there is no injustice to the minority and provided there is a full counting of the production and distribution of costs and benefits. The concept of opportunity costs forgone is not to be applied to minority would-be exploiters of the land, who are not now its owners, but to the present owners, the public. If this public uses a site on the commons as one kind of resource and cannot simultaneously use it as another kind of resource, then it must consider opportunity costs forgone, especially if such opportunities cannot be had elsewhere. But opportunity costs forgone need not apply to consumptive opportunists on public lands. That is why we should not pit concentrated costs against diffuse benefits but turn the issue around and pit concentrated benefits against diffuse costs.

Aspen groves enhance the scenic Rocky Mountains, being one of the few deciduous trees among the conifers, providing a delicate green in spring and a brilliant gold in autumn. Their white trunks grace the winter woods; deer and elk browse on twigs and bark; and other wildlife, such as tree swallows and wrens, favor the groves. Aspen regenerates well after fires, cloning from roots and tolerating open sun; it is (at least typically) replaced by spruce and fir, which grow up in the shade of the aspen in a succession that takes more than a century. During the rapid settlement of Colorado in the last century, fires were suppressed, and the Colorado groves are increasingly middle-aged and elderly.

The Louisiana-Pacific Corporation has opened a waferboard plant at Kremmling, Colorado, with a large appetite for aspen: twenty-five million board feet per year. Craig Rupp, chief forester of the Arapaho-Roosevelt National Forest and a demonstrated friend of wilderness preservation, argues that aspen should be clear-cut with discretion in nonwilderness forests in order to regenerate it, thereby mimicking the presence of fire. The chipboard plant could be used as a management tool to "treat" aspen so that the Forest Service can maintain the scenic beauty, benefit the wildlife, and sustain the general health of the ecosystem. There would also be income for the Forest Service to use for public goods. But this ought to be done even if taxpayers were to lose money (within reason) on the logging, since Louisiana-Pacific would be simultaneously helping to provide public benefits and satisfying their interest in purchasing timber.[8]

Others, including some ecologists, are not so sure and cite studies that some aspen stands are climax—that is, self-renewing—and not being replaced by spruce and fir. Others doubt that we know enough about succession, or about whether clear-cutting mimics fire, to plunge ahead with a heavy "hands on" management. So the facts are disputed as well as the values. If the facts go one way, this might be a case where economic and other values, including diffused ones, are noncompeting. If the facts go another way, it might be a case where (in the midst of confused rhetoric) concentrated private benefits (waferboard sales) are traded for diffuse public goods (scenic beauty).

Avoid irreversible change. Ecosystems are historical, and history is a one-way process in time. All change is irreversible, and change is inevitable, so in its strictest sense this maxim is impossible. But we can estimate the duration of the impact of policy (a decade for forage, a century for timber regeneration, 10,000 years for soil lost, forever for extinction). The longer the impact, the slower we should proceed. We want all the natural components so that we can put things back as they were, if we have to. There are often unforeseen bad consequences, especially as technology becomes more manipulative, chemicals less biodegradable, and mutagens more abundant. It is often easier to make changes (building a salt-water Panama canal, flying supersonic transports) than to foresee the results of the changes (extinctions from intermixing Atlantic and Pacific marine life, climatic changes following depletion of the ozone layer). This is especially true as we approach a carrying capacity of the commons.

Since we Americans (like those in many other developed or long-settled nations) have only 2 percent of our continental land remaining wild and almost no representatives of some ecosystems once abundant (virgin hemlock forests), it becomes crucial to save what wildness remains, just to guarantee that we do not make irreversible mistakes. "To keep every cog and wheel is the first precaution of intelligent tinkering," cautioned Aldo Leopold.[9] Since so much tinkering with the environment is going on elsewhere in the American economy, a responsibility of those who decide about the commons—public domain lands, multiple-use national forests, and especially relict wildlands—is to keep that tinkering intelligent and reversible by saving all the parts. We should leave room to reconsider; we should avoid radically closing options. Set that policy which allows us to redeem our mistakes. The chestnut and the passenger pigeon are gone forever; the starling and the English sparrow are here to stay. What next with our effluents in the salt marshes, with our acid over the Adirondacks? What links are being cut, what gene pools overshrunk? What eggshells are becoming too thin? What scientific studies of native ecosystems are no longer possible?

In Colorado national forests, pilot projects are testing whether water runoff can be substantially increased by managing timber harvests. With judicious cutting (often patch clear-cuts or strip-cuts), snowmelt and rainfall runoff can be increased up to 40 percent from water no longer used by the trees. Another method is to eliminate Engelmann spruce, a heavy water user, in favor of lodgepole pine, an efficient water user that produces more wood with less water. Deer also benefit from the openings, although in these subalpine and high montane forests deer populations are already limited by available winter forage at lower elevations, and summer forage is ample in uncut forests. These pilot projects have been done carefully, in some cases followed for nearly half a century.[10] It now seems possible to manage forests for better water production.

A decision that could lie ahead is whether to modify hundreds of thousands of acres of national forests to satisfy the demands of thirsty Denver and other Front Range cities, perhaps saving them just in the nick of time as they exhaust their underground aquifers. That sounds humane and foresighted, but it might also introduce irreversible, unforeseen changes of the first magnitude—especially after the cities, hooked on the water, demand ever increasing amounts of it, their politicians and developers pressing scientists to escalate water production. Large-scale intervention of this kind might only increase vulnerability, serving neither the social good nor individual goods in future generations, nor respecting the present integrity of the montane and subalpine ecosystems to be modified.

Optimize natural diversity. Mother Nature is a fecund producer of kinds—species, landscapes, ecosystems. Nature creates lots of niches and then puts evolutionary and genetic tendencies to work filling these with a kaleidoscopic array (species packing), as glancing through a butterfly guide will show. It would be a pity needlessly to sacrifice much, if any, of this pageant, especially if we get in return only more good like that of which we already have enough. Variety is a spice in life. That says something about human tastes, but it also recognizes the natural spices. (See "Diversity-Unity Values," Chapter 1).

Over evolutionary time nature has rendered most of her kinds extinct, only to generate others in their places, gradually increasing from zero to five or ten million species. This constructive tendency, little understood and mysterious, must in some sense be a good thing. Humans are an end result of it, as is the wonderland Earth. Environmental decisions should optimize existing, remnant diversity for the preservation of organismic and ecosystemic values, for the potential for human outdoor and wilderness encounters, scientific study, and religious experiences. This is the more true because anthropogenic extinction rates are accelerating. Some things are naturally rare (climbing ferns). Owing to human destruction of habitats, some things are artificially rare (the peregrine falcon). Both need to be protected, the latter more than the former, since there humans threaten to shut down the generative processes. Some wild environments are common (Douglas fir forests), some infrequent (tundra, water gaps), some rare (geyser basins), and one should favor unique natural environments. There are no substitutes available for the benefits they provide.

Diversity is a core idea that needs to be made more specific in various directions (species numbers, species abundance, community types, numbers of interactions and flow paths between species, redundancies and alternative food chains, varieties of experiences available to citizens). Here policy can optimize diversity in quality, even where the quantity of an environmental type must be sacrificed, seeing to it that all sorts of habitats, with a wide range of species, are located so that many persons have access to them.

There will be, and ought to be, many kinds of built environments, but an environmental policy insists that natural sectors be preserved and incorporated into the built environments—greenbelts in cities, rural areas, waterfalls and cascades, mountains on the skyline, seashores and lakeshores unspoiled by development, spits and headlands, islands, swamps, oxbow lakes, forests interspersed with pastures. All the junctions between land and water will be especially important (riverbanks, springs, lakes, shorelines, bogs, estuaries). These are typically rich wildlife habitats; the flow of water is the bloodstream of the ecosystem. We will leave the hardwoods along stream courses; we will establish corridors between wildlife preserves—perhaps using, where possible, abandoned railroad lines, power and pipeline rights-of-way. We will enact better laws to protect private lands for conservation in the public good.

Do not impoverish the system. This might earlier have favored development (and might still favor it in undeveloped countries), for development adds its riches too. But now it increasingly favors preservation in a nation that has only a fraction of the wildness it had a century ago, when its population was a fraction of what it is now.

Optimize natural stability. Ecosystems evolve slowly, becoming resistant to perturbations, naturally selected for stability over time. The unstable ones are extinct. Sometimes ecosystems oscillate from one equilibrium to another—they undergo succession; succession gets reset—and stability ought never to be interpreted as something static. Stability too is a core idea that needs to be made more specific in various ways (persistence of species kinds, constancy of species abundance, resistance of an ecosystem to change, resilience after change, amplitude of change from which a system can recover, degree of dynamic change without dramatic fluctuations, redundancies within the system). Sometimes actions we thought to be stabilizing (preventing forest fires, spraying insect infestations) have turned out to be destabilizing. Stability is only a short-range cross-section in a history where succession and evolutionary change are constant.

Still, ecosystems are resiliently interwoven, usually so that when one thread breaks the whole fabric does not unravel. This sometimes means that they can absorb human-caused interruptions well, as when the chestnuts were replaced by oaks. But they are not able to absorb all human interferences, and some ecosystems are much more fragile than others. The eastern deciduous forest is resilient; tundra is not. With the advent of monocultures (single crops grown over wide areas), humans can push the whole surrounding rural system toward a fragile simplicity. National forests managed as factory forests, growing timber species only, are easy to operate; they bring high yields and lower costs. But they have lower stability and high vulnerability to insect pests, diseases, droughts, and erosion. As the nation and its industry have expanded west, and on to Alaska and Hawaii, development patterns and technologies that would work in the temperate, humid East are destabilizing on arid lands, in the arctic, or on oceanic islands. (See "Stability and Spontaneity Values," Chapter 1.)

When moving into more fragile lands or when pressing even the familiar, temperate, humid ecosystems further and further toward their carrying capacities, we need to be careful because the chances are increasing proportionately that our disturbances will have some unintended bad consequences, probably with loss of stability. We need to "follow nature" in what we called the homeostatic sense (Chapter 1) and set policy accordingly. For instance, the regulations should specify that if a proposal has any measurable effect on the biocirculations (increased runoff, sedimentation, lower owl populations), this is a red flag, a prima facie reason for rejecting the proposal. At least, the burden of proof rests on those proposing interruptions that could be destabilizing. This might not be true on private lands, but it is on the commons. In this ecological sense, dynamic community stability trumps commodity resources.

Species have no owners; the state is their recent trustee. Near Hotchkiss, Delta County, in western Colorado, there is a large ranch on arid land. The owners were unaware that a few acres contained a rare plant species, *Eriogonum pelinophilum*, clay-loving buckwheat, discovered about 1970. The Nature Conservancy, involved in the discovery of the plants—known then only from that ranch—approached the ranchers asking to lease or purchase a few acres as a public trust. But the ranchers asked a highly inflated price, many times the land's normal worth per acre, on grounds that the land, including the rare species, was theirs, and they were entitled to get whatever they could, just as though oil had been discovered on their property. They later advertised the ranch for sale in newspapers at an increased price, noting that it contained a rare plant species. The property lies on Mancos shale, which is quite salty and otherwise considered scabland. *Eriogonum pelinophilum* has adapted to the peculiar soil. When the story made national news, the owners took steps to protect the plants from grazing. *Eriogonum pelinophilum* was officially listed as an endangered species in 1984. Later other populations were discovered, some on public land, and two of these are under study for designation as areas of critical concern.[11]

Do landowners own rare plant species that happen to occur on their land? By long tradition in the United States, the state holds all wildlife in trust for the people, although landowners can restrict access and specify who may hunt on their property. But game regulations are established by the state: if the ranchers were to shoot golden eagles that also inhabit their land, they would be prosecuted. The Federal Endangered Species Act prohibits the taking of endangered animal species but not of endangered plant species. Some state laws prohibit the taking of endangered plant species, sometimes making a distinction between what landowners and nonlandowners can do, sometimes making a distinction between what the landowners do directly and what their stock do indirectly. But Colorado has no such laws, and landowners may do what they please. Have landowners the right to let species be destroyed by grazing stock, or to demand an inflated purchase price for their acreage? Ought land ownership rights to be circumscribed by environmental policy?

At a minimum, even in a secondary environmental ethic, a species should be interpreted as a public, not a private, good. Individual organisms that are members of a species will sometimes be found on public, sometimes private property. Some species (grizzly bears) will move over both; some (*Eriogonum pelinophilum*) will be rooted in the earth. Wild animals and birds are (in the United States) regarded as being held in public trust by the state for the good of the people, though we sometimes think of farmers as owning the rabbits that reside in their fields. We do not think that farmers own the migratory geese that fly over their fields, stopping there temporarily to eat corn.

When we move to the level of species, all concepts of ownership ought to lapse. Landowners do not own species, whether fauna or flora, though they may own a field with individual plants in it, tokens of that type. *Land* can belong to citizens, interpreted as real estate by conventions of a culture. But *life*, especially the life processes at genetic, reproductive levels, is not and ought not to be any person's private property. It makes a limited sense to think of a farmer as owning the rabbits that are annually reproduced on his lands, perhaps owning the wildflowers that grow there every season. But a species, we must remember from Chapter 5, is a dynamic natural kind, a historical lineage persisting through space and time, typically with a half-life of ten million years. In that perspective, it is arrogant for even a nation to think of "owning" species. The United States (now over 200 years old) would be a quite latecoming owner of such species, and someone who has held property for perhaps the last decade seems a very tardy owner for a dynamic process stretching over millions of years.

Neither nation nor citizen should really be more than a trustee, though either can be a superkiller. We are still dealing, often, with a question of public or private *resources* when evaluating individual animals, trees, plants; but when we move to the level of species, and the speciating process, we rise to the level of evaluating *sources*. We pass from economics or recreation to evolutionary ecology and creation.

Since landowners are not the owners of species, the protection of species, regulated by the state, need not require compensation. Any redress to the landowner of "damages" resulting from public policy, newly introduced, is not to be modeled after eminent domain, where property may be taken from an owner but the owner must be compensated. Rather, species legislation is to be modeled after police power, designed to protect from harm, where right behavior may be enforced and public goods protected without compensation, since nothing owned is being taken away. Protection of species is not imposed to procure a public good (to gain for the public something they do not now own); rather, it is imposed to prevent a public loss, to prevent harm to the commons in which all share, a community that also contains biotic intrinsic and ecosystemic goods. Landowers do not have to be compensated for preventing harm to the public or to species and ecosystems. From this perspective, landowners do not have opportunity costs (benefits to which they were entitled but which must be forgone) as a result of legislation protecting species.

Such at least is the theory. In practice, given the novelty of legislation protecting endangered species, we may want to say that if new regulation is imposed during the tenure of a landowner, and if this regulation makes the land economically useless or an economic liability (as opposed to merely requiring other economic uses, including some that may make it less profitable than before), then that landowner (but not subsequent owners) may be entitled to compensation. One form of this might be tax exemption on reserved lands.

Notice that a different issue arises where the landowner is required to incur actual expenses (building a fence around endangered plants) to protect a public good or as trustee of an endangered species. Whether the state should bear those costs is negotiable.

In terms of our axiological model, the Colorado ranchers have no right to destroy the *Eriogonum pelinophilum* on their property, not only because social goods and preferences (evidenced in the Endangered Species Act) outweigh their personal preferences but also because the values of (and human duties to) endangered species override the values connected with individual preferences and associated market prices. Nor do they have a right to inflated market values as a result of the social goods accompanying the rare species on their property. This kind of environmental ethics may be written into policy.

Increase options. By doing so we increase human possibilities to actualize preferences (value$_{ip}$) and so increase freedom and the quality of life. Most Americans are oversupplied with market artifacts and undersupplied with sites for experiencing pristine nature. They live in an urban or rural environment some 99 percent of their time, in a wild environment 1 percent or less. Therefore, manage natural areas—especially wildlands—to meet needs that are unmet and unmeetable elsewhere (desires for a temporary exit from society, or to see wild bighorn sheep). This is more necessary when such needs are intense, even in a minority, and if society's meeting these needs involves doing little or nothing. Also, there is truth in the adage that one should manage for the specialized user (the fly fisherman, the backpacker) rather than the general user (the picnicker, the car camper), since it is likely that the former's interests will be keener, resulting in higher-quality experiences for which there will be no substitutes. Quality can sometimes trump quantity. On the Tennessee rivers there were twenty-two recreational lakes on which to water-ski within sixty miles of the Tellico Reservoir; there was but one wild, free-flowing river left in the Southeast; there was but one rare, small snail darter population (so far as was then known) when Congress voted to finish the dam. This decision decreased options. A society (and each individual citizen within it) is richer with twenty-two lakes and one wild river than with twenty-three man-made lakes.

Economic uses that consume natural lands destroy our liberties. Although society as a whole should increase all sorts of options, in environmental decisions we increase options for experiencing nature (among other things) alike for ourselves and for future generations. The pluralist model of "multiple use" means that on the commons we favor those multiple uses that increase options; on public lands these are likely to be the sorts of options that the economic sector is unlikely to supply. All this optimizes social diversity and permits following nature (for those who so choose) in the axiological and tutorial senses (Chapter 1). It also increases the educational value of nature, its capacity to lead the individual to novel experiences, and thereby increases individuality (Chapter 6).

A toxic threat is trumps. Not only the volume but the kinds of pollution dumped into the commons has markedly changed. From 1941 through 1977 the volume of manufactured synthetic chemicals increased 350 times in the United States, with many of these quite toxic to natural systems and to human biology. Even the most resilient local ecosystems cannot absorb our exhausts, pesticides, and herbicides; even global currents cannot flush out aerosol fluorocarbons and SST exhausts. All such pollutants ought to be regulated by policy, but the more they are poisonous, the more they are absolutely to be forbidden.

There is room to discuss what counts as acceptable risk, especially since minute pollutants are the most expensive to remove, but surely policy ought to be biased in favor of health over the production of extra goods, public or private. Given the pressures of capitalist competition, industry is pushed to dump wastes cheaply. Policy has to counteract this, else toxins and other poisons will be foisted unwillingly upon millions of persons not party to the benefits of particular business transactions. The aerial spraying of pesticides, which involves nearly two-thirds of their use (mostly on fiber crops, not food) increases the risk of those downwind, who derive little or no benefit from the spraying and who take the risks involuntarily. Especially in view of time lags here, involving the build-up across decades of delayed effects of small amounts of poisons, the margin of error ought to favor health by a wide margin.

Kesterson National Wildlife Refuge, located east of Gustine, California, retained some of the best riparian and wetland habitat in the United States. The freshwater marsh created by the overflowing of the San Joaquin River was a paradise for fish and waterfowl, important on migratory routes as well as for breeding ground. Agricultural drainwater from irrigation in the nearby San Joaquin Valley is selenium-laden and toxic in concentrated amounts. The San Luis Drain was initially to have carried water 200 miles into the San Francisco Bay. But funds ran out after eighty-five miles, the effect of the drainwater in the bay-delta area was controversial, and the drain stopped at Kesterson.

Since 1980 the selenium, with salts and pesticides, has built up, and over half the eggs in wildfowl nests fail to hatch; the embryos are crippled or dead. Coots, grebes, stilts, ducks, herons, blackbirds, raptors, mammals are often deformed. All the fish are gone except a species of tiny mosquito fish. Snakes and frogs are gone. Hunters are cautioned about eating waterfowl taken there; children and pregnant women are advised to eat none at all. The California Water Resources Control Board and the Department of the Interior have ordered the Bureau of Reclamation and the local water authority to come up with a solution that preserves the integrity of the wildlife refuge. The water, which is so heavily federally subsidized that users pay only 15 percent of project costs, is often being used on marginally productive lands. One solution is to construct evaporation ponds. Another is to sell the water to nonagricultural users and to use the land for grazing instead. The selenium is not toxic in nonconcentrated amounts, where it does not accumulate; some selenium may be essential to health.[12]

The need to handle high levels of trace elements was unforeseen (like so much else that results when humans press ecosystems to their carrying capacities), and the present situation can be corrected only at considerable cost. But the toxic threat here overrides other considerations because all the values that the wildlife refuge can provide are at stake. Its use as a toxic dump takes over all other uses, whether human or nonhuman. On the axiological model, the values$_{es}$ and values$_{or}$ on this relict wildland override all the human values. Humans have already claimed (destroyed) over 94 percent of the original wetlands habitat in the Central Valley of California, a key link in the Pacific flyway, and this score (94-6) loads the presumptions for the wildlife. Fortunately, but not accidentally, many human social and individual values (recreational, scientific, therapeutic uses) can be added to the intrinsic wildlife values to counter the benefits of cheap irrigation and the costs of a nontoxic solution. Farmers here have no right to damage a public good linked with a biotic community, especially when they use such heavily federally subsidized water to do so.

The more permanent the poison, the more it counters large amounts of immediate goods. The radioiodine in my thyroid kills me and moves on to others afterward. Plutonium remains lethal for fifty times longer than any civilization has yet survived, five times longer than *Homo sapiens* has yet survived. Poisons in the groundwater are almost impossible to remove. Even when such chemicals are natural in the sense that they are found in nature in minute amounts, they are unnatural in the volumes and concentrations in which they are used in industry and dumped into the environment. If a decision involves a poison that now or ever might be leaked into the environment, the decision touches basic givens in ecosystems on which life support depends (Chapter 1). The primacy of the well-being of organisms and the integrity of ecosystems, coupled with social and individual goods overriding individual preferences and market interests, make a toxic threat a veto.

Over the long haul, some violations in environmental ethics are more dangerous than those in traditional ethics because of the threat to so many generations. Since a poison erodes life and health, a little toxic threat overrides a lot of the pursuit of happiness. "Thou shalt not kill," and even life shortened or impaired is life taken. In repeated surveys, the public has preferred environmental protection over lower prices with pollution by about two to one, and a majority in all walks of life will say that environmental integrity at critical points must be maintained regardless of cost. But this will not happen without a policy that legislates at least a minimum morality. Industry cannot be expected to consider the long-range effects, especially no single industry, unless regulated by policy so that all industries act in concert; and even industries in concert must be constrained by larger social goods.

Government, too, not less than business, can be dilatory, and toxic threats can reach a point where ethical concern demands drastic action. Greenpeace activists in Everett, Massachusetts, broke the law (trespassing and disrupting the orderly conduct of business) to plug a discharge pipe pouring toxic wastes, released from a Monsanto chemical plant into the Mystic River. Monsanto was operating under a discharge permit that had expired several years before but was still considered valid because the Environmental Protection Agency had not amended its regulations. The protestors considered this to be agency and corporate culpable negligence. The following day, Monsanto officials agreed to convert the plant to closed-loop cooling and to cease discharging toxic wastes. The toxic-threat-is-trumps rule permits and even requires participation in activist protests of this kind.

Do not discount the future environmentally. Policy should place a check on the practice, used wisely enough in limited places in classical economics, of discounting the future. Initially a function of the interest rate, discounting can be defended economically because money in hand is worth more than the same amount in the future. Discounting can also be defended philosophically because future needs are uncertain, and resources shift with developing technologies. We excuse our present consumption of resources from the commons by saying that what persons desire varies over generations and that future persons will have to look out for themselves. Nor do we altogether use up natural resources; we partly convert them to capital, which others inherit.

Such justifications make some sense but fail when we begin to tamper with what have hitherto been the natural certainties. In any discounting, *today* trumps *tomorrow*, and there are seldom good reasons for permitting this with regard to environmental quality. Discounting future environmental quality is as mistaken as thinking that the nearest telephone pole really is the largest and that the further ones get smaller until the distant ones are insignificant. Such discounting counts future people as having less and less value until distant people count nothing at all, and this can be done only under moral illusion.

Perhaps we are not obligated to supply future generations with oil or timber; they may not need these as much as we do. But water, air, soil, genes, even landscapes are not in this class of resources, because they are more timeless and irretrievable. They define everything else, and there are no substitutes. There is a difference between cutting off a person's paycheck and cutting off his air supply, between eating the harvest and eating the seed corn. We have no duty to leave our grandchildren wealthy (with capital gained from resource depletion), but we ought to leave them a world no worse than we found it, like campers who use a campsite.

The issue is deceiving because we only gradually push the troubled skies and poisoned soils over onto the next generation. When the fifty-five-gallon drums storing our wastes rust out, their labels gone, and their contents have seeped into the groundwater, what then? If the Pharaohs had stored their plutonium wastes in the pyramids, these would still be 90 percent as lethal as when stored. Radiocontaminants from uranium tailings will be mutagenic for generations. Long-lived radium steadily emits short-lived but mobile radon gas, decaying into further contaminants. By dust, wind, leaching, runoff, irrigation, wildlife movements, these make their way into air, water, food. Our books may be in the black, the gross national product up, but how much of this is because of what we have charged to future generations? One should not make debts for others to pay, especially when there is no foreseeable way for them to pay such debts.

We do have to spend "mineralogical capital" by extracting ores and even "fossil capital," petroleum, but it is not clear that there ought to be any spending of "biological capital" at all— soils, air, water, forests, animal and plant species. These can be renewably used; where they are not, we are not following nature homeostatically (Chapter 1). We are not just using resources; we are shutting down our sources (Chapter 4). We are not respecting biotic community (Chapter 5) or projective nature (Chapter 6). To put it bluntly, we are stealing from tomorrow.

Policy concerns here are not merely about safety and a decent environment. They are also about freedom to enjoy the natural amenities. What if the politicians' grandchildren prefer warblers, eagles, parks, hiking, the seasonal rhythms of a countryside over the aging hydroelectric plants, dams, or exhausted strip mines left to them? They might complain that their grandparents bequeathed them no capital, no developments. They are more likely to complain that they took away their options in wildness, and that there are no substitutes for the wildlands sacrificed a generation before.

Do not allow steamrolling. "But we're already doing it!" Damage to the environment often becomes evident only after permissive practices are already underway, as has happened with acid rain and with the selenium at Kesterson. This is because there are frequent unknowns and long time lags, compounded causal links with additive, unforeseen results. There is a tendency to say that what is already going on ought to be permitted to continue, on the grounds of some "right" acquired in the past—perhaps to mine public lands, or clear-cut, or dump pollutants at a designated level. An environmental impact statement may turn up adverse effects only after property has been acquired for a new plant, the architect's drawings finished, construction ready to be bid, and the Chamber of Commerce elated about the new industry.

In the Tellico Dam case, the dam was already two-thirds finished when the snail darter was discovered, and the Tennessee Valley Authority continued further work until prohibited by the court from so doing. In a Georges Bank case in Massachusetts, while a consultation was underway on whether oil spills were likely to jeopardize endangered whales, the Secretary of the Interior proposed to go ahead and sell offshore oil and gas leases anyway. He was sued under amendments to the Endangered Species Act that prohibit "any irreversible or irretrievable commitment of resources . . . which has the effect of foreclosing . . . any reasonable and prudent alternative measures" while consultation is pending.[13] The suit failed, but the point remains that to sell leases and have leaseholders anxious about the outcome of the consultation could only make it harder to be objective about whether oil spills were likely to harm the whales.

Decisions get biased by momentum. The project or practice steamrolls on; something is done that would never have been done had the outcome been known at the start, or had objective reassessment been made during discoveries along the way, or had the proper studies been conducted in the proper sequence.

Some of this is unavoidable even with good faith on the part of all parties involved, but some results from deliberate efforts by protagonists to foreclose options by steamrolling. Policy ought be set to minimize decision by momentum.

Do not make decisions by default. Sometimes doing nothing is the cheapest thing to do and also protects values already in place. Often the burden of proof should be placed on those who propose a change. But there are occasions when doing nothing is an unstable policy. In many decisions there is a latency period; the results slowly become evident over decades. By that time decisions have been in place so long that people have gotten used to them, and it takes the least energy to leave them alone. Or perhaps no decision was ever explicitly made; there were only tacit, informal decisions that incrementally added up to a prevailing practice.

Such a history can mean that we now make decisions by default. Doing nothing is really a kind of deciding to continue the present practice, despite the changed situation and the new evidence, which really slips over into making another decision. Doing nothing was once believed to be stable in society and ecosystem, but evidence has been accumulating that it is not. To refuse to reassess this evidence may seem like doing nothing, but it is really deciding on an unstable future.

Keep remaining public wildlands off the market. The military, police, courts, schools, museums, churches, scientific societies, historical parks—all these cost money and have budgets but are not businesses expected to produce income in any cost-efficient sense, not even when they capture (by fees, admission charges, or contributions) part of the value of their services. Though we sometimes decide their worth in terms of dollars, their purposes are to produce nonmonetary values. Wildernesses and other preserved natural areas cost something to preserve, though only the minutest fraction of what these other social activities cost. Costs are largely opportunity costs forgone, so far as these cannot be achieved on the 98 percent of the country on the market.

Even on semiwild lands, it is a category mistake to compare market efficiency in a Weyerhaeuser timber tract with a national forest. Where national forests are quasi-market operations and little more, they should be sold or leased to private entrepreneurs, who will operate them better. Timber ought to be a private business, more and more (as bird watching cannot be). The days of "hunter-gatherer" forestry are over; forestry is silviculture. One can no more hunt for timber on the commons than he can hunt there for food. There really ought to be no expectation of forestry in the wild. In truly "national" forests we protect other values, and here market-style questions are awkward because what we want on wildlands is what the market never sells—a hiking trail, a trout stream, a scenic view, a wilderness experience.

While there is a good deal of private game ranching, and farmers may be encouraged to develop additional income from wildlife on their property, no one invests in land in order to lease it for bird watching or butterfly collecting, or for aesthetic or spiritual experiences. That is economic nonsense. The purpose of public wildlands is to provide benefits in concert that citizens cannot expect on the market. Wild rivers run by nature, but they must also run by act of Congress.

The point of a value analysis by democratic process is not to translate all or as much as possible of the values associated with nature into an economic common denominator but to display the wide spectrum of value types and levels and to give decision-makers and citizens a strengthened persuasion where these really do (or do not), in aggregate or gestalt, beat economic considerations on the fractional remaining wildlands. We want a policy to protect these value dimensions not because they are covert economic values but because they are not economic values at all.

Do not use remaining wildlands nonrenewably or consumptively to satisfy the basic needs of a minority in society. The way to feed the hungry is by a redistribution of produce from lands in private hands, not by further exploitation of the fractional public wildlands. Very few will be permanently put to work by wildland exploitation, and surely these can as well be employed elsewhere in the enormous American economy. In a free economy, left otherwise unchanged, it is impossible to assure that the benefits from sacrificing wildlands will go to the poor; indeed, they probably will not. What the disadvantaged (or middle or upper) classes think about trading wildland values to help the disadvantaged becomes irrelevant when considered apart from whether in the prevailing economy this transfer can reliably be expected to take place.

Nor will the individual economic gains of the poor (value$_{\text{ig,mp}}$), overcome the social losses (value$_{\text{sg}}$) in the fourteen value types of Chapter 1. Poverty problems should be solved where they arise: in the mainstream economic sector, not on wildlands. To pit the trivial pleasures of an elite (a few fit, wealthy backpackers) against the needs of many (starving in the ghettos) is confused. Such a choice may not be spurious in underdeveloped nations, but it is in the United States (and other developed countries), to which this analysis is applied.

Even elsewhere, unjust social structures will often prevent goods obtained by sacrificing wildlands from benefiting the poor in any long-term way. It is everywhere futile to sacrifice wildlands to benefit the disadvantaged unless the social structures are just enough to make it probable that this transfer will take place. Failing that, the issue is a smoke screen that merely protects vested interests; it sacrifices almost every kind of value type and level only to delay needed social reforms, keeping in place a social disvalue. The basic needs of all can be met, and would already be if the system were just. Social injustice, condoned, does not justify destroying natural values as yet unappreciated. Their loss is part of no stable, long-term strategy for the solution of human problems here; to the contrary, these values are lost because humans do not have any visible strategy for solving their problems. They have only an illusion of solution.

Especially considering the ratio of human conquest to remaining pristine nature (98 percent to 2 percent), we wrong both nonhumans and humans who appreciate nature when we try to solve interhuman distribution problems (arising from injustices, vested interests, institutional failures, carelessness) by the sacrifice of nonhumans (ecosystems, species). Two wrongs (injustice plus the sacrifice of relict nature) do not make a right (trickle-down benefits feeding a few Americans). Disproportionate distribution among humans is not to be cured by further disproportion of the human-built environment to the pristine natural environment.

Make explicit the latent value judgments in quantitative models. The numbers look hard: 11,176 visitor days, $4,175,000 in timber sales, willingness to pay $2.32 per person, discount rate 6.7 percent, preference 7.3 (scale of 10) in age group 25–35 with 12+ years of education. Although some will say that quantification makes values explicit, remember that the numbers are no harder than the theories out of which they come and are as limited as the concepts that generate them. Unless the theories and concepts are explored and remain visible in the discussion, the numbers can deceive. All numbers in science are theory-laden, in environmental and social science often laden with soft theories. The "facts" can be "artifacts" of the theory; indeed, they to some extent always are. They contain large empirical margins of error. When used to persuade, they arise from value-laden theories that need to be made manifest. To take visitor days as a value indicator concentrates on the value$_{ip}$ level, recreational value, and leaves unanalyzed all other levels and types. To use any discount rate prefers the present over future generations.

Quantitative techniques, when ineptly or mechanically used, can obscure important value relations; even when used at their best they can never substitute for judgment, intuition, scope of understanding, and verbal assessment. Only the latter skills can suggest, at the start, what values are worth quantifying and how to try to quantify them, and in the end only the latter can interpret the numbers that emerge. Any dollar signs assume that a host of problems have been overcome interrelating value$_{sg}$ to value$_{mp}$. The "number values" are meaningless except in the context of an interpreted narrative of values. Numbers are usually thought to make values explicit, but numbers can disguise rather than expose value judgments. Indeed, the numbers are sometimes little more than tropes, used for the sake of giving life or emphasis to an idea but used in a different sense from the way numbers are usually used—not to count empirical things exactly at all but only symbolically to stand for values when they are felt to be real but the amount present, though important, is unverifiable. We should distrust any numbers for which there is only one indicator, since there is no cross-checking, and the cramped value judgments are less easy to expose.

In the end, environmental decisions are not a data-driven process; rather, the data are caged by a value-driven theory. The data seldom change anyone's mind, but they are gathered and selected to justify positions already held, ignored or reinterpreted if in conflict with favored positions. We should decide first about the latent ideology, only secondarily about the number analysis.

Protect minority interests, especially where doing so is nonconsumptive and requires doing nothing. Consumptive minority interests, particularly those that require expensive action (building a road to keep a local mill going) should not override nonconsumptive majority interests. On the other hand, nonconsumptive minority interests (mountaineering, bird watching) can be satisfied by doing almost nothing, are cheap and easy to protect, and are noncompeting between the noneconomic value types. And in this case doing nothing is a stable strategy. The protection of such minority interests is a long-standing majoritarian American value. Nothing is actually taken away from the majority in protecting these interests, although opportunity costs may be forgone. These may be significant to a few, but are not likely to be great to the community as a whole.

Opportunity costs forgone (value$_{mp}$) make sense as real social costs (value$_{sg}$) only where these opportunities are available nowhere except on the site in question. From the perspective of value$_{sg}$, the timber lost on a wilderness site is no irretrievable disvalue if, by better management techniques, an equal amount might have been grown elsewhere—even though managers have been too inefficient or uninterested to attempt it.

Similarly, in assessing the costs of the Cranberry Wilderness in West Virginia at $30.77 per visitor day, it makes little sense to count as by far the largest factor $223,609 per year in opportunity costs of coal left underground and unmined, since there is a 300-year supply of coal elsewhere in the Appalachian coal strata and no reason to think the Cranberry coal needs to be mined soon in order to meet national needs.[14] Nor should one forget, when development takes place and these opportunity costs become dollar benefits instead, that a spectrum of other opportunity costs (in noneconomic values) appears, opportunities lost perhaps forever.

Any delay, moreover, brings an opportunity to see whether even the majority do not gain in other value types more than they lose in opportunity costs. We gain benefits for the minority and the benefits of waiting for the majority. This rule protects against a danger in what otherwise seems so democratic—settling things by referendum. One purpose of government is to see that the fully considered will of the majority is done, where there is no injustice; another is to see that majority will is not imposed on the minority unjustly. A strategy for ensuring this might be, for instance, to prefer nonconsumptive minority interests over consumptive simple majority interests. We might require a two-thirds majority, on grounds that consumptive use of the commons—especially of relict wildlands—requires more caution and a quite unequivocal assertion that it is in fact the considered majority view, that it is a use worth imposing on the minority at irreversible sacrifice to them and with irreversible loss of option to the majority.

Policy here should also favor nonconsumptive minority interests over consumptive minority interests, since those who want to "lock up" the land delay but do not irrevocably destroy the option of developing it, while developers who "use up" the land irrevocably erode the original set of wild values carried by it, values accruing to both humans and nonhumans.

Recognize that environmental decisions must be one place where the model (myth?) of the perpetually expanding economy is broken. Four hundred and fifty years ago Europeans began to enter what they naively called an empty continent. Abetted by the industrial revolution in the last 200 years and the explosion of science and technology in the last 100, the American economy has been on a growth trip unprecedented in the history of the world. Americans have lauded rugged individualism, entrepreneurs, private property, development. A national tradition conflicts with the preservation of commons and of wildland values. Many people cry, "More!" Those who set policy on the commons, and especially wildland managers, besides the values they positively protect, have negatively to say, "Enough!" It will often be possible temporarily to increase the GNP by eroding the commons, always possible to increase it a bit by sacrificing wildlands. A politician can frequently gain votes by so doing. But on the commons is the place to say: "We must learn to accept no-growth sectors of the economy." At the boundaries of the wildland remnants is the place to say: "This far, but no further with the expanding economy."

Expand it, if you must, on nonwild lands—though even there, especially on the commons, a steady-state economy is more ecological, more realistic than an ever-growing economy. Some sorts of growth may occur forever, as advancing technology makes new products possible. Our supply of materials is finite (even if we develop space mining), but materials can be recycled and substituted; and energy in principle is in generous supply, although in practice difficult to get cheaply. The growth of know-how may be unlimited, given the ingenuity of hand and brain. At the same time, some sorts of growth have limits, and here policymakers ought to mix savvy with conscience to know what growth to subdue before limits are thrust upon them. There are sixty-nine dams on the Tennessee and Cumberland river systems; perhaps there should be no more.

It would be especially futile to sacrifice the relict wildlands, and then to confront only after they are gone the collapsing growth myth. To confront it early will save so much in the noneconomic value types. It will help policy to anticipate the steady-state economy and not to tumble into it by default and catastrophe. We have no reason to think that the last fraction exploited will leave us any nearer to satisfied consumer desires in a system designed ever to escalate those desires. Americans are already rich and need to learn when enough is enough. In this sense, wildland decisions are not peripheral "recreational" matters but front-line challenges to a governing paradigm. Wildland managers are not simply supplying values additional to those generated in the domestic economy; they are confronting the slowdown and, at wildland boundaries, the breakdown of a traditional economy in favor of noneconomic values. Wildland decisions are rewriting history, terminating and reevaluating the transcontinental growth trip. At the wilderness boundary we should post a sign: "Enter the wilderness. Abandon the GNP rat race. Learn to be wilderness-rich."

One frequently hears proposals that developers and preservationists ought to meet each other halfway. Compromise is frequently necessary and often moral in policy decisions, but there is no logic by which on the commons fairness is always a matter of meeting each other halfway or by which conflicting values are usually optimized by compromise. There is even less reason to believe this in wildland disputes, where 98 percent of the country is developed and developers propose to preservationists that they should meet halfway over the remaining 2 percent.

Further, according to the axiological model, the issue is not merely development-humans against preservationist-humans; the issue is humans versus wildlife, wildlands. One should remember the score—*humans 98; wilderness 2* (or at best, 96 to 4)—and set an ethic in that context, because what it is now right to do depends on what has already been done in the history of our nation so far. Too much of a good thing can become a bad thing, if development means the wiping out of wilderness. Any further gains for humans should be in those value types that humans can gain at no losses to wild nature.

Expect environmental decisions to awaken previously latent and newly emerging values. Gail L. Cramer and Clarence W. Jensen, in a chapter on natural resources in an economics textbook, conclude:

> Natural resources are all those resources provided by nature including land, water, minerals, plants, animals, and humans themselves. A natural resource has value only when an economic use has been discovered for it. . . . Natural (or other) resources in themselves have no value; they are valued, and command a price, only because they are capable of producing goods and services people want and are willing to pay for.[15]

That is the economic model that an ethic of the commons has to overthrow, replacing even in a secondary environmental ethic the all-consuming commodity model with a much more comprehensive humanistic ethic about the values carried by nature, and at length transforming even that with a primary environmental ethic informed by intrinsic, instrumental, and systemic values in biotic communities and historic, evolutionary ecosystems.

Environmental values are on a growing edge toward things once taken for granted, naively appreciated, or unappreciated. Not until developers threatened the mountain on the skyline did we realize what it meant to us, and in noneconomic terms. Not until they proposed to drain the marsh could we say that we would rather have it left alone, and even now it is difficult to articulate why. We never miss the water until the well runs dry. We learn what is at stake only when we learn that it *is* at stake. We awaken to goods when their opposites threaten, or to inconsistencies in our own value sets when we cannot have our cake and eat it too.

In these matters we can hardly expect a congressional mandate ever to be as groundbreaking as it ought to be, though we can reasonably expect it to express social preferences over economic interests. One cannot get anything through Congress that is very complex or controversial. The earliest growth in value awareness comes somewhere back in the grassroots, but decision models need to help it along. Policymakers should find the trend, not the mean; they should lead, not just follow; they should set principles, not just sum preferences.

Sometimes this approach will reverse existing priorities. Montana livestock operators sued the U.S. Fish and Wildlife Service, angry at a ruling that wildlife on the Charles M. Russell National Wildlife Refuge should have priority over livestock grazing on public land. A Federal District Court found in favor of the grazers, ruling that livestock and wildlife should have "equal access" to the refuge, as had been the policy for more than forty years. But the U.S. Ninth Circuit Court of Appeals reversed the lower court, finding that Congress in recent legislation involving wildlife refuges intended to give priority to antelope and sharptail grouse over livestock grazing, up to populations of 1,500 antelope and 400,000 grouse.[16] There are various ways of reading this case philosophically; one is to see the court as affirming a coupling of human recreational value with intrinsic values carried by antelope and grouse plus the systemic value in an ecosystem, all overriding the economic values of livestock on a wildlife refuge. The court decision, based on a reassessment by Congress, reflects an awakening to new priorities in value.

We close with a factual claim and a plea. Something approximating this axiological model (Figure 7.1, above the solid line) and these rules is a trend in Congressional legislation over the last twenty-five years, usually expressed vaguely as a desire to protect "environmental," "ecological," or "amenity" values from economic usurpation. The Federal Land Policy and Management Act of 1976 "declares that it is the policy of the United States that" there be "a combination of balanced and diverse resource uses . . . without permanent impairment of the productivity of the land and the quality of the environment with consideration being given to the relative values of the resources and not necessarily to the combination of uses that will give the greatest economic return."[17] The 1964 Wilderness Act affirms that Americans want to preserve the "primeval character and influence" of the wildernesses set aside "where the earth and its community of life are untrammeled by man, where man himself is a visitor who does not remain."[18] Though these wildernesses are also spoken of as "resources," this language seems to begin to recognize intrinsic values in the wildlands themselves. Perhaps this is what the concept of a wildlife "sanctuary" should involve, a place where nonhuman life is sacrosanct: that is, valued in ways that surpass not only economic levels but transcend resource use in the ordinary senses.

What is novel here is adding the understory of natural value, which, while not explicit in the legislation, is permitted by and consistent with it and more ethically advanced (nonanthropocentric) than can yet be expected of congressional legislation. What we still need (because we have only hints of it in present legislation) is a kind of emancipation proclamation for the wilderness that remains, which could be issued in the full assurance that the benefits to the emancipators would outweigh their costs, with these to be added to the benefits to the emancipated (as was true with the Emancipation Proclamation of 1863). We need to recognize that the human commons is the wild commons too. What we really want is an ethic of the community, not just of the commons. This is a call for humans to respect the plenitude of being that surrounds us in the wild world, once so vast and now so quickly vanishing.

Faced with public interest or with alleged values in and duties to fauna, flora, ecosystems, the landowner may claim, "It's my land and I have a right to do what I please on it." The citizen, on public land, may say, "It's our national land and we are free to use it, collectively choosing our maximum benefits." The human superiority we have defended (Chapter 2) can seem to justify these attitudes. But there is something incongruous in a landowner insisting on being free himself and a tyrant over his 400 acres, without a thought whether the wild creatures on his land have their freedom too. There is something morally immature in a land dedicated to liberty for its citizens and to the total conquest of nature, maximizing fauna and flora as nothing but (economic) resources. At least in symbolic places—in wildernesses and wildlife refuges, on the wing, on the run, prowling in the night, singing at dawn, bursting forth in spring—nature ought to be free. Liberty cuts both ways: those who only get and never give it cannot understand it; indeed, they do not yet fully have it themselves.

Can humans genuinely gain by exploiting the fractional wilds that remain? What does it profit to gain the world, only to lose it? to gain it economically, to fence it in, pave it over, harvest it, only to lose it scientifically, aesthetically, recreationally, religiously, as a wonderland of natural history, as a realm of integral wildness that transcends and supports us—and perhaps even to lose some of our soul in the tradeoff?

8 *Environmental Business: An Ethic for Commerce*

 IN NATURE, every organism must "earn its way"—consuming its environment, exploiting and capturing values—and business activity follows the natural imperative that humans must labor for food and shelter. This much of what *is* the case we can also endorse as what *ought to be.* What nature requires (that we work), what *is* the case (that we must work), we also morally command (one *ought* to work). Otherwise humans cannot flourish, and, in extremes, we die. That much of a bread-and-butter "work ethic" properly opposes a romantic naturalism that wants to leave nature untouched. It can celebrate how marvelously labor and management have brought the environment under human control.

At the same time, every organism must be a natural fit, integrated into a life-support system. In the wild, misfits cannot flourish and are eventually eliminated. However much human business revises spontaneous nature, primarily by deliberately adapting the environment to humans rather than humans to the environment, humans do not escape the fundamental requirement of inclusive fitness to their surroundings. They have many options among ways to do this but sooner or later must do it one way or another, for better or worse for themselves and the fauna, flora, and ecosystems in which they reside.

Some ways are more appropriate, and more moral, than others. Though humans must and should work, not all human working is equally "fitting." Its appropriateness can be judged on two scales, and this leads to two kinds of environmental ethics. We have met these already, but now we see how they fit into an ethic for commerce.

First, *on the humanistic side,* we must and ought to work because we and other humans benefit when we do and suffer when we do not. The sorts of work humans can morally do are limited by considering benefits and costs to themselves and to other humans. Only those kinds of work are permissible that do not degrade our environment, destroy our inclusive fitness. Any business activity that contributes, even incrementally, to a reduced fitting of humans into the natural system does not really contribute to a better standard of living. It may gradually imperil human survival. An upset of Earth's carrying capacity is a prospect for today and tomorrow that was seldom a fear for business yesterday. Here labor and management must become sober environmentalists. We move from what *is* the case (how life is ecologically grounded) to what *ought to be*. Given a humanistic environmental ethic, business ought to be environmentally sensitive. Locally and globally, humans are interlocked with their Earth, with material and energy inputs, throughputs, and outputs; balanced budgets are required in biology not less than in accountants' offices. In that sense *economic* activity sooner or later must be and ought to be deeply *ecological* activity, both adjectives having the sense of life prospering in a home place. All that, however, can remain an ethic for the use of the environment, a resource ethic in which our ultimate concern is how far humans are helped or hurt by the condition of their environment. The environment in itself is only secondary.

Second, in a primary environmental ethic *on the naturalistic side*, some natural objects (whooping cranes) count morally in their own right, apart from human interests. Ecosystems (the Great Smoky Mountains) contain systemic and intrinsic values—dynamic stability, integrity, biotic community, speciating power—from which humans derive a duty to respect "the land." The sorts of work that business ought to do will sometimes be limited by considering benefits and harms done to fauna and flora, to species, ecosystems, landforms.

Since business began, some ways of making money have been judged morally unacceptable, because in one way or another they place unacceptable costs (losses in some larger sense, often noneconomic) on operators, employers, employees, buyers, sellers, or other persons. But only in recent decades has business been pressed to cope with environmental prohibitions. These are keyed to the concern of Congress, emerging in recent decades, for "environmental values" (noted in Chapter 7). The ethic of the commons produces an ethic for commerce. The Environmental Protection Agency and related regulatory agencies have become major federal powers. There are many state and local environmental rules. Environmental regulation has become a daily fact of business life.

For the most part, such rules are intended to enforce extensions of traditional ethics. Humans have duties to other humans;

given the massive powers of environmental alteration that business has recently attained, we must by legal and moral imperatives take care that there is no injustice to other humans, today or tomorrow. But that is not all. Among the citizens who support these regulations are advocates of a deeper environmental ethic who are further concerned about the integrity of the environment, or this or that component of it, for what it is in itself. There is some moral awakening going on here, analogous to the awakening to the evils of slavery, child labor, apartheid, or discrimination against women.

People in business are by custom bound to consider the anthropocentric ethic but not the naturalistic one. Yet those in the world of business eventually will encounter the latter ethic—principles advocated by their most vigorous critics and that we have been advocating in preceding chapters. Even those who operate out of humanistic motives may find that they sometimes share sympathies with and find some logic in what the naturalists recommend.

We begin with some principles in a humanistic environmental ethic as these apply to business, follow with some rules in a more naturalistically oriented ethic, then note the special complexity of the ethical interplay between business and the environment. Owing both to the nature of business in our industrial society and to the nature of environmental interactions, complications arise that require ethical judgments in less familiar, more demanding contexts than ethicists sometimes face. Our final group of guidelines offers some advice for business persons in the complexities of environmental affairs. A mosaic of ideas—humanistic and naturalistic concerns, theory and practice, idealism and pragmatism, individual and corporate responsibility, obligations to future generations, shared risks, and so forth—has to be kept in focus if we are to form a clear picture of "the facts" and "the values." Stand too close and we see some details but lose the overall pattern. Stand too far away and we see the shape but lose the substance. The challenge is to command a clear view.

We have already sketched an environmental policy for the commons and set out some guidelines there. Those form a background for what follows. The ethic for the commons overrides, where applicable, the ethic for commerce: for instance, if our policy is to avoid irreversible change or not to discount the future environmentally, or if a toxic threat is trumps, then business ought to operate within those collective choices as constraints. The ethic for the commons, however, covers a wider territory, ranging over realms of nature that are off the market, out of the commercial sector. Further, an ethic for commerce needs to be more specific about commercial forces in the private sector, off the commons, about the institutional pressures of business. So the two ethics are separate sets but have an intersection.

Business corporations, like government, play a large role in our lives and have enormous environmental impact; unless an ethic can get lodged there, it will be ineffective. Sometimes one hears the protest that neither governments nor businesses are moral agents; only persons are, so all that is needed or possible is a personal ethic practiced by the individuals who engage in business or run the government. It is sometimes said that when persons act collectively in businesses, no moral criticisms can be made of their actions.

But in institutions there emerge ethical patterns and responsibilities that overleap individuals. There is an ethic "writ large" in the business firm or the government agency. Persons are influenced by, as much as they influence, these social forces with their ethical components. The institution itself becomes a normative system, placing demands on us. Individuals enmeshed in a corporate system inevitably, sometimes uncomfortably, mingle private ethics with those of the office; often, the higher up the agent, the more this is so. Business executives stand for more than themselves; willingly or reluctantly, they uphold the policy, tradition, bias—the norms—of their company. The institutional pressures make it difficult for individuals to face issues and options squarely. They make us play roles. They make it hard to say how far we are behaving rationally and how far we are rationalizing behavior. Authority shapes behavior. One cannot advance without affirming the organization's priorities. Those above us do not promote their adversaries; we do not hire troublemakers.

All this means that if we are to control these institutional forces morally, we have to write rules at the level of the business firm (just as we have to write regulations for government agencies) as well as at the level of the individual. Often what may first seem to be routine and nonmoral environmental matters, *just business*, turn out to involve deeper ethical puzzles about what is *just in business.*

Business and a Humanistic Environmental Ethic

Environmental ethics connects us with a problematic theme: how to harmonize the sometimes dissonant claims of private interests and public goods. An old ambivalence in the Judeo-Christian mind about profitmaking, and how this mixes doing unto one-self with doing for others, has reappeared in recent discussions about the social responsibility of business. If moral philosphers have nearly agreed to anything, they agree that ethical egoism (I ought *always* do what is in my enlightened self-interest) is both incoherent and immoral. If ethically enlightened executives have nearly agreed to anything, they agree that profitmaking cannot be the *sole* business of business, however much it is a necessary one and however unsettled the extent of their social responsibil-ity. There is a tendency for need to slide into greed; even the duty to fulfill needs (economic and noneconomic) must be balanced and sometimes checked by moral constraints.

In a narrow sense, the personal ethic most opposed by ethicists seems to be the bottom line of all business. But in a broader sense, much business is possible that simultaneously serves private in-terests and public goods. It is hard for a large business to stay in operation, whatever its profits, unless the managers and employ-ees bring themselvess to believe that the firm is contributing to the public good. Otherwise, negatively, they must regard them-selves as trapped or bury themselves in their own anxiety. But, positively, this means they will try to choose a route that at once serves their profit and the public good, more or less.

Some business is profitable within moral constraints, and when businesses act in concert (perhaps because they are reg-ulated so by government or moral custom), responsible appre-ciation of environmental quality is usually affordable without heavy costs at all—especially in the already prosperous Western economies. That much agreement, admittedly rough, reconciles business and moral philosophy enough to let us apply environ-mental ethics to business.

"Environmental and other social problems should get *at least* as much corporate attention as production, sales, and finance. The quality of life in its total meaning is, in the final reckoning, the only justification for any corporate activity."[1] That demand, with its emphasis, comes from the former chairman of the board of the world's largest bank, Louis B. Lundborg. What would it mean to write environmental ethics into company policy? If that ethic is humanistic, the following maxims would be first considerations.

Assess costs suffered by persons not party to your business trans-actions. Social costs do not show up on companies' or customers' books, but someone pays them sooner or later. Dumping pollutants into the air, water, and soil amounts to having free sewage. A business exports pollution, more or less of it depending on how much the company can get past current regulations. The EPA classifies over half of the 50,000 market chemicals as hazardous if inadequately disposed of, with perhaps only 10 percent being safely handled. Divide or multiply their figures by two or three, and the threat is still serious. Someone has to suffer impaired health, a blighted landscape, and reduced property values and must pay clean-up bills or medical costs. The acid rain falls downwind at home or abroad. Governor George Wallace once remarked, as the winds blew east to waft pollution through the Alabama capitol's corridors, that the odor wasn't so bad; in fact, it was "sweet" because it was "the smell of money."[2] He could more accurately have said that it was the smell of money changing pockets from the hapless victims, who must pay for the damages, to those of the business operators who profited the more from their free sewage.

Here a good company will follow the urging of Henry B. Schacht, chairman of the board at Cummins Engine Company, to consider the stakeholders as well as the stockholders.[3] But it is easy to forget this because of the concentrated benefits and widespread costs. The costs are heavy but too thinly dispersed to keep focused against the lesser but concentrated benefits. Lots of persons are hurt, but they may not be hurt very much or able to show easily the origin of their hurt. Individuals may be too scattered to organize themselves well against the offending company. Concern for stakeholders as well as stockholders enjoins concern about all this.

Allied Chemical Corporation, operating an eastern Virginia plant, was charged with intentionally violating environmental protection laws by releasing Kepone into local waters. Denying the charges, the firm pleaded no contest and was fined $13.2 million, the largest fine ever imposed in an environmental case. Judge Robert R. Merhige, Jr., wrote: "I disagree with the defendants' position that all of this was so innocently done, or inadvertently done. I think it was done because of what it considered to be business necessities, and money took the forefront. . . . Allied knew it was polluting the waters."[4] Allied was refusing to count the stakeholders in order to please the stockholders.

The Kepone fine illustrates the legal penalties that are developing because business has been notoriously slow to police its spillover. The Superfund legislation of 1980 and 1986 provides large sums to clean up a hundred orphaned sites inherited from (knowingly or unknowingly) irresponsible practices of earlier years. Many chemical and petroleum companies have backed this legislation, a bit grudgingly, perhaps hoping thereby to deal with the tip of an iceberg; they will get off cheaper this way than if the full extent of old costs hidden at 50,000 sites ever becomes evident. One business by itself can only partially (to use an economist's catchword) internalize these externalities, but every business can as a matter of policy work in concert with others here. Almost every citizen is carrying in his or her body some of the burden of this problem, so there ought to be none unwilling to weigh the moral burden.

Do not assume that what is good for the company is good for the country. The aphorism of Charles E. Wilson, a famous GM executive, that, "what's good for General Motors is good for the country," is half true, even mostly true.[5] But its untruth sufaces in environmental affairs, where we give the word "country" a grassroots twist to include the people in their urban, rural, and even wild places. We want an ethic for "the land" in cultural and natural senses. The United States automakers steadily resisted stronger pollution standards and fuel-efficient cars, foot-dragging all the way—even though cleaner air is good for the city, the countryside, and all inhabitants of both and though small cars are less demanding on petroleum reserves. Their reason was that compliance took extra work and put a crimp in the industry's profits. Every developer, realtor, purchaser of minerals and fibers, user of energy, and disposer of wastes will find some ways of doing business better, some worse for the countryside—and here one ought to love his country more than his company.

Each business, like each person, lives, eats, and breathes in and on a public reservoir. In this sense there is no such thing as a private business. Garrett Hardin has described in a sad phrase, "the tragedy of the commons," how individuals and their companies, each doing what is in their own immediate self-interest, can all together gradually destroy the public domain, "the commons," including their neighborhood and countryside, its air, water, soil, forests, resources. They end by destroying themselves.[6] To prevent such disaster, we have placed an ethic of the commons, one for the country and countryside, ahead of this ethic for the company. We have also placed social goods ahead of economic goods and even, on relict wildlands, ecosystemic goods ahead of social goods.

Do not keep company secrets that may vitally affect those from whom the secrets are kept. Following this rule permits a healthy outside environmental audit. A company has a limited right to keep trade secrets and to classify its affairs, but there is a lamentable tendency under this guise to conceal information that might prove detrimental to the company. The reluctance to count spillover costs and to take the trouble to distinguish the goods of company and country make it important to get out the facts, and lack of them, for the purpose of open debate. This is especially important if those who may be hurt are to have the chance to defend their own interests.

It took the Freedom of Information Act to disclose that (in 1976) 8,000 pounds of plutonium and bomb-grade uranium were unaccounted for in the United States, enough for the construction of hundreds of nuclear weapons.[7] A corporate polluter once claimed that the amount of sulfuric acid his company dumped into the Savannah River was a trade secret; others have claimed that the public had no right to know what was coming out of their smokestacks. The National Science Foundation's Panel to Select Organic Compounds Hazardous to the Environment sent a survey to industries in 1975 and found that only 28 percent gave replies that were usable as answers in compiling data, owing largely to the tradition of secrecy in the chemical industries.[8] Subpoenaed documents have often shown companies to be telling less than the whole truth.

Love your "enemies" here because they are in the long run your friends—unless you really don't care whether you harm innocents. Company policy should volunteer relevant files cooperatively, even if doing so may reduce company profits. It forces you to take more care, but the threat of potential harm to innocents overrides reduced profits by operators. The rule also requires individual employees to reverse, even to violate, policy that maliciously, tacitly, naively makes truth the first casualty in an environmental contest. It may require whistle-blowing.

The secrets here are sometimes about secrets. For example, the administrators of a nuclear reactor may fail to reveal that they do not know the extent, and cannot diagnose the threat, of contaminants released in an accident. It is hard to maintain credibility when ignorance and mistakes are exposed, but still harder to recover it once you are found to have lied or mismanaged the news.

Do not disclaim responsibility in inherited problems. Many mistakes were made before hazards were understood. An individual who joins a firm inherits all its problems (often coinciding with its opportunities) proportionately to his or her influence with that company, the degree of which may advance over time. When a firm enters the market, it inherits all its problems (also its opportunities) proportionately to its share of the market. Both individuals and firms will find themselves with problems for which they are not responsible; previous actors produced the present situation. We have a rationalizing tendency to conclude that we are not responsible *in* the inherited mess if we are not responsible *for* it. The employee may not have been born or the company in business when the now-orphaned wastes were carelessly dumped. But present operators, both single companies and all in concert, can do something about reversing these conditions, as the firms backing the Superfund illustrate.

Creatively doing what we can is our responsibility. When we wake up to sufficient environmental deterioration to alarm us morally, the problem is well underway. It is not "our" fault, if we restrict the scope of "our" to present employees and firm, but it is still "our" problem. Voluntarily to join a company is voluntarily to assume responsibility for the effects of its past decisions. This is part of the mingling of personal ethic and corporation ethic that we earlier noticed. Inaction can be irresponsible as well as action.

Optimize nonconsumptive goods. Consumption is what business and even life is all about, for we all consume to live. But in another sense, consumption is a kind of wasting disease, a matter of ineffective use. Perhaps permitted levels of consumption can rise gradually over time as broader resource bases, recycling methods, and energy techniques are discovered. Then the luxuries of the fathers can become the necessities of the children. Nevertheless, at any given decision point, it is better to favor the least consumptive alternative. Some things can be used without being used up, the difference between a cloth and a paper towel. Many wildlife photographers but only one trophy hunter can "shoot" the same buck; therefore, fiscal concerns being equal, an optics manufacturer might prefer telephoto lenses to crosshair scopes. Often, the less consumptive a good is (a day spent hiking the Appalachian Trail), the higher its quality. Amenity use tends to be nonconsumptive, while commodity use tends to be consumptive. A realtor who resolves to keep goods as public and permanent as possible will not seek to convert into posted, exclusive cabin plots land suitable for a state park or essential to the trail.

One alarm clock may last two years, another twenty. In our lavish yet cheap, throwaway economy, business has hardly urged efficiency upon its customers. The market is full of planned obsolescence, with far more time spent hooking the gullible buyer into consumption than is spent considering alternative, possibly equally profitable, ways of making goods more durable. We too often have (to adapt a computing term) a *gigo* economy—garbage in, garbage out—because the stuff is not only junk when discarded; it is junk when sold. Some products should hardly have been made at all. It is unlikely that electric carving knives have really benefited one in a hundred of their purchasers. The advice to eliminate consumptive goods is ridiculous, but the effort to maximize consumptive goods is equally so and unethical as well. Maximizing tendencies sometimes have to be checked; they can be consumptive in the bad sense.

Optimize recycling. Make it so it will last, but then again, make it so it won't. When junked, can it be remanufactured? Of otherwise comparable materials, which one may be more economically reused? General Motors has had a task force looking for ways to improve the recyclability of cars by changing the materials. Ecologically, one material may be biodegradable, another not. The hamburger must be eaten, but does it need to be wrapped in so majestic a petroplastic carton, used for twenty-five seconds to carry it from the counter to the table, then tossed away to lie in a trash heap for decades? The hamburger is digested and eliminated, the nutrients recycled; the wrapper, indigestible by man or microbe, outlasts the life of the burger eater. For that matter, does an eat-in hamburger need to be wrapped? Even biodegradable paper packaging requires the lavish use of wood pulp.

The soda pop consumed on the trail is soon gone, the aluminum tab tossed there lasts nearly a century. It might have been manufactured affixed to the can, and the can packed out and recycled by deposit or buy-back incentives. A single wood-handled carving knife will outlast half a dozen electric ones; it gives its user needed exercise and no expense. If it ever wears thin, the wood can rot and the steel be remelted, while the plastic from the electric gadgetry lies useless at the dump.

An economist needs to be mindful of what an ecologist calls "throughput" in the system, the movement of energy and materials so that the valuable constituents nowhere choke up but keep being reused in the systemic flows. From one viewpoint this is a matter of expediency and efficiency, but from another it is also a moral concern. How do we spend a resource so as to keep it from being spent forever? How do we recycle value? Nature's bounty and invisible hand once took care of these things reasonably well, but no longer. So business has a new duty.

The more vital an irreplaceable resource, the more worthwhile the use to which it should be put. No resources should go through the economy too cheap to meter, but some are dear enough to need metering by more than market supply and demand. Of those nonrenewable and difficult to recycle, some are more crucial than others. The more one does business in this type of resource, the less one ought to manufacture transient, trivial goods; the more one ought to lock it into the capital of the economy.

Molybdenum is in relatively short supply, its ores uncommon. An area known as "Oh Be Joyful" near Crested Butte in Colorado high mountain country—desirable for wilderness, for watershed, for ski development—is believed to have high potential for the ore. Retained as wilderness, the area would be used nonconsumptively; if developed for skiing, it could be lightly used with high public turnover. If prospected and later mined, as urged by AMAX (formerly the Climax Uranium Company), the area has to be destroyed, with drastic social effects as well on the small town.

And what becomes of the molybdenum? It goes into solar collectors, which can assist energy independence. It goes into ICBMs, but don't we have enough? It goes into sporting rifles so trophy hunters can shoot up their game, and into the electric carving knives we already have too many of. Wilderness is in short supply, but the molybdenum is needed, so the area might be sacrificed for true but not for false progress. Solar development, even if it destroys the wilderness, may be more important than skiing, which doesn't. But if the wilderness is to be destroyed, then the vital mineral should not be indifferently used.

In our present capitalist economy, unfortunately (as socialists rightly lament), there is no way to ration the use of such a resource. Until there is, perhaps by selective taxation, the business community needs to develop some conscience about priority uses for our more critical resources. That is admittedly a difficult assignment, and many will shrug their shoulders and say they can do nothing about the demand for and uses of their products. But that is only to acquiesce in an unjust and clumsy market system.

Accept no-growth sectors of the economy. A corollary for business from the environmental policy reappraising the perpetually expanding economy (Chapter 7, pp. 285–86) is that there are limits to growth. There may be no limits to some growth of technology; newly discovered resource uses, substitute resources, economies of scale, and better recycling techniques may be forever possible. But there may sometimes be no available options: some sectors of the market may saturate, or increased markets, though possible, may not be socially desirable. Value at the level of social good (we recall from the axiological model in the preceding chapter) is produced by markets but also overrides market value—a value hierarchy that we can now apply to commerce generally, as well as to the commons.

Again, a stinging criticism made by socialists is that capitalists are wedded to mindless growth, whether or not it is in the considered interests of the society that business serves. An economy that is bent on escalating desires is likely to find that it escalates desires faster than it can fulfill them, or that it has to advertise to create "needs" (really only desires) as it creates products. The results compound growth willy-nilly, and this escalates consumer appetites for the environment. Corporate needs determine the individual needs, not the other way round. Individuals are lured into needs, unmodulated and undisciplined by the realities of their environment.

Perhaps there should not be any additional per capita consumption of electricity, not at the present cost in environmental degradation. Perhaps there never need to be three television sets in every home, with their increased advertising clout. American cars should never have been the two-ton, tail-finned dinosaurs they were in the 1960s. Perhaps we do not need to fly across the continent in supersonic transports in less time than we take going to and from airports at each end of the flight. An environmental ethic has many doubts about the all-pervasive consumerism in business.

Think steady, when enough is enough. Think small, when less is more. The satisfactory condition is not always the maximum. A sign of the adult state, surpassing juvenile years, is that physical growth is over, while a more sophisticated intellectual and social growth continues. In the mature years physical growth may be nonfunctional, even cancerous. Growing is a natural thing, up to a point; but the organism or population that must always get bigger to survive is in trouble. Steady-state resource use is also a natural thing. And so with business: some businesses will always be waxing, some waning; but a business system in which only those that get ever bigger can survive is in trouble. It "has consumption." It knows nothing of the law of the steady state.

Business and a Naturalistic Environmental Ethic

A humanistic ethic may be viewed as a matter of fouling or feathering our own nest. It insists on considering a public, not merely a company, nest. But ethical concern deepens with the claim that we have comprehensive duties to consider the natural community and its diverse sorts of inhabitants. In this community we humans no doubt have our interests, but these interests are, as it were, investments in a bigger corporation. Here we humans are major but not exclusive stockholders. The place of lesser subsidiaries has to be recognized. In a humanistic ethic we had only to pull environmental concerns under social values already more or less in place. When human interests are the sole measure of right and wrong, nature is but the stage upon which the human drama is played.

When nonanthropocentrism comes to the fore, however, the plot thickens to include natural history. We have to pull social values under an inclusive environmental fitness. The humanistic ethic will still be needed, but if exclusive, it will be pronounced shallow. Any business is wrong that asserts self-interest at cost to the whole public welfare. We have already conceded that. Now we move the argument one step up. The whole human business is wrong if, likewise, it asserts its corporate self-interest at the expense of the biosystemic whole, disregarding the other stake-holders. This does not mean that humans have no right or duty to capture values from nature but only that, as in interhuman ethics, some forms of exploitation are permissible, some are not. We need an enriched moral calculus reconciling human and natural systems, economic and ecological ones.

What values would a naturalistic environmental ethic in business recognize and seek to foster? This is what the next list of maxims attempts to identify. These value judgments will affirm the worth of objective characteristics in nature (life, species, diversity, complexity) and deny that nature is in the usual economic sense only a collection of resources. But adding to our moral puzzlement, we will find that nearly all these maxims have a humanistic rider. Some benefits may come to humans who recognize the natural excellences. This fits the age-old observation that to respect the integrity of another person is often to gain a benefit. Nevertheless the benefit is often nebulous and iffy, soft and intangible, never very impressive before hard and immediate economic pressures. Humanistic motives are here weak and subordinate. They must combine with some appreciation of nature to bring you to endorse a maxim. This leaves us confused about our motives and principles, but it may nevertheless leave us with operational guidelines that allow us to do business with ecological satisfaction.

Respect an ecosystem as a proven, efficient economy. Business and labor use resources resourcefully, and this effort spent transforming nature sometimes leads us, unreflectively, to see raw nature—apart from human occupation—as a useless wasteland. But an ecosystem is an economy in which the many components have been naturally selected for their efficient fitness in the system. There is little waste of materials and energy. Wherever there is available free energy and biomass, a life form typically evolves to fill that niche and exploit those resources. The economies we invade are durable; they have worked about as they do for tens, even hundreds of thousand of years, and in this sense each is a classic.

Nature is a sort of tinkerer, adapting this to that, seldom starting from scratch but using trial and error to experiment with odds and ends on hand, pragmatically insisting that a thing keep working, surviving, or tearing it up and making something else. There is relentless pruning-back by a sort of cost-efficient editing process, so that only the fittest survive. Detroit engineers do a lot of this sort of tinkering, pressed toward efficiency, defeated if their trials are structurally or functionally unsound. Even business in general operates much like this.

A sensitive naturalist will say that ecosystems as classics with long histories of efficient resource use call for an admiring respect, something to be considered when humans do business there. One ought to admire what is already there, modify it though we must; one ought to modify it with some deference for what it spontaneously is.

When a business interrupts an ecosystem, it should take care lest there be bad consequences (linking up with the policy to optimize stability, Chapter 7), consequences perhaps needlessly bad for the ecosystem and needlessly bad for humans. Even Ph.D.'s in engineering can be like the foolish natives who burn off semi-arid grassland savannas, plant marginal soils, and wonder why the desert advances and their economies fail. As tropical deforestation progresses, the Brazilians may soon be asking why their lateritic soils have lost their fertility.

One analyst even warns, "The survival of man may depend on what can be learned from the study of extensive natural ecosystems."[9] That is perhaps extreme, but it is likely that our economy can be improved by attention to the efficiency of nature's economy. Again, appreciation of what nature objectively is has a spinoff. Those who prefer to say that the effect on human welfare is all that is valuable here may nevertheless endorse this maxim, only giving a more pragmatic twist to the word "respect." Even in modern business we can ponder an aphorism coined long ago at the start of the technological age by the English philosopher Francis Bacon: "Nature is not to be commanded, except by being obeyed."[10]

On a ranger-naturalist hike along the rim of the Grand Canyon, the guide in her interpretive comments returned again and again to how this animal or that plant made efficient use of resources. The ponderosa pine is adapted to conserve water; the squirrel's fir conserves heat; dung beetles make a resource out of wastes dropped by the burros that carry tourists down the trail. The efficient are naturally selected for; nature eliminates the inefficient. "Good ecology," I thought. But the lessons came so repeatedly and with such hints of a moral that I began to suspect more. Quizzing the ranger at the end of the hike, I found policy behind the ecology.

Those were the years of the oil crisis, of an emphasis on resource sustainability, of worries about running out; they were years of anxiety about national self-sufficiency in resources, about the inroads of foreign trade. An executive order "from the top" had urged including lessons about efficient resource use in ranger talks all across the country. The theme was, "The future belongs to the efficient!" It was taught as a lesson to be learned from nature. Is it legitimate to derive a lesson for economics from ecology? Is this a command of nature to be obeyed? If so, perhaps we also learn here some admiring respect for the efficiencies displayed in ecosystems.

The rarer an environment, the lighter it ought to be treated. Nature's habitats are unevenly distributed. Grasslands are common, desert springs infrequent, salt lakes rare. Human development has increased the rarity of them all; we have only scraps of once common ones (virgin hemlock forests). The Little Tennessee, now feeding a lake at the Tellico Dam, was one of the last really wild rivers in the East. The rarer an environment, the more carefully we ought to do business there. This will impose minimally on business in general, though it will vitally affect the few companies who work in rare environments.

Weyerhaeuser, "The Tree Growing Company," with a generally positive environmental record, owns timberland areas collectively as large as Massachusetts. A few holdings are subalpine forests interfingered with alpine meadows; others are cathedral groves of virgin growth. The former were always relatively rare, the later are now. Weyerhaeuser has been clear-cutting both, and its director of environmental affairs, Jack Larsen, maintains that while there is a public interest in preserving such forests, doing so is "not the responsibility of a private land owner" but "a function of government."[11] But this is too simple a shifting of responsibility. Proportionately as these forests are rare, they ought to be cut by selection or remain uncut, whether or not the government is alert to the situation. The managed, regrown forests that may slowly succeed the primeval ones will not be the equal, either for wilderness experience or for scientific study, of the rare virgin forests sacrificed for a quick crop.

The rare environments are not likely to be essential to regional ecosystems; hence we can do without them. But they may serve—like relics, fossils, and keepsakes—as clues to the past or to alien and twilight worlds. They are planetary heirlooms that hark back to the wonders of nature, to our broader lineage. They add diversity and options. Their serendipitous benefit, as environments under special stress, is that they are often good indicators of the first negative effects that humans introduce, good laboratories of exotic survival.

The dropping water levels in desert springs indicated trouble ahead for agricultural and urban water users; the pupfish in such springs, endangered by the dropping water table, have been studied for their kidney adaptation to salt levels and for their extremes in evolutionary adaptation. Given our bent for radical technologies, it is hard to predict just where the next stress points will appear and what will be the best laboratories in which to study them. At this point, rare environments are often revealing ones.

The more beautiful an environment, the more lightly it ought to be treated. Every business person has stood at some scenic point and been glad for the pristine, unspoiled beauty. Teddy Roosevelt exclaimed before the Grand Canyon, "Leave it as it is. You cannot improve on it. The ages have been at work on it, and man can only mar it."[12] The really exceptional natural environments do not need any business development at all. Tastes in beauty differ, but a survey of what most people think will usually do for business decisions. In tougher cases, the witness of experts with enriched aesthetic sensitivities can be sought. Places that stimulate an experience of the sublime warrant particular care, as that experience is infrequent in rebuilt environments.

Some art is priceless, and all art is awkward to price. Natural art is not really an economic resource but is better understood in romance. The technological, businesslike relation of humans to nature is not the only one; sometimes we wish not to show what we can do but to be let in on nature's show. Nature's show is always aesthetically stimulating, and sometimes this display (projective nature; systemic, intrinsic, and instrumental values in ecosystems, species, fauna, and flora) overrides economic values (Chapter 7).

Where natural places are not left alone, we ought to work in and on them with deference to their beauty. The philosopher Alfred North Whitehead lamented a half-century ago, "The marvellous beauty of the estuary of the Thames, as it curves through the city, is wantonly defaced by the Charing Cross railway bridge, constructed apart from any reference to aesthetic values." Society suffered the loss of natural beauty here because "in the most advanced industrial countries, art was treated as a frivolity," and "the assumption of the bare valuelessness of mere matter led to a lack of reverence in the treatment of natural or artistic beauty." In any socially progressive business, "the intrinsic worth of the environment . . . must be allowed its weight in any consideration of final ends."[13]

The more fragile an environment, the more lightly it ought to be treated. This maxim is a corollary for business of the policy to optimize stability, and it further extends the respect (both admiring and pragmatic) that humans have for ecosystems as spontaneous economies. Sometimes we find ecosystems where life, though flourishing, is a fragile thing, where the struggle for life is especially intense and adverse. This becomes a constraint on business, both a moral and a prudential one. Admiring respect requires us to be gentle-men.

Natural ecosystems have considerable but not equal stamina. Industrial society developed in Europe and the eastern United States where (and in part because) the soils were fertile, the climate temperate, the waters abundant. This sort of ecosystem is especially self-healing, and those environments took a lot of punishment and offal. Society moved into the arid West; industrial expansion went multinational, seeking raw materials even under the tundra and the sea. We have discovered, often sadly, that old ways of doing business will not transplant to fragile soils. The Alaska pipeline crosses eight hundred miles of arctic vegetation. Some gashes will be there long after the oil is burned, even after the men who made them are dead.

The oil from shale found in the plateaus of western Colorado is proving difficult to extract without mutilating the terrain. The shale has to be heated: if this is done above ground, the spent shale is hard to revegetate because of the low precipitation and chemical changes in the retorting; if it is done underground, the chemicals prove toxic in the limited water in the aquifers that feed the few creeks and watering holes. Technologies that might work with thirty inches of rain and cannot be used where there is only an eight-inch rainfall.[14]

This rule is, in the first instance, the prudent preventing of a boom-and-bust cycle. But it can be a reluctance to go bulldozing in a china shop, lest what is shattered be "ruined"—a reluctance perhaps because of its beauty or rarity; perhaps in appreciation for the intensity of the life struggle; perhaps to avoid irreversible change, or to maintain diversity, or to appreciate the extra regimen in a natural economy so soon subject to our distressing it. Fragility alone, like rarity, is hardly a value word. But it has a way of figuring in a constellation of natural qualities; and in the whole pattern we may find some respect for the integrity of a natural place. We may resolve to do our civil business with less insult, less savagery. Vandalism is possible on nature, even in a businesslike way.

Respect life, the more so the more sentient. The capacity for quality of experienced life seems to parallel the sophistication of the central nervous system. Pleasure and pain become more intense as we go up the phylogenetic tree. It has seemed self-evident to moral philosophers that pleasure by itself must be a good thing and pain by itself must be bad. But if it is evil for persons, then why not for sentient animals? It will not do to say: "Because they are not persons." That indeed is inhumane anthropocentric insensitivity. Jeremy Bentham's question, with which we began the consideration of duties to sentient life (Chapter 2) is a relevant moral consideration for business firms as well as for individuals: "Can they suffer?"

In fact, business pressures have pushed employers and employees toward increasingly callous and inhumane treatment of animals, wild and domestic; modern industry often asks employees to treat animals in ways that they would never agree to outside of business. The fence destroying the antelope herd at Red Rim, threatening thousands with starvation in a cruel winter, would never have been built except under the pressures of business (Chapter 2).

The principle of the homologous nonaddition of suffering (developed in Chapter 2) constrains business. Does the business-inflicted suffering exceed routine natural suffering? Like human activities more comprehensively, business is permitted to capture the values in nature, and in this capture innocent life will sometimes suffer. But business-imposed suffering must be comparable to ecologically functional suffering—comparable in the duration and intensity and also in the basic or serious needs met by the sacrifices involved. Important differences need to be marked out between domestic and wild animals: the former would not even exist without human care; the latter sometimes suffer terribly in their natural ecosystems. Those who build an environmental ethic on animal rights and those who build it on the characteristics of natural ecosystems do not always agree. But we need not resolve all such problems in order to conclude that one ought not needlessly increase suffering beyond that probable in the ecosystems from which the animals were or are taken. Does not the Golden Rule reach at least this far?

Limited animal suffering will sometimes be justified by sufficient human benefits, as is regularly the case in food and medical uses of animals. Even then, we ought to do business so as to cause the least pain. We should, for instance, choose the least sentient animal that will do for the purpose of our testing and research.

Some human goods may not justify the suffering they require. Calves are confined in constricted stalls and, except for two daily feedings, kept in darkness for their entire lives in order to satisfy a gourmet preference for pale veal—which is neither tastier nor more nutritious than darker veal. In a procedure called the Draize test, cosmetics are tested by dripping concentrates into the eyes of unanesthetized rabbits until their eyes are swollen or blinded. The gourmet, the restaurateur, and the perfumed lady who know these things might be less callous. Faced with growing public criticism, Revlon has funded a $750,000 grant to find a substitute for the Draize test. (Consider again the cases of Merck Sharp & Dohme versus the chimpanzees, or waterfowl and the manufacturers of lead shot, Chapter 2.) Industry toxicologists are making serious efforts to reduce the use of animals in testing, with some impressive results.[15]

Perhaps industries that manufacture or use pesticides ought also fund research to discover products that sterilize in preference to those that kill—especially those (such as cyanide and 1080) that slowly and painfully kill vertebrate pests with highly developed nervous systems. This would involve two costs to industry, agriculture, and consumers: the expense of the research (with risk of failure) and, even with success, losses while sterilized pests yet continue to live. The benefit would be increased respect for life. It would not seem unreasonable to ask industry to fund research that an independent panel of experts sees as having more than a fifty-fifty chance of success, especially in cases where industrial or agricultural intervention has made "pests" out of sentient animals (coyotes, groundhogs, prairie dogs, pigeons, rats) that once had places in natural ecosystems. Likewise, industry should fund research for products that kill pests more selectively, with less killing of nonoffending wildlife. As a rule, any pesticide that kills half as many innocents as pests ought to be discouraged, even banned. At least the burden of proof should lie with users who desire an exemption to a policy forbidding its use.

Respect life, the species more than the individual. Three-quarters of adult Americans (the customers and stockholders of business) believe that endangered species must be protected even at the expense of commercial activity.[16] That alone makes it good public relations to protect rare and endangered species in the process of doing business. We have already met some of their reasons: extinction is irreversible; we lose diversity, beauty, a genetic resource, a natural wonder, a souvenir of the past. But underlying these there is another, really a religious reason: life is a sacred thing, and we ought not be careless about it. This applies not only to life with the capacity for experience, but to the lesser zoological and the botanical species. Species enter and exit the natural theater but only over geologic time, to fit evolving habitats. Individuals have their intrinsic worth, but particular individuals come and go, while that wave of life in which they participate overleaps the single life span millions of times. Nature treats individuals with brief lives but prolongs the type until it is no longer fit. Lost individuals can be replaced, but the species is irreplaceable, and the loss of critical habitat and a shrinking breeding population dooms a species.

Extinction of species (as we argued in setting forth duties to species, Chapter 4) is a kind of superkilling, since it kills natural kinds beyond individuals, types beyond tokens, "essences" beyond "existences." Artificial extinction (including industry-caused extinction) shuts down speciation. It shuts down the projective sources in nature, beyond the loss of human resources. It is thus radically different from the natural extinction that has occurred throughout evolutionary history in the context of replacement speciation. Industry needs a superjustification to destroy, even incrementally, the creative biological processes.

Yet one to three species vanish every day, and within a decade that could be one per hour. If the accelerated extinction rate is unabated, 20 percent of all species on Earth could be lost within twenty years. About half these losses result from tropical deforestation, which is pressed by industrial forces; the second greatest cause is pollution. The threat cuts to the quick in our respect for life. The question now is not, Are they sentient? but, Are they rare? "We had to decide which was more important: saving a rare bird, or pumping more oil and gas from an area which is that creature's only known nesting place in North America. I decided in favor of the bird."[17] So reported Walter Hickel, Secretary of the Interior, in a 1970 decision for the California condor. "For the birds!" The oil tycoon will say that derisively. "For the birds indeed!" The naturalist will say it too, but more respectfully.

Some companies have opted for the birds, however. The Weyerhaeuser Company (which we criticized earlier in this chapter) has set aside over 900 acres in Washington and Oregon—representing over $9 million in unharvested timber—to protect eighty bald eagle nesting sites, and devotes about one man-year per year to managing them. Weyerhaeuser also claims costs of $115,000 as a result of reserving 155 acres in southern states to protect twenty-two colonies of the endangered red-cockaded woodpecker, plus 100 man-days annually to manage the area. These woodpeckers prefer to nest in prime timber, eighty-year-old pine forests, and the timber cycle has to be less than optimum to accommodate them. In eastern Virginia, Union Camp Corporation has set aside 200 acres of timber to maintain two birds, plus their annual young; Gray Lumber Company and Perry Lumber Company too have set aside land there and worked closely with ornithologists.[18]

Think of nature as a community first, a commodity second. That ecosystems are intricate communities is an established biological fact, a principle of ecology, which those doing business in nature often encounter—sometimes to their regret. In the Pacific Northwest, loggers have clear-cut forests only to discover that on some sites, the forest cannot be regenerated. They did not understand the undercover shielding, needed for seedling regrowth, that is provided by the interaction of multiple species, sometimes weedy ones; or they did not understand the nitrogen economy, failing to recognize how the seemingly useless lichens found primarily on old-growth trees are critical fixers of nitrogen that fertilize the forest. In southeastern pine forests, mycorrhizal root fungi are similarly crucial. An ecosystem is a community where parts fit together in symbiosis.

Nature operates its economies in a corporate mode, if also in a competitive mode. This does not mean that the individual members of the community are aware of the process, much less endorse it, but only that natural systems are selected to form a kind of togetherness. The strivings of the parts are overridden, and collective behavior and functioning result. After Darwin, some might have said that nature is a jungle, a free-for-all where issues are settled by pulling and hauling. But after ecology, we get a revised picture of checks and balances that pull the conflicts into an interdependent community. This goes beyond seeing natural systems as tight and proven economies, beyond the efficiency recognized in the first maxim in this section. We think now of a community, a web of life, of life forms as flourishing only when interlocked in biological pyramids. In terms of the root metaphor of the word "ecology," a root shared also by "economics," we all live in a *household* (Greek: *oikos*).

Does any ethic follow from all this? Those who accept the prevailing anthropocentric ethic will still treat things like property and resources, but once they know about this coacting, they may become more prudent in extracting resources or eliminating wastes. Others, more naturalistically inclined, endorse the natural principle of life-in-community not only as a given but as a good. We examined that theory and the resulting duties to ecosystems in Chapter 5. That account is more sophisticated and sensitive to the complexities of evolutionary ecosystems than we can expect to take into the corporation board meeting; but we can give an abbreviated account.

This account runs as follows. Even in humanistic ethics it is always individuality-in-community upon which ethics rests. There can be overly atomistic views that posit only self-interested individuals looking out for themselves, and some may think that business should be like popular conceptions of Darwinian nature, a field of competition where the fittest survive. But surely a more appealing view is one that can generate some sense of the individual welfare as inseparable from the good of the community, recognizing on a moral level in human affairs the symbiosis in biology. We have a doubtful business ethic where an individual treats all fellow persons like so many commodities, forgetting that his life is in a community.

But when we turn to natural systems, we find the same sort of thing. The competitions take place in a cooperating community, not a moral or conscious one but a good one, and when we humans come to do our business there, the principle of community membership—known already in human affairs—is to be continued because it fits well with the biological patterns we find: that life is always life-in-community. Though there are relevant differences between interhuman ethics and intraspecific ethics, the cultural and natural domains feature in common an interdependence in which individuals are what they are in their natural or social environments. Business is constrained by community in society and by community in nature.

This may not derive ethics from natural facts, but it at least tries to fit an ethic to natural modes of operation. In nature there are movements of self-interest that are quite properly present, but these are superintended nondeliberately in ecological systems by nature's overriding hand in favor of an interdependent whole. When humans, as moral beings, enter to evaluate the natural scene, they continue by endorsing the principle of interdependent life. We have the right to treat nature as a resource but also the responsibility to respect the community (the source) in which all life is sustained. A business needs prudently to recognize the limits imposed by ecological laws. It is even better if fitted by moral temper for its place in the whole natural community of which it is a part. Nature is really the ultimate corporation, a cooperation, into which humans ecologically must and morally ought to fit.

Love your neighborhood as you do yourself. The surrounding countryside is, as Augustine said of God, that in which we live, move, and have our being. We should not be either irreverent or provincial about this. The local neighborhood is our nearest responsibility; there the impact of a business for good or ill is likeliest to be felt. But the successes of big business, the powers of technology, and the revelations of science have shrunk the world so that our neighborhoods are larger and interlocked. The ultimate neighborhood is the parental Earth, shown us so hauntingly in pictures from space. This Earth has generated us and continues to be our life support. It should be the object not only of our prudent care but of our love.

Though in one sense this commandment is quite down to earth, in another sense it is rather philosophical and general. Still, there are immediate, practical applications. We give local care to natural items that have become cultural symbols of home (the Shenandoah, the Mississippi, the bald eagle, Mount Monadnock) but also to landforms just because they are the home in which life is set, to life forms just because they are our "neighbors"—in the biblical sense. For the average American, already well-heeled and comfortable, from here on these natural things are increasingly worth saving; if a business continues to destroy them, whatever benefits it provides are not likely to outweigh the harm it does. Even for the average world citizen, who has real physical needs that business ought to meet, the quality of life cannot really be raised if the quality of the environment declines thereby.

There actually is no such thing as a healthy economy in a sick environment; it appears so only where industry can rape and run, rape one environment and run to another. But after a while there is no place left to run. If we damage the biosphere, we end by damaging ourselves. Humans and Earth have entwined destinies, and loving one is entwined with loving the other. Sooner or later, ethics and business must attend to the appropriate unit of survival, and that cannot be less than the whole Earth, the womb of all.

Ethical Complexities in Business and Environmental Concerns

Moral responsibility in environmental affairs is as complex and novel as any responsibility a business executive is likely to face. It demands decisions that weigh technical, fiscal, social, and moral judgments, often made over long hauls and in the face of unknowns, breaking new ground with an amalgam of humanistic and naturalistic interests. We face two kinds of ethical difficulties. One is where we know what ought to be done but not how to get the company to do it. The other is where we do not know what is right. We do not know the facts, or how to weigh the facts, especially statistical ones. We do not know the probabilities for development of future technologies. We do not know how to attach values to facts, or how to trade this good off against that one. Decisions will not be ideologically pure but rather messy. Yet there is some good news with the bad. The business executive will never be replaced by a computer on which these ethical and valuational decisions are programmed. There will be an increasing need for business heads that can do hard thinking.

Someone may object that the maxims given so far are useless because they are too general and imprecise. It is well to recall that ethics is not geometry and that we should not expect of one what we require of the other. Remember that even a general principle or warning can have value. Though we cannot derive from these maxims concrete solutions for every case, they nevertheless provide a background against which we can explore and assess our practical decisions. Those who share some or even most of them may sometimes disagree in practice, but still they have reference points against which to work, a background against which to sketch the shape of their differences.

These maxims must be brought into cross-play between themselves and more traditional injunctions. One rule may collide with or sideswipe another. These are not maxims from which we can compute exact solutions, but neither are they empty. They lay moral constraints on available options. For actual decisions, we have further work to do. But these prima facie directives clearly preclude some wrong choices. We cannot eliminate but we can reduce ambiguity by maxims such as these.

Notice that whether an act is *expedient* or *moral* needs to be specified with reference to the actor, the affected class, and the time span. All these are complicated in business morality. Here individuals, who are morally responsible, act for the company, which is owned by themselves, by employers, by stockholders. The company itself has some explicit or tacit policy, and serves the community over both short and long terms, a community populated with changing individuals. A particular decision may be immoral but expedient for stockholders this year; its reverse, a decision that is moral though inexpedient now, may prove expedient five years hence, given ensuing public opinion and governmental regulation. Meanwhile, the body of stockholders has changed somewhat, and different persons fill some company jobs, "offices."

As a rule of thumb, the further one looks ahead, the broader the group considered within the company, and the more effective social critics become, the more the moral and the prudent will coincide. As a rule, too, the bigger and more long-lived the corporation, the more fuzzy the line between private and public concerns, which increasingly interlock. Thus it tends to become true for such businesses that what is ethical is self-serving—not in the way that ethical egoists maintain, but because smaller, shorter-range individual concerns fade into bigger, longer-range corporate and social ones, with trickle-down benefits to individuals for decades. Meanwhile also, no businesses and no persons within them escape immediate short-range pressures that sometimes pull them toward making shortsighted decisions.

Where moral decisions become complex, they often cease to be absolutely and unambiguously right or wrong, and we seek to judge what is the best of competing but mutually incompatible goods or to choose the least of evils. There is some good to be accomplished by either alternative: some profit (which too is a good) but also some products delivered and services rendered that fill public needs. We need the power, the pesticide, the plastic, or the paper pulp, but then again, can we really afford it at this social cost and consequence? Someone is going to get hurt by either alternative. It is tempting to deliver the goods, give persons what they want (or seem to want), and let *them* assume the responsibility. But here, even more than in traditional ethics, the good is the enemy of the best.

One has to be alert and compensate for the tendency to underestimate the diffused values (Chapter 7). Values that are quite important, even of the highest kind, but dispersed and soft, get trampled down before values that are not really any more important but concentrated and hard, easy to get into calculations, and marketable. We have to trade off clear scenic vistas against smoggy ones with cheaper power.

Sometimes too the actions of business executives can be well-intended and yet, when their actions combine with those of other executives, do ill environmentally. Nevertheless, at other times a great deal of environmental carelessness and even crime stem from rationalizing selfishness. Neither a humanistic nor a naturalistic ethic allows abdicating individual and corporate responsibilities, and the following maxims will help to maintain a sense of responsibility despite the complexities of environmental concerns, in which it is easy (and sometimes convenient) to get lost.

Do not use complexity to dodge responsibility. Environmental causal links are multiple, incremental, and long-term. Their discovery is slow. Any verification is more or less partial, statistically probabilistic, and backtracking. One can steadily deny that the sulfur dioxide from his smokestack had anything to do with the acidity of a pond 200 miles away. One can point to closer plumes that sometimes blow that way, cite better-buffered watersheds where the fish still flourish, notice that volcanoes emit some SO_2, argue about the level of statistical significance used, and for perhaps a decade debunk the evidence.

Insisting that we get *all* the evidence before making a decision can postpone decision indefinitely, which amounts to keeping in place old decisions that were made on even *less* evidence than we now have. As one is forced toward compliance, lag times for design, delivery, and installation of antipollution technology are easily used to create delays and confusions. With compliance mandated, one can build the stacks higher, if this is cheaper than scrubbers, and airmail the contaminants farther downwind past the local monitors, claiming that they are now diluted to a harmless level. Then the dispute has to start over to determine whether this is so.

Add to all this the complexity of the corporation, its business links, and its role in society. Various levels of management can deny authority, since this is often partial, or claim to be not principals but only agents for the stockholders, whose will seems to be known (to maximize profits by recalcitrant compliance) but who are too diffuse a body upon which to fix responsibility.

Compliance will require financing, but will the lending agencies attend to the soundness of the projects they finance? Most banks resist the claim that they have any environmental responsibility; these matters are too complex for them to get involved in. The John Hancock Life Insurance Company, the Equitable Life Assurance Society, and Aetna Life and Casualty have, however, paid considerable attention to the environmental impact of projects they have financed and have sometimes voted the stock of companies in which they have holdings with that impact in view.[19]

Of course, causal links and corporate responsibilities need to be clearly defined, for there is usually no single cause or villain, but business complexities should not be a hiding place used to postpone responsibility or to subvert the law.

Do not use PR to confuse yourself or others. Every company lives and dies not only in the market but also by its image. For public relations purposes it is tempting to opt for symbolic solutions rather than substantive ones, then to advertise this legitimate but minor cleverness while ignoring—deliberately or tacitly—the major environmental problems that still lie unsolved. The company builds a model new plant, meanwhile continuing to run thirty in noncompliance. It can exaggerate the cost of sound solutions; plead foreign competition, the unlikelihood of better technical solutions; feature the jobs lost in a plant closure, its solicitousness for employees, low profits in that subsidiary. Through it all the company can so advertise the good will of the firm as to look better than it actually is. Diversionary PR may fool others about your worthiness; perhaps it even fools you. But the ethical person insists on judging the reality behind the image and, more than that, judges phony image-seeking to be unethical.

Diversionary PR is not only directed outside the company. The deep need of employees to believe that they are contributing to the public good can be a virtue—but it can also be a vice because, owing to this need, employees are easily deceived by company pep talks about its environmental awareness, about its progressiveness before obstructionist Luddites, elitist bird watchers, and canoe freaks. The need for personal self-justification, coinciding with the company's need for a positive image, gives employees a tendency to rationalize and adds further to the company tendency to contrive token solutions and to cover things up with rhetoric. But all this only confounds the problem.

At the core of management, those in charge know the intricacies, possibilities, and costs of environmentally sound business better than the agencies who are regulating them or the environmentalists who are suing them; if they don't, they *ought* to—an *ought* with elements of both job competence and morality. A nuclear power consortium should focus on these things rather than publish a promotional pamphlet exclaiming that God must love nuclear reactors because in the stars he made so many of them,[20] which only diverts attention from whether we ought to build this reactor three miles—not ninety-three million miles—from an elementary school.

Morality often exceeds legality. "There's no law on the books that says we can't." But environmental novelties are still unfolding; they ignore jurisdictions; and one can expect here a lag time between legislation and the developing conscience. Nor will the law at its best ever embody more than the minimum negative public ethic. Law forbids the most serious violations, but it cannot command the second mile of good citizenship. Even the conservative Milton Friedman, doubtful of any social responsibility for business, recommends that business "make as much money as possible while conforming to the basic rules of the society, both those embodied in law and those embodied in ethical custom."[21]

His statement recognizes the gap between the legal and the moral but is too conservative, because in environmental ethics what is already embodied in ethical custom, beyond the law, is likely to be archaic. Unprecedented sorts of damages may be done before the law and public opinion wake up, but the managers of an offending business may be able to sense and correct trouble much sooner. In this ethic, a business leader is called to live on the frontier. The best will be ahead of government, which itself is often subject to delay and malfunction. Law and politics can be quite as flawed as business, often more so, and the moral business person will not take advantage of outdated law, bureaucratic dawdling, or a do-nothing legislature.

That may seem too much challenge, but consider the alternative. A company that announces (or demonstrates in its behavior) its intention to make all the legal profits it can, though it concedes modest attention to ethical customs, waves a red warning flag. Everyone knows that such a business has to be watched like a hawk, past good faith in law and custom, in order to push its directors toward any deepening ethical insight. People assume that the business will become less ethical with increasing market insecurity. The company will increase its morality only at the irritation of its critics, and such a firm can expect to do business in an atmosphere of hostility. The courts, public interest groups, and the press rightly conclude that they will have to draw such a firm along by steady legal and social pressures lest it fling its legal acid into the wind or clear-cut whatever is legal in Oregon or Brazil; they will consider it always in the rear, always callous in attending to the fragility or beauty of the environment, to rare species and amenities.

Is this the reputation business wants? Unless your firm really is out for pure black profit, it is better to move voluntarily toward compliance and even to go the second mile, especially in those cases where you are soon going to be forced to it anyway. Those both inside and outside the firm will feel better about a morality that exceeds legality.

Recognize a shifting burden of proof in environmental decisions. When the first New England settlers did business with Yankee ingenuity, they posed little threat to the ozone layer, about which they knew nothing. The twentieth-century manufacturers of aerosol fluorocarbons have endangered that protective layer. Early Virginia farmers hardly knew that the South Pole existed. Modern agribusiness in the South used DDT that made its way into penguins in Antarctica. The more massive the manipulative power, the nearer industry and agriculture approach the carrying capacity of the commons, the more far-reaching the unintended, amplifying consequences are likely to be. Chemicals, unlike persons, are not innocent until proven guilty but suspect until proven innocent. So the burden of proof shifts, and it is now up to the industrialists to dispatch it. This puts them again on the frontier, technologically and morally. Formerly, nature's "invisible hand" ruled over these things, but this is no longer so.

One might have hoped that as our competence increased, risks would diminish. But the depth of upset advances, and we remain ignorant of our reach. Uranium was mined by the Climax Uranium Company (now AMAX) from 1951 through 1970 on the south edge of Grand Junction, Colorado. The tailings, containing 85 percent of the original radioactivity but thought harmless, were widely used as construction materials in thousands of homes, in schools, and in sidewalks. Not until 1970 did physicians notice a marked increase in leukemia, cleft lip and palate, and Down's syndrome. These causal links are still vague but established enough for federal and state governments to take emergency action. The regulatory authorities could have made better guesses about just what remedial action to take if they had had the latest report of the National Research Council's Advisory Committee on the Biological Effects of Ionizing Radiations (BEIR III), but during their deliberations the report had not been published, because of the inability of members of the committee to reach a consensus.[22]

With ever higher technology, it seems that our power to produce changes overshoots increasingly our power to foresee all the consequences. The latter takes much more knowledge. It is easier to make Kepone than to predict what it will do in the ecology of the James River estuary, easier to mine uranium and make reactors than to predict where the mutagens in the tailings will end up and what damage will result. In a way, our ignorance outpaces our knowledge; thus, we are asking for trouble unless we slow down the introduction of potentially more potent novel changes with adequate pretesting. The unforeseen consequences outnumber the foreseen consequences, and the bad unforeseen consequences greatly outnumber the good unforeseen consequences. Serendipity is rare in high technology.

Many persons in business are paid to introduce changes, to develop new products, and the quicker the better. But few are employed to foresee adverse consequences and caution against them. There is little pay attached either to conservative care or to rational consideration of the best social option. There is no pay at all attached to the defensive appreciation of nature, although in these low-pay and no-pay areas there is much of value to be defended. The government regulates to widen by law the margin of safety and to assure the preservation of environmental values. But caution is also a moral requirement in these circumstances.

DDT causes cancer in mice, but it is difficult to show that it does or does not in humans, for we cannot experiment much on humans, and everyone is already carrying a DDT load from its previous use. Does one conclude that, since there is no hard evidence, we should continue to use it anyway—at least where it is legal, outside the United States? We would then, in effect, be experimenting on humans, and making a profit during the experiment! Or does one accept the burden of proof to show that although carcinogenic in mice it does not cause human cancer? This might perhaps be done by experiments on more anthropoid mammals, or by comparative studies with similar synthetic chemicals that humans regularly contact, that we have no reason to think are carcinogenic in humans, but that do prove to be carcinogenic in mice. It might be done by comparing more refined measurements of cancer rates with existing DDT loads as these fluctuate within diverse populations, or as they flush out across a period of years.

The point is that it is moral to err on the safe side and that business has the responsibility to argue that the risks are minimal, not to presume so and chance the damage. Our grandparents when in doubt could risk a new pesticide, but we as conscientious grandchildren must increasingly refuse to act until we prove the limits of our effects. This applies to effects not only on life's necessities but also on the natural amenities, which have never before been so threatened.

The asymmetry in the burden of proof arises from an asymmetry in decisionmaking. Often one has to keep on deciding *no* (not to build the dam, not to store the hazardous wastes underground, not to build SSTs, not to spray with DDT). Once one decides *yes* (and builds the dam, pours wastes deep underground, flies SSTs, sprays fields with DDT), the decision is irreversible. When doing something is more irreversible than not doing it (Chapter 7), the burden of proof shifts to those who wish to introduce the changes.

Extend moral judgments through the whole event in which your business plays a part. While the buck should not pass outside a given company, the scope of judgment should not stop at the boundaries of that business. One should think as far outside one's business as one can. We cannot tell just by looking at the effects of our own actions, considered in isolation, whether we are acting well. Each of us is a link. Parts tied into wholes cannot be judged in themselves but must be judged in the resulting pattern that they constitute.

Hitherto, an entrepreneur could skimp on this principle because the results of his enterprise were reasonably evident to immediate parties, and any unintended consequences were likely to be neutral. But we can no longer assume that new technology or more growth is likely to be positive, or even neutral. What might look good in itself, what has always been good in past contexts, may be bad when seen full circle. Even when technology succeeds, the promised sweetness increasingly comes with much that is sour. The workers have jobs, but everyone for miles around suffers blighted health and landscapes. Almost invariably, when high technology fails, the benefits are lost and their opposites arrive with a vengeance. We need to consider what will be left economically if the gamble does not pay off. The Kepone was intended for better crops and a stronger economy, but the result is a crippled company and a poisoned James River basin. The failed reactor can no longer deliver its power; worse, the legacy is expensive and even impossible to clean up. Society is not only not in the black; it is not even back to zero. We are deep in the red.

Ethical judgment needs to reach for the compound unit. There is no point in surviving on a sinking ship, little point in prospering in a deteriorating environment. Formerly, we might have thought that the relevant unit to consider was merely the company and its customers. Now, given our sophistication and a sense of danger, it needs to be society, the country, the global Earth!

Think for decades. There are strong pressures to see what the charts look like this quarter, even this week. The higher the interest rate on money, the more difficult it is to think about conserving the future, and there is always at least *some* interest rate, some pressure for profit now. And scarce resources drive prices up, often driving interest up too. Some say that the successful business eye has to be myopic. But this is never entirely so and is increasingly less so with the size and longevity of the modern corporation, where collective interests overleap even the lives, let alone the interests, of individuals who play company roles. The

Weyerhaeuser timber cycle is half a century. No big company can afford less than telescopic vision—to make it clear that the telephone poles are not shorter in the distance, that the goods of future generations are just as important as our own (see Chapter 7, pp. 277–78).

Nor do stockholders care only about the next dividend. Most are holding their investments for ten or twenty years; the more dynamic the corporation, the more likely it is that they can retire on these investments and bequeath them to their children. They want the firm to make it through the year but to do so in such a way that the long outlook is promising. They will take reduced profits if they believe that the company is innovative, that it is a good fit in its society and countryside, and that this increases the quality of the environment in which they retire and in which their children, who inherit those investments, will live. Commercial and home loans are for twenty or thirty years. Why should the lending company think its clientele uninterested in the business stability and the quality of the neighborhood during and after the time that these loans are being repaid? Environmental spending, like that for military defense, is immediately a nonproductive cost; its benefits are general and longer-range.

The corporate and composite character of the big firm can permit exactly the demanded time scale. The company itself needs what is also required by social and naturalistic concerns. Generations in the future may not have much moral or biological hold on us, but if one can see as far as grandchildren, that will do operationally in the present case. Meanwhile, the company need not age and die; it can be revitalized forever. Couple this with the fact that many of its owners and operators are on board for decades; couple that with the tendency of expediency and morality to coincide over time, and a good business head will think for decades.

If this perspective seems rather general, consider the following as a specific corollary. A company should invest as much in finding new options as in reducing options: one ought not to shrink a nonrenewable resource base more rapidly than it is being expanded by technology (new extractive techniques or recycling technology discovered, new reserves prospected, substitutes found). Hence a business duty (as well as prudent policy) is to invest in research and development commensurate with the extraction required by production. To do otherwise is really a kind of freeloading, leaving the world worse off than you found it.

Impose on others lower risks than you yourself are taking. Some fishermen work both the James River and uncontaminated tributaries, mix their catches for public sale, but carefully take home a batch of the uncontaminated fish. They represent a multitude who own and operate businesses that require a hazardous waste site but who refuse to live near one, who demand power but from faraway reactors and coal-fired plants. They want goods but not risks. But no one should accept goods and not bear the risks. In fact, we should do this risk-bearing without consideration of fiscal costs and their distribution. My profit never permits your poisoning; a toxic threat is trumps. But set profit aside: how then do we divide the risks that remain? You ought not impose on others risks you are unwilling to take yourself, whatever the public benefits. Further, we have to consider not just degrees of risk but whether it is distributed equitably, undergone voluntarily or involuntarily.

Most persons do not wish to live within 100 miles of a hazardous waste dump or nuclear plant, and such persons should not demand power or goods that require others to do so. A company that sites dumps or plants any closer to a local population will impose upon those people, and operators ought not to do so unless they themselves live within such a radius of risk. Removing pollutants escalates in cost with the percentage removed, and zero risk is impossible. Some risk is unavoidable, more risk profitable, and there will be cost pressures to set tolerances high. So let the maximum permissible concentration be set by researchers, themselves among the susceptible, who are ignorant of the costs and who must long breathe the air whose toxicity they define.

Business is now playing with toxins, mutagens, carcinogens. Let all those involved join in the risks proportionately to the public, never merely private, interests. One ought not to settle environmental *lulus* (locally unwanted land uses) by property rights or legal statutes alone. Without his or her consent, one does not gamble with somebody else's happiness, not if the odds are one in a hundred; nor with someone else's life, not if the odds are one in a thousand. A risk imposed on others should be several orders of magnitude below one for which you will volunteer.

Work for benefits that can be had only in concert. There is not much point in removing the sulfur from one stack if a hundred remain. One developer may drop an area upon finding that the Nature Conservancy is trying to get an option on it, but a dozen still bid. Not only is the intended effect lost by the noncooperation of others, but the environmentally sensitive firm is disadvantaged in the market. You cannot always do the better thing and survive if others are doing wrong cheaply; competitiveness here becomes a vice because it encourages gain by eating up the commons. Yet what one firm cannot afford, all together can. Both the environmental and the economic contexts require that businesses act in concert. Moral success depends on the interplay of many wills. Associations of manufacturers, power companies, and realtors often have considerable persuasive force for broad policy-setting.

Still higher, there may be governmental regulations, zoning codes, pollution standards, taxes, quotas. The historical tendency of free enterprise has been to resist all of these, but surely they are morally required where the alternative is private profit at public loss. The capitalism that cannot incorporate working for benefits in concert is doomed, sooner or later, to fall before socialism if not into totalitarianism. If an association of firms proves to be only the self-interest of companies all over again, a lobby rather than conscience in concert, then we can expect once more the social antagonism that confronts announced legal profiteering. One should work for "mutual coercion, mutually agreed upon."[23] Perhaps no industry can be trusted entirely to police itself; perhaps we need to recognize this for ourselves and our successors as we face unknown pressures ahead. No company is an island; the bell that tolls for one tolls for all.

Stay critical of corporate pressures. A corporate structure tends to deaden and fragment moral awareness. This is so because of the individual's partial involvement, because of a firm's limited functions and claims, because of its collective impersonal nature, because our paychecks lie there; it is so even though a corporation's long-lived semipublic character permits more moral reach than the individual can have. For many, morality goes off (or soft) when the business suit goes on, when the time card goes in. It is always risky to question authority.

We may be given, and want, a job description with sharply defined responsibilities. There are some questions you may not be encouraged to ask; you get the message that nobody here can handle them; you are socialized to forget it and get on with the job. The corporate climate may foster more interest in loyalty than in truth. Capitalism does force us sometimes to make decisions in a context narrower than we need in order to make them morally, socially, environmentally. Perhaps we get moral fatigue, our nerve fails, but what we ought to do is to ask all the questions we would as a parent, citizen, or consumer and answer them as we would if we were not working for the company.

Some say that philosophy makes a person unfit for business; actually it makes one unfit only for unfitting sorts of business. Philosophy urges business by "one able to judge" (Greek: *kritikos*), and judgment is a high-class business skill. Like the university, government, or church, the corporation that cannot welcome and include its critics will grow dogmatic and archaic. There can be reformation only by those who question authority, and if the critics stay noisy, the moral and the expedient tend to coincide over time. Rachel Carson was right about DDT; Ralph Nader was right about automobile exhaust and air pollution. Our cars, towns, and countryside are the better for them. The Alaska pipeline is better built because of its critics. Conservative business operators said, a century back, they could not afford the abolition of slavery and child labor. They say now they cannot afford environmental responsibility. But the more philosophical executives are setting this right. The profit pressures do need moral watching. Whitehead remarked, "A great society is a society in which its men of business think greatly of their functions."[24] That has now come to include "thinking environmentally."

Remember that the bottom line ought not to be black unless it can also be green. Given that there is no healthy economy built on a sick environment, we can rewrite an earlier, faulty slogan. What's good for the countryside is good for the company—not for all companies, but we use the axiom to test for the good ones. Running in the black is not enough if it requires our running out of the green, green being here the color of the natural currency. T. V. Learson, former president of IBM, argues for "the greening of American business" and concludes:

> In the end, therefore, the whole question of the environment boils down to a value judgment, a priority setting, and the will to do something about it. Most businessmen I know have made that value judgment. They want a cleaner environment as much as anyone else. I believe they will have the *will* to press on for it, too, and to help, through business leadership, in stiffening the national will.[25]

The demand for bottom-line green is valid because the oceans, forests, and grasslands are the lungs of the Earth. But the reasons are more than obviously pragmatic ones. Business relations are only one of our manifold human relations with nature. This one should not preempt the others that go on before and after business hours, or when we are no longer consuming. Other ways of pursuing happiness are scientific, recreational, aesthetic, appreciative, pastoral, and philosophical. Both in order that business may continue and in order that we may live well after business is done, we need an environment clean enough to be green.

Clean has two meanings here: clean in the nonpolluted sense, and clean in a noninterrupted sense. Some areas ought to be absolutely and others relatively clean of human management and intervention. The world is not solely an arena for human satisfaction, much less solely for doing business. Some spaces should remain rural, some wild. There should be mockingbirds and cottontails, bobwhites and pristine sunsets, mountain vistas and canyonlands. There should remain much of that sort of business which went on for the millions of years before we modern humans arrived. In this sense green is the color of life, the most fundamental business of all.

Business and Nature

Sometimes it is said that in business mathematics the numerator can be a public or environmental good, but the denominator must be a dollar mark. Perhaps that is true locally on any one company's account books, but in broader perspective it is truer to say that while the numerator can be a dollar mark, the denominator must be an ecosystem. That is, every economy is superimposed on an ecology, and although that ecology can be transformed by the economy, it cannot be escaped as the business location.

Bertrand Russell claimed, "Every living thing is a sort of imperialist, seeking to transform as much as possible of its environment into itself and its seed."[26] Such an overstatement, taken alone, leads to a social Darwinism thrusting atomistic egos and their firms into aggressive competitiveness, with nothing more. Nature has not so equipped or inclined any one form to transform very much of the environment into itself and its seed. Each life form is specialized for a niche, limited to its own sector but woven into a web so that it depends on many other species in a pyramidal, flowing biomass. Recent biology has emphasized not so much aggression and struggle as efficiency and habitat fitness. Many animal populations limit themselves to suit their resources. If not checked from within, a species' genetic impulses are checked from without by the "natural corporation" that keeps every living thing in community.

All this is premoral. So what are we to say when at the top of the pyramid there emerges *Homo sapiens*, so powerful and unspecialized that, culturally evolving to where we now are, we almost can transform the Earth into ourselves and our seed? The answer lies in nature's simultaneously equipping us with a conscience, not given to nonhuman creatures. Perhaps this conscience can now wisely direct the magnificent, fearful power of the brain and hand. A naturalistic ecological ethic seeks to realize that conscientious human activity, business included, ought to be a form of life that both fits and befits—however much it also extends—what has previously, premorally been the case. Each life form is constrained to flourish within a larger community.

The planetary system carries humans most gloriously, but it cannot and ought not to carry humans alone. The best of possible worlds is not one entirely consumed by humans but one that has place for the urban, rural, and wild. Only with moral concern for the whole biological business can we do our work of living well. This ethic defends human life by balanced resource budgets. But more, it defends all life in its ecosystemic integrity.

Humans were made for Earth (if not also by it), and this gives us both the power and the duty so to act that we continue to fit this Earth, the substance, the sustainer of life.

9 Down to Earth: Persons in Natural History

THE ETHICS FOR POLICY and commerce, developed in the two preceding chapters, have been public and social; the argument was that a private ethic is not sufficient in environmental ethics, where government and business with their collective choices have such powerful environmental impact. But a public, corporate ethics, though necessary, is not sufficient. Further, the ethics developed in earlier chapters concerning fauna, flora, species, ecosystems, and landscapes had universal intent; we constructed a philosophy of values in nature as objectively as possible, from which duties could be derived that are binding on all moral agents. But something specific has to follow, or else genuine universality is nothing but abstract generality.

At the end of our search for an ethic, at ground level, there must be local, personal ethics practiced by individuals resident in their environments. An ethic must have an owner. Ethics is not just theory but conviction. In closing, we couple the philosophy of nature with a philosophy of life, turning to environmental ethics as self-involving and life-orienting. Who am I? Where am I? What must I do? We hope to put persons in their places.

The end of a book, and the end of ethics, is more life. We seek an increased quality of life in habitat, more experience of neighborhood. In this last chapter, environmental ethics is not a discovery of theory, not a set of arguments, not a levying of duties, neither rules to keep nor values to conserve—though we have had to travel through such analysis in preceding chapters. Such ethical principles are the algorithms that spin and govern the biographies of persons in natural history. This ethic concludes in a rich residence on Earth. The conclusions we lead toward are not those of arguments but those enacted in stories.

A disembodied argument may still be an argument, but a disembodied ethic is nothing at all. Value exists when humans are not around; ethics does not. Ethical systems overleap individuals, of course; a person never constructs his ethics alone. An ethics be-

328

longs to a community, a heritage; it cannot be functional unless it survives, reproducing itself over generations. But this means that ethics requires embodiment in individuals, as do life and species. All exceed but require particular individuals. One part of the truth necessary in an ethic is value judgment based on adequate description, an evaluator making a correct (if partial) assessment of intrinsic, instrumental, and systemic values present. The other necessary part of the truth is an actor who is "true to," faithful to, these valued environmental lives and processes. An ethic has to be inhabited, as much as an environment. It is a place one lives, part of a niche, which is not just an address but an occupation.

We have been discovering how to fit our world. The concept of fitness is initially a biological one but can subsequently be extrapolated into morality. Appropriate conduct fits the situations encountered. In both biology and ethics, life demands suitable behavior—right actions. In a way this equivocates on words such as "fit" and "right." A prairie dog's behavior is *right* (or good) in its grasslands niche; a person's conduct is *right* (or good) in sharing scarce resources. The first use *just* means nonmorally adapted to an ecosystem, as a nut fits a bolt. The other use means *just*, ethically considerate of other persons.

Still, granted that prairie dogs are not moral agents, the question remains: In what way does moral agency, when it emerges in humans, contribute to human fitness? Perhaps when humans are moral in their social and natural environments, this is functionally homologous at a higher level to the nonmoral fitness of animals in habitat. Both are considerations about a life form being good-of-its-kind, being good-in-its-kind-of-place, and being in a good kind of place, and these add up to the question of well-placed goodness; they could be value-optimizing questions in different but analogous ways. We are trying here to get ethics naturalized.

Humans Resident in Nature and Culture

An Ethical Fitness before Compounded Values

Man is a political animal, as Socrates discovered, awakening to the city as the niche for humans. Culture is not present in prairie dogs, even though they have a society and live in "towns"; culture appears in humans. But man is an earthling; Earth is his residence as surely as is the *polis*. Humans ought to be *cosmopolitan* in the fullest sense of that word; they should live both in a *cosmos*, a world, and in a *polis*, a city. In an environmental as well as a political sense, a man without a country is a personal tragedy. We need to belong where we live and not just to count our environment, like our artifacts, among our belongings. Persons need to be natives. Browning was as wise as Socrates:

> I am earth's native:
> No rearranging it![1]

It is true that culture is carved out against nature; there are dimensions of conflict. Every organism is set against its world, and culture intensifies this opposition. Humans in culture gain dominion over nature. We rearrange Earth to make it a city. But this is a dialectical truth: the thesis is nature; the antithesis is culture; and the synthesis is culture situated in nature, the two forming a home, a *domicile* (Greek: *oikos*, the root of "ecology"). From struggle to fitness—that sums up aphoristically the revision in paradigms that has characterized biology as early Darwinism has matured into evolutionary ecoscience. Something similar needs to characterize a maturing ethics. An ethic of conflict—humans as the resourceful conquerors of nature—has to become an ethic of complementarity: humans as completing and appreciatively residing in nature.

On Earth, humans ought to seek an optimally satisfactory fit. Involving both nature and culture, we can think of that fit as an ellipse with its two foci (Figure 9.1), though a diagram like

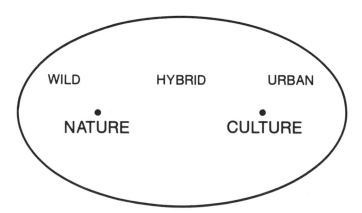

FIGURE 9.1 *The arena of values.*

this gives no sense of history; it only sketches the stage on which the dramas of natural, cultural, and personal histories can be played. Some of the area of values is generated under the control of a focus that we can label *culture;* such values are in the *urban* zone, where "urban" marks those arts and achievements to which the contributions of spontaneous nature are no longer evident in the criteria of value—though they remain among the precursors of value. The urban zone includes widespread social, personal, and interpersonal goods—for example, listening to a symphony orchestra, serving in the state legislature, or getting a pay raise.

The other focus, spontaneous *nature*, generates a *wild* zone of value. Humans value natural things for what they are in themsélves—for example, enjoying a field of wildflowers, listening to loons call, or experiencing the sublime fury of a storm at sea. Although humans come to own such values through the mediation of their cultures, they seek to admire value generated under the natural focus of the ellipse.

A domain of hybrid values is generated under the simultaneous control of both foci, a resultant of integrated influences from nature and culture. These values are so diverse that no single word characterizes them; they derive from domesticating nature as a cultural resource. Nature is redirected into cultural channels, pulled into the cultural orbit. This happens when human labor and craft put natural properties to use in culture, mixing the two to good effect in agricultural, industrial, scientific, medical, and technological applications. This domain includes rural and pastoral environments but equally the suburban life, the blending of town and country. It is a zone of what we earlier called value capture. Examples might include landscaping a home, taking penicillin, or going skiing.

This mingling of nature and culture means that ethics cannot be isolated from either metaphysics or science. All the historical world outlooks that orient persons' lives (examples of which we soon examine) are cultural products. This fact involves not just a cultural principle but an ecological one as well. Everything is what it is in relation to other things, however much integrity it may have of its own. Any outlook has a cultural coefficient; this permits a discovery of fact and value in the natural world. We may describe what an ecosystem is, or what a jaguar is in its niche, and find it to be inseparable from what a good ecosystem or a good jaguar is. We must then notice that we have gained both description and prescription here through a culture (with its botany, zoology, philosophy) that helps us to interpret and evaluate nature in terms of ecosystems, and jaguars in terms of niches, discovering integrity in both.

Perhaps, strictly speaking, there are no purely urban values, since some contribution of natural properties can be noticed in every cultural activity (the muscles that move the violinist's arm at the symphony). Even in town we never cease to reside in nature. Also, strictly speaking, humans may have no access to purely wild values, since even a wilderness is enjoyed with cultural supports (Gore-Tex jackets, matches, bird guides, the training in botany that permits hikers to understand where they are). We cannot revert entirely to nature and remain human. Nevertheless, some values push far into the urban area; others push far on the wild side, and many lie in between.

Environmental ethics is concerned with wild values and the natural components of resource-obtained values. This nowhere denies a cultural focus of value in the comprehensive account. (For another model of the same terrain, see Figure 6.6, which better depicts how cultural values are superposed on foundational natural values.)

Karl Barth held that a crucial difference between humans and nonhumans is that although humans belong to their environment, as do animals, humans do not merge into their environment. Culture is a mark of this nonassimilation.

> Real man cannot merge into his environment. He cannot surrender to it and be assimilated into it. If he did, or even if he could, he would cease to be real man. He is this creature, and as such he is not another, or a mere component part of a total creaturely reality. Although he belongs to the latter, he is marked off in specific ways from his fellow-creature.[2]

That is half the truth; humans are not like beasts immersed in a niche. In a sense humans have no niche at all. They make in culture an exodus from nature. Humans are standouts in a nature they are not wholly of. We recognized in Chapter 2 a legitimate human superiority, and we will soon be saying that humans are moral overseers on Earth.

The other half of the truth is that real (authentic) humans need to inhabit an environment. Persons need a place of residence, and valued activity there, a need with both nonmoral and moral components. Biologically and materially, without a world as a resource, without an ecology, there can be no human life. Philosophically and ethically, human life is less than it can and ought to be where valuing never transcends the human. Humans are not to be free *from* their environment but to be free *in* their environment. Unless they can sometimes follow nature they will miss marvelous values in their world. They will not see who and where they are. Humans do not merge into their environment, but with their emergent culture they ought appropriately to fit it.

Ethical Priorities in Nature and Culture

The emergent *polis* and this culture that makes humans standouts are of high value, and this can tempt humans to say that interhuman ethics is primary and interspecific ethics secondary. Sometimes, when soberly concerned with urgent issues arising when persons confront other persons, involving human welfare, life, and culture (making war, distributing food, or rationing medical care), ethicists can smile at those concerned for chipmunks and daisies. Environmental ethicists may seem to have taken a romantic retreat from serious issues; their concern for nonhumans accentuates the peripheral. Only marginally, it might seem, is this ethics.

But not so. As humans seek an intelligent residence on Earth, the four most critical issues we are currently encountering are peace, environment, development, and population. All are intertwined. Human desires for maximum development drive population increases, escalate exploitation of the environment, and fuel the forces of war. Those who are not at peace with one another find it difficult to be at peace with nature, and vice versa. Although environmental ethics operates in the arena of nature, not culture, interhuman ethics and interspecific ethics quickly overlap in practice. Those without moral principles who exploit in one arena will typically exploit in the other. Humans who seek peace with condors will seldom have to be urged to seek peace with their fellow humans.

Environmental ethics lies not on a fringe but on a frontier. It is not secondary but foundational. Humans who smile at concern for fauna, flora, species, ecosystems, landscapes need pity; they cannot see beyond their own affairs; they do not know the country where they belong. Interhuman ethics is not mandatory and environmental ethics optional. Nor does justice require interhuman ethics and charity permit an environmental ethic. Duty demands

both. All ethical agents who seek mature character are required
to develop an environmental ethic as well as a cultural ethic.

Some issues in cultural ethics may be more urgent than some
in environmental ethics. The duty to curb the arms race is more
significant than the duty to preserve condors. But in scope though
not always in intensity, issues in environmental ethics (in the primary sense) can be as critical as issues within interhuman ethics.
Extinction of species by aggressive development may pose as
great a threat of long-term loss as does nuclear war. Further, environmental ethics is critical because it enlarges the area of moral
vision, stretching human past their own class self-interests. Environmental ethics presses a cutting edge of moral concern.

Though environmental ethics urges nonoptional duties, each
person does have options about where to intensify his concern
for values within the area of the ellipse. Choosing to live in New
York City does not absolve one from responsibility for endangered
species. But New Yorkers, like everyone else, cannot be concerned
about everything equally, and each person's burden of concern is
partly at his or her discretion; it will develop in the details of
an autobiographical ethic in a storied world. Even in interhuman
ethics, one person may develop a concern for refugees from Central America, another devote time to local senior citizens, and still
another pursue justice by preventing toxic threats to future generations. The three benefit various persons, whom we may consider
equally valuable, but no benefactor helps them all equally.

Similarly, given the large area of the comprehensive ellipse,
some persons will spend their lives among the more urban values
and some among the wilder values; all will enjoy a host of hybrid values. Three-dimensional persons will know them proportionately. Some persons will have a more narrowed perspective,
at the risk of becoming one-dimensional persons but with the possible reward of being "expert" (more fully experienced) in a single
area.

Though obligations in environmental ethics have universal intent, they are not categorical, not absolute and independent of
circumstances and beliefs about the world. They are systemic,
and the systemic components are both natural and cultural. Do
x, because you believe y about the world, that z is a fact and v
is of value there. We move from believed facts to believed eval-
uations and thence to believed duties. In this respect, environmental ethics is not different from interhuman ethical systems,
though these other ethical systems, focusing on human relation-

ships, sometimes allege that they are independent of metaphysics or natural facts. Those who think that environmental ethics is peripheral, or that their ethical systems are autonomous, think this way because they have quite metaphysical background assumptions about who and where humans are. Any natural science in which they share is generated by, and quickly put in the service of, defending human values.

Humans as Moral Overseers on Earth
Apical Value and an Apical Role in Natural History

Humans have little instrumental value in the ecosystems they inhabit. To the contrary, they typically have instrumental disvalue, disrupting these ecosystems to capture and reform natural values for culture. Yet humans are highly endowed with evolutionary achievements. The Earth system, projective nature, has historically (at least in top trophic rungs) intensified organic individuality, sentience, even freedom and mentality (see Chapter 5, pp. 182–86). The human hand and brain are evolutionary products that result in culture, and fortunately so; hence the large area of resource-based and urban values in the value ellipse.

But when humans build their cultures, they continue to reside in nature, and what is the standing of those who stand on top? Has this anomalous species without a typical role some apical role? Can we describe the human type-specimen? Can we evaluate the distinctively human values?

An answer long favored in ethics is that humans are not to be judged for their instrumentality even in culture, much less in nature, but are to be judged intrinsically. Persons have value in themselves. Their roles are ends, not (just) means to ends. Kant thought that our capacity to say "I" raised humans infinitely above all other earthly kinds (Chapter 2), and philosophers who have tried to identify human intrinsic values have often sought for something peculiar to or "within" human life that warranted ethical claims. If the central idea in intrinsic value is that such value inheres in its holder, one will not need to assess the environment to justify intrinsic value. To be a person is a good thing, and this can be known without asking about origins or consequences or environmental relationships or any further contributory reference. Personality is a good thing in itself, as a point experience in the display of phenomena that results when nature gives way to culture.

Additionally, however, according to a recent corollary to the long-standing philosophical judgment, this high value can be defended not only by noting what persons are in themselves but by noticing where they are in their ecosystems. They reside at the summit of the Earth system. Personality is a point experience at the top of the global ecosystem, a lofty evolutionary achievement. The last are first, so to speak. In this way recent ecology bulwarks traditional ethics. Consider a passage by Fraser Darling:

> Man is biologically an aristocrat. He has dominion over the creatures, the plant cover and the very landscape of his planet. Man, indeed, is privileged. Ecologically, he occupies the summits of food chains and pyramids. Man is the lord of the living manor and privilege is implicit in superiority. I do not think aristocracy is a human conceived notion but an observable phenomenon.[3]

That is true, but a truth, Darling cautions, that requires careful handling. It can lead to counting human intrinsic value either as transcending the Earth system or as lording it over the rest of the planet. The focus of moral concern can turn inward to human class interests. Within the judgment that humans enjoy superior intrinsic values and that they ought to honor such values among themselves, the distortion can arise that this superior value is one of privilege without responsibility. The exclusive, humanistic view of value does not really see from the summit; it rationalizes superiority into self-importance; it commits the sin of pride.

This ecological truth about humans at the summit ought, by logic, to point in outward and downward directions, to bring an inclusive, global view, leading to a sense of aristocratic responsibility for the natural world. So we have been striving to fit intrinsic values of all kinds—natural and cultural—into instrumental and systemic values, insisting that intrinsic value, though in some sense on its own—a point experience without necessary further contributory reference—is in another sense embedded in an environment. Neither in an ecology nor in an ethic is anything really on its own. We want responsible intrinsic value, humans appreciating their Earth world. There is a dialectic of freedom and responsibility.

Some ethical responsibility does, of course, arise even within a misconceived aristocratic entitlement. Interhuman ethics develops to pull the focus of concern off self-center and bring into focus others in the community of persons. The single self must find a situated cultural fitness; a person ethically adapts to his or her neighbors. That is what ethics to date has largely tried to accomplish—honoring the intrinsic worth of persons. Humans struggle with impressive, if also halting, success in an effort to evolve altruism in fit proportion to egoism. That has yielded a sense of ethical priority, often ethical exclusivism, toward humans. Humans are on top; only humans count. Love your (human) neighbors as you do yourself.

A wider, ecosystemic perspective sees such a rationale as oblivious to the way the system has hitherto contained myriads of species in interdependent tension and harmony, with nothing maximizing itself except by optimizing a situated environmental fitness. From this more comprehensive perspective, persons operating with the prevailing ethical systems are blind to their place of storied residence, blind to most of their neighbors. All the rest of projective nature and the products of the evolutionary ecosystem are counted as resources.

From a narrow, organismic perspective, that conclusion seems right, since in the prehuman world everything is making a resource of everything else, so far as it can. Culture is impossible except as built on value capture from nature. Every other living natural kind defends only its own kind; humans behave that way too, maximizing their own kind—and justifying (defending) their position by claiming to be the only species with and of moral concern. Always prefer humans; culture outweighs nature.

Ethical Transcendence Emergent in Natural History

But human ethicists who argue like this only halfway emerge from their environment. They elevate human intrinsic values above all else. They are right about the human excellences, but they defend only their own kind, and in this respect they do not *emerge;* they just *merge* and play by the rules of natural selection. They become moral agents in encounter with other humans, but they do not become moral agents in encounter with nature. They do not discover their emergent fit in their place of residence. Trying to defend the high human value, they act like beasts. The traditional, anthropocentric ethics tries to make humans the sole loci of value, transcending the otherwise valueless world. In this aggressive attempt it stunts humanity, because it does not know genuine human transcendence—an overarching care for the others. Humans become myopic when they ought to be synoptic.

Plainly, humans have expanded their territories all over the globe. But what is an appropriate lifestyle for residing in this globally occupied territory? To maximize the high intrinsic value of their kind? Nothing more? The better answer, found in environmental ethics, is that humans ought to be ideal observers—using the excellent rationality and morality peculiar to their niche in such way that these lead to a dominion involving genuine transcendence, a worthwhile emergence that makes peace with and befits its environment. Rather than using mind and morals as survival tools for defending the human form of life, mind forms an intelligible view of the whole and defends ideals of life in all their forms. *Humans* are cognate with the *humus*, made of dust, yet unique and excellent in their aristocratic capacity to view the world they inhabit. They rise up from the earth and look over their world (Greek: *anthropos*, to rise up, look up). Persons have their excellences, and one way they excel is in their capacity for overview.

The novelty in the human emergence is class altruism emerging to coexist with class self-interest, sentiments directed not simply at one's own species but at other species fitted into biological communities. Humans ought to think from an ecological analogue of what ethicists have called the original position, a global position that sees Earth objectively as an evolutionary ecosystem. In occupying this position, human subjects meaningfully interpret and play roles in the storied achievements on Earth. Interhuman ethics has spent the last two millennia waking up to human dignity. As we turn to a new millennium, environmental ethics invites awakening to the greater story of which humans are a consummate part.

This is a novel ethical issue (at least in the mainstream West), and two considerations drive its urgency: first, the vastly increased understanding of natural history that humans have gained in the last century with the appearance of evolutionary biology and ecology; second, the vastly increased powers of technology, both for good and for ill, also brought by recent science.

Humans have oversight; they are world-viewers—more than they have ever been before. From this, morality follows as a corollary—more than before. This is what human dominion potentially meant in Genesis, or should have meant, and what dominion should mean now. It takes humans past *resource* use to *residence* and constrains their policy, economics, science, technology. Being a "resident" is something more than maximum exploitation of one's environment, though it requires resourceful use. Humans want to be "residents," something more than "citizens." The latter word is too narrowly political, a word only for the urban-dominated area of the ellipse. Residing as an overseer in a community takes us past management questions to moral questions.

Humans want to be inhabitants who appreciate (in double senses of *finding value in* and *adding value to*) their habitats. Humans are value-able, *able to evaluate* the world, able to discover (as well as invent) value there. They can keep life wonderful (Chapter 1, p. 26) because they have the capacity for wonder. This subjective capacity is fittingly exercised in Earth's objective wonderland. Humans bring subjectivity to intense focus to complement objectivity. Humans can be "let in on" more value than any other kind of life. They can share the values of others and in this way be altruists. Humans are of capstone value because they are capstone evaluators.

In earlier eras humans needed an exodus out of nature into culture, but now they want to be liberated out of egoism, out of humanism, into a transcending overview that sees Earth as a blessed land exuberant with life, a land filled with integrity, beauty, dynamic achievement, and storied history. That is not a leaving of nature; it is an exodus within a promised land. This dominion over nature follows nature.

In this sense, humans are or can be superior, superb, supervenient, even (in a provocative sense) supernatural, super-to-the-natural. They transcend the spontaneous environment because they have oversight of it; they have transcendence in immanence. To continue to play with words, humans are spectacular because they emerge to see the spectacle they are in. Animals have the capacity to see only from their niche; they have mere immanence (as we claimed in Chapter 2, pp. 71–73). Humans can have a view from no niche. Skeptics and relativists may say that humans merely see from another niche, and it is certainly true that when humans appraise soil or timber as resources, they see from within their niche. But humans also see other niches and the ecosystems that sustain niches; they study warblers, or see Earth from space. No other species has such supersight, such spectacular oversight.

Resident Environmental Altruism

Without denying that there is value superiority *within* humans, environmental ethics says more. It not just our capacity to *say I*, to actualize a self, but our capacity to *see others*, to oversee a world, that distinguishes humans. Kant knew something about others, but, eminent ethicist though he was, the only others he could see were other humans, others who could say "I." Environmental ethics calls for seeing nonhumans, for seeing the biosphere, the Earth, ecosystem communities, fauna, flora, natural kinds that cannot say "I" but in which there is formed integrity, objective value independent of subjective value. Environmental ethics advances beyond Kantian ethics, beyond humanistic ethics, in that it can treat as ends others besides humans. Environmental ethicists see further morally. They can see *without* as well as *within.* They see the "whole great ethic" that Victor Hugo and Albert Schweitzer envisioned.[4] They really see the neighbors Jesus commanded us to love, the sparrows whose fall God notices, the lilies of the field so splendidly arrayed. In this sense the capacity for thoughtful residence, for experiencing community with nonhuman others, is as requisite for ethics as any capacity for human self-actualizing. That very self-actualizing in this ethic seeks human self-transcending.

We can put this provocatively by saying that Kant was still a residual egoist in the objects of his ethics; although he recommended to ethical subjects that they be humanistic altruists, he was not yet the genuine altruist he hoped to be. He could count morally only "egos" (persons); he did not have enough moral vision to count real "others" (nonhumans)—trees, species, ecosystems. He was an altruist only humanistically speaking, not yet an altruist environmentally. But a really exciting difference between humans and nonhumans is that while animals and plants can count (defend) only their own lives, with their offspring and kind, humans can count (defend) life and even nonlife with vision of greater scope.

Animals and plants do not have egos; they have at most selves—typically objective, somatic selves, though in some of the highest animals these sponsor subjective selves. Plants and animals reach no genuine altruism, not even intelligent animals that learn to cooperate in their mutual self-interest. This does not fault animals or plants, for they are not and cannot be moral agents, but it does recognize a difference crucial for understanding the human possibilities in the world. Humans can achieve genuine altruism; it begins when they recognize the claims of other humans—whether or not such claims are compatible with their own self-interest—but is not complete until humans can recognize the claims of nonhumans: fauna, flora, species, ecosystems, landscapes. In that sense environmental ethics is the most altruistic form of ethics. It really loves others. It transforms residual egos into resident altruists. This ultimate altruism is, or ought to be, the human genius. In this sense the last becomes the first; this late-coming species with a latter-day ethics is the first to see the story that is taking place. This late species takes a leading role.

On Earth, it is only humans who, by means of their rationality, morality, world views, their *subjective* experiences interpreting and admiring the natural world, *can* be *objective* (to some extent at least) about the skills, achievements, lives, values present in nonhumans from organisms to ecosystems, and that *subjective* capacity (capacity of *subjects*) to be *objective* (appreciate world *objects*) is a superiority worthy of extra valuing. That valuable capacity ought to be exercised, with grace and without pride. That is simultaneous privilege and responsibility, simultaneous participation and detachment.

Storied Residence on Earth

Developing an ethics is a creative act, the writing of an appropriate chapter in an ongoing story, whether the "writer" lives in culture or in nature. In the latter the human career requires environmental interpretation; that is, no one can or should live without an outlook on nature that drives an ethos, a way of life. This happens for better or worse; it ought to happen for the better. Life has, and ought to have, other dimensions—a family ethic, a business ethic, a community ethic, a meaningful career—and we have recognized that special concerns may be differentially developed. Still, the moral life is not complete without a sensitive approach to one's place—to the fauna, the flora, the landscapes surrounding one's life.

One human role is to enrich the environment by appreciating it. Classical ethics urges living in one's own space culturally. Environmental ethics urges living in one's own space naturally. Complementary with recognizing intrinsic values apart from the human presence, this ethics also demands existential adequacy, fitness, in the human presence. Humans ought to have experiences appropriate to the world facts, a human subjectivity to fit the natural objectivity, spirit incarnate in place, where the passage of consciousness through nature in time takes narrative form.

An ethics should be rational, but rationality inhabits a historical system. The place that is to be counted morally has a history;

the ethics that befits such a place will take on historical form; the ethics will itself have a history. The place to be mapped (to return to an ellipse as a model) will have twin foci. One focus will be nomothetic, recurrent; the other will be idiographic, uniquely particular.

Under the idiographic focus, ethical concern will be directed toward historical particulars, with minimal appeal to types or universals. Humans protect the Grand Canyon because it is the particular place it is, one of a kind, warranting a proper name—not because it is a representative canyonland, hardly because it exemplifies uniformitarianism. Under the influence of both foci, the ethic will mix the generic and the specific. One protects that whooping crane with legs banded blue, red, gold—banded at Gray's Lake in Idaho, now migrating through the San Luis Valley in Colorado—because it is a living individual exemplifying intrinsic value and also because it is a token of a vanishing type. Under the nomothetic focus, the ethic will value natural forces and tendencies or type specimens. A reason for protecting relict wildlands is that they are living museums of the processes of natural history, and this is true in all the particular wilderness areas preserved.

The rationality of the ethic, as well as the area to be mapped, will be historical. That is, logic will be mixed with story. The move from *is* to *ought*, which logicians have typically thought it their job to solve before any naturalistic ethics could be judged sound, is transformed into movement along a story line. It becomes a move from *is* to *becoming*, and that historical movement is part of the *ought-to-be*. The ethic becomes an epic.

An ethic, it may be insisted, has to be formal, general, universal, applicable without regard to time and place, true all over Earth, true on all planets where there are moral agents. Keep promises. Tell the truth. Do to others as you would have them do to you. Do not cause needless suffering. Respect life. Yes, but ethics is not lived like that. Such principles are used to narrate and evaluate biographies. Each person lives in a particular time and place, and such abstractions are not yet a flesh-and-blood ethic but only a skeleton. An ethic too has an environment, a niche to inhabit. Like a species, it is what it is where it is. Ethics evolve, as do species, and have storied development.

Nonhuman Storied Residence in Natural History

Prehuman nature is already historical in form (see Chapter 4, pp. 135–36; Chapter 5, pp. 177–79). Storied residence does not begin with humans. At long ranges, over millennia that humans have begun to appreciate only within the last century, evolutionary ecosystems have been dramatically eventful in spinning stories on Earth that are never twice the same. Only in a short-range perception is there seasonal recurrence, recycling, homeostasis, dependable patterns, repeated order. In that sense, words such as homeostasis, conservation, preservation, stability—even species and ecosystem—are only penultimate in environmental ethics, although they are the words with which environmental ethics was launched. The spontaneous system generates order with novelty, and spins stories. The ultimate word is *history*.

R. G. Collingwood and G. W. F. Hegel say, "Nature has no history."[5] Karl Barth claims, "Being in history is human being alone"; "Existing in this history, the being of man is plainly separated and distinguished from all others."[6] True, plants and animals do not know their histories. Their DNA, a logical and normative set, codes these stories (Chapter 3). The genome is a historical set but without awareness. Plants and animals are historical beings objectively but do not know this subjectively. Some animals have memories, so animal life may have precursors of historical consciousness. Still, humans are the only historical subjects in a historically objective world. When humans become historians, they fit the world better if they decipher natural history as well as remember their own cultural heritages.

The story of applied science has been one of learning to remake the world in human interests, to use it resourcefully; but the story of pure science has been one of discovering the nature of nature, learning the story of our sources. Early science thought this nature to be lawlike and repetitive, but recent science has learned the evolutionary Earth history, indeed the history of our universe. And this story is still taking place. Life is still arriving. Earth is not so much a syllogism with premises and conclusions as it is a text to be interpreted. It is stories being told.

Like the books in our cultural libraries, the landscapes are to be read, palimpsests of the past. As with stories in our newspapers, there are new events regularly to be reported. Biological science has cleverly detected much of the past; it reads present events out of the historically produced landscape. But bioscience can present little argument explaining this history that has gone before—little logic (tracking causes) by which there came to be a primeval Earth, Precambrian protozoans, Cambrian trilobites, Triassic dinosaurs, Eocene mammals, Pliocene primates, eventuating in Pleistocene *Homo sapiens*. No theory exists, with initial conditions, from which these follow as conclusions. And bioscience cannot predict the critical events in future natural history.

To the contrary, from the viewpoint of the best available theory—natural selection with its descriptions how, and demands that, the fittest survive—the whole odyssey seems some hybrid between a random walk and a tautology. The theory neither predicts outcomes, nor, looking back after the outcomes are known, retrodicts why this course of events occurred rather than thousands of others equally consistent with the theory. Perhaps one way of interpreting events is that nature moves from the general (particles, gravitation, elements, covalent bonding, stars, galaxies, planets) more and more to the particular (cytochrome-C molecules, trilobites, Neanderthal man, Henry David Thoreau). That is one way of interpreting its tendencies toward complexity and individuality.

Likewise, passing from science to ethics, environmental ethics can present no ethical argument why these stories ought to have taken place. We will have to accept them as good stories, perhaps to reform the stories by which we catch what is going on. We may even come to love the epic and prefer narrative over argument, over some theory by which natural history would follow as either an inevitable conclusion or just a statistically probable one. In that sense, neither science nor ethics can present an argument that either necessitates or justifies the existence of each (or any!) of the five million species with which we coinhabit Earth. But we can begin to sketch nesting sets of marvelous tales. There is no logic with which to defend the existence of trilliums or mayapples, squids or lemurs; but each in its niche enriches Earth's story. That alone is enough to justify their existence.

Humans as Natural Historians

When humans appear, an emergent activity of high value results from the human capacity to tell stories about what is going on. From his earliest traces, man has been a great storyteller. In the past, at profoundest levels, these have often been myths about the Earth humans inhabit. Whether and in what sense these myths, even in prescientific eras, have been true and false we cannot here examine. At present, an exciting part of the story of science is that the history of Earth is being better told, despite the fact that the weakest skills of science are the historical ones. In that sense, though *Homo sapiens* once arrived millions of years ago, we are still arriving, still figuring out where we dwell and what our roles here are.

Science can present only fragments of argument explaining how humans arrived, nothing really approaching any logical scheme (tracking causes) by which the Earth story eventuates in *Homo sapiens*. No theory exists, plus initial conditions, from which we follow as conclusions. That has troubled many in Darwin's century, who have disliked the thought that humans may be here by accident. The truth seems rather that humans are one of the headings of the system, along with diversifying speciation and increasing individuality (paths traced in Chapters 4, 5, and 6). But we have to put this in story form; it cannot be deduced from theory, although it is in some sense an implication of the Earth system.

Likewise, passing again from science to ethics, philosophical ethics can give no argument why humans ought have arrived here. What philosophy can do is join science in inviting humans as historical subjects to appreciate the objective stories that lie in, with, and under the Earth they inhabit, to enrich the saga by telling it and taking a role within it. Humans can be a microcosm of the macrocosm and enjoy their storied residence here. Perhaps they may even come to prefer that role to a lesser one by which humans are empirically necessary as outcomes of deterministic processes, or probable as outcomes of statistical tendencies, or the result of some random walk.

Indeed, this much, with nothing more said (though there is much more to say) might justify human existence. Just the telling of the story might make the human part in the story seem right, fitting, appropriate behavior. Taking a narrative role might make the story, and the human part in it, seem meaningful, despite the lack of sufficient logical premises or theory with which to reach the human presence as a conclusion. Perhaps we may come to prefer that historical, systemic account of sources to one that counts the human existence alone as intrinsically valuable and everything else as instrumental resources.

Personal Residence in an Environment

Their role as historical overseers identifies the place of *Homo sapiens*, the wise species, at the turn of a new millennium, discovering from the revelations of recent science who and where we are, and creating a new ethic (and epic) of place. But this high role may seem to require too advanced a reconstruction of natural history, too much scientific education, skills in environmental interpretation well past the capacities of most of Earth's residents. Only a minority of humans have had, or can have, such a global overview; most persons in their built environments live most of the time with little sense of evolutionary time, hardly indeed even with a sense of ecological time over decades of succession. Can we bring the sense of residence into focus at native range? How is a local environment to be lived through? Turning to personal presence on the local scene, what is the logic of residence in a more immediate territory? Even though we think globally, we have to live locally. We need an art of life to go with the science of natural history.

A rural New Yorker once reflected upon his environment, in late November, with a strong sense of satisfactory residence:

> The wind sweeps out of the west, with the faint breath of blizzard far away; but the skies are clear, without even the shredded, high-flying clouds of storm. And so November leans toward December, and late autumn creeps past, silent as the stars. The hush of winter approaches, and short days lie upon the land.
>
> Now is the time that the countryman has the country to himself. The visitors are gone, vacations over. Even the migrant birds are gone. The squirrels go quietly about their business. And a man has time to survey his world and understand his own place in it, if he is ever to understand.
>
> Now it becomes clear that it isn't the little pleasures of the country that make life worth living there. It is rather the big assurances. The little pleasures are for the casual visitor; but one must live with the wind and the weather and know the land and the seasons to find the certainties. The flash of a goldfinch or the song of an oriole can delight the senses; but the knowledge that no matter how sharp or long the winter, they will be back again for another spring provides an inner surety. To see a hillside white with dogwood bloom is to know a particular ecstasy of beauty; but to walk the gray winter woods and find the buds which will resurrect that beauty in another May is to partake of continuity. To feel the frost underfoot and know that there is both fire and ice in the earth, even as in the patterned stars overhead, is to sense the big assurances.
>
> Man needs to know these things, and they are best learned when the silence lies upon the land. No one can shout them. They need to be whispered, that they may reach the questing soul.[7]

Residence in a local environment senses the recurrent universals particularly displayed in that place—the seasons, the regenerative, vital powers of life, the life support, the proportions of time and place. It enjoys these big assurances exemplified in local areas. A human in his biography—as much as an ecologist with a field grid, a geneticist with a breeding experiment, a taxonomist with a type species, or a mathematician with a set of algebraic equations—is a detection device for catching something of the richness and integrity of what is taking place on the landscape.

There follows a sample test of the scope of your resident environment. The items are only suggestive; some will apply at particular seasons and places.

- Name a half-dozen wildflowers currently in bloom in a nearby natural environment you frequently visit. Where can violets first be found in the spring? What will be the last flowers of autumn?
- Recall an experience appreciating nature aesthetically—a sunset, a cumulus cloud, a snowflake, the flair of an elm, a flight of geese overhead—within the last week.
- Do you have a sense of seasons passing (beyond calendar dates), a sense of the day passing (beyond o'clock)? Do you ever check time by looking at sun or sky, or think seasons by looking at a flower or bird that has arrived, or disappeared? Do equinox and solstice pass without your notice? When was your last experience of geological time?
- Recall a natural place—a swimming hole, a waterfall, a tree or boulder in the meadow, a mountain summit, a country road, a shoreline, a bay—that you enjoyed as a child, one to which you could not return without bringing goose pimples on your skin or a lump to your throat.
- Name a half-dozen birds now resident in, or migrating through, your environment. Where is the nearest active bird's nest? What birds now present will leave, come winter or summer?
- What large mammal did you last see in the wild? Small mammal?
- What encounter with an animal, bird, or plant recently took you by surprise, so much so that you turned aside from what you were doing to observe it?
- What fauna and flora inhabited the landscape on which your home is located before humans lived there? Where is the nearest that each of these can now be found? Can you name your native ecosystem?

- What species are especially characteristic of your ecosystem—not found or more difficult to find when you travel further north, south, east, or west? What is your state animal, flower, bird?
- What species are endangered in your state? Which are not officially listed but ought to be?
- What local natural area that you formerly enjoyed has been so much degraded by development that you are disappointed when you return there?
- If all the human-made noises were to cease, what cries, calls, or natural sounds could you expect to hear after dark at your home or in a nearby natural area? In what phase is the moon now?
- Where is the nearest wild or semiwild area large enough that it would take a day on foot to cross it? How much time have you spent in this area?
- What part of your local natural environment—birds, flowers, insects, trails, fishing spots, tackle, flies and baits to use, hunting areas, drainage patterns and names of streams, types of flowers and vegetables that grow best in your climate—do you know particularly well, so much so that others seek you out for information?
- What did you eat last that came directly from the soil, without being marketed? Did you prepare it?
- What pictures, patterns, arrangements of flowers, wildlife, or landscapes ornament your home?
- Recall a recent newspaper story or television feature dealing with biological or environmental conservation.
- When did you last write a congressman or other official about a matter of environmental concern? Of what conservation group are you a member? Have you made any recent contribution toward environmental conservation?
- What was the most recent natural area in your state to be protected by federal, state, or private designation? For what areas is protection still being sought?
- What has the business for which you work, or a company in which you own stock, recently done that benefits or harms the natural environment?
- What is the next outing you plan that will increase your familiarity with your natural environment? What has been your most memorable such outing this year?
- How many hours did you spend last week with your feet on the ground? With the sky over your head?

■ When did you last act, or refuse to act, in encounter with nature out of moral conviction?
■ When was your last encounter with birth or death in the natural world? When did you last pause with a sense of mystery before nature? With a sense of assurance, or a shudder? Recall a recent experience of the sublime or a religious experience outdoors. Where, if you could, would you most like to be buried?

An environmental ethic does not want merely to abstract out universals, if such there are, from all this drama of life, formulating some set of duties applicable across the whole. An ethic demands a theory of the whole, an overview of Earth, but not a unity that destroys plurality, not the sort of moral law that forgets history. Far from remaining uncolored by the agent's own history, cultural identification, personal experiences, and choices, an ethic rather requires a theory that can rejoice in that color. The moral point of view must survey the levels—humans, animals, organisms, species, ecosystems—but it also must belong to a person with a proper name who lives in Montana, Utah, Newfoundland; on the tall grass prairie or the Cape Cod coastline. We said before that we want an ethic that is cosmopolitan; now we want one that is provincial. An ethic requires a world view but is lived along a world line. An ethic is not just a theory but a track through the world. An ethic has to be instantiated in individuals, just as does a species. Humans are moral overseers but also moral travelers. They must pass through their world; they ought to do so ethically.

Ethics must be written in theory with universal intent, but the theory must permit and require ethics to be lived in practice in the first person singular. This person will not be the solitary Cartesian ego, isolated from its world, but the subjective "I" in singular communion with its objective world. The logic of the home, the ecology, is finally narrative, and the human career will not be a disembodied reason but a person organic in history. Character always takes narrative form; history is required to form character. This is perhaps more familiar to us in culture but not less true in the human relations with nature. The standing of humans in nature is not, after all, that of detached ideal observers. In dialectic with what was claimed before, now we specify an ideal of humans inseparably entwined with particular times and places. If a holistic ethic is really to incorporate the whole story, it must systematically embed itself in historical eventfulness, or else it will not really be objective. It will not be appropriate, well-adapted to the way humans actually fit their niches.

No two human careers are identical, because over historical time nature changes and cultures change. Genetic sets, choices, circumstances, contingencies differ. A contemporary backpacker cannot confront the environment as did Jim Bridger, even if both camp at the same spot in pristine wilderness. An American does not have the same environment as does an Australian. Two New Englanders may walk the same trail together; one knows the wildflowers, the other knows birds, and their experiences differ correspondingly. Endlessly singular human subjects confront an endlessly singular environment. The practical, applied character of environmental ethics will have to recognize this singularity to do justice to the form of the world and of human life in it. This is, in a way, the ultimate in fitness—to fit one's environment not just systemically but idiographically. It is the ultimate production of individuality.

In the understory of the human story, nature itself is never twice the same. Whatever the annual and diurnal repetitions, each new year, each day, is historically different. Whatever their repetitions, each locality, each ecosystem, is unique. The formative topographical and biological forces project distinctive differences in every mix of land, fauna, flora—the Ozarks, the Grand Tetons, Okefenokee Swamp, the Finger Lakes. No two waterfalls, mountains, beaches, bays, creeks, or maple trees are identical. As J.R.R. Tolkien put it, "In every wood in every spring there is a different green."[8] Sometimes the differences are trivial, and even when they are notable, we may want to abstract out covering laws or general trends. Sometimes we think that the idiographic elements, punctuating the nomothetic elements, are noise in the system. But they are not really noise; they are news, good news—because this historical and topographic variation elevates nature into a place for storied residence.

These story lines are not simply found, though many lie there to be found. They must also be constructed, authored as they are detected by complex persons localized in the complex ecosystems they inhabit. We write the narratives as we travel, prose mixed with poetry, even when we interpret the environment. With artistry, we paint the pictures we see. Nature can seem loose, open, unfinished, even chaotic; so it is in part. But just this element is freedom on a providing ground, freeing and providing for persons to be educated to and by their environments (see Chapter 6, pp. 212–13).

At times humans in the midst of their world can seem only to stand in kaleidoscopic variety, but life can and ought to be more than that. Kaleidoscopes have beauty, but they spin no history. By contrast, persons in nature live careers in their places. Some events are episodes, perhaps valuable without further contributory reference. A person does not have to justify a sunset, a picnic at a waterfall, or a joyous warbler's song by placing it in a narrative career. Still, the world is full of fragments of stories, intersecting, colliding with one another, forming nested sets of story possibilities, only some of which actualize at any length. Superimposed on some of the causal linkages, supported by the ecosystemic webs, furthered by cultural lines, and despite wayward paths, many stories develop.

A principal characteristic of human life is that it develops into biography. In that sense, humans do not want their values in nature, any more than they want other goods in life, to come seriatim, like beads on a string—intrinsic goods without meaningful interconnection. Humans want a storied residence in nature where the passage of time integrates past, present, and future in a meaningful career. This does not make nature mere instrument in a human story, any more than it makes the fellow persons in our drama merely tools. Rather, we have reached the richest possible concept of life in community, one in which all the actors contribute to storied residence.

Complementing now the global oversight considered earlier, we seek a local view, not as ideal observers looking on from some original position, but as living participants in stories of our time and place. We must complement transcendence with immanence. I do not expect or desire, in this sense, that my views will be shared by everyone. My views have been those of Appalachia and the Rocky Mountain West; Henry David Thoreau's views were those of Walden Pond; and John Muir's were those of the high Sierras and a thousand-mile walk to the Gulf. John James Audubon's views were of birds; Rachel Carson's of the sea. A. J. Grout saw mosses as few have seen them before or since. Albert Bierstadt's eye was for landscapes; Paul Ehrlich's is for butterflies. Wendell Berry sees Kentucky, and Barry Lopez the Arctic. David Brower knew Glen Canyon as the place no one knew.

In this sense, an envionmental ethic needs roots in locality and in specific appreciation of natural kinds—not always rooted in a single place, but moving through particular regions and tracks of nature so as to make a narrative career, a storied residence. The life of every naturalist-environmentalist will be, or ought to be, more than episodic; life will be stories superimposed over day-to-day events, some of which cohere as puzzle pieces in a bigger picture. Without such integration, even the richest experiences grow fatiguing. This storied residence gives a person standing.

Environmental ethics itself will have a history entwined with these biographies of particular individuals. Such a code of ethics will have its rationality embedded in the historical developments in which environmental ethicists reside. There are specific cases (Hetch Hetchy, the Indiana Dunes, the antelope fence at Red Rim), conservation groups (the Wilderness Society, the Desert Fishes Council) with their founders and directors, contests followed by memorable court rulings (Tellico Dam, the Devil's Hole Pupfish), state and federal agencies charismatically excited by significant individuals (Stephen Mather, Gifford Pinchot, Phil Pister), the laws passed by legislators on particular dates (the Wilderness Act, 3 September 1964; the Federal Land Policy and Management Act, 21 October 1976), the Rachel Carsons and Paul Erringtons whose names become attached to the sea and to the land. But leaders require followers in support, and environmental concern has from the first been a grassroots movement where the leaders are only symbols for sentiments widespread across the countryside, because citizens are discovering meanings in their resident environments.

Aldo Leopold concluded his *Sand County Almanac* with a call for a "land ethic," and he concluded his land ethic with a general principle: "A thing is right when it tends to preserve the integrity, stability, and beauty of the biotic community. It is wrong when it tends otherwise."[9] Leopold's principle is properly, deeply embedded in his love for the Wisconsin sand counties. It is no accident but essential to the ethic that the earlier pages of his *Almanac* have remembered a January thaw, the spring flowering of *Draba*, the April mating dance of the woodcock. Leopold's biographical residence is the personal backing to his ethic, as John Rodman notices:

> We cannot simply abstract from the last part of this carefully composed book the notion of extending ethics to the land and its inhabitants. The land ethic emerges in the course of the book as an integral part of a sensibility developed through observation, participatory experience, and reflection. It is an "ethic" in the almost forgotten sense of "a way of life." For this reason it would be pretentious to talk of a land ethic until we have let our curiosity follow the skunk as it emerges from hibernation, listened with wonder at the calls of the wild geese arriving at the pond, sawed the fallen ancient tree while meditating its history, shot a wolf (once) and looked into its eyes as it died, recognized the fish in ourselves, and strained to see the world from the perspective of a muskrat eye-deep in the swamp only to realize that in the end the mind of the muskrat holds for us a mystery than we cannot fathom.[10]

Different persons, with differing residential experiences in the same locality, with experiences in diverse localities, and, more comprehensively, differing cultures over geographical places and historical times, bring to expression differing positive sensitivities to the natural world—all this enriches the human global community, *Homo sapiens* in its responsive, responsible community with the natural world. This enrichment and diversity bring into existence, sustained over place and time, a still higher complex of values than exists in nonhuman nature. The story of nature, with appropriate stories of cultural appreciation, brings into being valued events greater than those possible in either nature alone or in culture alone.

This is a systemic, communitarian achievement. It happens in millions of minds in millions of encounters with nature, though each encounter takes place in a single mind and a particular place. Like the ecosystems that we praised (in Chapter 5) where the skills and achievements, the adventures and world lines of many diverse individual parts are vitally integrated, with satisfactory fit and with enough looseness ·to preserve individuality, now too in the cultural community, the storied residences of a host of persons are integrated into a global overseeing of natural history, surpassing anything reached by any one human, though each contributes his or her share. The valued event that occurs formally, generally, universally (the human overseeing of Earth) is an integration of differential, local, particular, individual biographies. What goes on in the heads of individuals integrates into something that goes on over the heads of any of us. The human culture corporately in its storied residence is *Homo sapiens*, the wise species. There are many storied residences, but one story of humans on Earth. That private ethics on which we are insisting results in this sense in a corporate ethics again, but only as, and just because, these personal residences accumulate into a global overseeing. With this local and global residence, ethics will be naturalized. *Homo sapiens* will optimize the good of its kind by being good in its kind of place. The story is of the exodus of spirit, incarnate in place, inheriting a promised land.

Our role is to live out a spacetime, placetime ethic, interpreting our landscapes and choosing our loves within those landscapes. We endorse the world with our signatures. In this sense we want an emotive ethic but not, as that term usually conveys, an ethic that is nothing but emotion. Emotive environmental ethics lives in caring response to the surrounding natural places and times, an appropriate fit of the tripartite mind—reason, emotion, will—creatively corresponding to the nature in which mind is incarnate. In this ethic, knowledge is power, as also is love, with faithfulness. There is a penultimate place for superior human standing, and the ultimate lesson is that the meek inherit the Earth. The fittest survive in an optimally satisfactory environment. But this is no submission that is unnatural or inhuman; it is in truth an adventure in love and freedom—the love of one's world and freedom in it. This is, ultimately, what the evolutionary epic has been about, now consummated in environmental ethics: an adventure in the love of life and in increasing freedom in one's environment, entwined in biotic community. Such a world might even be the best of possible worlds.

Notes

PREFACE

1. Albert Schweitzer, *Out of My Life and Thought: An Autobiography* (New York: Holt, Rinehart & Winston, 1949), pp. 158-59.

CHAPTER 1

1. See Holmes Rolston, III, "Is There An Ecological Ethic?" *Ethics* 85 (1975): 93-109, reprinted in Rolston, *Philosophy Gone Wild* (Buffalo, N.Y.: Prometheus Books, 1986), pp. 12-29.

2. Karl Marx, *Grundrisse* (New York: Random House, 1973), p. 366.

3. S. R. Kellert and J. K. Berry, *Knowledge, Affection and Basic Attitudes toward Animals in American Society*, Phase 3 of a U.S. Fish and Wildlife Service Study (Washington, D.C.: U.S. Government Printing Office, 1980).

4. T. D. Brock, "Life at High Temperatures," *Science* 158 (1967): 1012-19.

5. A. F. Coimbra-Filho, A. Magnanini, and R. A. Mittermeier, "Vanishing Gold: Last Chance for Brazil's Lion Tamarins," *Animal Kingdom* 78, no. 6 (December 1975): 20-27, citation on p. 25.

6. Aristotle, *Poetics* 1451.

7. Edith Cobb, "The Ecology of Imagination in Childhood," *Daedalus* 88 (1959): 537-48, a summary of *The Ecology of Imagination in Childhood* (New York: Columbia University Press, 1977).

8. N. R. Scott, "Toward a Psychology of Wilderness Experience," *Natural Resources Journal* 14 (1974): 231- 37.

9. A. L. Turner, "The Therapeutic Value of Nature," *Journal of Operational Psychiatry* 7 (1976): 64-74.

10. Edward Young, *Night Thoughts* (Edinburgh: James Nichol, 1853), pp. 286-87.

11. Gifford Pinchot, *Breaking New Ground* (New York: Harcourt, Brace, 1947), p. 103.

12. P. G. K. Kahn and S. M. Pompea, "Nautiloid Growth Rhythms and Dynamical Evolution of the Earth-Moon System," *Nature* 275 (1978): 606-11.

13. William Wordsworth, "Lines Composed a Few Miles above Tintern Abbey" (1798).

14. Kellert and Berry, *Knowledge, Affection and Basic Attitudes toward Animals.*

15. William F. Baxter, *People or Penguins: The Case for Optimal Pollution* (New York: Columbia University Press, 1974), p. 5.

16. Barry Commoner, *The Closing Circle: Nature, Man, and Technology* (New York: Knopf, 1972), p. 41.

17. Ralph Waldo Emerson, *Journals* (Cambridge, Mass.: Riverside Press, 1910), vol. 3, p. 208.

18. John Stuart Mill, "Nature" (1874), in *Collected Works* (Toronto: University of Toronto Press, 1963–77), vol. 10, pp. 373–402, citation on p. 400.

19. William James, "The Moral Equivalent of War," in *Memories and Studies* (New York: Longmans, Green, 1911), pp. 267–96; "Is Life Worth Living?" in *The Will To Believe* (New York: Longmans, Green, 1897), pp. 43–44.

20. See Holmes Rolston, III, "Can and Ought We to Follow Nature?" *Environmental Ethics* 1 (1979): 7–30, reprinted in *Philosophy Gone Wild*, pp. 30–52.

21. Rolston, "Is There an Ecological Ethic?"

22. Mill, "Nature," p. 381.

23. G. E. Moore, *Principia Ethica* (Cambridge: Cambridge University Press, 1903, 1956), pp. 36–58, 188, 193, 195–98, 200, 206.

CHAPTER 2

1. Jeremy Bentham, *The Principles of Morals and Legislation* (1789; New York: Hafner, 1948), chap. 17, sec. 4, p. 311.

2. Aristotle, *Politics* 1256b.

3. Proverbs 12.10.

4. For the clearest separation of animal rights concerns from environmental ethics, see J. Baird Callicott, "Animal Liberation: A Triangular Affair," *Environmental Ethics* 2 (1980): 311–38.

5. Nicholas Wade, "New Vaccine May Bring Man and Chimpanzee into Tragic Conflict," *Science* 200 (1978): 1027–30, citation on p. 1030.

6. Charles S. Elton, *The Ecology of Invasions by Animals and Plants* (New York: Wiley, 1958), p. 143.

7. Arne Naess, "A Defence of the Deep Ecology Movement," *Environmental Ethics* 6 (1984): 265–70, citation on p. 266.

8. John C. Lilly, *Lilly on Dolphins* (Garden City, N.Y.: Anchor Books, 1975), p. xiv.

9. Constance Holden, "Assertion of Dolphin Rights Fails in Court," *Science* 199 (1978): 37.

10. The best treatment is Tom Regan, *The Case for Animal Rights* (Berkeley: University of California Press, 1983). The book that sparked the contemporary debate, based on utilitarian theory rather than on rights, is Peter Singer, *Animal Liberation* (New York: New York Review Books, 1975). Other leading sources, in addition to those below, are Tom Regan and Peter Singer, eds., *Animal Rights and Human Obligations* (Englewood Cliffs, N.J.: Prentice-Hall, 1976); Bernard E. Rollin, *Animal Rights and Human Morality* (Buffalo, N.Y.: Prometheus Books, 1981); Stephen R. L. Clark, *The Moral Status of Animals* (Oxford: Oxford University Press, 1977, 1984): R. G. Frey, *Interests and Rights: The Case against Animals* (Oxford: Clarendon Press, 1980); H. J. McCloskey, "Rights," *Philosophical Quarterly* 15 (1965): 115–27; *Philosophy* 53, no. 206 (October 1978); and *Inquiry* 22, nos. 1–2 (Summer 1979).

11. U.S. Fish and Wildlife Service, *Final Environmental Statement: Proposed Use of Steel Shot for Hunting Waterfowl in the United States* (Washington, D.C.: U.S. Government Printing Office, 1976), and *Final Supplemental Environmental Impact Statement: Use of Lead Shot for Hunting Migratory Birds in the United States* (Washington, D.C.: U.S. Fish and Wildlife Service, 1986).

12. Ted Williams, "Who Killed 10,000 Caribou?" *Audubon* 87, no. 2 (March 1985): 12–17; "The Drowning of Caribou in the Caniapiscau River on September 28 and 29 1984," a report by SAGMAI, Gouvernement du Québec, Secrétariat des activités gouvernementales en milieu Amérindien et Inuit.

13. Greg Early, quoted in an Associated Press release, 4 December 1986.

14. Peter Miller, "Do Animals Have Interests Worthy of Our Moral Interest?" *Environmental Ethics* 5 (1983): 319–33, citation on p. 330.

15. Details from Mary Meagher, Yellowstone Park Research Biologist, Yellowstone National Park, Wyoming. See also Tom Thorne, "Born Looking for a Place to Die," *Wyoming Wildlife* 51, no. 3 (March 1987): 10–19.

16. Steve F. Sapontzis, "Predation," *Ethics and Animals* 5, no. 2 (June 1984): 27–38, citation on p. 36.

17. Immanuel Kant, *Anthropology from a Pragmatic Point of View* (The Hague: Nijhoff, 1974), p. 127; *Lectures on Ethics* (New York: Harper & Row, 1963), p. 239.

18. Michael Polanyi, *The Tacit Dimension* (Garden City, N.Y.: Anchor Books, 1967), p. 47.

19. G. G. Simpson, *The Meaning of Evolution* (New Haven, Conn.: Yale University Press, 1949), p. 284–85.

20. W. H. Murdy, "Anthropocentrism: A Modern Version," *Science* 187 (1975): 1168–72, citation on p. 1172.

21. Charles Darwin, *The Descent of Man* (New York: D. Appleton, 1895), pp. 48–49, 619. Darwin also penned himself a memo about

describing the natural history of creation: "Never use the words *higher* and *lower*" (Francis Darwin and A. C. Seward, eds., *More Letters of Charles Darwin* [London: John Murray, 1903], vol. 1, p. 114n).

22. Paul W. Taylor, "The Ethics of Respect for Nature," *Environmental Ethics* 3 (1981): 197–218, citations on pp. 215–16, 218, See also Taylor, *Respect for Nature* (Princeton, N.J.: Princeton University Press, 1986).

23. Richard and Val Routley (now Richard Sylvan and Val Plumwood), "Human Chauvinism and Environmental Ethics," in Don Mannison, Michael McRobbie, and Richard Routley, eds., *Environmental Philosophy* (Canberra: Research School of Social Sciences, Australian National University, 1980), pp. 96, 189.

24. Albert Schweitzer, *Civilization and Ethics* (London: A. & C. Black, 1923), part II: *The Philosophy of Civilization*, trans. John Naish, p. 254.

25. John Muir, *A Thousand-Mile Walk to the Gulf* (Boston: Houghton Mifflin, 1916), p. 139.

26. Stephen Jay Gould, *Ever Since Darwin* (New York: Norton, 1977), p. 13.

27. Gordon G. Gallup, Jr., "Self-Awareness in Primates," *American Scientist* 67 (1979): 417–21.

28. F. G. Patterson, "The Gestures of a Gorilla: Language Acquisition in Another Pongid," *Brain and Language* 5 (1978): 72–97; Francine Patterson and Eugene Linden, *The Education of Koko* (New York: Holt, Rinehart & Winston, 1981); Herbert S. Terrace, *Nim* (New York: Knopf, 1979).

29. Theodosius Dobzhansky, "The Pattern of Human Evolution," in John D. Roslansky, ed., *The Uniqueness of Man* (Amsterdam: North-Holland, 1969), pp. 41–70, citation on p. 43.

30. Peter Singer, *Animal Liberation*, pp. 2–3.

31. This is approximately (though more boldly put) the argument of Murdy, "Anthropocentrism."

32. Aldo Leopold, *A Sand County Almanac* (New York: Oxford University Press, 1949, 1969), pp. 204, 223, 110.

33. Callicott, "Animal Liberation," p. 330.

34. Karen DeYoung, "Ritual Slaughter Sparks Debate," *Washington Post*, 27 December 1985, pp. A19–20.

35. Details from Ted Joanen, Louisiana Department of Wildlife and Fisheries, Rockefeller Wildlife Refuge, Grand Chenier, Louisiana.

36. Paul Watson, "Pirate Whalers Rammed out of Business," *Greenpeace Chronicles* (Vancouver, B.C.), September 1979; Jim Mason, "Sea Shepherd Crew Fined, Jailed," *Agenda* 4, no. 2 (March/April 1984): 1, 6–7.

37. Details from Bill Clark, California Department of Fish and Game, Wildlife Investigations Laboratory, Rancho Cordova, California.

38. Joseph Wood Krutch, *The Best Nature Writing of Joseph Wood Krutch* (New York: William Morrow, 1969), p. 148.

39. Stephen R. Kellert, *Public Attitudes toward Critical Wildlife and Natural Habitat Issues*, Phase 1 (Washington, D.C.: U.S. Fish and Wildlife Service, 1979), p. 107.

40. Genesis 9.3; Exodus 20.13.

41. Jose Ortega y Gasset, *Meditations on Hunting* (New York: Scribner, 1972), pp. 110–11.

42. "Maine's Moose Controversy," pamphlet prepared by the National Wildlife Federation, Washington, D.C., 1983.

CHAPTER 3

1. Lewis Thomas, *The Lives of a Cell* (New York: Bantam Books, 1975), p. 12. Thomas, however, holds that the ant colony, as distinct from individuals, shows intelligence. For an introductory account of the marvels of ant life, see Edward O. Wilson, *Biophilia* (Cambridge, Mass.: Harvard University Press, 1984), pp. 23–37.

2. Peter Singer, *Practical Ethics* (Cambridge: Cambridge University Press, 1979), p. 92, and *Animal Liberation* (New York: New York Review Books, 1975), p. 188.

3. Mark 5.1–20, 11.12–25; Matthew 8.28–34; 21.18–22. The fig tree story was probably originally a parable, and the destruction of the pigs need not have been Jesus' intention but rather a popular misunderstanding of whatever took place. Elsewhere Jesus teaches that God cares for sparrows, lilies, and the grass of the fields, and that humans are worth much more than sparrows. The Noah story is in Genesis 6–9, the quotation from Genesis 9.10. See also Hosea 2.18.

4. The Iowa Pleistocene snail, a relic of preglacial times, survives in a population of a few thousand in northeastern Iowa's nonglaciated driftless area, notably in a cave in Bixby State Park. The species was first described as a fossil and later found to have survived the Ice Age. A search for the extent of this species discovered several new species, also Ice Age relicts. See *Endangered Species Technical Bulletin* 3, no. 8 (August 1978): 5, with further details from Dean Roosa, State Ecologist, State Preserves Advisory Board, Des Moines, Iowa. These species survive by the double good luck that, during the Ice Age, some snails chanced to live in a nonglaciated area and, later, during subsequent climatic warming, some chanced to live in cool environments, like cave entrances, that resembled the Pleistocene period. That they survive by freakish accident can make one wonder about duties to preserve them.

5. Two useful discussions are Kenneth E. Goodpaster, "On Being Morally Considerable," *Journal of Philosophy* 75 (1978): 308–325; Robin Attfield, "The Good of Trees," *Journal of Value Inquiry* 15 (1981): 35–54.

6. W. K. Frankena, "Ethics and the Environment," in K. E. Goodpaster and K. M. Sayre, eds., *Ethics and Problems of the 21st Century* (Notre

Dame, Ind.: University of Notre Dame Press, 1979), pp. 3-20, citation on p. 11).

7. Peter Singer, "All Animals Are Equal," in Tom Regan and Peter Singer, eds., *Animal Rights and Human Obligations* (Englewood Cliffs, N.J.: Prentice-Hall, 1976), pp. 148-62, citation on p. 154.

8. Peter Singer, "Not For Humans Only: The Place of Nonhumans in Environmental Issues," in Goodpaster and Sayre, *Ethics and Problems*, pp. 191-206, citation on p. 200.

9. Frankena, "Ethics and the Environment," p. 11.

10. Joel Feinberg, "The Rights of Animals and Unborn Generations," in William T. Blackstone, ed., *Philosophy and Environmental Crisis* (Athens: University of Georgia Press, 1974), pp. 43-68, citation on p. 53.

11. David W. Prall, *A Study in the Theory of Value*, University of California Publications in Philosophy, vol. 3, no. 2 (Berkeley: University of California Press, 1921), p. 227.

12. Wilhelm Windelband, *An Introduction to Philosophy*, trans. Joseph McCabe (London: T. Fisher Unwin, 1921), p. 215.

13. Ralph Barton Perry, *General Theory of Value* (Cambridge, Mass.: Harvard University Press, 1926, 1954), pp. 125, 115-16.

14. W. M. Urban, "Value and Existence," *Journal of Philosophy, Psychology and Scientific Methods* 13 (1916): 449-465, citation on p. 453.

15. William James, *Varieties of Religious Experience* (New York: Longmans, Green, 1925), p. 150.

16. Perry, *General Theory of Value*, p. 116.

17. J. Baird Callicott, "Non-anthropocentric Value Theory and Environmental Ethics," *American Philosophical Quarterly* 21 (1984): 299-309, citation on p. 305.

18. J. Baird Callicott, "On the Intrinsic Value of Nonhuman Species," in Bryan G. Norton, ed., *The Preservation of Species* (Princeton, N.J.: Princeton University Press, 1986), pp. 138-172, citation on pp. 142-43, 156.

19. Ibid., pp. 143, 160.

20. This kind of account is given by Frankena, "Ethics and the Environment," pp. 13-19, where it is called "inherent value" as opposed to "intrinsic value." See also Robin Attfield (*The Ethics of Environmental Concern* [New York: Columbia University Press, 1983], pp. 151-53), who accepts both "inherent value" and (nonanthropogenic) "intrinsic value."

21. This is the traditional terminology. "No objective existent has strictly intrinsic value; all values in objects are extrinsic only. . . . The goodness of good objects consists in the possibility of their leading to some realization of directly experienced goodness" (C. I. Lewis, *An Analysis of Knowledge and Valuation* [LaSalle, Ill.: Open Court, 1946], p. 387). All that nonsentient organisms offer is the standing possibility of valuation; they do not have intrinsic value, nor do they gain it by human conferral.

22. Thomas E. Hill, Jr., "Ideals of Human Excellence and Preserving Natural Environments," *Environmental Ethics* 5 (1983): 211–24.

23. R. D. Guthrie, "The Ethical Relationship between Humans and Other Organisms," *Perspectives in Biology and Medicine* 11 (1967): 52–62, citation on p. 53.

24. Paul W. Taylor, "In Defense of Biocentrism," *Environmental Ethics* 5 (1983): 237–43, citation on p. 242.

25. Quoted in an Associated Press release from Chicago, 12 February 1984.

CHAPTER 4

1. John Rawls, *A Theory of Justice* (Cambridge, Mass.: Harvard University Press, 1971), p. 512.

A shorter version of this chapter appeared as "Duties to Endangered Species," *BioScience* 35 (1985): 718–26, © AIBS 1985; reprinted in Rolston, *Philosophy Gone Wild* (Buffalo, N.Y.: Prometheus Books, 1986), pp. 206–20. For an introduction to these issues, see Bryan G. Norton, ed., *Preservation of Species* (Princeton, N.J.: Princeton University Press, 1986).

2. Council on Environmental Quality and the Department of State, *The Global 2000 Report to the President* (Washington, D.C.: U.S. Government Printing Office, 1980), vol. 1, p. 37; vol. 2, pp. 327–33.

3. Endangered Species Act of 1973, sec. 2 (a) (1) Public Law 93–205, 87 Stat. 884.

4. TVA v. Hill, 437 U.S. 153 (1978) at 173, 184, 185.

5. Stuart Hampshire, *Morality and Pessimism* (New York: Cambridge University Press, 1972), pp. 3–4.

6. Joel Feinberg, "The Rights of Animals and Unborn Generations," in W. T. Blackstone, ed., *Philosophy and Environmental Crisis* (Athens: University of Georgia Press, 1974), pp. 43–68, citation on p. 56. Feinberg holds that the duty to preserve species is more important than any rights of individual animals but is not a duty that can properly be attributed to species as a whole.

7. Paul Ehrlich and Anne Ehrlich, *Extinction* (New York: Random House, 1981), pp. xi–xiv.

8. Norman Myers, *The Sinking Ark* (Oxford: Pergamon Press, 1979).

9. "Statement of Thomas Eisner," *Endangered Species Act Oversight*, Hearings, 8 and 10 December 1981 (Washington, D.C.: U.S. Government Printing Office, 1982), pp. 295–97.

10. James Fisher, Noel Simon, Jack Vincent, and IUCN staff, *Wildlife in Danger* (New York: Viking Press, 1969), p. 19.

11. Norman Myers, "Conserving Our Global Stock," *Environment* 21, no. 9 (November 1979): 25–33.

12. National Science Foundation, "The Biology of Aridity," *Mosaic* 8, no. 1 (January/February 1977): 28–35, citation on p. 28.

13. *Endangered Species Technical Bulletin* 3, no. 1 (January 1978): 5.

14. "Statement of Peter H. Raven," *Endangered Species Act Oversight*, pp. 290–95.

15. On the other hand, the public shows a surprising sympathy for the protection of endangered species, even at economic cost. See Stephen R. Kellert, *Public Attitudes toward Critical Wildlife and Natural Habitat Issues*, Phase 1 (Washington, D.C.: U.S. Fish and Wildlife Service, 1979); Kellert, "Social and Perceptual Factors in the Preservation of Animal Species," in Norton, ed., *Preservation of Species*, pp. 50–73; Robert C. Mitchell, *Public Opinion on Environmental Issues* (Washington, D.C.: Council on Environmental Quality, Department of Agriculture, Department of Energy, and Environmental Protection Agency, 1980).

16. Paul A. Opler, "The Parade of Passing Species: A Survey of Extinctions in the U.S.," *Science Teacher* 43, no. 9 (December 1976): 30–34.

17. Estimates of standing diversity in the Permian Period range from 45,000 to 240,000 marine species, with mass extinction of perhaps 80 percent of species (36,000 to 192,000); see D. M. Raup, "Size of the Permo-Triassic Bottleneck and Its Evolutionary Implications," *Science* 206 (1979): 217–18. Projections of extinctions by the year 2000 run 15–20 percent (much lower proportionately) or between 500,000 and 2,000,000 species (a much higher total); see *Global 2000 Report*, vol. 1, p. 37. Paleontologists are not agreed how rapid the catastrophic extinctions were. Spread over 50,000 years, the natural extinction rate then was lower than the artificial rate has been in the last 100 years. Further, respeciation was simultaneously taking place during the natural extinctions.

18. That these extinctions are more careless than deliberate makes matters worse. The Office of Endangered Species estimates, on the basis of consultations so far, that by careful consideration 98 percent of conflicts can be resolved without serious loss to humans and without loss of endangered species. These odds make callousness all the more unscrupulous.

19. Charles Darwin, *The Origin of Species* (Baltimore, Md.: Penguin Books, 1968), p. 108.

20. A J. Shaw, "*Pohlia andrewsii* and *P. tundrae*, Two New Arctic-Alpine Propaguliferous Species from North America," *Bryologist* 84 (1981): 65–74.

21. A. B. Shaw, "Adam and Eve, Paleontology, and the Non-Objective Arts," *Journal of Paleontology* 43 (1969): 1085–98, citations on pp. 1085, 1098.

22. G. G. Simpson, *Principles of Animal Taxonomy* (New York: Columbia University Press, 1961), p. 153.

23. Ernst Mayr, *Principles of Systematic Zoology* (New York: McGraw-Hill, 1969), p. 26; "The Biological Meaning of Species," *Biological Journal of the Linnean Society* 1 (1969): 311-20, citation on p. 318.

24. Michael Ghiselin, "A Radical Solution to the Species Problem," *Systematic Zoology* 23 (1974): 536-44; David Hull, "A Matter of Individuality," *Philosophy of Science* 45 (1978): 335-60; Ernst Mayr, *The Growth of Biological Thought* (Cambridge, Mass.: Harvard University Press, 1982), pp. 46, 253.

25. Niles Eldredge and Joel Cracraft, *Phylogenetic Patterns and the Evolutionary Process* (New York: Columbia University Press, 1980), p. 92.

26. Details from Richard C. Bishop, "Endangered Species: An Economic Perspective," in Kenneth Sabol, ed., *Transactions of the Forty-Fifth North American Wildlife and Natural Resources Conference* (Washington, D.C.: Wildlife Management Institute, 1980), pp. 208-18, esp. '.15-16.

27. Juanita Greene, "Fast Growth of Civilization Threatens Panther Survival," and Mark Obmascik, "Protecting Panther Could Cost $112.5 Million," both in *Miami Herald* (International Edition), 12 November 1984, pp. 1A, 7A. Further details from Gary Evink, Florida Department of Transportation, Tallahassee, Florida. In another facet of this case, James E. Billie, chairman of the Seminole Indian tribe, shot, killed, and ate a panther, and was charged with violating the Endangered Species Act. But Billie claims he had a right to kill and eat the panther as part of a religious ritual, under Indian treaty rights and under freedom of religion rights from the First Amendment. See Philip Shabecoff, "Killing of a Panther: Indian Treaty Rights Vs. Law on Wildlife," *New York Times*, 15 April 1987, pp. A1, A24.

28. Details from Jan Larson, Natural Resources Manager, Naval Air Station, North Island, San Diego, California.

29. Details from Edwin P. Pister, California Department of Fish and Game, Bishop, California.

30. Feinberg, "Rights of Animals and Unborn Generations," pp. 55-56.

31. Peter Singer, "Not for Humans Only: The Place of Nonhumans in Environmental Issues," in K. E. Goodpaster and K. M. Sayre, eds., *Ethics and Problems of the 21st Century* (Notre Dame, Ind.: University of Notre Dame Press, 1979), pp. 191-206, citation on p. 203.

32. Tom Regan, *The Case for Animal Rights* (Berkeley: University of California Press, 1983), p. 359.

33. Nicholas Rescher, "Why Save Endangered Species?" in *Unpopular Essays on Technological Progress* (Pittsburgh, Pa.: University of Pittsburgh Press, 1980), pp. 79-92, citation on p. 83. Rescher holds that there is an *ethical* (distinguished from *moral*) duty to conserve the value associated with species, but this is a responsibility not *to* species but *for* species, derived from a generalized duty to protect value.

34. G. R. Fraser, "Our Genetical 'Load': A Review of Some Aspects of Genetical Variation," *Annals of Human Genetics* 25 (1962): 387–415.

35. The American wapiti, *Cervus canadensis*, has been recently regrouped by some taxonomists with the red deer of Europe, *C. elaphus*.

36. Defenders of Wildlife vs. Andrus, 428 F. Suppl. 167 (D.D.C. 1977).

37. Organized Fisherman of Florida v. Andrus, 488 F. Suppl. 1351 (S.D. Fla. 1980).

38. 16 *United States Code*, sec. 410 (c) (1982, vol. 6, p. 251).

39. D. M. Raup and J. J. Sepkoski, Jr., "Mass Extinctions in the Marine Fossil Record," *Science* 215 (1982): 1501–3.

40. R. H. Whittaker, "Evolution and Measurement of Species Diversity," *Taxon* 21 (1972): 213–51, citation on p. 214.

41. D. V. Ager, *The Nature of the Stratigraphical Record* (New York: Wiley, 1973), p. 100.

CHAPTER 5

1. Aldo Leopold, *A Sand County Almanac* (New York: Oxford University Press, 1949, 1969), pp. 224–25. A shorter form of this chapter has appeared as "Duties to Ecosystems," in J. Baird Callicott, ed., *Companion to A Sand County Almanac* (Madison: University of Wisconsin Press, 1987), pp. 246–74.

2. Leopold, *Sand County Almanac*, pp. viii–ix.

3. F. E. Clements, *Research Methods in Ecology* (Lincoln, Neb.: University Publishing, 1905), p. 199.

4. H. A. Gleason, "Delving into the History of American Ecology," *Bulletin of the Ecological Society of America* 56, no. 4 (December 1975): 7–10, citation on p. 10.

5. See an early essay (never published by Leopold himself), "Some Fundamentals of Conservation in the Southwest," *Environmental Ethics* 1 (1979): 131–41. In *A Sand County Almanac*, Leopold has abandoned any philosophy of organism.

6. A good summary of current thought about the nature of ecosystems is Jonathan L. Richardson, "The Organismic Community: Resilience of an Embattled Ecological Concept," *BioScience* 30 (1980): 465–71. Good discussions of conceptual issues are: Esa Saarinen, ed., "Conceptual Issues in Ecology, pts. 1, 2, *Synthese* 43, nos. 1, 2 (January, February 1980), a collection largely reprinted as Esa Saarinen, *Conceptual Issues in Ecology* (Dordrecht: D. Reidel, 1982); and R. V. O'Neill, D. L. DeAngelis, J. B. Waide, and T. F. H. Allen, *A Hierarchical Concept of Ecosystems* (Princeton, N. J.: Princeton University Press, 1986).

7. John Passmore, *Man's Responsibility for Nature* (New York: Scribner, 1974), p. 116.

8. Donald H. Regan, "Duties of Preservation," in Bryan G. Norton,

ed., *The Preservation of Species* (Princeton, N.J.: Princeton University Press, 1986), pp. 195–220, citation on p. 198.

9. Garrett Hardin, "The Tragedy of the Commons," *Science* 162 (1968): 1243–48.

10. D. F. Owen and R. G. Wiegert, "Do Consumers Maximize Plant Fitness?" *Oikos* 27 (1976): 488–92; D. F. Owen, "How Plants May Benefit from the Animals That Eat Them," *Oikos* 35 (1980): 230–35; D. F. Owen and R. G. Wiegert, "Mutualism between Grasses and Grazers: An Evolutionary Hypothesis," *Oikos* 36 (1981): 376–78, and 38 (1982): 253–59, forum; W. J. Mattson and N. D. Addy, "Phytophagous Insects as Regulators of Forest Primary Production," *Science* 190 (1975): 515–22; S. J. McNaughton, "Serengeti Migratory Wildebeest: Facilitation of Energy Flow by Grazing," *Science* 191 (1976): 92–94; S. J. McNaughton, "Grazing as an Optimization Process: Grass-Ungulate Relationships in the Serengeti," *American Naturalist* 113 (1979): 691–703; Eugene P. Odum and Lawrence J. Biever, "Resource Quality, Mutualism, and Energy Partitioning in Food Chains," *American Naturalist* 124 (1984): 360–76; A. J. Belsky, "Does Herbivory Benefit Plants? A Review of the Evidence," *American Naturalist* 127 (1986): 870–92; K. N. Paige and T. G. Whitham, "Overcompensation in Response to Mammalian Herbivory: The Advantage of Being Eaten," *American Naturalist* 129 (1987): 407–16.

11. Leopold, *Sand County Almanac*, p. 203.

12. P. W. Gilbert, "Observations on the Eggs of *Ambystoma maculatum* with Especial Reference to the Green Algae Found within the Egg Envelopes," *Ecology* 23 (1942): 215–27, and further comment 25 (1944): 366–69.

13. L. P. Brower and S. C. Glazier, "Localization of Heart Poisons in the Monarch Butterfly," *Science* 188 (1975): 19–25.

14. Leopold, *Sand County Almanac*, p. 173.

15. Clements, *Research Methods in Ecology*, p. 265. An analogue of this in evolutionary development is the tendency of winners to overspecialize and to become extinct in changing environments, losing out to the less specialized.

16. Henry S. Horn, "Markovian Properties of Forest Succession," in Martin L. Cody and Jared M. Diamond, eds., *Ecology and Evolution of Communities* (Cambridge, Mass.: Harvard University Press, 1975), pp. 196–211.

17. H. E. Wright, Jr., "The Roles of Pine and Spruce in the Forest History of Minnesota and Adjacent Areas," *Ecology* 49 (1968): 937–55.

18. A. G. Tansley, "The Use and Abuse of Vegetational Concepts and Terms," *Ecology* 16 (1935): 284–307, on p. 290.

19. Leopold, *Sand County Almanac*, p. 203.

20. Ibid., p. 211.

21. Ibid., p. 216.

22. G. G. Simpson, *The Meaning of Evolution* (New Haven, Conn.: Yale University Press, 1964), pp. 243, 341.

23. C. S. Elton, *The Pattern of Animal Communities* (London: Methuen, 1966), p. 62.

24. Simpson, *Meaning of Evolution*, p. 341.

25. Sam Iker, "New Life from Old Junk," *National Wildlife* 24, no. 2 (February–March 1986): 12–17.

CHAPTER 6

1. Plato, *Phaedrus* 230d., trans. H. N. Fowler, *Plato*, vol. 1, Loeb Classical Library (Cambridge, Mass.: Harvard University Press, 1914, 1977), pp. 423–24.

2. John Muir, *The Story of My Boyhood and Youth* (Madison: University of Wisconsin Press, 1965), p. 228.

3. Edward O. Wilson, introduction to special issue, "What's a Species Worth?", *Nature Conservancy News* 33, no. 6 (November–December 1983): 4. See also E. O. Wilson, *Biophilia* (Cambridge, Mass.: Harvard University Press, 1984), pp. 13–17.

4. B. J. Carr and M. J. Rees, "The Anthropic Principle and the Structure of the Physical World," *Nature* 278 (12 April 1979): 605–12, quotations on p. 605, 609.

5. B. J. Lovell, "In the Centre of Immensities" (presidential address to the British Association for the Advancement of Science, 27 August 1975), published in part as "Whence?" in *New York Times Magazine*, 16 November 1975, pp. 27, 72–95, citation on pp. 88, 95.

6. Mike Corwin, "From Chaos to Consciousness," *Astronomy* 11, no. 2 (February 1983): 14–22, citations on pp. 16–17, 19.

7. P. C. W. Davies, *The Accidental Universe* (Cambridge: Cambridge University Press, 1982), pp. 90, 110.

8. George Wald, "Fitness in the Universe: Choices and Necessities," in J. Oró, S. L. Miller, C. Ponnamperuma, and R. S. Young, eds., *Cosmochemical Evolution and the Origins of Life* (Dordrecht: D. Reidel, 1974), pp. 7–27, citation on p. 9.

9. Manfred Eigen, "Selforganization of Matter and the Evolution of Biological Macromolecules," *Die Naturwissenschaften* 58 (1971): 465–523, citation on p. 519.

10. David Hume, *Dialogues Concerning Natural Religion*, ed. Henry D. Aiken (New York: Hafner, 1948, 1972), p. 79.

11. K. G. Denbigh, *An Inventive Universe* (New York: Braziller, 1975).

12. Peter Humphrey, "The Ethics of Earthworks," *Environmental Ethics* 7 (1985): 5–21; Allen Carlson, "Is Environmental Art an Aesthetic Affront to Nature?" *Canadian Journal of Philosophy* 16 (1986): 635–50; Alan Sonfist, ed., *Art in the Land: A Critical Anthology of Environmen-*

tal Art (New York: Dutton, 1983); Elizabeth C. Baker, "Artworks on the Land," *Art in America* 64, no. 1 (January–February 1976): 92–96; Christo, *The Running Fence Project* (New York: Abrams, 1977), and *Valley Curtain* (New York: Abrams, 1973).

13. For what follows, see Holmes Rolston, III, "Are Values in Nature Subjective or Objective?" *Environmental Ethics* 4 (1982): 125–51, reprinted in Rolston, *Philosophy Gone Wild* (Buffalo, N.Y.: Prometheus Books, 1986), pp. 91–117.

14. John Dewey, *Experience and Nature* (1929; New York: Dover Publications, 1958), p. 4a.

15. Jacques Monod, *Chance and Necessity* (New York: Random House, 1972), pp. 112–13, 138.

16. Stephen Jay Gould, "Chance Riches," *Natural History* 89, no. 11 (November 1980): 36–44; "Extemporaneous Comments on Evolutionary Hope and Realities," in Charles L. Hamrum, ed., *Darwin's Legacy: Nobel Conference XVIII* (San Francisco: Harper & Row, 1983), pp. 95–103, citation on pp. 101–2.

17. This seems to be the view of George Santayana, *The Sense of Beauty* (1896; New York: Modern Library, 1955), pp. 21–24, 150–54.

18. Samuel Alexander, *Beauty and Other Forms of Value* (1933; New York: Thomas Y. Crowell, 1968), pp. 30–31. Alexander holds, however, that certain nonaesthetic values may exist in nature (pp. 285–99).

19. Alfred North Whitehead, "The Study of the Past—Its Uses and Its Dangers," *Harvard Business Review* 11 (1932–33): 436–44, citation on p. 438.

20. John Locke, *The Second Treatise of Civil Government* (1690; Oxford: Basil Blackwell, 1948), secs. 42, 43, pp. 22–23.

21. John Stuart Mill, "Nature," (1874), in *Collected Works* (Toronto: University of Toronto Press, 1963–77), vol. 10, pp. 373–402, citation on p. 398.

22. David M. Raup, "Biological Extinction in Earth History," *Science* 231 (1986): 1528–33, on p. 1532.

23. Loren Eiseley, *The Firmament of Time* (New York: Atheneum, 1960), p. 171.

24. U.S. Government Printing Office, Poster 751–269 (1981).

25. J. Ronald Engel, *Sacred Sands* (Middletown, Conn.: Wesleyan University Press, 1983).

26. Wilderness Act of 1964, sec. 2 (c) Public Law 88–577, 78 Stat. 891.

27. Henry David Thoreau, "Walking," in *The Portable Thoreau* (New York: Penguin Books, 1947, 1980), pp. 592–630, citation on p. 609.

28. Bunny McBride, "If people be killing killing . . .," *Sierra* 70, no. 2 (March–April 1985): 64–68, esp. p. 66.

29. Immanuel Kant, *Critique of Judgment* (New York: Hafner, 1966), p. 196.

30. A computer-generated picture of a DNA molecule is on the cover of *Science* 222, no. 4630 (23 December 1983). For computer-enhanced

pictures, see G. A. Briggs and F. W. Taylor, *The Cambridge Photographic Atlas of the Planets* (Cambridge: Cambridge University Press, 1982).

31. John Muir, *Our National Parks* (Boston: Houghton Mifflin, 1901), p. 4.

32. William Morris, *Art and the Beauty of the Earth* (London: Longmans, 1898), p. 24.

33. Allen Carlson, "Nature and Positive Aesthetics," *Environmental Ethics* 6 (1984): 5–34, citation on p. 5. Carlson's is the best treatment of this issue.

34. Lewis Carroll, *The Annotated Alice* (New York: Potter, 1960), p. 38.

35. John Muir, *A Thousand-Mile Walk to the Gulf* (Boston: Houghton Mifflin, 1916), p. 98.

36. James McNeill Whistler, *The Gentle Art of Making Enemies* (London: William Heinemann, 1904), p. 143.

37. R. Burton Litton, Jr., *Forest Landscape Description and Inventories—A Basis for Land Planning and Design*, Forest Service Research Paper PSW-49 (Berkeley, Calif.: USDA Pacific Southwest Forest and Range Experiment Station, 1968), p. 2.

CHAPTER 7

1. Garrett Hardin, "The Tragedy of the Commons," *Science* 162 (1968): 1243–48. A portion of this chapter previously appeared as "Valuing Wildlands," *Environmental Ethics* 7 (1985): 23–48, reprinted in Holmes Rolston, III, *Philosophy Gone Wild* (Buffalo, N.Y.: Prometheus Books, 1986), pp. 180–205. The earlier essay contains more extensive criticisms of economic valuations of wildlands.

2. U.S. Congress, Office of Technology Assessment, *Technologies to Maintain Biological Diversity*, OTA-F-330 (Washington, D.C.: U. S. Government Printing Office, 1987), pp. 11–14. The assistance of Michael J. Bean, Environmental Defense Fund, Washington, D. C., and of Diane Davenport Huning, The Wilderness Society, Washington, D.C., is acknowledged in preparing the list of environmental legislation.

3. Designated wilderness includes 23.4 million acres of the 1,888 million acres in the contiguous U.S., or about 1.2 percent, some in national parks, some in national forests, a small amount in wildlife refuges, virtually none as yet on Bureau of Land Management holdings. Another 1 percent is de facto wilderness or under serious study. National forests form 8 percent of the lower forty-eight states, of which 14 percent is wilderness, with other areas kept semiwild, most put to multiple use. Even including Alaska, only about 4 percent of the nation is designated or de facto wilderness.

4. Estimates from Richard C. Bishop, "Endangered Species: An Economic Perspective," in Kenneth Sabol, ed., *Transactions of the*

Forty-Fifth North American Wildlife and Natural Resources Conference (Washington, D.C.: Wildlife Management Institute, 1980), pp. 208-18, esp. pp. 211-12.

5. Palila v. Hawaii Department of Land and Natural Resources, 471 F. Suppl. 985 (1979), again 639 F. 2d 495 (1981).

6. TVA v. Hill, 437 US 153 (1978) at 174; Endangered Species Act of 1973, sec. 2 (3), Public Law 93-205 87, Stat. 884.

7. "EPA Approves Acid Rain Study in Wilderness Areas," *On the Wild Side*, June 1985, p. 1.

8. Details from Craig Rupp, Regional Forester (now retired), Arapaho-Roosevelt National Forest, Fort Collins, Colorado.

9. Aldo Leopold, "The Round River," in *A Sand County Almanac* (New York: Sierra Club/Ballantine Books, 1970), p. 190.

10. Robert R. Alexander et al., *The Fraser Experimental Forest, Colorado: Research Program and Published Research 1937-1985*, General Technical Report RM-118 (Fort Collins, Colo.: USDA Rocky Mountain Forest and Range Experiment Station, 1985).

11. Details from J. Scott Peterson and Stephen O'Kane, Rocky Mountain National Heritage Inventory, Denver, Colorado. *Eriogonum pelinophilum* was described by James L. Reveal, "A New Subfruticose Eriogonum (Polygonaceae) from Western Colorado," *Great Basin Naturalist* 33 (1973): 120-22.

12. Richard W. Wald, "Cleaning Up Kesterson," *Resources*, no. 83 (Spring 1986): 11-14; Lori Wheeler, "Tale of a Toxic Marsh," *Not Man Apart* 15, no. 3 (March-April 1985): 10-11. See also *Final Environmental Impact Statement: Kesterson Program*, 2 vols. (Washington, D.C.: U.S. Bureau of Reclamation, U.S. Fish and Wildlife Service, and U.S. Army Corps of Engineers, 1986).

13. Commonwealth of Massachusetts v. Andrus, 481 F. Suppl. 685 (1979). The quotation is from the 1978 Endangered Species Act Amendments, sec. 7 (d), Public Law 96-632, 92 Stat. 3751.

14. R. W. Guldin, "Predicting Costs of Eastern National Forest Wildernesses," *Journal of Leisure Research* 13 (1981): 112-28.

15. Gail L. Cramer and Clarence W. Jensen, *Agricultural Economics and Agribusiness*, 3d ed. (New York: Wiley, 1985), pp. 279, 259.

16. Schwenke v. Secretary of the Interior, 720 F. 2d 571 (1983).

17. Federal Land Policy and Management Act of 1976, secs. 102, 103, 90 Stat. 2743 at pp. 2744, 2746 (Public Law 94-579). There is similar language in the Multiple Use Sustained Yield Act of 1960, sec. 4 (a), Public Law 86-517, 74 Stat. 215.

18. Wilderness Act of 1964, sec. 2 (c), Public Law 88-577, 78 Stat. 891.

CHAPTER 8

1. Louis B. Lundborg, *Future without Shock* (New York: Norton, 1974), pp. 128-29. Parts of this chapter are from "Just Environmental

Business," in Tom Regan, ed., *Just Business: New Introductory Essays in Business Ethics* (New York: Random House, and Philadelphia: Temple University Press, 1984), pp. 324–59, © 1984; reprinted in Holmes Rolston, III, *Philosophy Gone Wild* (Buffalo, N.Y.: Prometheus Books, 1986), pp. 144–79.

2. See a report by Marshall Frady in *Harper's* 240, no. 1440 (May 1970): 103.

3. Henry B. Schacht and Charles W. Powers, "Business Responsibility and the Public Policy Process," in Thornton Bradshaw and David Vogel, eds., *Corporations and Their Critics* (New York: McGraw-Hill, 1981), pp. 23–32.

4. October 5, 1976. U. S. District Court, Eastern District of Virginia. Richmond. Judge Merhige's statements were made from the bench at the time of sentencing. The fine was technically reduced to $5 million when Allied placed $8 million into a fund to reduce damages. See also Marvin H. Zim, "Allied Chemical's $20-Million Ordeal with Kepone," in *Fortune* 98, no. 5 (11 September 1978): 82–90; Frances S. Sterrett and Caroline A. Boss, "Careless Kepone," in *Environment* 19, no. 2 (March 1977): 30–37, and references there.

5. See *Time*, 6 October 1961, p. 24. More accurately, Wilson once reported, "For years I thought that what was good for our country was good for General Motors, and vice versa."

6. Garrett Hardin, "The Tragedy of the Commons," *Science* 162 (1968): 1243–48.

7. David Burnham, "The Case of the Missing Uranium," *Atlantic* 243, no. 4 (April 1979): 78–82.

8. *Final Report of the National Science Foundation Workshop Panel to Select Organic Compounds Hazardous to the Environment* (Washington, D.C.: National Science Foundation, 1975), p. 8.

9. H. E. Wright, Jr., "Landscape Development, Forest Fires, and Wilderness Management," *Science* 186 (1974): 487–95, citation on p. 494.

10. Francis Bacon, *Novum Organum* in *Works* (New York: Garrett Press, 1968), vol. 1, p. 157; cf. vol. 4, p. 47.

11. Quoted in Robert Cahn, *Footprints on the Planet* (New York: Universe Books, 1978), p. 107.

12. Theodore Roosevelt in a speech delivered there, recorded in *New York Sun*, 7 May 1903.

13. Alfred North Whitehead, *Science and the Modern World* (New York: Mentor Books/New American Library, 1925, 1964), p. 175.

14. For the difficulties of heavy technology on fragile land, see Congressional Office of Technology Assessment, *An Assessment of Oil Shale Technologies* (Washington, D.C.: U.S. Government Printing Office, 1980).

15. Constance Holden, "Industry Toxicologists Keen on Reducing Animal Use," *Science* 236 (1987): 252.

16. Attitudes of Americans toward endangered species are reported in Stephen R. Kellert, *Public Attitudes toward Critical Wildlife and Natural Habitat Issues.* Phase 1 (Washington, D.C.: U.S. Fish and Wildlife Service, 1979); Kellert, "Social and Perceptual Factors in the Preservation of Animal Species," in Bryan G. Norton, ed., *Preservation of Species* (Princeton, N.J.: Princeton University Press, 1986), pp. 50–73. See also Robert C. Mitchell, *Public Opinion on Environmental Issues* (Washington, D.C.: Council on Environmental Quality, Department of Agriculture, Department of Energy, and Environmental Protection Agency, 1980), esp. p. 18.

17. Walter J. Hickel, *Who Owns America?* (Englewood Cliffs, N.J.: Prentice-Hall, 1971), p. 151. The decision halted further oil and gas leasing in the Sespe Condor Sanctuary, 9 March 1970.

18. *Hearings before the Subcommittee on Fisheries and Wildlife Conservation and the Environment of the Committee on Merchant Marine and Fisheries.* House of Representatives, 97th Cong. 2d Sess., Serial 97-32, 22 February, 8 March 1982 (Washington, D.C.: U.S. Government Printing Office, 1982), pp. 230–62, esp. 235, 261–62. See also Wilford Kale, "Some Firms Aware of Threatened Birds," Richmond (Virginia) *Times-Dispatch*, 9 October 1986, pp. 1, 13.

19. Cahn (*Footprints on the Planet*, pp. 124–40) surveyed environmental policies in banking and finance and reports that only six in thirty of the major commercial banks have environmental policies, none of these very specific. He also found the positive records of John Hancock, Equitable, and Aetna.

20. William G. Pollard, "A Theological View of Nuclear Energy" in the *Let's Talk about . . .* series interpreting nuclear power to the public, published by the Breeder Reactor Corporation, an association of 753 electrical power systems, Oak Ridge, Tennessee.

21. Milton Friedman, "The Social Responsibility of Business Is to Increase Its Profits," *New York Times Magazine*, 13 September 1970, pp. 32–33, 122–26, quotation on p. 33.

22. See the *Progress Report on the Grand Junction Uranium Mill Tailings Remedial Action Program*, prepared by the U.S. Department of Energy's Division of Environmental Control Technology, the DOE Grand Junction Office, and the Colorado Department of Health, February 1979, and available from the National Technical Information Service. The report of the Committee on the Biological Effects of Ionizing Radiations, *The Effects on Populations of Exposure to Low Levels of Ionizing Radiation: 1980* (BEIR III), has since been published (Washington, D.C.: National Academy Press, 1980), but the much-troubled report was never released without dissent among committee members.

23. Hardin, "Tragedy of the Commons," p. 1247.

24. Alfred North Whitehead, *Adventures of Ideas* (New York: Free Press, 1967), p. 98.

25. T. V. Learson, "The Greening of American Business," *Conference Board Record* 8, no. 7 (July 1971): 21–24, quotation on p. 22.

26. Bertrand Russell, *An Outline of Philosophy* (New York: New American Library, Meridian Books, 1974), p. 30. Cf. the anthropocentric biocentrism argument in Chapter 2, p. 77.

CHAPTER 9

1. Robert Browning, "Pisgah-Sights," *Poetical Works* (London: Oxford University Press, 1905, 1967), p. 531–32.

2. Karl Barth, *Church Dogmatics*, vol. 3, pt. 2 (Edinburgh: T & T Clark, 1960), p. 78.

3. F. Fraser Darling, "Man's Responsibility for the Environment," in F. J. Ebling, ed., *Biology and Ethics*, Symposia of the Institute of Biology, No. 18 (London: Academic Press, 1969), pp. 117–22, citation on p. 117.

4. See the Victor Hugo and Albert Schweitzer citations in this book's epigraph and Preface.

5. R. G. Collingwood, *The Idea of History* (New York: Oxford University Press, 1956), p. 114, endorsing G. W. F. Hegel.

6. Barth, *Church Dogmatics*, vol. 3, pt. 2, pp. 174, 78.

7. Editorial, *New York Times*, Sunday, November 28, 1948, p. 8B. For some personal accounts of satisfactory residence, see Holmes Rolston, III, *Philosophy Gone Wild* (Buffalo, N.Y.: Prometheus Books, 1986), pp. 221–61.

8. J. R. R. Tolkien, *Fellowship of the Ring* (New York: Ballantine, 1965), p. 364.

9. Aldo Leopold, *A Sand County Almanac* (New York: Oxford University Press, 1949, 1969), pp. 224–25. See also Chapter 5, p. 160.

10. John Rodman, "The Liberation of Nature," *Inquiry* 20 (1977): 83–131, citation on pp. 110–11.

Selected Bibliography

The following bibliography contains principally books; a few articles of particular significance are included. For additional articles, the reader should begin by consulting the journal *Environmental Ethics*.

Robin Attfield. The Ethics of Environmental Concern. New York: Columbia University Press, 1983.

Ian G. Barbour. Technology, Environment, and Human Values. New York: Praeger, 1980.

William T. Blackstone, ed. Philosophy and Environmental Crisis. Athens: University of Georgia Press, 1974.

Robert Cahn. Footprints on the Planet. New York: Universe Books, 1978.

J. Baird Callicott. "Animal Liberation: A Triangular Affair." *Environmental Ethics* 2 (1980): 311–338.

———. "Non-Anthropocentric Value Theory and Environmental Ethics." *American Philosophical Quarterly* 21 (1984): 299–309.

Stephen R. L. Clark. The Moral Status of Animals. Oxford: Oxford University Press, 1977, 1984.

Bill Devall and George Sessions. Deep Ecology. Salt Lake City, Utah: Peregrine Smith Books, 1985.

David Ehrenfeld. The Arrogance of Humanism. New York: Oxford University Press, 1978.

Robert Elliot and Arran Gare, eds. Environmental Philosophy. State College: Pennsylvania State University Press. 1983.

Albert J. Fritsch et al. Environmental Ethics: Choices for Concerned Citizens. New York: Doubleday, 1980.

K. E. Goodpaster and K. M. Sayre, eds. Ethics and Problems of the Twenty-First Century. Notre Dame, Ind.: University of Notre Dame Press, 1979.

Philip P. Hanson, ed. Environmental Ethics: Philosophical and Policy Perspectives. Burnaby, B.C.: Simon Fraser University, Institute for the Humanities, 1986.

374 *Selected Bibliography*

H. J. McCloskey. *Ecological Ethics and Politics.* Totowa, N.J.: Rowman & Littlefield, 1983.

Don Mannison, Michael McRobbie, and Richard Routley, eds. *Environmental Philosophy.* Canberra: Australian National University, 1980.

Arne Naess. "The Shallow and the Deep, Long-Range Ecology Movements: A Summary." *Inquiry* 16 (1973): 95–100.

Roderick Nash. *Wilderness and the American Mind.* 3d ed. New Haven, Conn.: Yale University Press, 1982.

Bryan G. Norton, ed. *Preservation of Species.* Princeton, N.J.: Princeton University Press, 1986.

Ernest Partridge, ed. *Responsibilities to Future Generations.* Buffalo, N.Y.: Prometheus Books, 1981.

John Passmore. *Man's Responsibility for Nature.* New York: Scribner, 1974.

Tom Regan. *All That Dwell Therein.* Berkeley: University of California Press, 1982.

———. *The Case for Animal Rights.* Berkeley: University of California Press, 1983.

———, ed. *Earthbound: New Introductory Essays in Environmental Ethics.* New York: Random House, 1984.

Bernard Rollin. *Animal Rights and Human Morality.* Buffalo, N.Y.: Prometheus Books, 1981.

Holmes Rolston, III. *Philosophy Gone Wild.* Buffalo, N.Y.: Prometheus Books, 1986.

Donald Scherer and Thomas Attig, eds. *Ethics and the Environment.* Englewood Cliffs, N.J.: Prentice-Hall, 1983.

Kristin Shrader-Frechette. *Environmental Ethics.* Pacific Grove, Calif.: Boxwood Press, 1981.

Peter Singer. *Animal Liberation.* New York: New York Review Books, 1975.

Christopher D. Stone. *Earth and Other Ethics.* New York: Harper & Row, 1987.

Paul W. Taylor. *Respect for Nature.* Princeton, N.J.: Princeton University Press, 1986.

Donald VanDeVeer and Christine Pierce, eds., *People, Penguins, and Plastic Trees.* Belmont, Calif.: Wadsworth, 1986.

Edward O. Wilson. *Biophilia.* Cambridge, Mass.: Harvard University Press, 1984.

Index